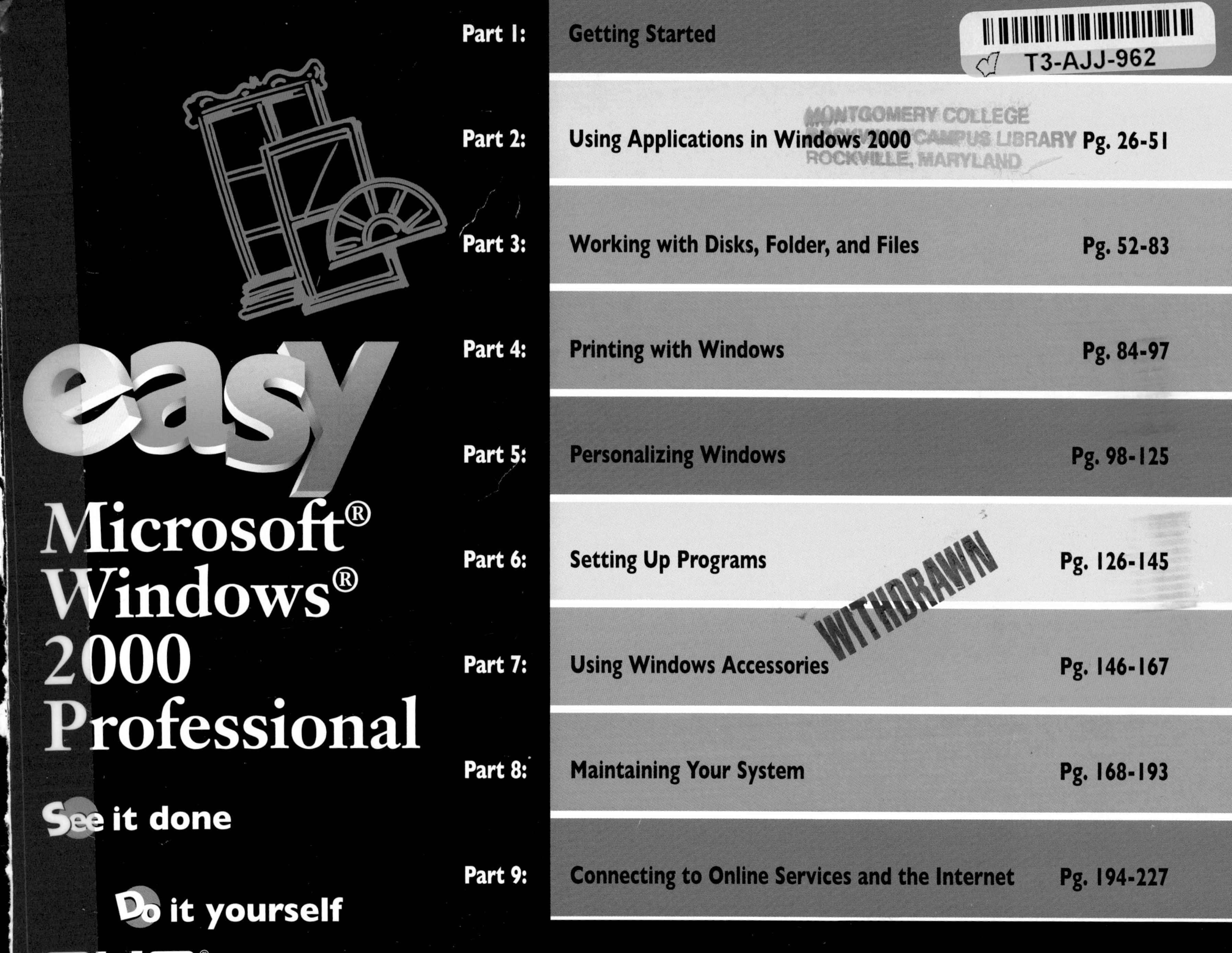

easy
Microsoft® Windows® 2000 Professional
See it done
Do it yourself
QUE®

Part 1: Getting Started

Part 2: Using Applications in Windows 2000

Part 4: Printing with Windows

Part 5: Personalizing Windows

Part 6: Setting Up Programs

Part 7: Using Windows Accessories

Part 8: Maintaining Your System

Part 9: Connecting to Online Services and the Internet

International Standard Book Number: 0-7897-2187-2

Library of Congress Catalog Card Number: 99-63897

Printed in the United States of America

First Printing: March 2000

02 01 00 4 3 2 1

Trademarks

Warning and Disclaimer

About the Author

Shelley O'Hara is the author of more than 80 books, mostly relating to computers. She has had several best-selling titles, including *Easy Windows 98*.

Dedication

As Abraham Lincoln once said, "All that I am or hope to be I owe to my mother."

Acknowledgments

Big hearty thanks and good luck to the best editor around, Kate. Special thanks also to Chris Will for inviting me to do this project.

Executive Editor
Greg Wiegand

Development Editor
Kate Shoup Welsh

Managing Editor
Thomas F. Hayes

Project Editor
Leah Kirkpatrick

Copy Editor
Kelli Brooks

Production
Jeanne Clark

Indexer
Greg Pearson

Technical Editor
John Purdum

Production Designer
Eric S. Miller

Book Designer
Jean Bisesi

Cover Designers
Anne Jones
Karen Ruggles

Illustrations
Bruce Dean

How to Use This Book

It's as Easy as 1-2-3

Each part of this book is made up of a series of short, instructional lessons, designed to help you understand basic information that you need to get the most out of your computer hardware and software.

1 Each step is fully illustrated to show you how it looks onscreen.

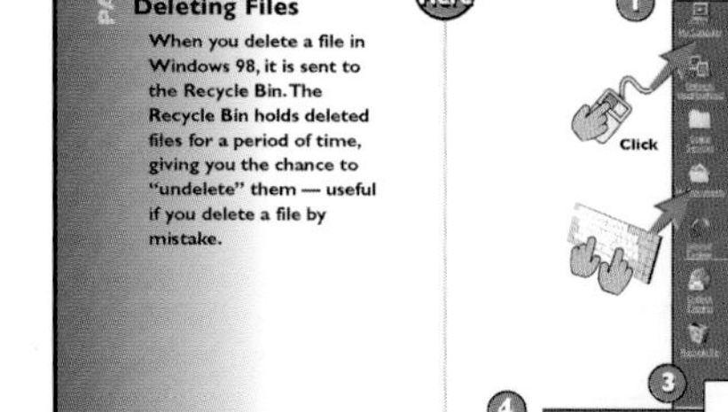

Click: Click the left mouse button once.

Double-click: Click the left mouse button twice in rapid succession.

Tips and Warnings give you a heads-up for any extra information you may need while working through the task.

Right-click: Click the right mouse button once.

Each task includes a series of quick, easy steps designed to guide you through the procedure.

Pointer Arrow: Highlights an item on the screen you need to point to or focus on in the step or task.

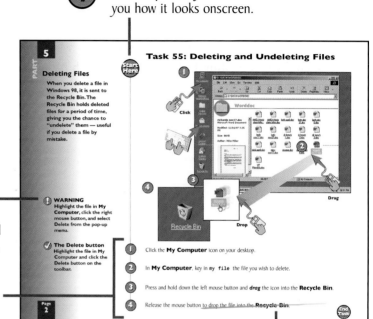

3 Items that you select or click in menus, dialog boxes, tabs, and windows are shown in **bold**. Information you type is in a `special font`.

Selection: Highlights the area onscreen discussed in the step or task.

Click & Type: Click once where indicated and begin typing to enter your text or data.

How to Drag: Point to the starting place or object. Hold down the mouse button (right or left per instructions), move the mouse to the new location, then release the button.

Next Step: If you see this symbol, it means the task you're working on continues on the next page.

End Task: Task is complete.

Introduction to *Easy Microsoft Windows 2000 Professional*

Becoming proficient with a new operating system—such as Windows 2000—can seem like a daunting task. There's so much to learn: How do you create and edit documents? How can you customize the desktop? How do you connect to the Internet? Sometimes these questions can seem overwhelming.

That's why *Easy Microsoft Windows 2000 Professional* provides concise, visual, step-by-step instructions for handling all the tasks you'll need to accomplish. You'll learn how to get started in Windows 2000, how to use applications, how to organize your materials, how to print, how to personalize your system, how to set up programs, how to use Windows accessories, how to maintain your system, how to connect to online services, and more.

The *Easy* books have been proven best-sellers because they help the ordinary user get started, troubleshoot problems, and learn new skills. You can choose to read the book cover to cover, or use it as a reference when you encounter a piece of Windows 2000 that you don't know how to use. Either way, *Easy Microsoft Windows 2000 Professional* lets you see it done and do it yourself.

PART I

Getting Started

Windows 2000 is the newest version of Windows. Introduced in 1999, this version includes some new features designed to make your computer easier to use. If you purchased a new computer recently, this is the version you most likely have. You can also upgrade to Windows 2000 by purchasing the new version from a retail store or from Microsoft.

Other than turning on your PC, you don't need to do anything to start Windows 2000. When you turn on your computer, Windows starts automatically, and you see a screen called the *desktop*. The desktop is your starting point. Here you find the key tools for working with your computer. From your Windows desktop, you can open and switch between applications, search for specific folders, print documents, and perform other tasks. This section covers the basics of working with the desktop.

Tasks

Task 1: Displaying the Start Menu

The taskbar, located at the bottom of your screen, contains the Start button. Clicking the Start button enables you to start applications, open documents you recently had open, customize settings in Windows, get help, and more. You use the Start button to begin most tasks in Windows.

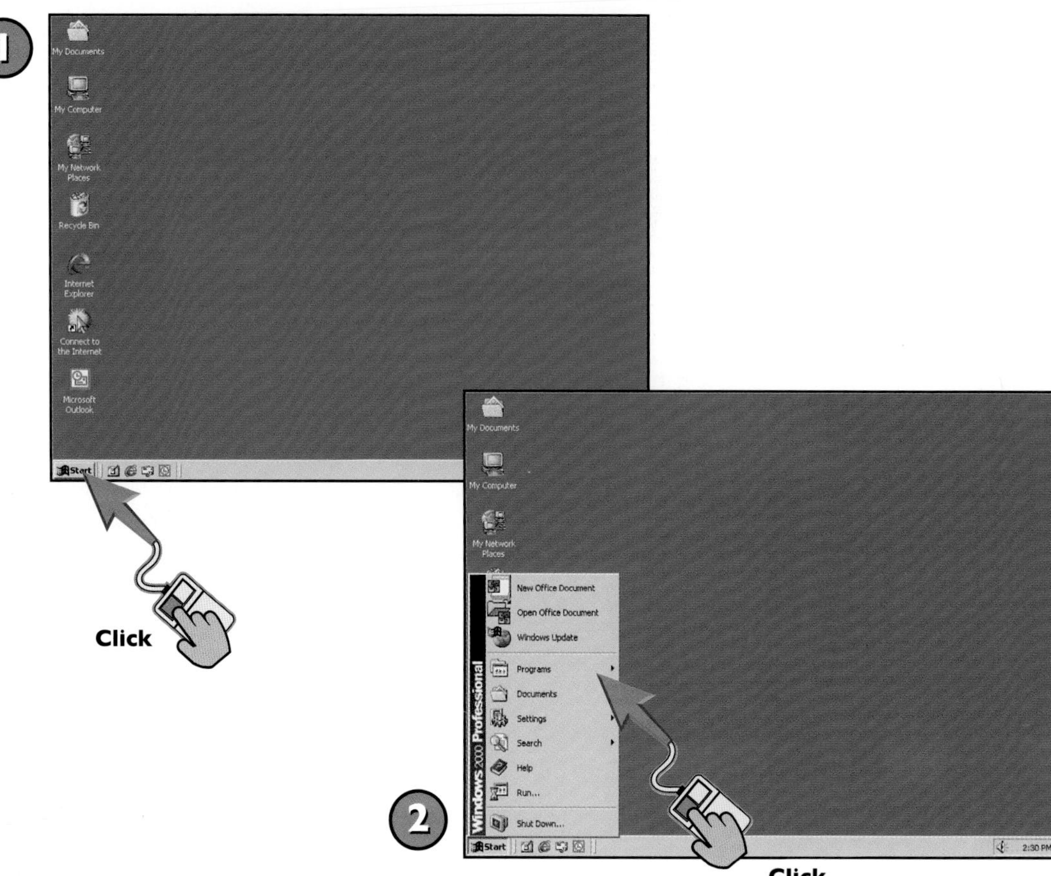

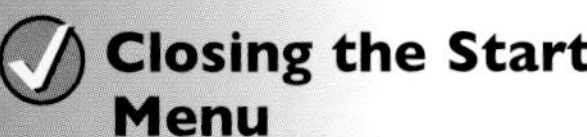

Closing the Start Menu

If you click the **Start** button by mistake and want to close the Start menu without choosing a command, simply click outside the menu.

1. Click the **Start** button.

2. Click the command you want.

Task 2: Opening a Window

Double-Click

Windows 2000 displays all its information in onscreen boxes called *windows*. To work with any of the information on your computer, you must know how to display (or open) these windows. Many windows are represented onscreen by small pictures called *icons*. You can double-click an icon to display the contents of the window the icon represents.

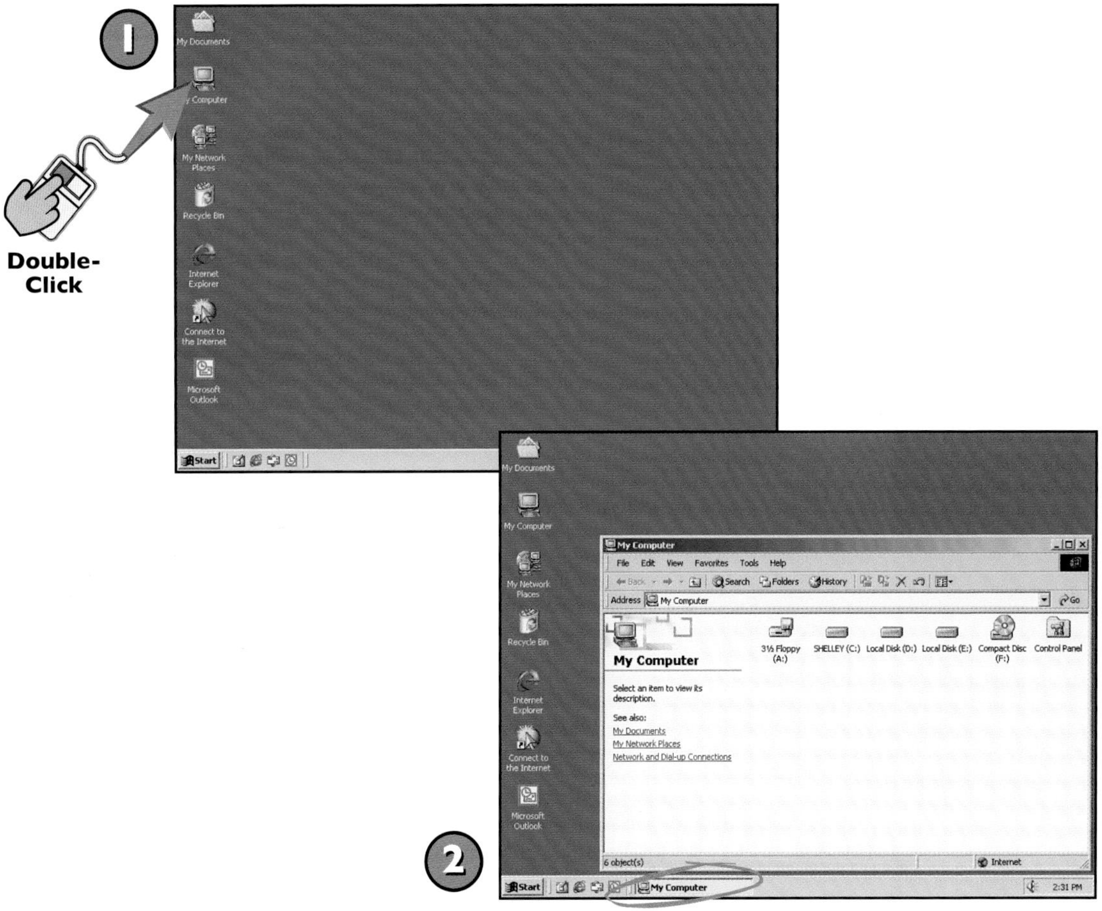

1 Double-click the **My Computer** icon.

2 The contents of this icon are displayed, and a button for the My Computer window appears on the taskbar.

Nothing Happens?
If nothing happens when you double-click an icon, it might be because you did not click quickly enough or because you single-clicked, moved the mouse, and single-clicked again. You have to click twice in rapid succession. A good way to practice using the mouse is to play Solitaire.

Single-Click?
If you have your system set up for single-clicking, you can simply single-click to open an icon. See Task 12, "Changing How the Mouse Works," in Part 5, "Personalizing Windows."

Task 3: Closing Windows

You close a window after you finish working with it and its contents. Too many open windows clutter the desktop as well as the taskbar.

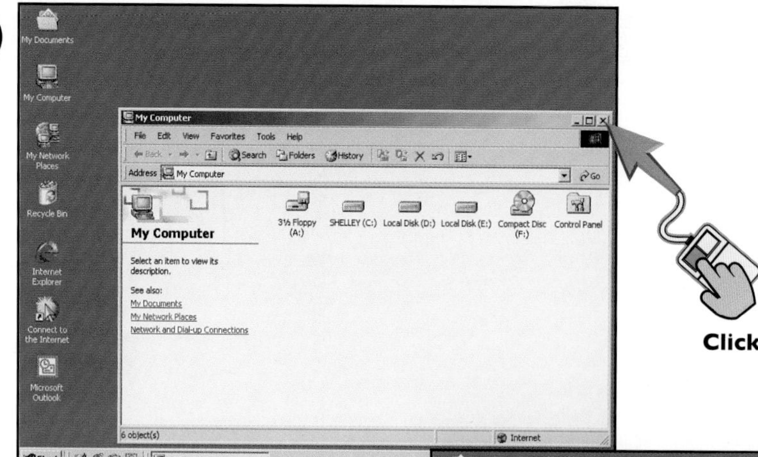

1 Click the **Close** button (the button marked with a × in the top-right corner of the window).

2 The window is closed, and the button for the window no longer appears in the taskbar.

Using the Control Menu

The Control menu, located in the upper-left corner of the title bar, contains commands related to the open window, such as Restore, Move, Size, Close, and so on. To close the window via the Control menu, click the **Control** menu icon and then choose **Close** from the menu. Alternatively, you can press **Alt+F4**.

Task 4: Minimizing a Window

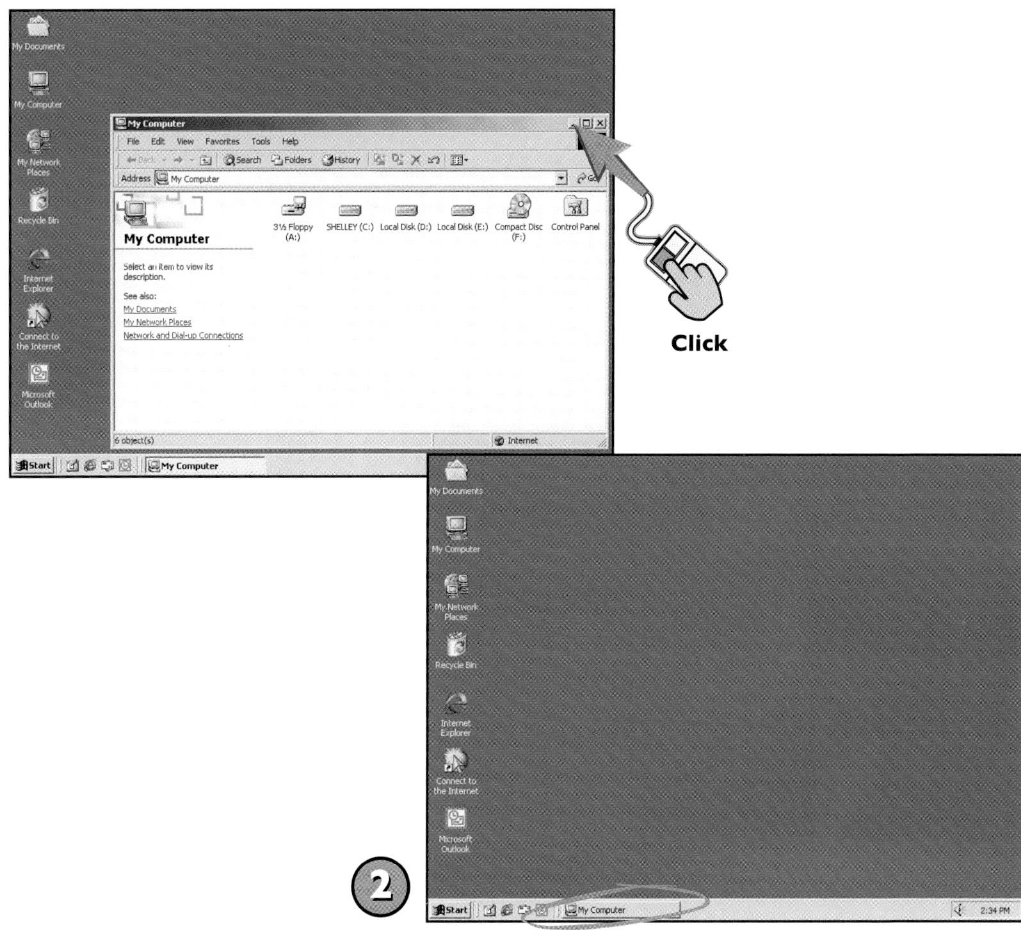

You can reduce (minimize) a window so that it is still available as a toolbar button, but is not displayed on the desktop. You might want to minimize a window to temporarily move it out of your way but keep it active for later use.

1 Click the **Minimize** button in the window you want to minimize.

2 The window disappears from the desktop, but note that a button for this window remains on the taskbar.

Checking Out the Taskbar

You can tell which windows you have open by looking at the taskbar.

Task 5: Maximizing a Window

You can enlarge (maximize) a window so that it fills the entire screen. Doing so gives you as much room as possible to work in that window.

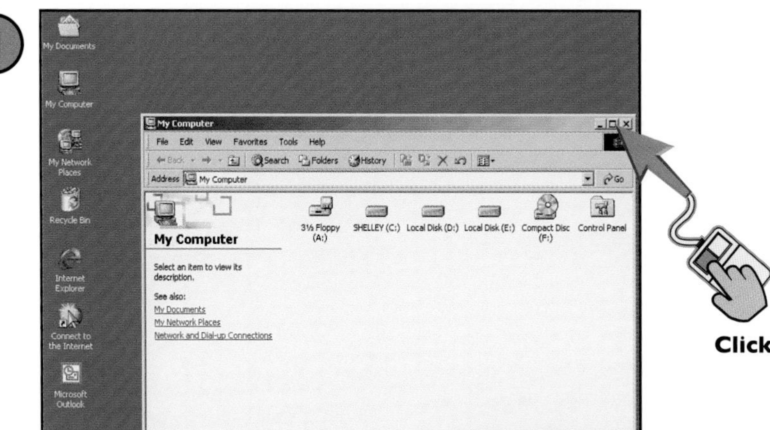

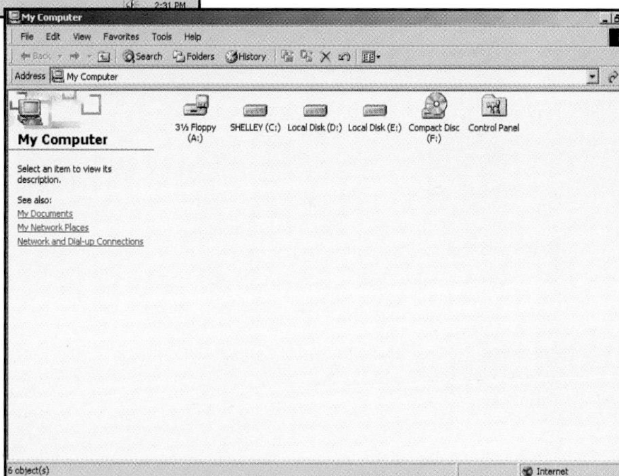

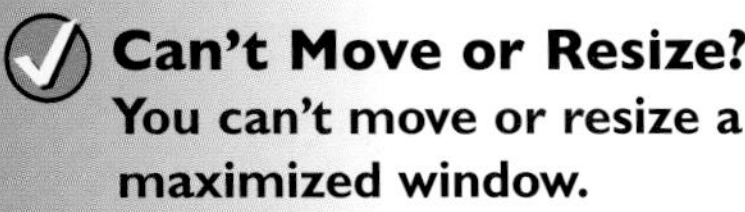

Can't Move or Resize?
You can't move or resize a maximized window.

1. Click the **Maximize** button.

2. The window enlarges to fill the screen, and the Maximize button changes to the Restore button.

Task 6: Restoring a Window

If you maximize a window, you can easily restore it to its original size.

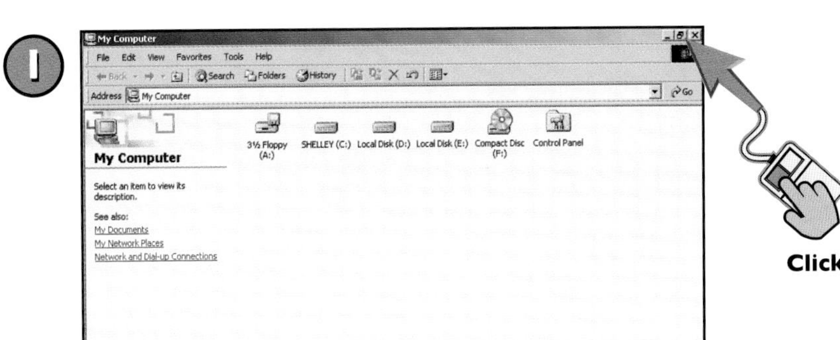

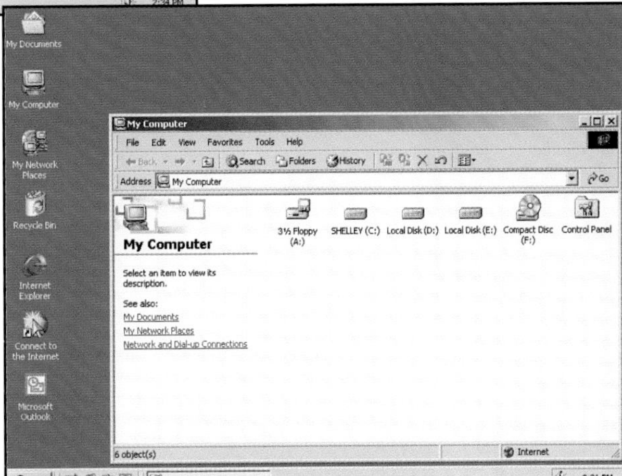

1 In a maximized window, click the **Restore** button.

2 The window is restored to its original size.

Task 7: Moving a Window

As you add more applications, folders, shortcuts, and so on to the desktop, you'll need more room to display these elements. You can easily move the windows around so you can see all the open windows at one time.

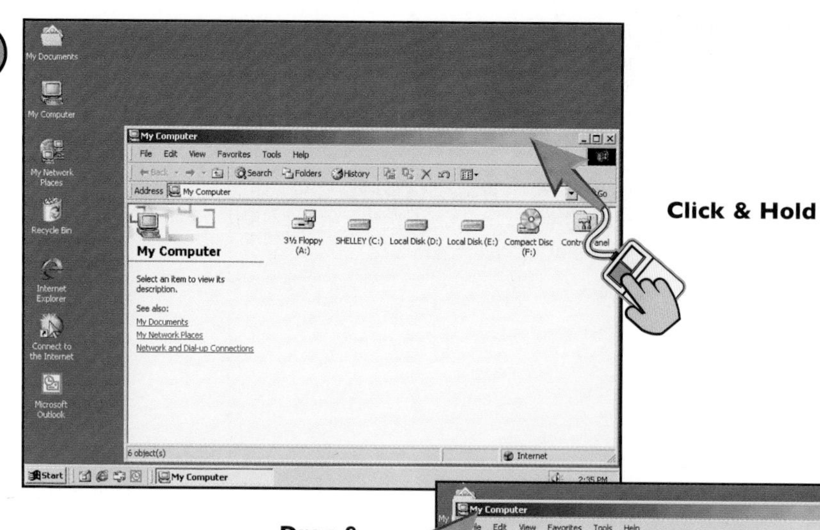

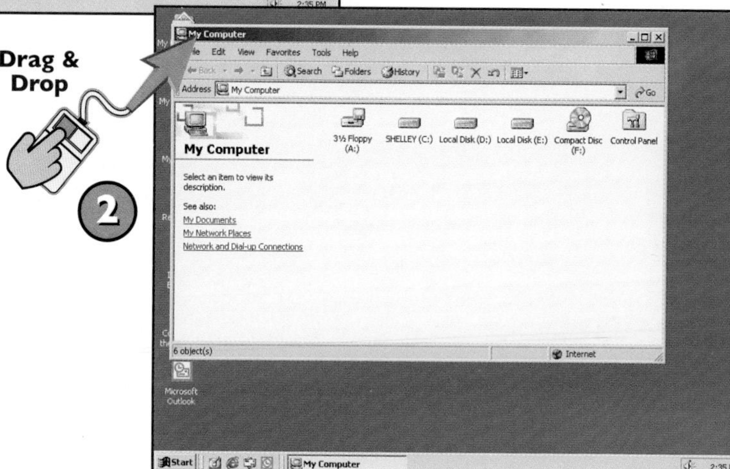

1. To move an open window, click on its title bar.
2. Drag the window to a new position. Release the mouse button. The window and its contents appear in the new location.

Save Memory

The more windows you have open, the more memory is used. Minimize is more efficient, memorywise.

Pointing to the Title Bar

Be sure to point to the title bar. If you point to any other area, you might resize the window instead of moving it.

Task 8: Resizing a Window

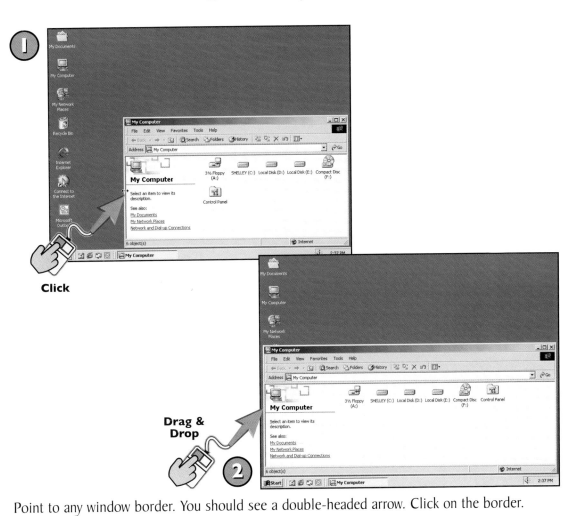

In addition to being able to move a window, you can resize a window to whatever size you want. Resizing windows is helpful if you want to view more than one window at the same time.

Click

Drag & Drop

1 Point to any window border. You should see a double-headed arrow. Click on the border.

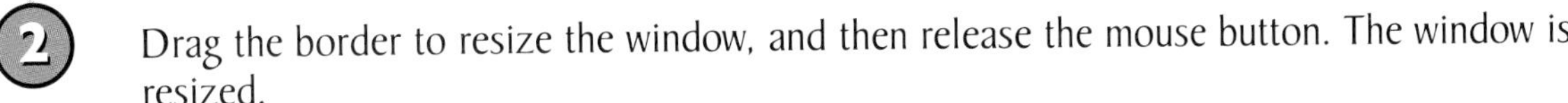

2 Drag the border to resize the window, and then release the mouse button. The window is resized.

Dragging a Corner
You can drag a corner of the window to proportionally resize both dimensions (height and width) at the same time.

Cannot Resize Maximized Windows
You cannot resize a window that is maximized. If you don't see borders, you cannot resize the window. If you want to resize the window, simply restore it and then resize it.

Task 9: Scrolling a Window

If a window is too small to show all its contents, a vertical *scrollbar* appears along the edge of the window. You can use this bar to scroll through the window to see the other contents.

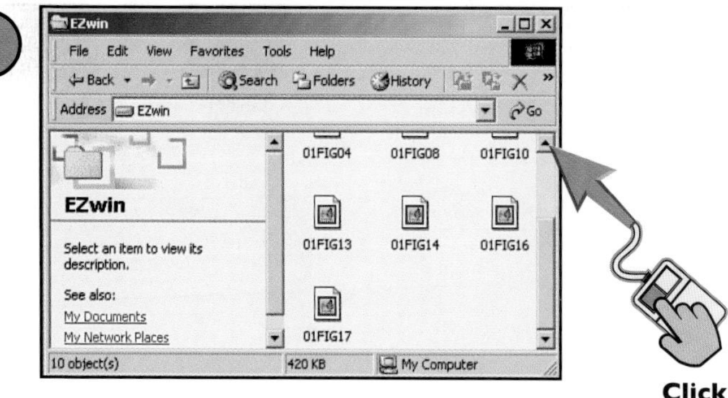

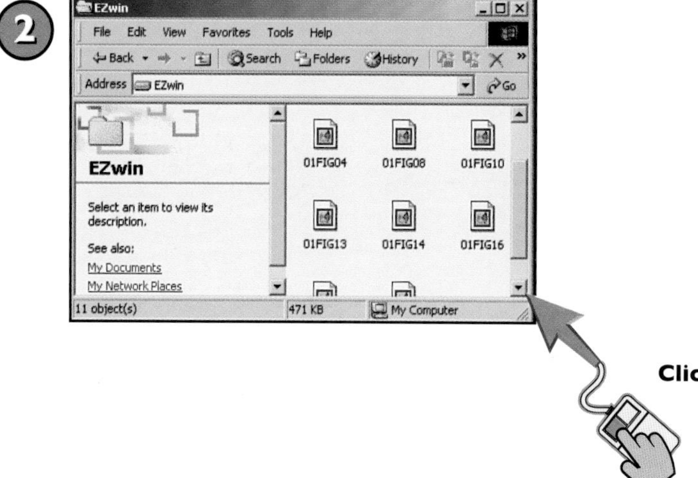

Clicking in the Scrollbar
You can click anywhere in the scrollbar to jump in that direction to another part of the window. You can also drag the scroll box to scroll quickly through the window.

Scrollbars for the Other Pane
Depending on how you have set up your folders for viewing, you might see two panes of information. You might also have scrollbars for the first pane. You scroll this part of the window in the same way.

1. Click the up arrow to scroll up through the window.

2. Click the down arrow to scroll down through the window.

End Task

Task 10: Arranging Windows on the Desktop

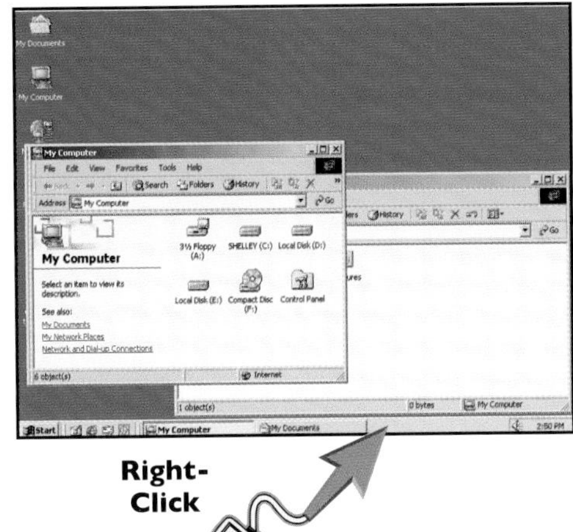

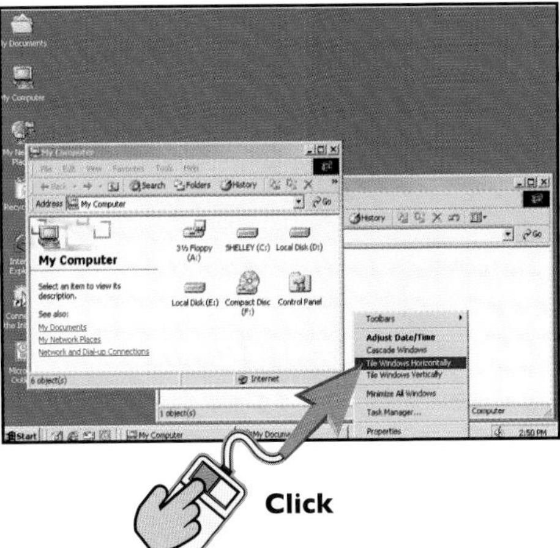

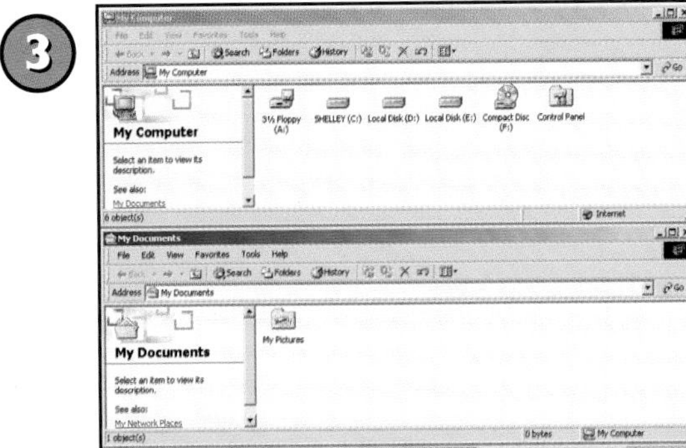

1. With multiple windows on the desktop, right-click a blank area of the taskbar.
2. Click the arrangement you want.
3. Windows arranges the windows; here they are tiled horizontally.

As you work, you will often have several windows open on the desktop at one time. The windows probably overlap each other, which can make it difficult to find what you want. To make your work easier and more efficient, Windows enables you to arrange the windows on the desktop in several different ways.

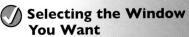

Selecting the Window You Want

To work in any one of the open windows, click the desired window to make it active. The active window moves to the front of the stack, and its title bar is a different color.

Clicking a Blank Area

Be sure to right-click on a blank area, not on a button.

Undoing the Arrangement

You can undo the arrangement by right-clicking again and choosing **Undo**.

Task 11: Using Menus

Although you can perform many tasks by clicking the mouse on different onscreen objects, you must choose commands to perform the majority of Windows tasks. Commands are organized in menus to make them easy to find. Most windows contain menu bars that list the available menus; each menu then contains a group of related commands.

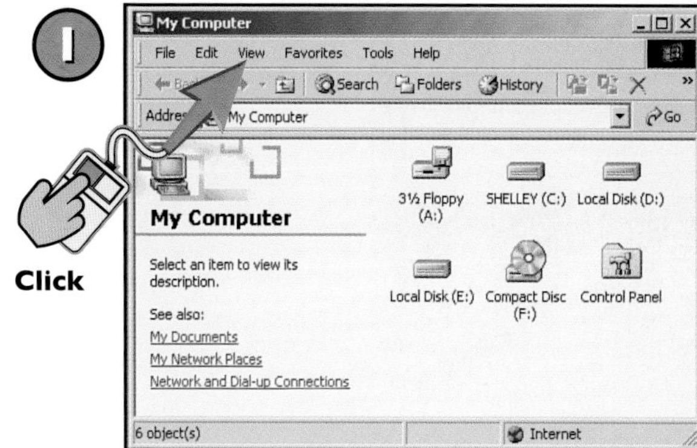

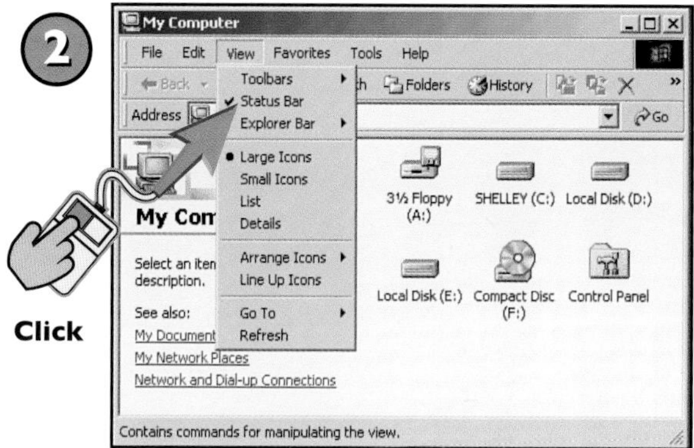

1. In the window or program, click the menu name (in this case, the menu name is **View**).
2. Click the command you want.

Using the Shortcut Keys

Menus also list shortcut keys. Also, selecting a command that is followed by an arrow displays a submenu. Clicking a command that is followed by an ellipsis displays a dialog box.

Closing the Menu

To close a menu without making a selection, press the **Esc** button on your keyboard or click outside the menu.

Task 12: Using Shortcut Menus

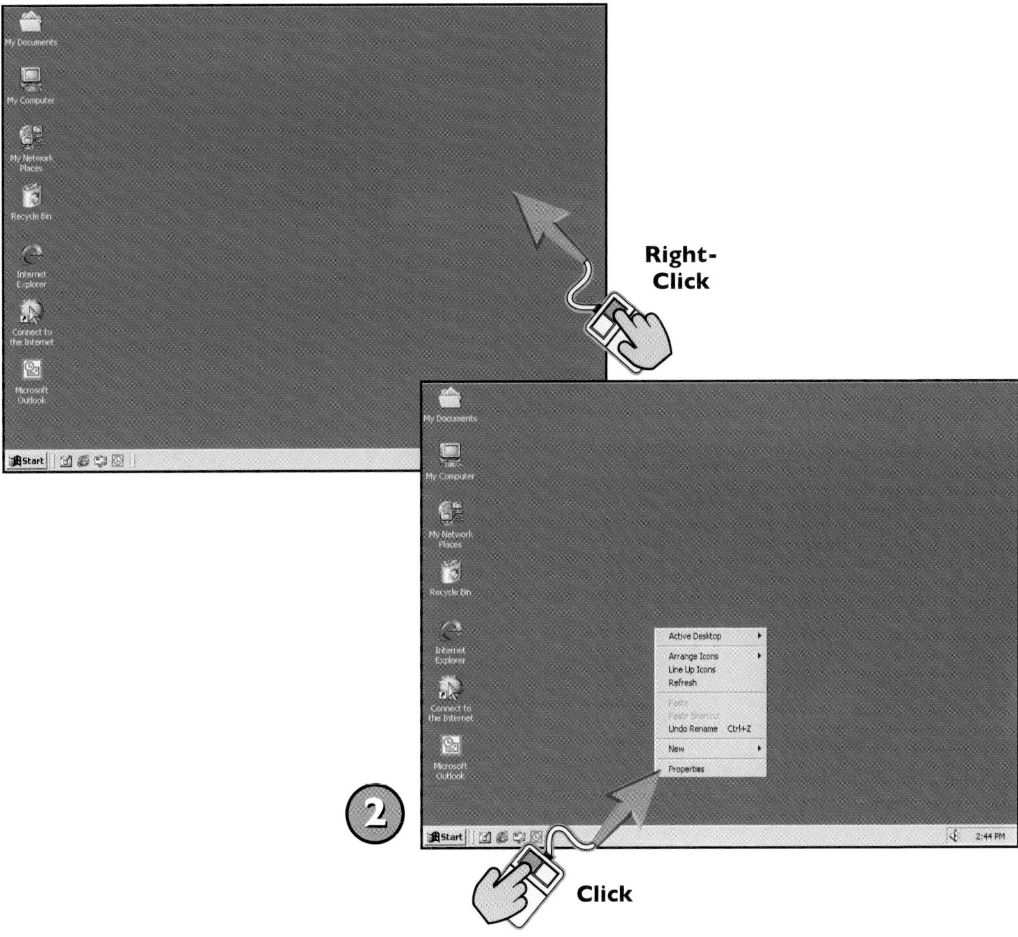

Shortcut menus, also called *quick menus* or *pop-up menus*, provide common commands related to the selected item. You can, for example, quickly copy and paste, create a new folder, move a file, or rearrange icons using a shortcut menu.

Right-click the item for which you want to display a shortcut menu. For instance, right-click any blank part of the desktop.

Click the command you want.

Commands Will Vary
Different shortcut menus appear, depending on what you're pointing to when you right-click the mouse.

Task 13: Using a Dialog Box

When you choose certain commands, a dialog box appears to prompt you for additional information about how to carry out the command. Dialog boxes are used throughout Windows; luckily, all dialog boxes have common elements, and all are treated in a similar way. When a dialog box appears, you must make your selections. Different dialog boxes will have different options. The figures in this section are meant to show the types of items you might find in a dialog box.

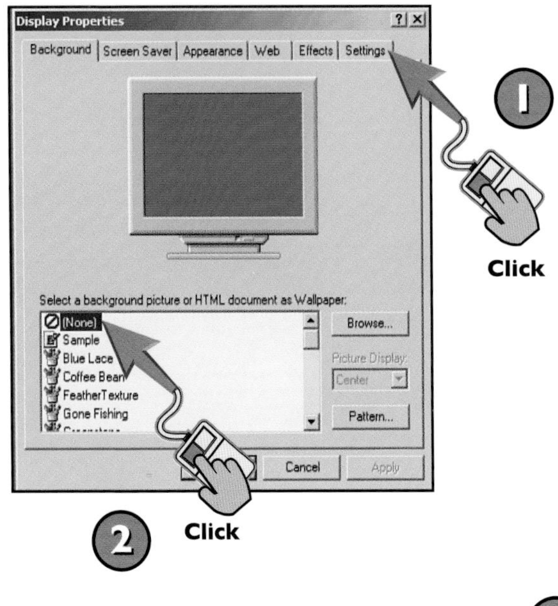

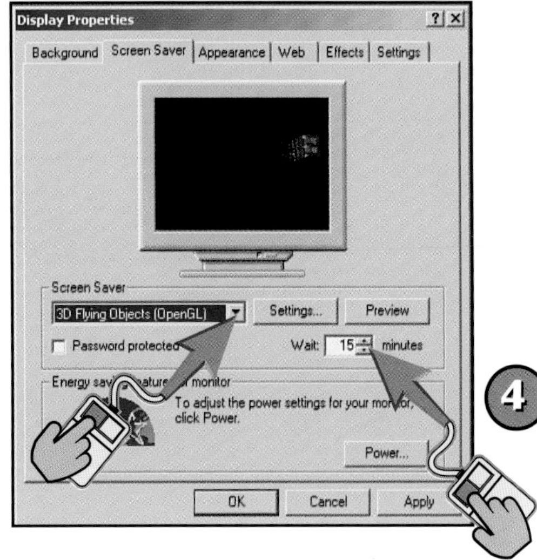

Closing the Dialog Box
When a dialog box is open, you cannot perform any other action until you accept any changes by clicking the **OK** button. To close the dialog box without making a selection, click the **Cancel** button.

1. To view a tab, click it.
2. To use a list box, scroll through the list and click the item you want to select.
3. To use a drop-down list box, click the arrow and then select the desired item from the list.
4. To use a spin box, click the arrows to increment or decrement the value or type a value in the text box.

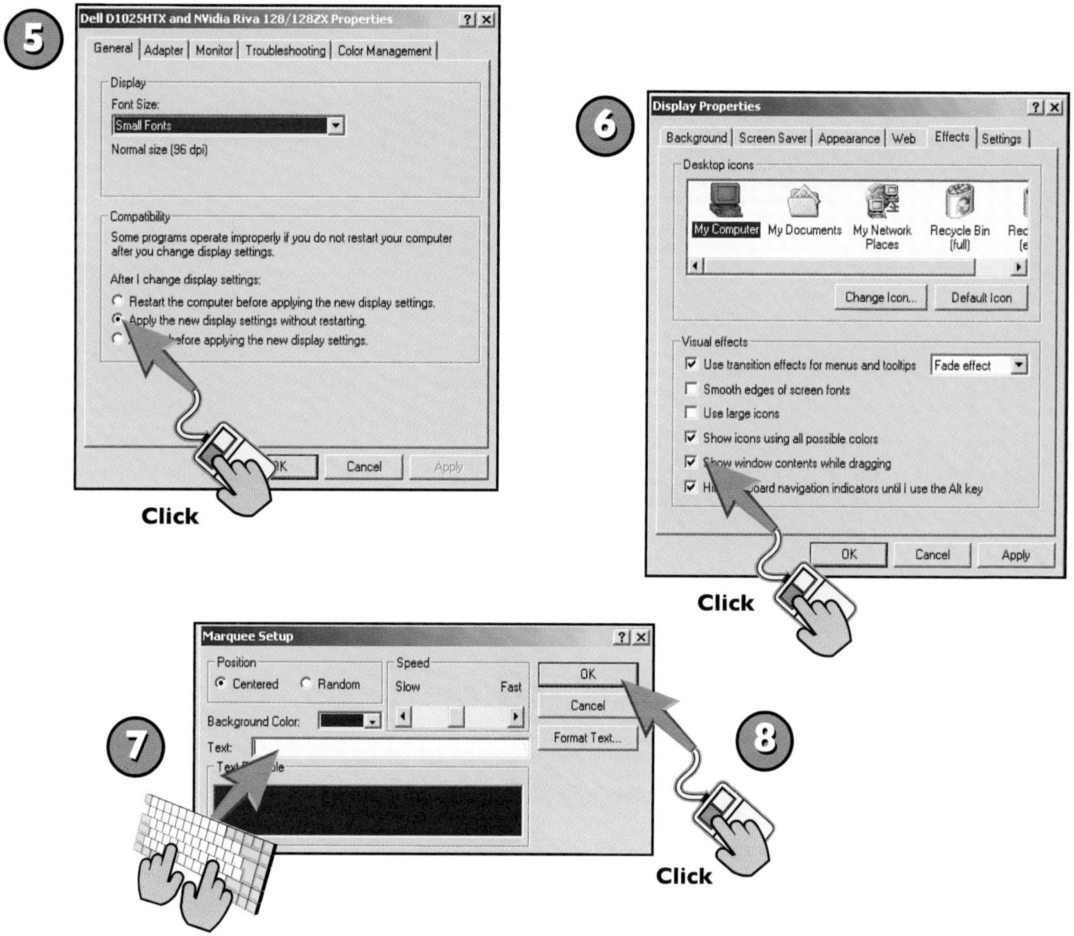

5 Click a radio button to activate it.

6 Click a check box to select it (or to deselect a check box that is already checked).

7 Type an entry in a text box.

8 After you make your selections, click the **OK** button.

Radio Buttons Versus Check Boxes

Dialog boxes contain various types of elements, including radio buttons and check boxes. You can choose only one radio button within a group of radio buttons; choosing a second option deselects the first. However, you can select multiple check boxes within a group of check boxes.

Task 14: Getting Context-Sensitive Help

When you open a dialog box, you might not know what each of the options do. If you have a question about an option, you can view a description of that option by following the steps in this task.

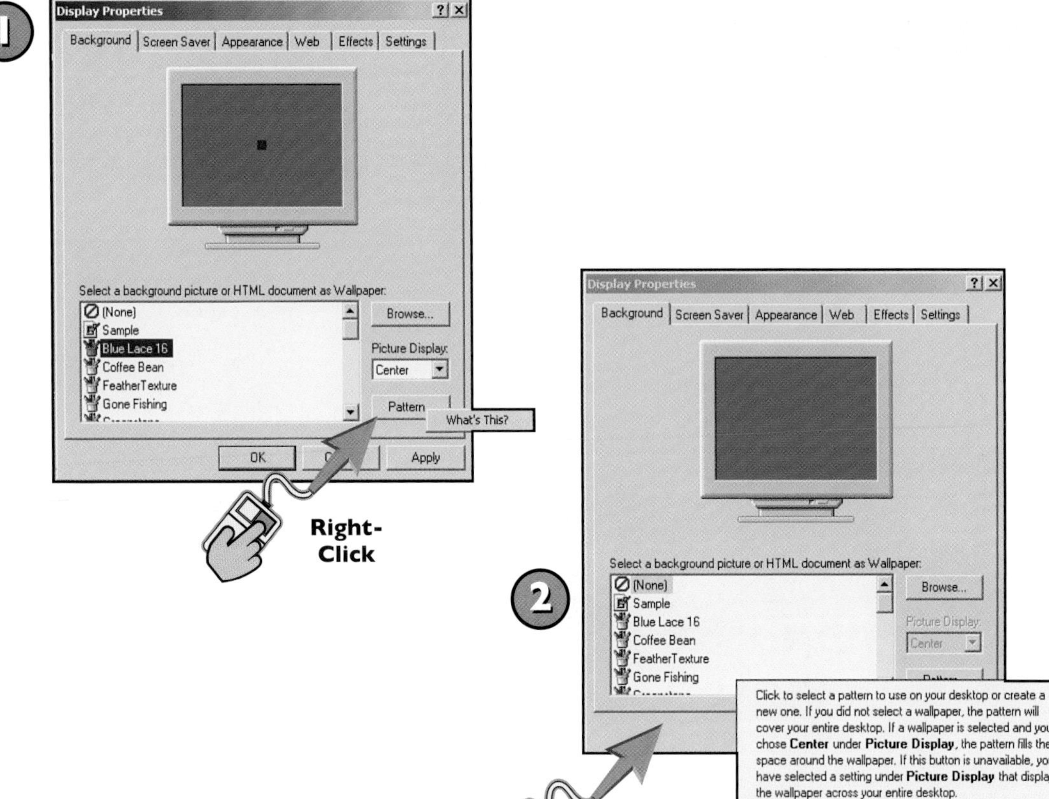

In a dialog box, right-click the option you want help on, and then click the **What's This?** button.

After you review the material in the pop-up explanation, click anywhere within the dialog box to close the pop-up box.

Task 15: Looking Up a Help Topic in the Table of Contents

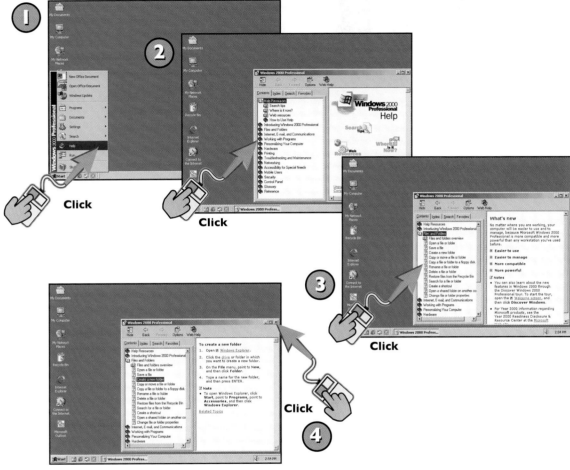

Use the Contents tab to locate help for performing specific procedures, such as printing a document or installing new software. The specific topics included in the Contents tab quickly refer you to everyday tasks you might need to perform in the program.

1. Click the **Start** button, and then select **Help**.
2. Click the topic you want help on.
3. Continue clicking book topics until you find the exact help topic you need, and then click that help topic.
4. After you review the help information, click the **Close** button to close the Help window.

Printing a Help Topic
Click the **Options** button and then choose **Print** to print the help topic.

What the Icons Mean
Subtopics are indicated with a book icon. Help topics are indicated with a question mark icon.

Displaying a Definition
You can click any of the underlined text in the help area to display a definition of that term or to display related help information.

Task 16: Looking Up a Help Topic in the Index

Start Here

If you want to find help on a specific topic, such as storing files by size or editing text, use the Index tab in the Help window. Topics listed in the index are in alphabetical order. You can quickly scroll to see topics of interest.

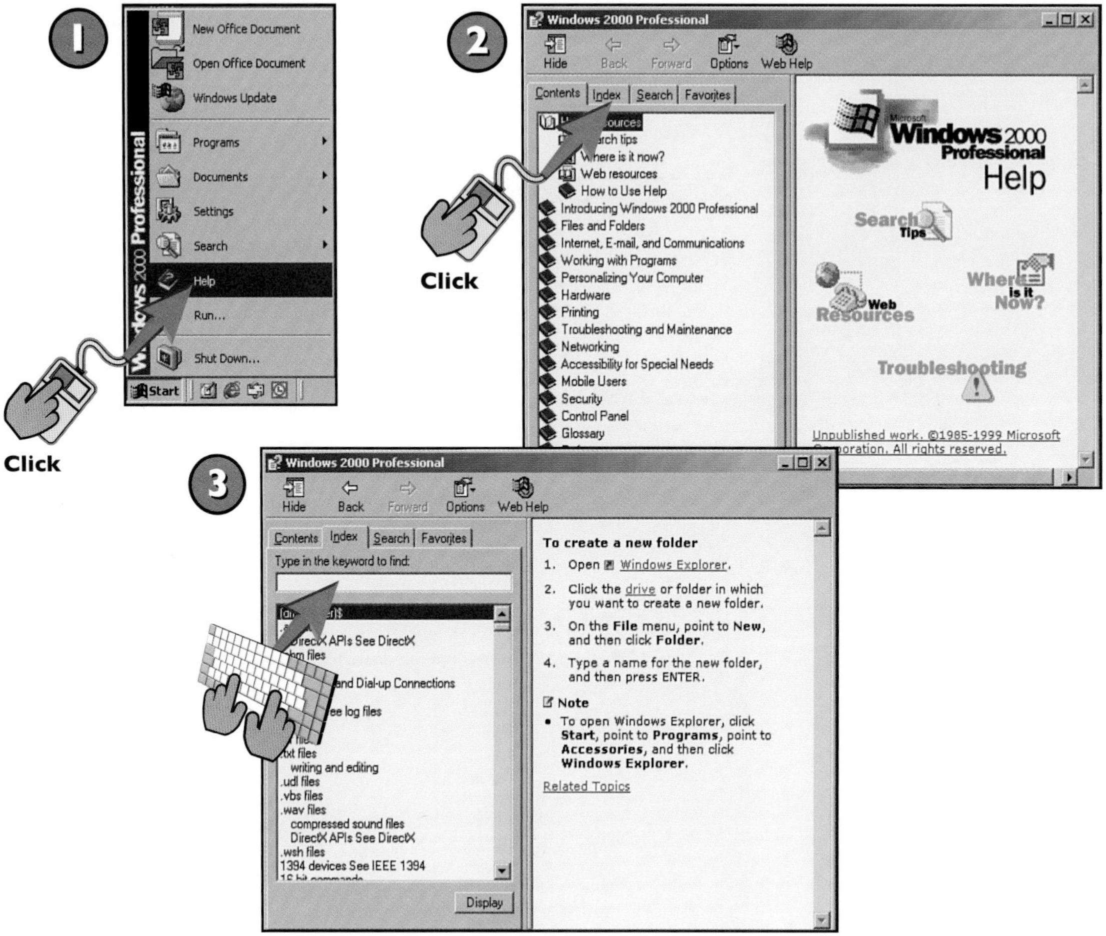

1. Click the **Start** button, and then select **Help**.
2. Click the **Index** tab.
3. Type the topic for which you want to find help. The list below the text field jumps to the topic you type.

Scrolling Through the Index

You can scroll through the list of topics on the Index tab. Click the scroll buttons or drag the scrollbar.

Going Back a Page

You can also click the **Back** button to go back to the previous help page.

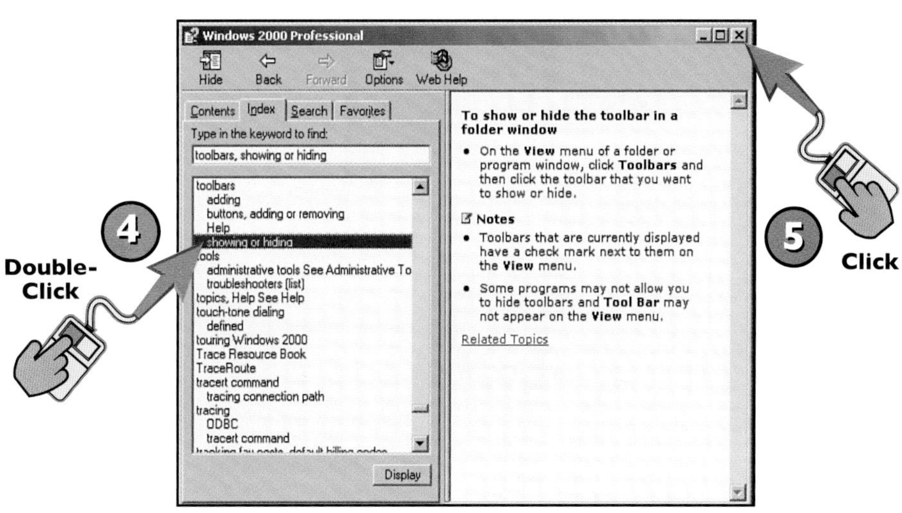

4. Double-click the topic you want to review and then look over the help information.

5. After you review the help information, click the **Close** button to close the Help window.

Task 17: Searching for a Help Topic

If you don't find the topic in the table of contents or index, try searching for it. Windows will display a list of topics that contain what you are looking for; you can then select the one you want.

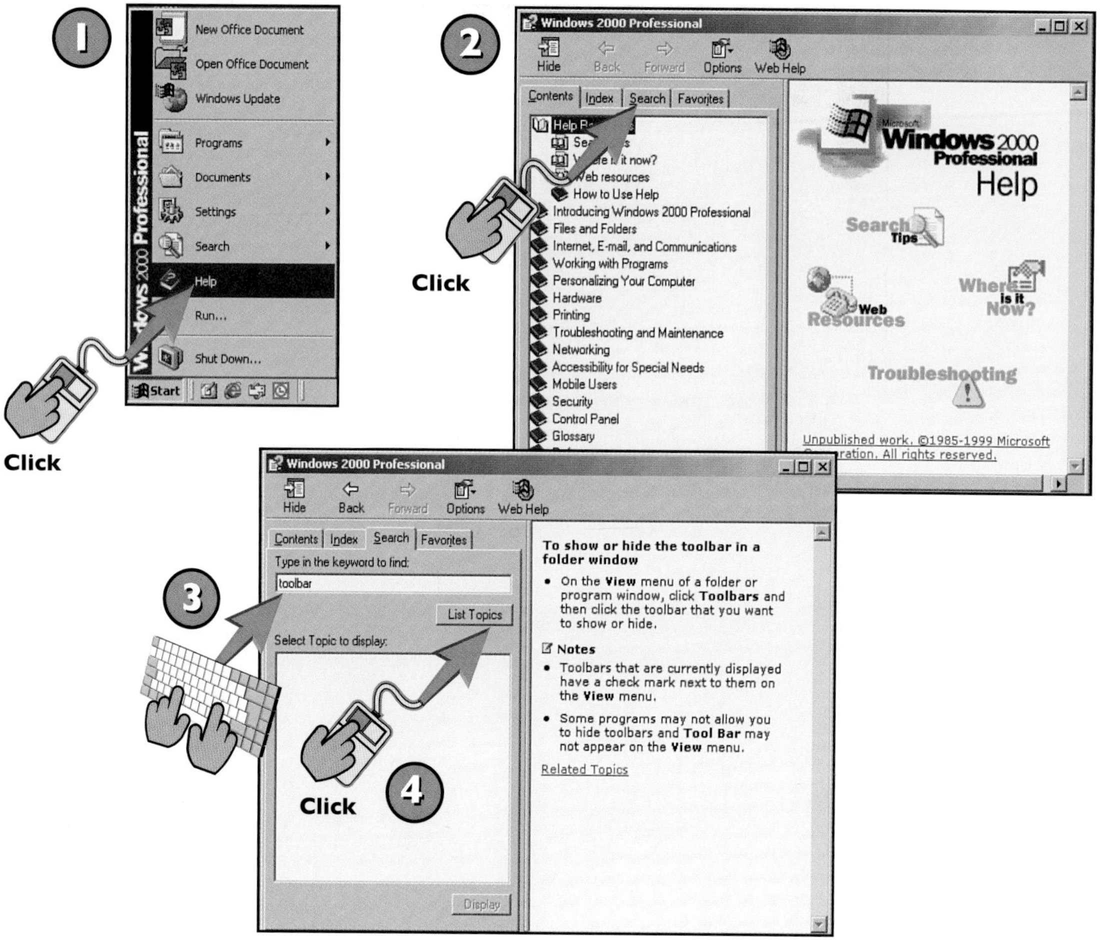

Start Here

Getting Help in Other Applications

Windows help works in the same way throughout most Windows applications. If you master help basics, you can apply these same skills to other programs.

Getting Web Help

If you are connected to the Internet, you can use Web help to get product support from Microsoft's Web site. Click the **Web Help** button and then click the **Support Online** link. For more information on the Internet, see Part 9, "Connecting to Online Services and the Internet."

1. Click the **Start** button, and then click **Help**.
2. Click the **Search** tab.
3. Type the topic you want to find.
4. Click the **List Topics** button.

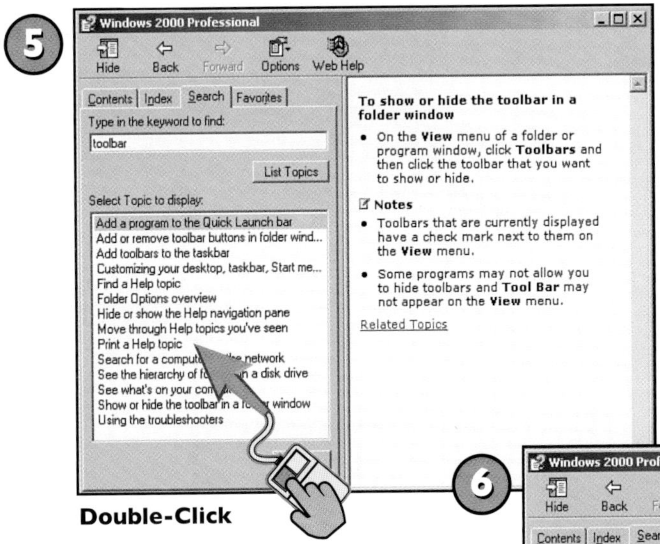

Double-Click

Click

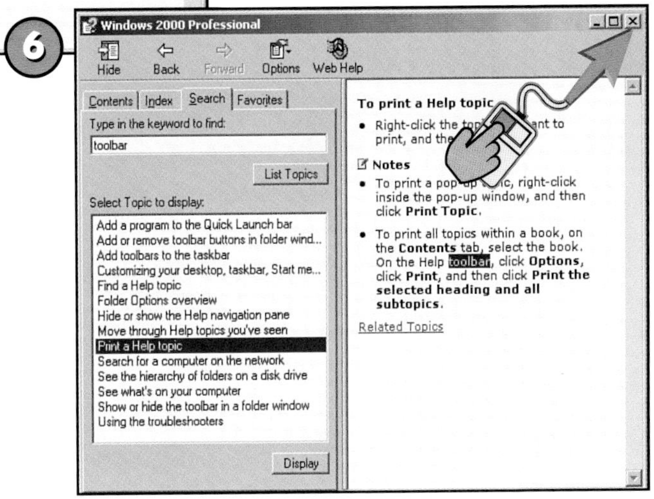

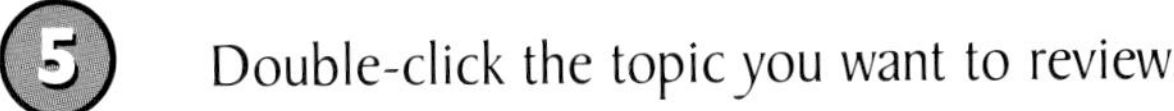

5 Double-click the topic you want to review.

6 Review the help information, and then click the **Close** button.

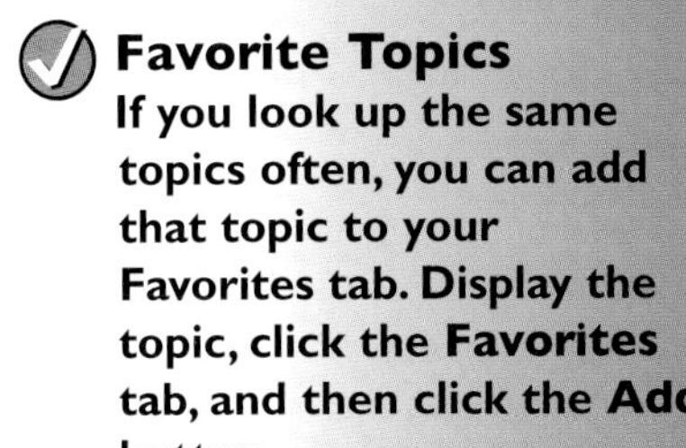

Favorite Topics

If you look up the same topics often, you can add that topic to your Favorites tab. Display the topic, click the Favorites tab, and then click the Add button.

Task 18: Shutting Down the Computer

If you turn off the power to your computer before you properly shut the computer down, you could lose valuable data or damage an open file. Windows provides a safe shutdown feature that checks for open programs and files, warns you to save unsaved files, and prepares the program for you to turn off your computer. You should always shut down before you turn off the power.

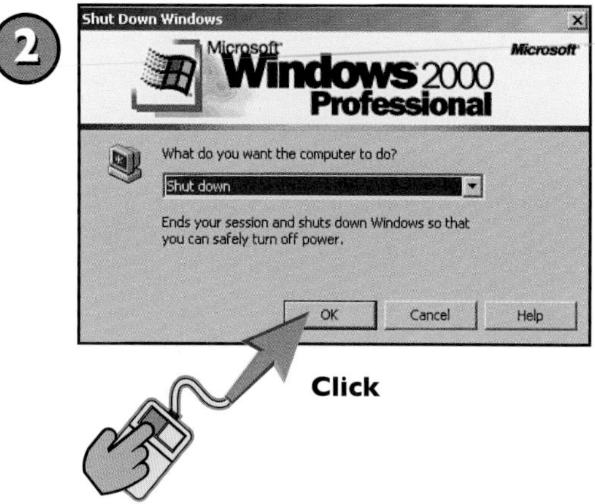

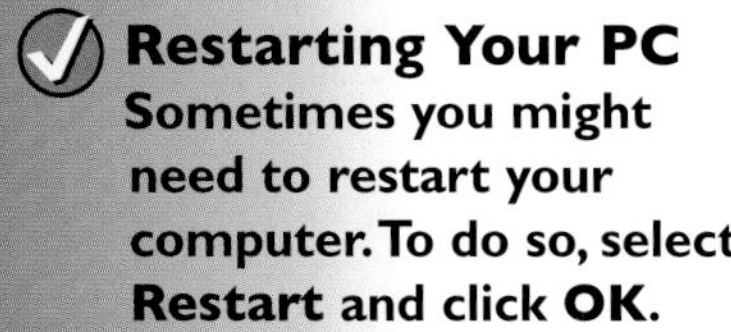

Restarting Your PC
Sometimes you might need to restart your computer. To do so, select **Restart** and click **OK**.

1. After you've closed down all open programs, click **Start** and then **Shut Down**.

2. Select **Shut Down** from the drop-down list and click **OK**. Windows is shut down, and you can turn off your PC.

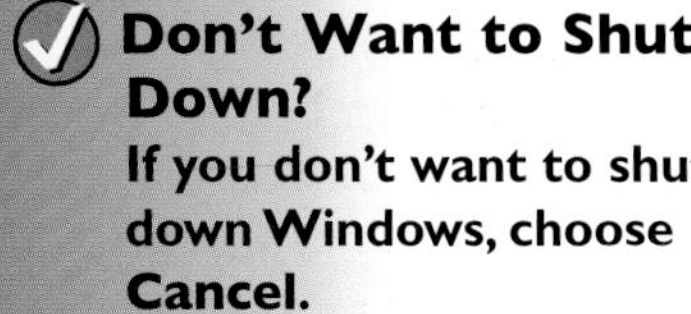

Don't Want to Shut Down?
If you don't want to shut down Windows, choose **Cancel**.

Task 19: Restarting the PC

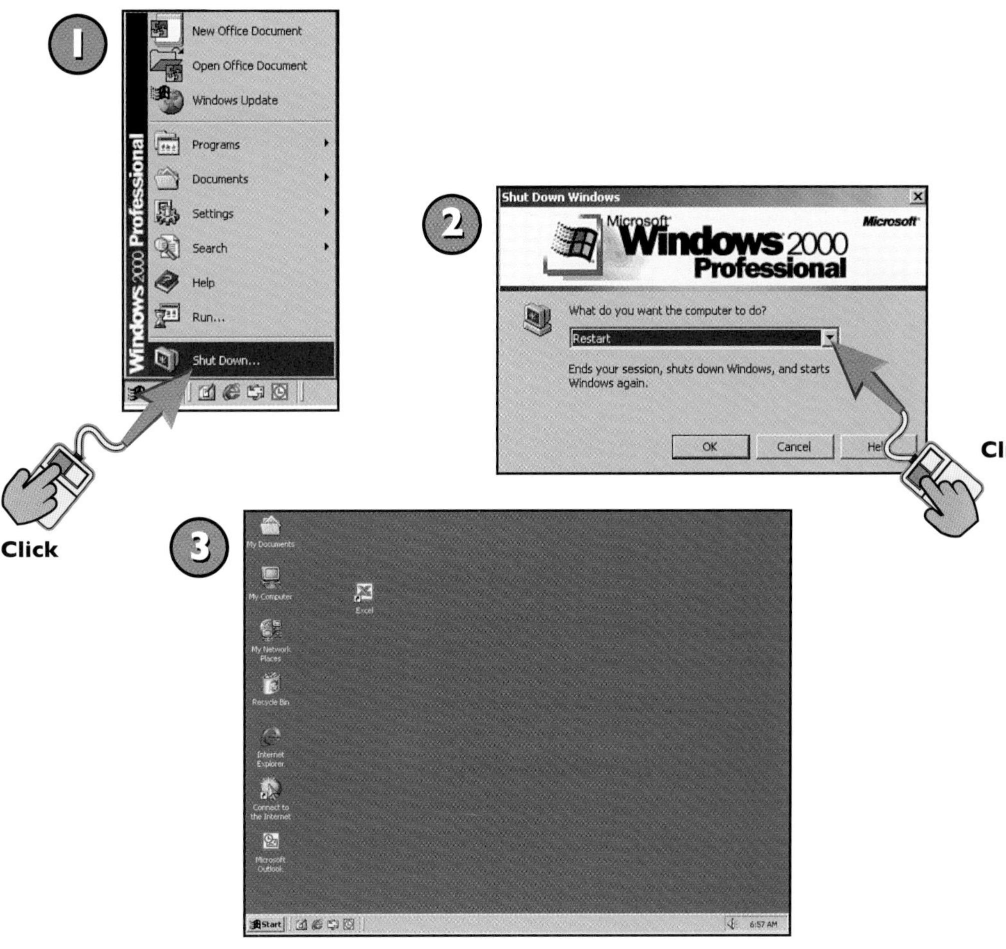

If you make some system changes, you might need to restart your computer so that the new settings are in effect. Before you restart, save all documents and exit all programs.

1. After you've closed down all open programs, click **Start** and then **Shut Down**.
2. Select **Restart** from the drop-down list and click **OK**.
3. Windows will go through its startup routine. You will see the Windows desktop after Windows has restarted.

Don't Want to Restart?
If you don't want to restart Windows, choose **Cancel**.

Computer Stuck?
If your computer gets stuck, and you cannot click the Start button, you can press **Ctrl+Alt+Delete**. Click the **Shut Down** button. In the Shut Down Windows dialog box, select **Restart** or **Shut Down** from the drop-down list and then click **OK**.

PART 2

Using Applications in Windows 2000

One advantage of using Windows is the enormous number of available Windows applications. You can use many word-processing, database, spreadsheet, drawing, and other programs in Windows. This variety of applications provides you with all the tools you need to perform your everyday tasks.

Windows applications are easy to open and use, and enable you to save data in files of different names and in various locations on your hard disk or a floppy disk. You can open a file at any time to view, edit, or print it. This part covers starting and working with applications.

Tasks

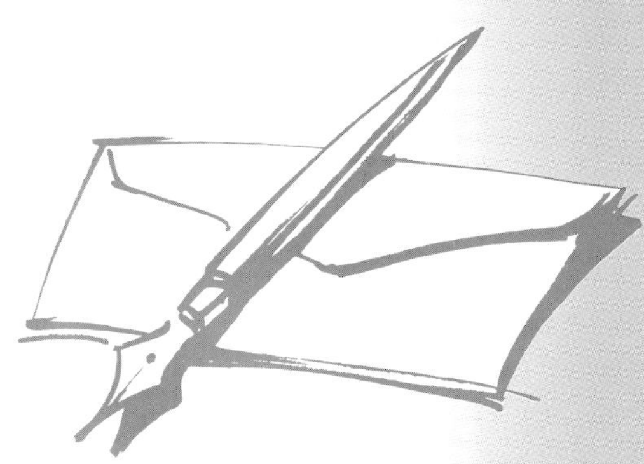

Task 1: Starting an Application from the Start Menu

Start Here

Most of the time you spend using your computer will be with an application. You can start an application in any number of ways, including from the Start menu. When you install a new Windows application, that program's installation procedure sets up a program folder and program icon on the Start menu.

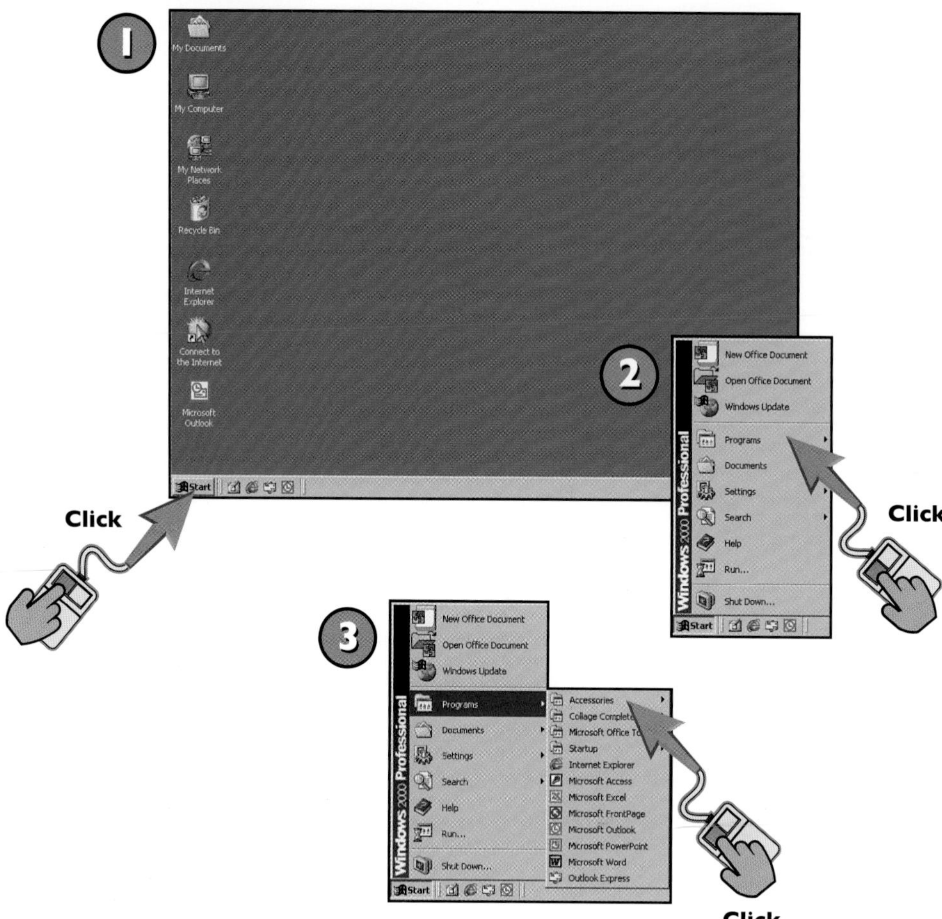

Closing the Start Menu

To close the Start menu without making a choice, simply click outside the menu.

Program Not Listed?

If you don't see your program icon listed, you can easily add programs to the Start menu. For more information about how to handle this, see Part 6, "Setting Up Programs."

1. Click the **Start** button.
2. Click the **Programs** command.
3. Click the program group that contains the application you want to start.

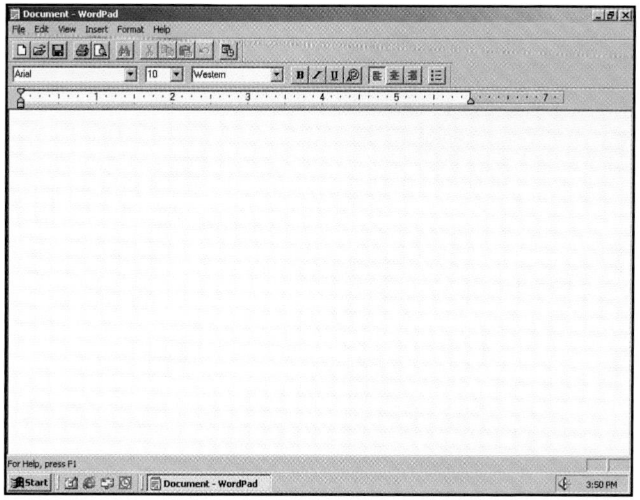

4 Click the application you want to start.

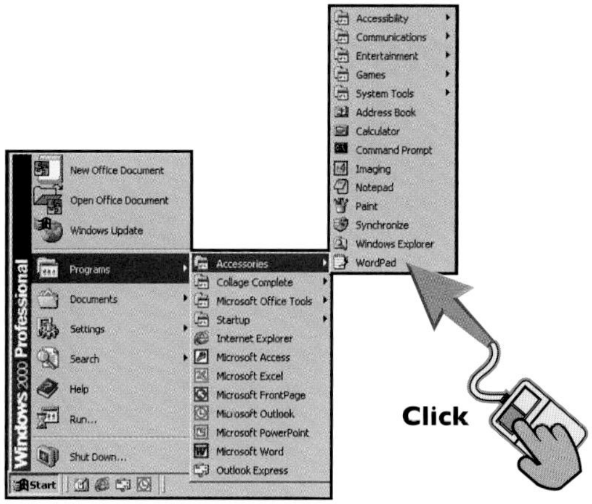

5 The application opens in its own window (here, WordPad).

Task 2: Starting an Application from a Shortcut Icon

Start Here

If you frequently use a certain program, you might want to be able to access that program right from the desktop. To do so, you can set up a shortcut icon for the program (covered in Part 6) and then start the program by double-clicking that icon. Also, some programs have shortcut icons set up for you automatically.

Double-Click

1. Double-click the shortcut icon on the desktop.
2. The application is started and displayed in its own window.

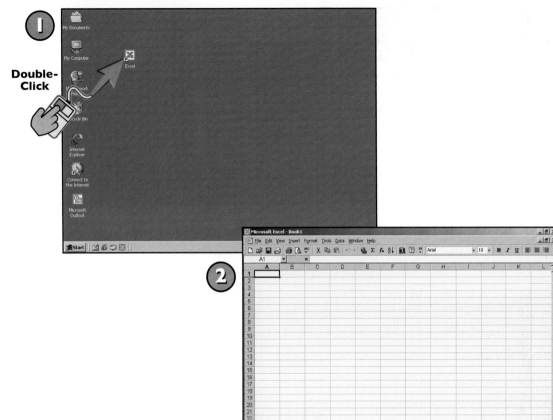

Nothing Happens?
If nothing happens when you double-click the icon, or if the icon moves, it might be because you haven't clicked quickly enough or because you clicked and dragged by accident. Be sure to press the mouse button twice quickly.

Task 3: Starting an Application and Opening a Document

1

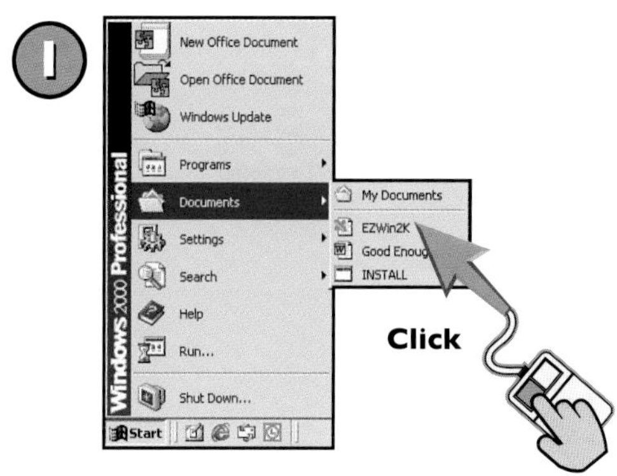

2

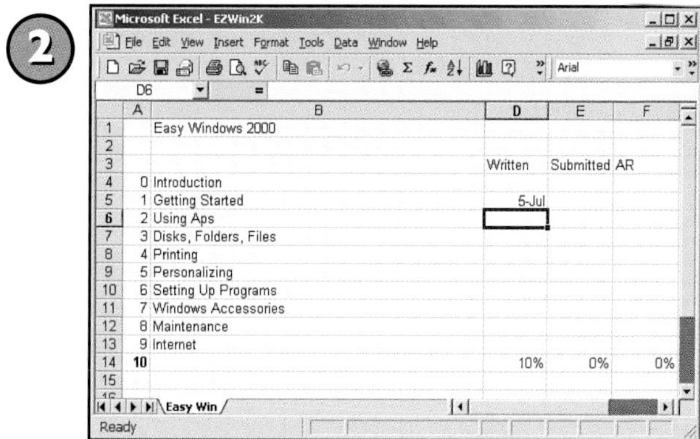

1. Click the **Start** button, click **Documents**, and then click the document you want to work on (in this case, **EZWin2K**).
2. The program for that document is started and the document is opened.

If you want to work on a document that you recently had open (in Excel, for example), you can use a shortcut to both start Excel and open the document. Windows 2000's Documents menu lists the 15 documents that you have opened most recently.

Clearing the Documents Menu

To clear the Documents menu, click the **Start** menu, choose **Settings**, and then choose **Taskbar & Start Menu**. Click the **Start Menu Options** tab and click the **Clear** button.

Document Not Listed?

If the document you want to use is not listed, it's probably because it's not one of the last 15 you have worked on. In this case, simply start the program you need and then open the document. Alternatively, you can display the document in My Computer or Windows Explorer and then double-click the document's icon.

Task 4: Switching Between Applications

Start Here

Because you most likely work with more than one type of document, you need a way to switch from one program to another. For example, you might want to compare price figures from an Excel worksheet with a price list you've set up in Word. Switching between applications enables you not only to compare data, but also to share data.

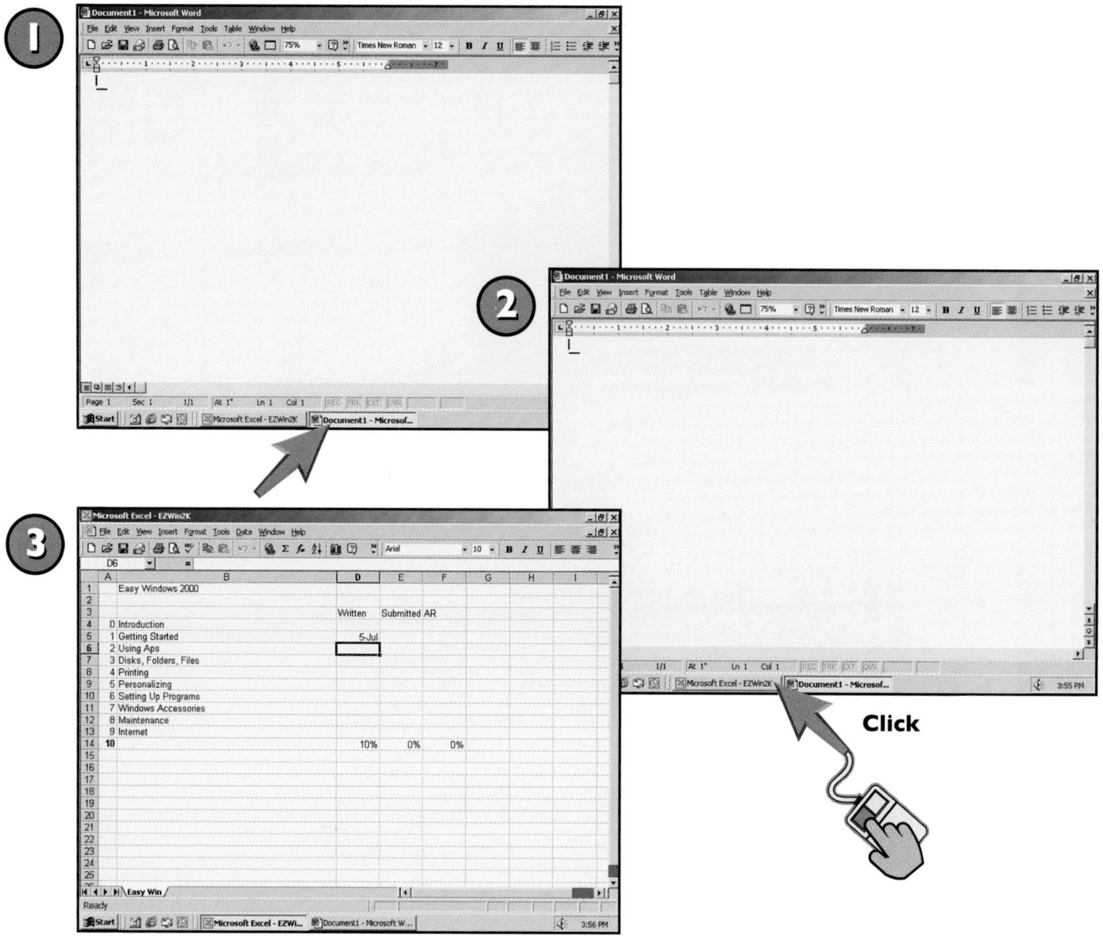

Click

Looking at the Taskbar

You can tell what programs are open by looking at the taskbar. Each open program is represented by a button; the button representing the program you are currently using is selected.

How Many Programs Open?

The number of programs you can have open at any one time depends on the amount of RAM (random-access memory) in your system.

1. After you've started two programs, look at the taskbar. You should see a button for each program. In this case, the Microsoft Word button is selected; Microsoft Word is displayed onscreen.
2. Click the button for the program you want to switch to (in this case, Microsoft Excel).
3. Excel becomes the active program.

Task 5: Closing an Application

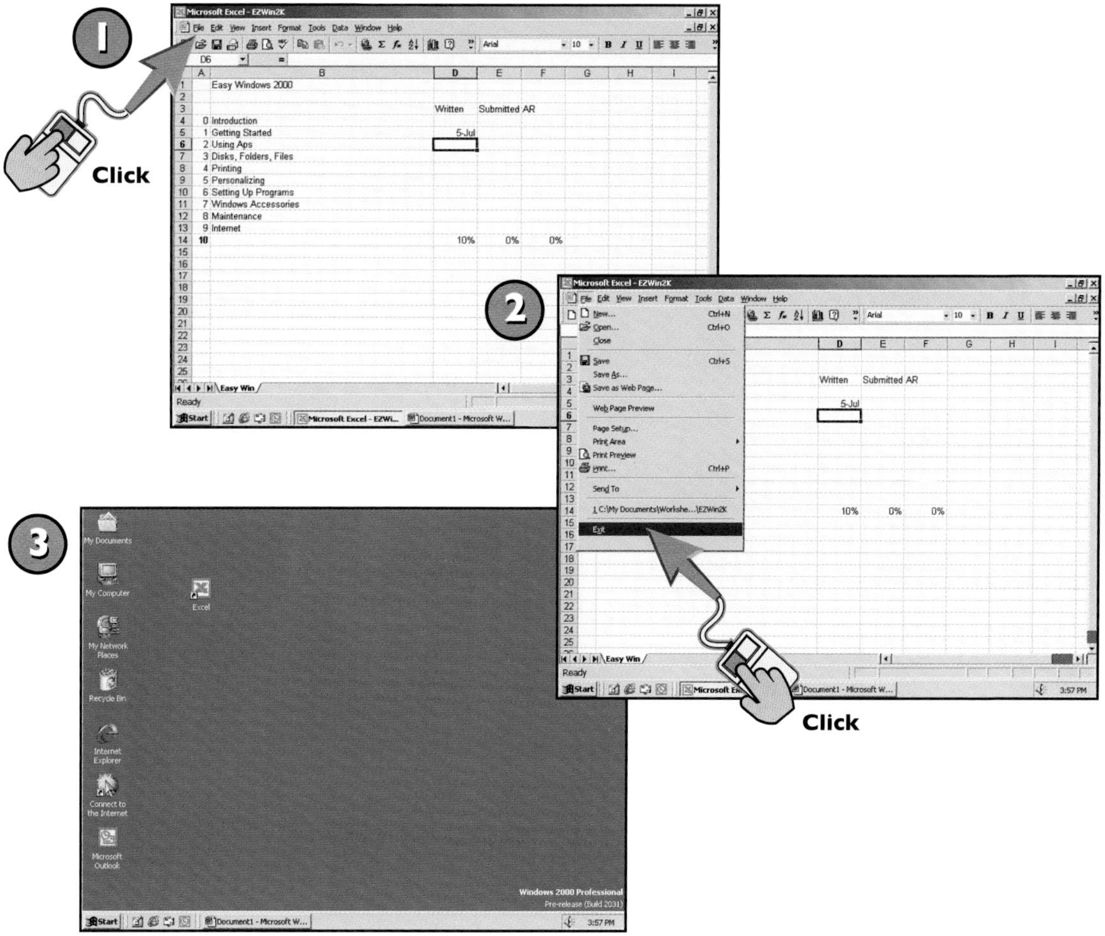

When you finish working in an application, close it to free system memory. Too many open applications can tax your system's memory and slow the computer's processes, such as saving, printing, switching between applications, and so on.

Click

Click

1 Click **File**.

2 Click the **Exit** command.

3 The program is closed. Notice that the taskbar button for Excel has disappeared.

Other Methods
To close an application, you can also press **Alt+F4** or click the **Close** (×) button in the application's title bar.

Forgetting to Save?
If you have not saved a file and choose to close that file's application, a message box appears asking if you want to save the file. If you do, click **Yes**; if not, click **No**. If you want to return to the document, click **Cancel**. For more information, see Task 8, "Saving a Document," later in this part.

Task 6: Closing a Stuck Program

Start Here

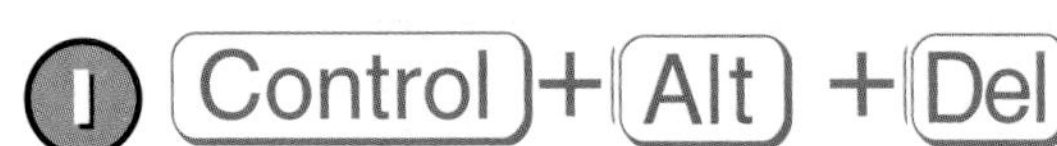

Sometimes (and who knows why) a program gets stuck. Nothing happens when you press a key. The program just does not respond. If this happens, you can use the Task Manager to close the stuck program.

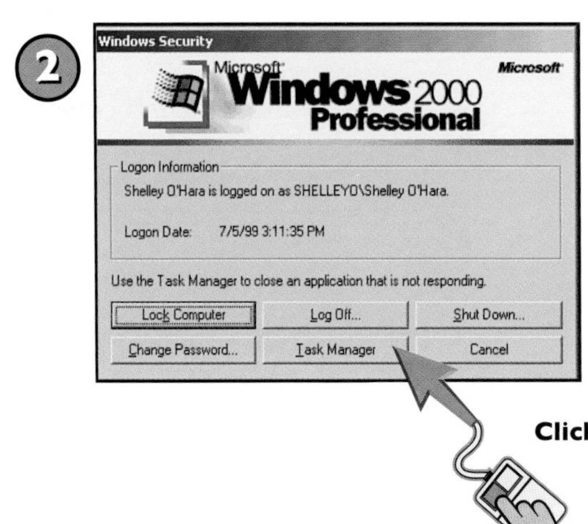

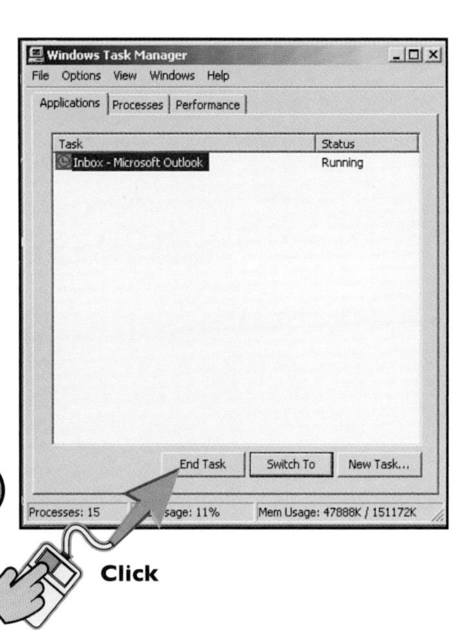

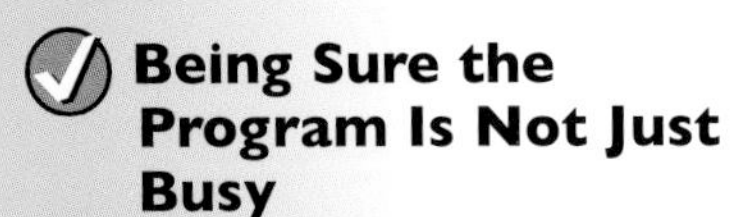

Being Sure the Program Is Not Just Busy

Before you restart, be sure the program is stuck and not just busy. Check the disk activity light. Listen for the disk. If you hear the disk whirring or see the disk light blinking, the program might just be busy.

Program Not Responding

You can also try to close the program from the taskbar. Right-click its button and then click **Close**. If you see a message that says the program is not responding, click the **End Now** button.

1. Press **Ctrl+Alt+Delete**.
2. In the Windows Security dialog box, click the **Task Manager** button.
3. Click the program you want to close and click the **End Task** button.

End Task

Task 7: Closing a Document

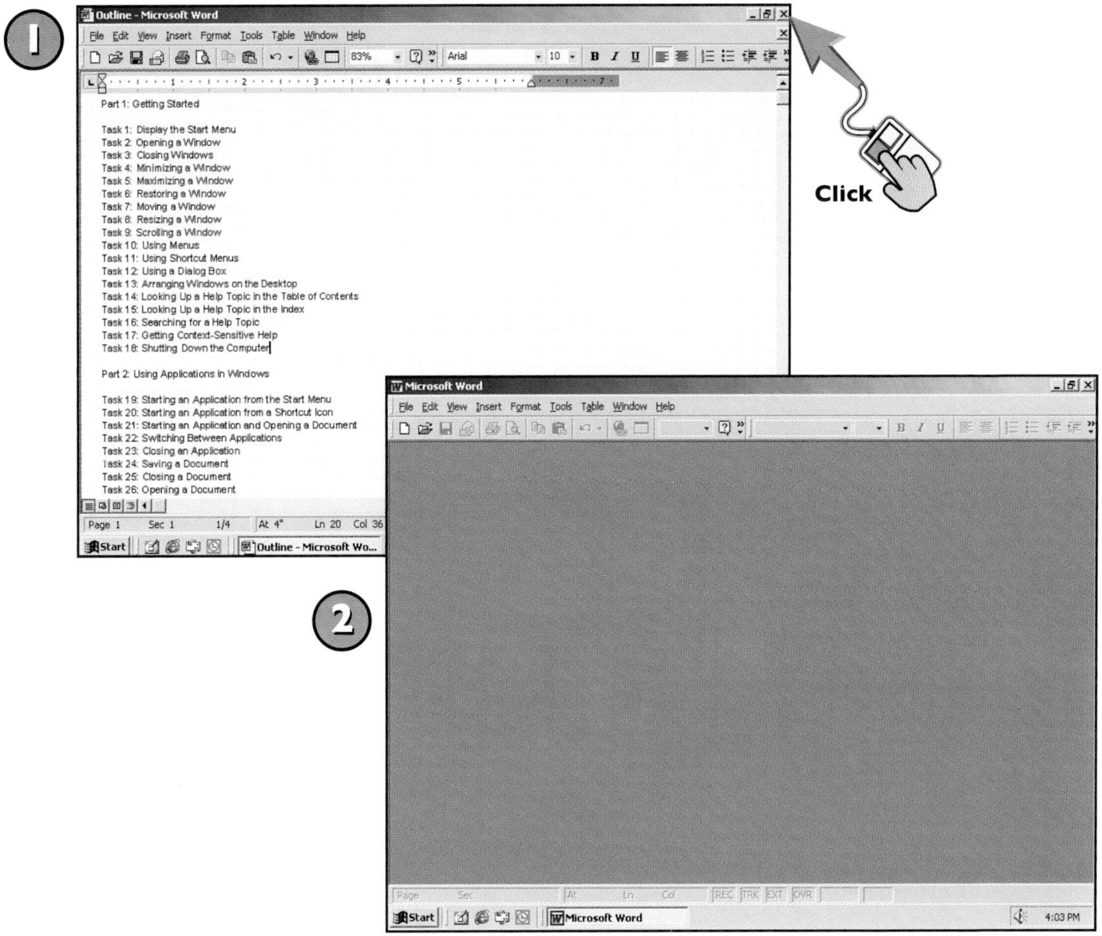

Click

When you save a document, that document remains open so that you can continue working. If you want to close the document, you can easily do so. You should close documents that you are no longer using to free up memory.

1. Click the **Close** (×) button.

2. The document is closed, but the program remains open. You can create a new document or open an existing document.

Don't Click the Program Window's Close Button

If you click the **Close** (×) button on the program window, you exit the program. Be sure to use the button for the document window if you want to remain in the program but close the document.

Task 8: Saving a Document

Start Here

You save documents and files so that you can refer to them later for printing, editing, copying, and so on. The first time you save a file, you must assign that file a name and folder (or location). You save documents pretty much the same way in all Windows applications; this task shows you how to save a document in Word.

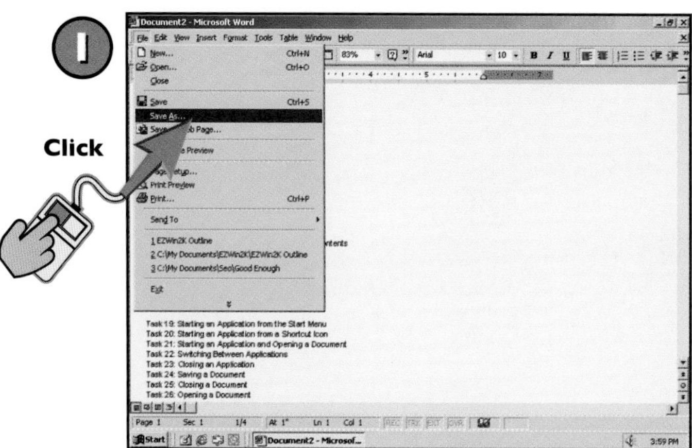

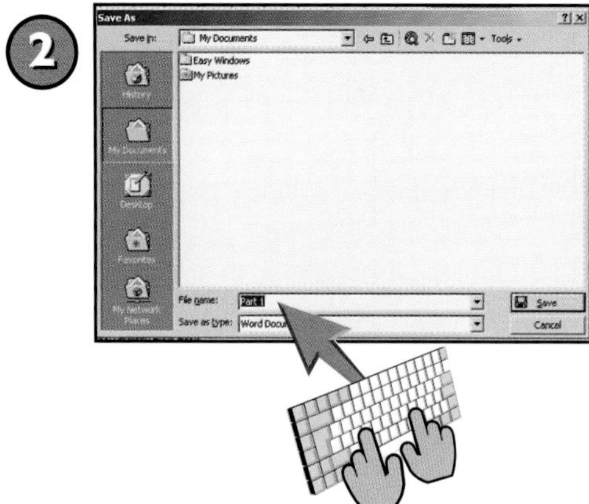

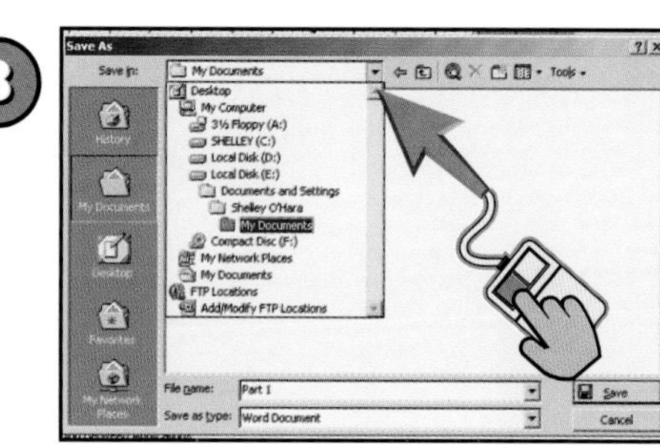

Saving with a Different Name

To save a file with a different name or in a different location, use the **Save As** command and enter a different filename or folder.

Don't Use These Characters

You cannot use any of the following characters in a filename: :
" ? * < > / \ ¦
You can, however, use spaces, letters, and numbers.

1. Click **File**, and then click the **Save As** command.
2. The program might propose a name for the file. You can either accept this name or type a new name.
3. To save the document in another drive, click the **Save In** drop-down list and select the drive you want.

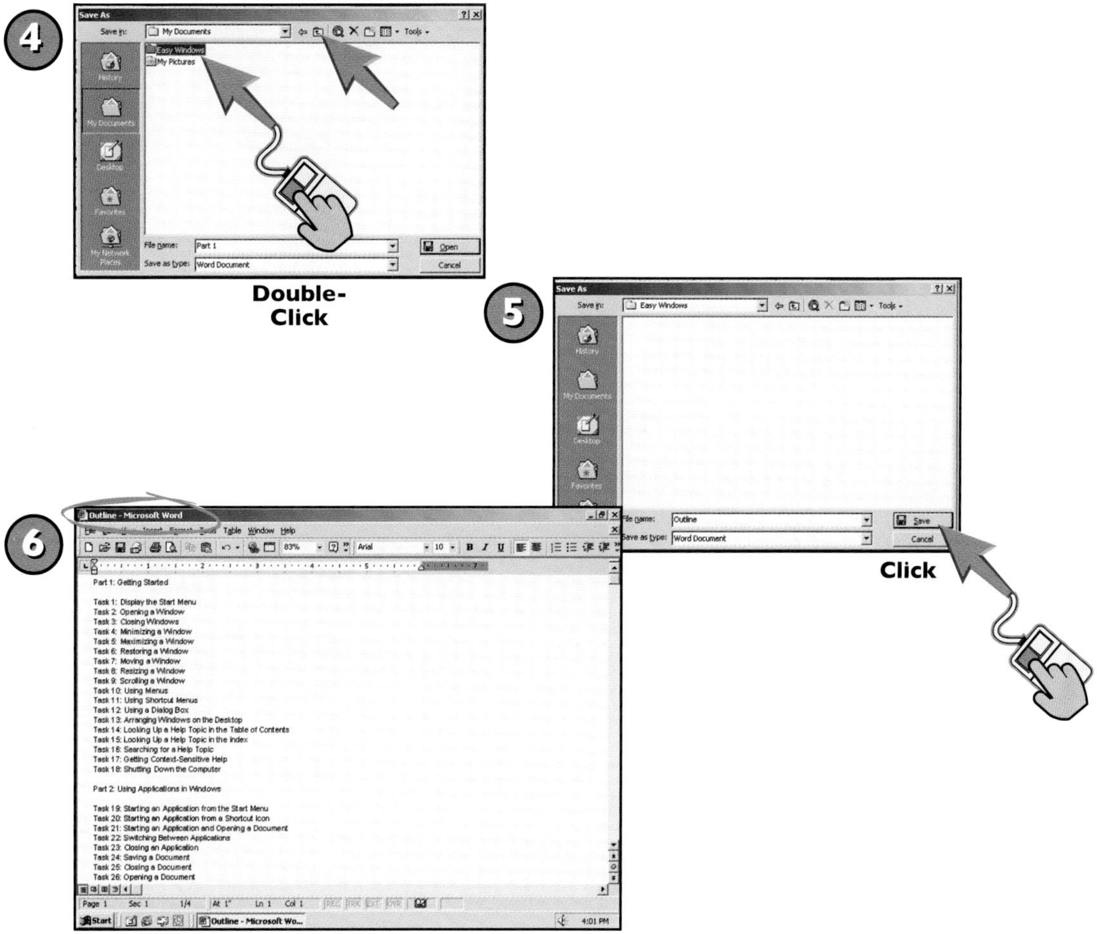

Double-Click

Click

4 To save the document in another folder, double-click the desired folder in the list. To move up through the folder structure, click the **Up** button and then double-click the folder you want.

5 Click the **Save** button.

6 The application saves the file and returns to the document window. The document name is listed in the title bar.

Saving Again

After you've saved and named a file, you can simply click File and select Save to resave that file to the same location with the same name. Any changes you have made since the last save are reflected in the file.

Task 9: Opening a Document

Start Here

The purpose of saving a document is to make it available for later use. You can open any of the documents you have saved by selecting **File** and choosing the **Open** command.

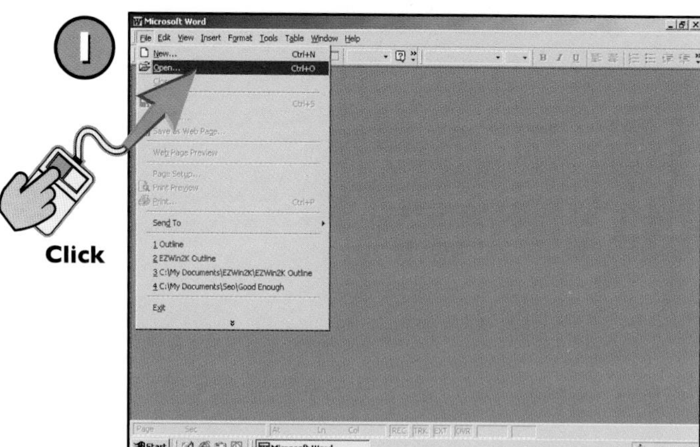

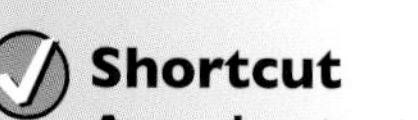

Can't Find the File?

If you can't find the file you want to work with, it could be because you did not save it where you thought you did. Try looking in a different drive or folder. If you still can't find it, try searching for the file (for more information about searching for files, see Part 3, "Working with Disks, Folders, and Files").

Shortcut

As a shortcut, click **File**. You'll notice that the last files opened are listed near the bottom of the menu. You can open any of these files by clicking them in the File menu.

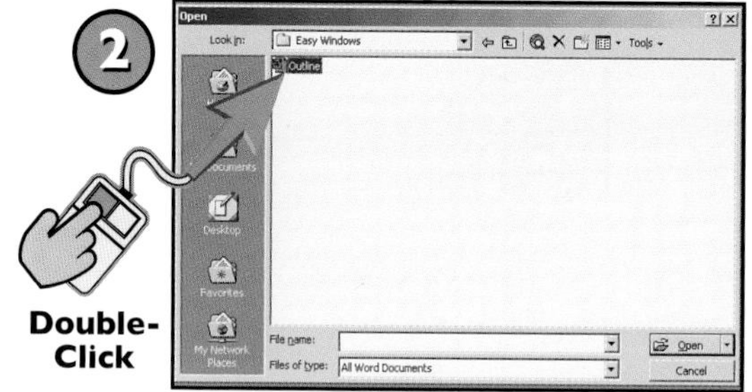

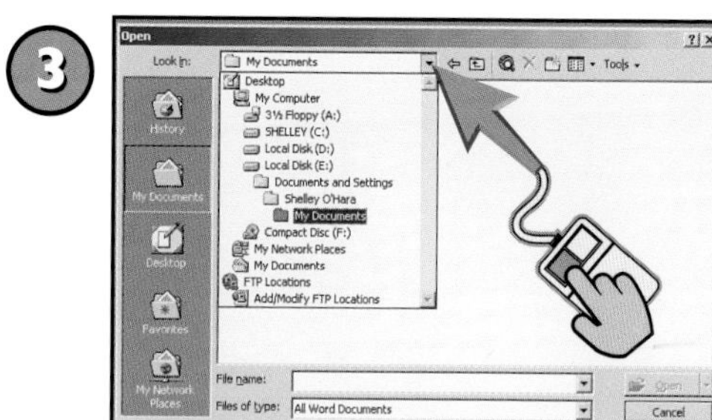

1. Click **File** and then click the **Open** command.
2. If the file you need is listed in the dialog box, double-click it and skip the remaining steps.
3. If the file is not listed, display the **Look In** drop-down list and select the drive where you placed the file.

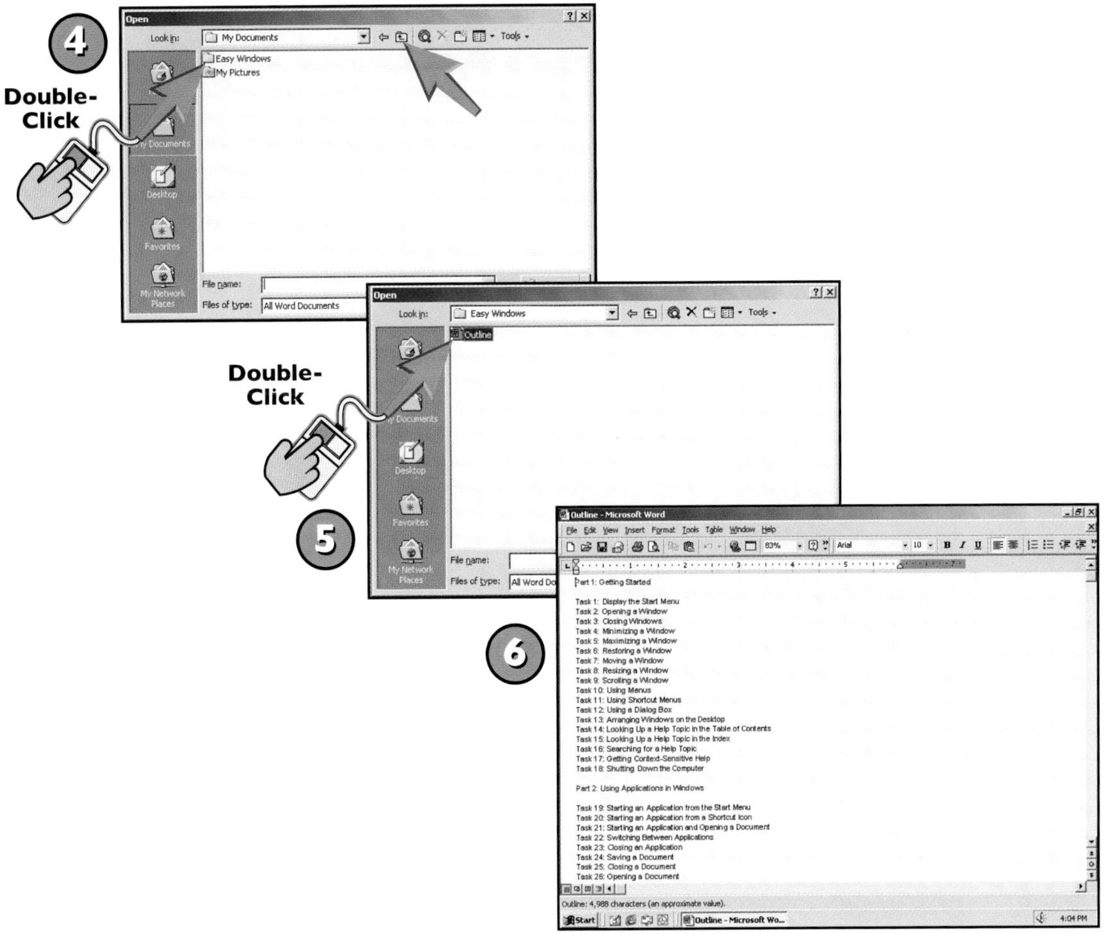

4 Double-click the folder name where you placed the file. You can use the **Up** button to move up through the folder structures.

5 When you find the file you seek, double-click it.

6 The file is opened.

My Documents and Favorites Folders

In Office applications, you can use the buttons in the Places bar to display certain folders, including the My Documents folder and the Favorites folder. Click the button to display that folder.

Task 10: Switching Between Open Documents

Start Here

Just as you can work with several sheets of paper on your desk, you can work with several documents in your application. Simply click File and select the Open command to open the files you want to work with. Then you can easily switch between any of the open documents.

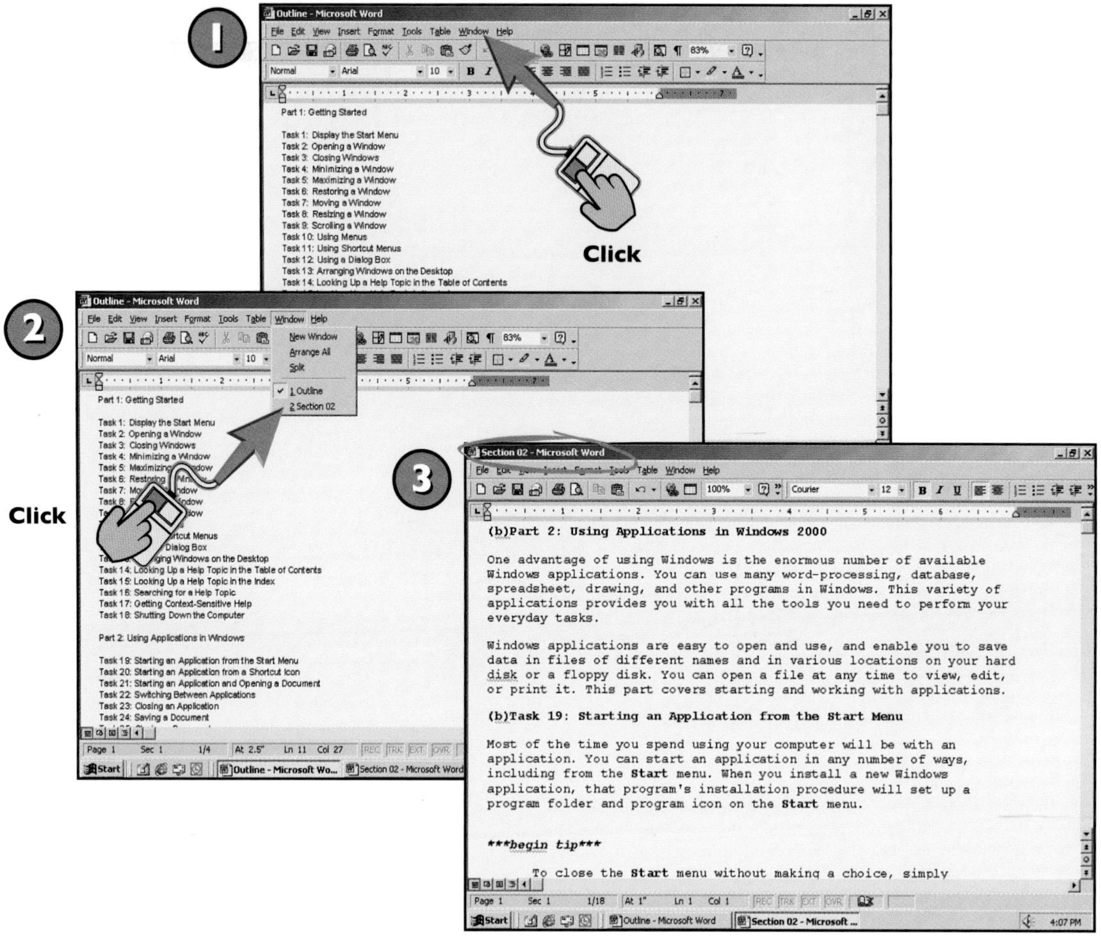

Switching Programs Versus Switching Documents

Don't confuse switching between documents with switching between programs. To switch programs, use the taskbar. For more information, refer to Task 4, "Switching Between Applications."

Arranging All Open Documents

You can arrange all open documents in the window to make your desktop easier to manage. Simply click Window, select the Arrange All command, and then choose the arrangement you want.

1. Click **Window**.

2. Notice that the current document has a check mark next to its name (here the document named Outline). Click the document that you want to switch to (in this case, the document called Section 2).

3. The document you just clicked in the Window menu becomes the active document (here the document named Section 2).

Task 11: Creating a New Document

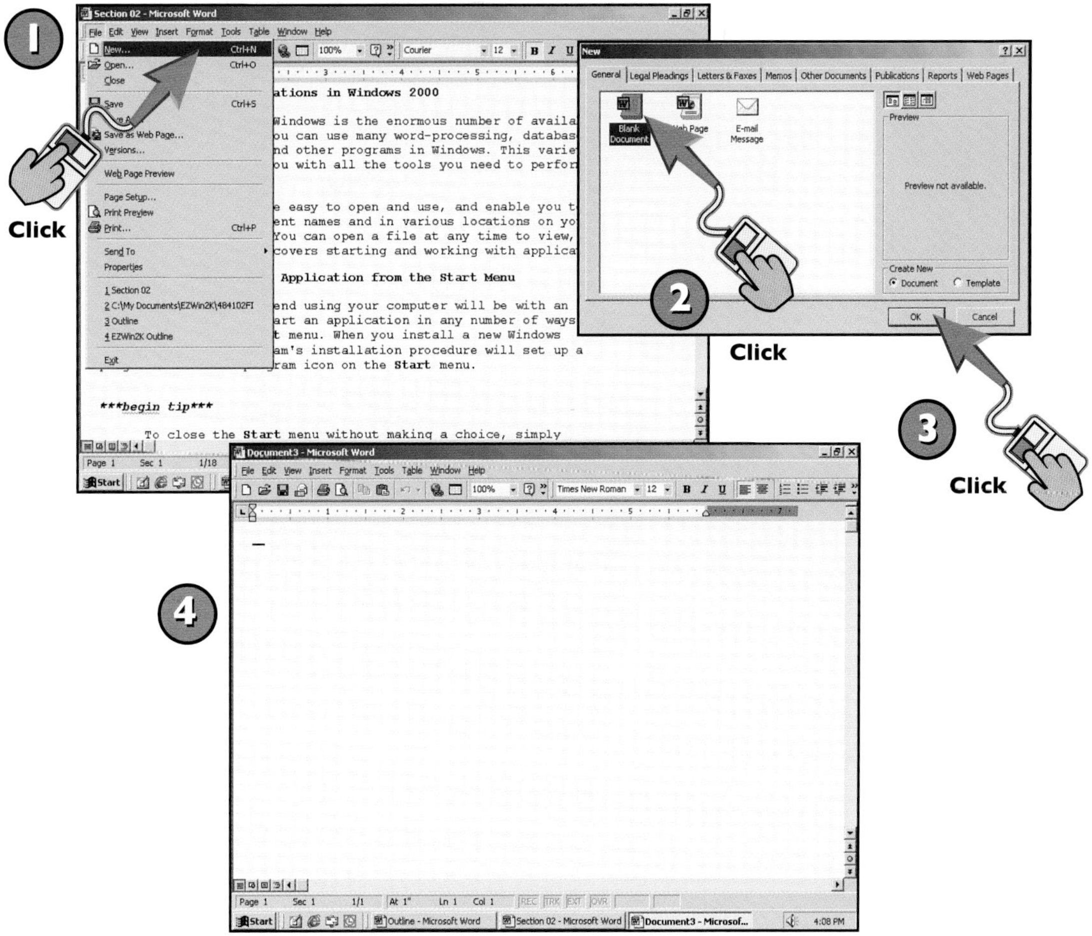

When you want a new "sheet" of paper, you can create a new document. For complex programs like PowerPoint (a presentation program) and Access (a database program), you might be prompted to make some selections before the new document is created. For others, you simply select the template you want. (A *template* is a pre-designed document.)

1. Click **File** and then click the **New** command.
2. If you see a New dialog box, click the type of document you want to create.
3. Click the **OK** button.
4. A new document is displayed.

Shortcut
As a shortcut, you can click the **New** button to create a new document based on the default template.

Task 12: Copying Text

Start Here

One of the most common editing tasks is to copy text. You can copy text and paste the copy in the current document or in another document.

Click & Drag

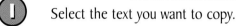

Click

Click

Copying to Another Document

To copy data from one open document to another, select the text and then move to the document where you want to paste the text using the **Window** menu.

Copying to Another Application

For information about copying data from one application to another, see Task 14, "Copying Data Between Applications."

1. Select the text you want to copy.
2. Click **Edit** and then select the **Copy** command. Windows copies the data from the document and places it in the Clipboard, a temporary holding spot.
3. Click the spot in the document where you want to put the copied data.

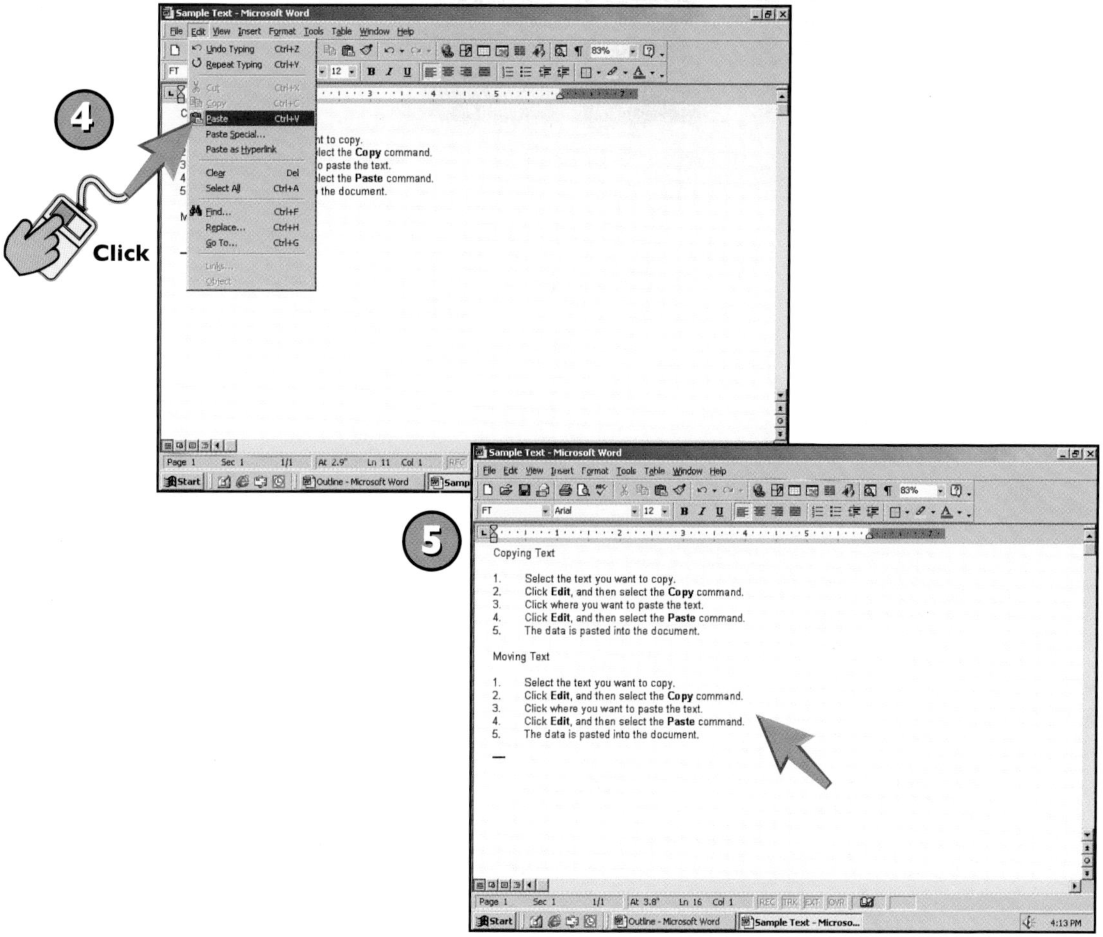

4

Click

5

4 Click **Edit** and then select the **Paste** command.

5 The data is pasted at the location you selected.

Shortcuts

You can also use the keyboard shortcut Ctrl+C to copy and use the keyboard command Ctrl+V to paste. Look also for toolbar buttons for Copy and Paste.

Task 13: Moving Text

Just as you can copy text, you can move text from one location in a document to another location in the same document. You can also move text from one document to another. Moving text is similar to copying text, except that when you move something it is deleted from its original location.

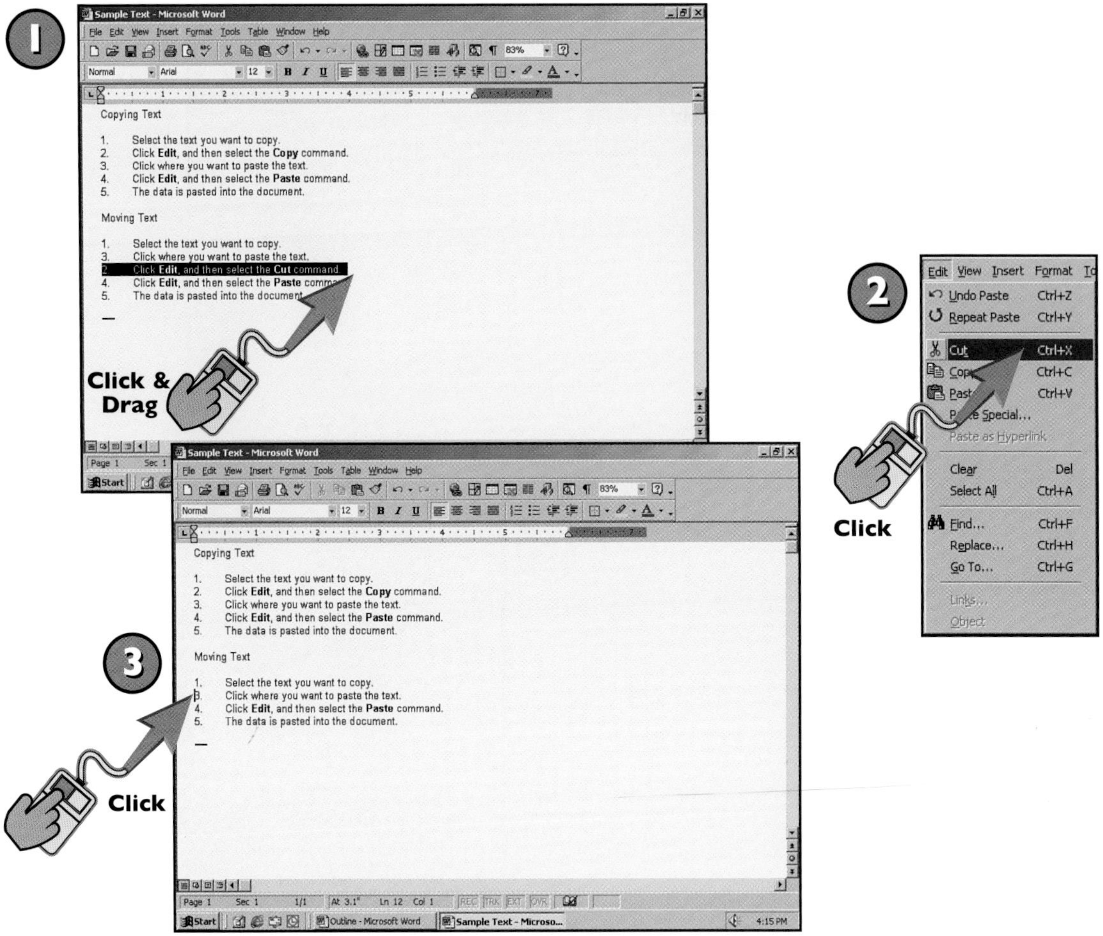

Start Here

Moving to Another Document
To move data from one open document to another, select the text and then move to the document where you want to paste the text using the **Window** menu.

Moving Text to Another Program
For help on moving data from one application to another, see Task 15, "Moving Data Between Applications."

1. Select the text you want to move.
2. Click **Edit** and then click the **Cut** command. Windows deletes the data from the document and places it in the Clipboard, a temporary holding spot.
3. Click in the document where you want to place the text.

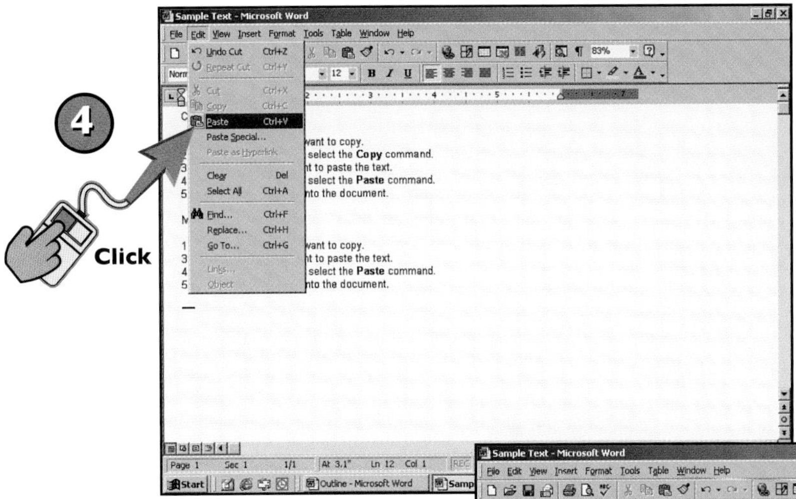

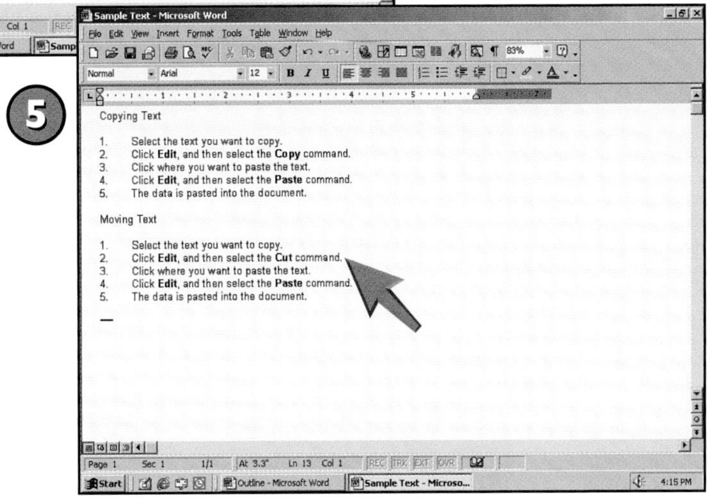

4 Click Edit and then select the Paste command.

5 The text is pasted into the new location.

Shortcuts

You can also use the keyboard shortcut **Ctrl+X** to cut and use the keyboard command **Ctrl+V** to paste. Look also for toolbar buttons for **Cut** and **Paste**.

Undoing a Move

You can undo a paste operation if you change your mind after performing the action. Simply click **Edit** and then select the **Undo Paste** command to remove the text you just pasted.

4 Click **Edit** and then select the **Paste** command.

5 The text is pasted into the new location.

Task 14: Copying Data Between Applications

Start Here

You can copy data from a document in one application and paste it into another document in another application to save time typing. In addition to being able to copy text, you can copy spreadsheets, figures, charts, clip art, and so on. Using copied text and graphics saves you time in your work.

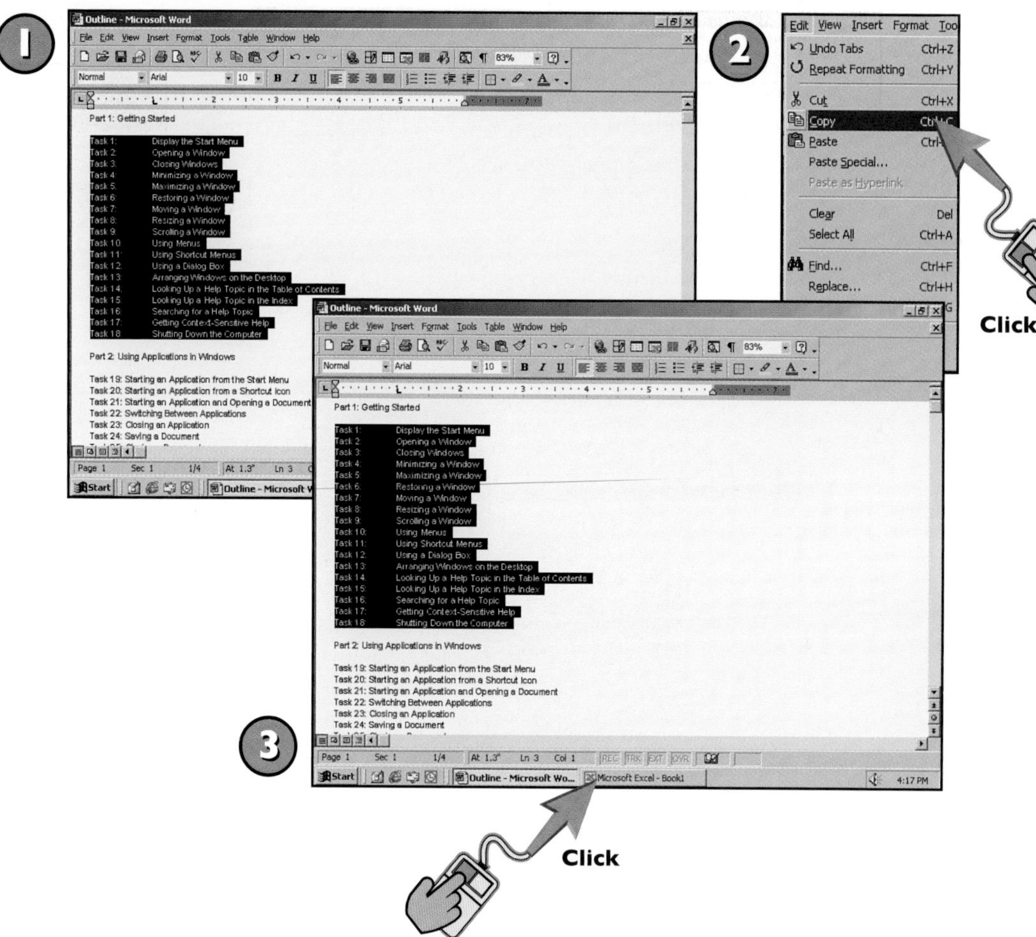

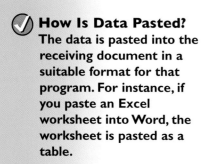

How Is Data Pasted?

The data is pasted into the receiving document in a suitable format for that program. For instance, if you paste an Excel worksheet into Word, the worksheet is pasted as a table.

1. Select the data you want to copy.
2. Click **Edit** and then click the **Copy** command.
3. Click the taskbar button representing the program you want to switch to (in this case, **Microsoft Excel**). If the program isn't started, start the program.

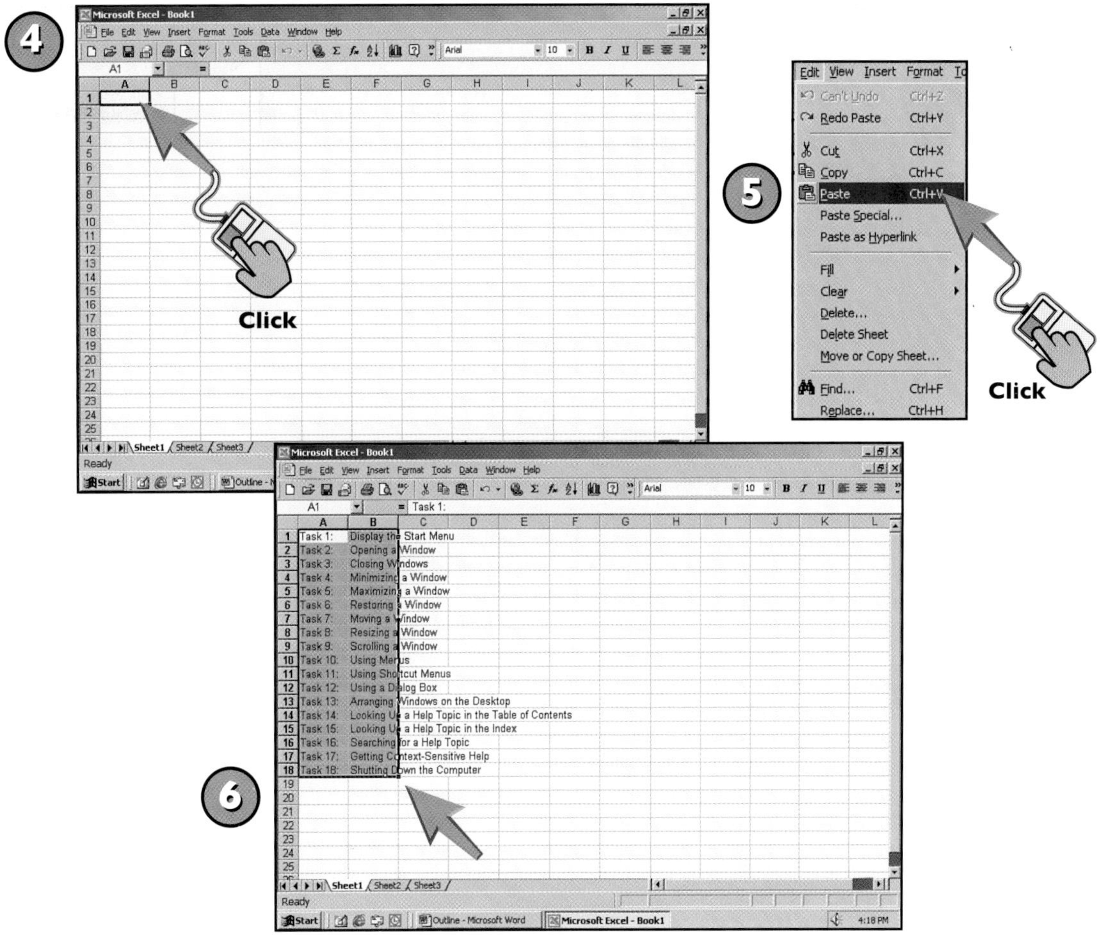

4 In the document, click the location where you want to paste the copied data.

5 Click **Edit** and then click the **Paste** command.

6 The data is pasted into the document.

Paste Command Not Available?

If the Paste command is grayed out, it means you have not copied anything. Be sure to click Edit and then select the Copy command before you try to paste the text.

Task 15: Moving Data Between Applications

You can move information from one application to another. For instance, you can cut a table of numerical data from Excel and paste it into a report in Word.

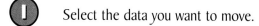

Start Here

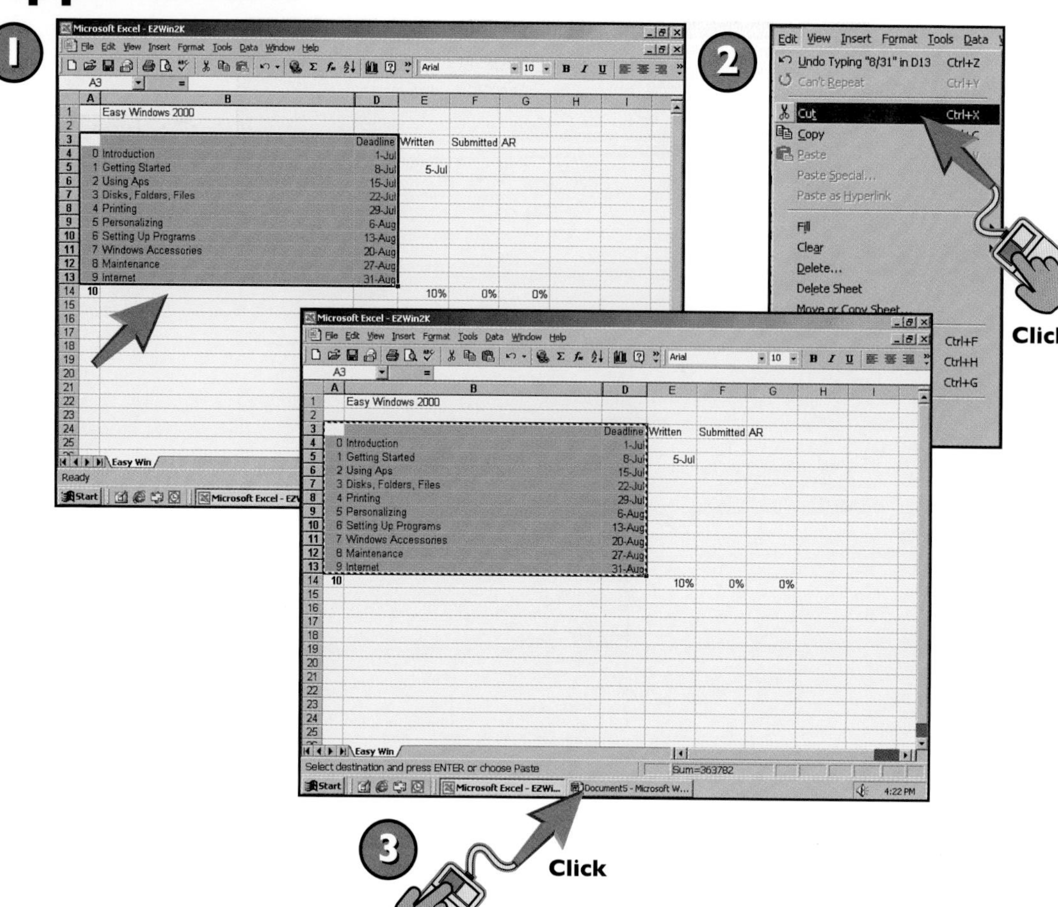

Program Not Started?
If the program to which you paste the data is not started, click the Start button, select Programs, and then click the program icon. Then you can paste the data into a new document or open a document and paste the data into that document.

1. Select the data you want to move.

2. Click **Edit** and then click the **Cut** command. Windows deletes the data from the document and places it in the Clipboard, a temporary holding spot.

3. Click the taskbar button representing the program you want to switch to (in this case, **Microsoft Word**).

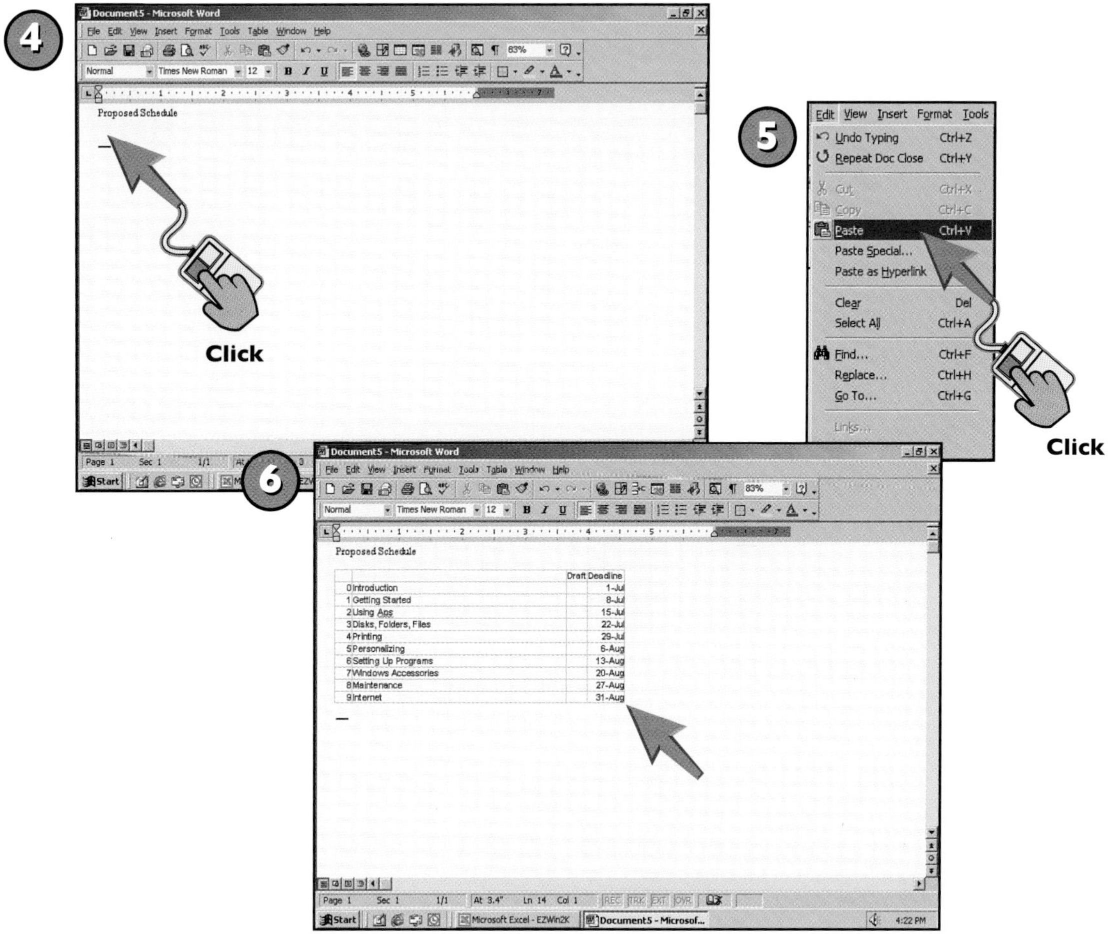

4 Click in the document where you want to place the data.

5 Click **Edit** and then click the **Paste** command.

6 The data is pasted into the document.

How Is Data Pasted?
The data is pasted into the receiving document in a suitable format for that program. For instance, if you paste an Excel worksheet into Word, the worksheet is pasted as a table.

Task 16: Linking Data Between Applications

You might link data between applications if you want the data to be updated automatically when you edit or add to the source document. Linking data saves you time because you only have to edit the information once; Windows then updates any linked files for you.

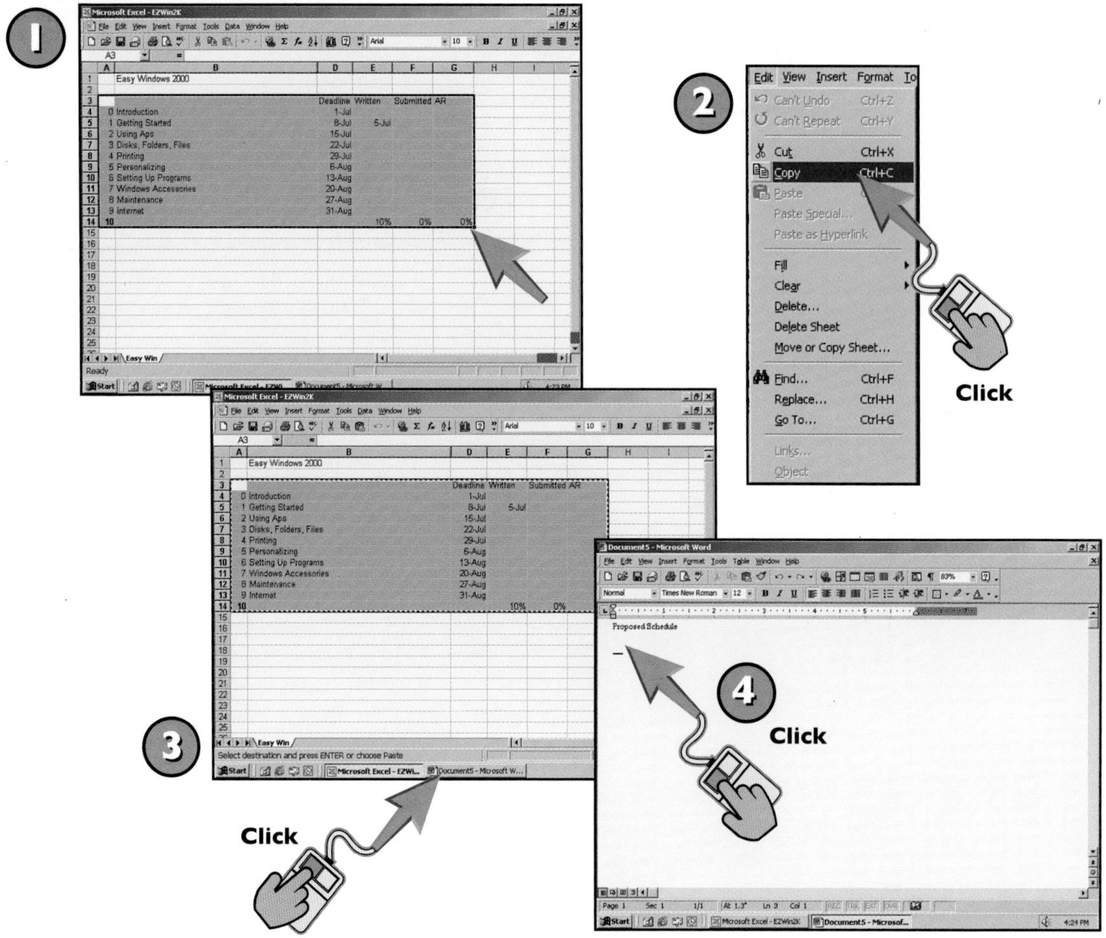

Start Here

Click

Click

Click

1. In the source document, select the data you want to link.
2. Click **Edit** and then click the **Copy** command.
3. Click the taskbar button representing the program and document where you want to paste the linked data.
4. Click in the document where you want the linked data to go.

Embedding Data

You can use embedding when you do not already have a source document for the data you want to share. Creating a source document within the destination document makes it easy for you to edit data quickly and efficiently. Open the **Insert** menu and select the **Object** command for embedding data.

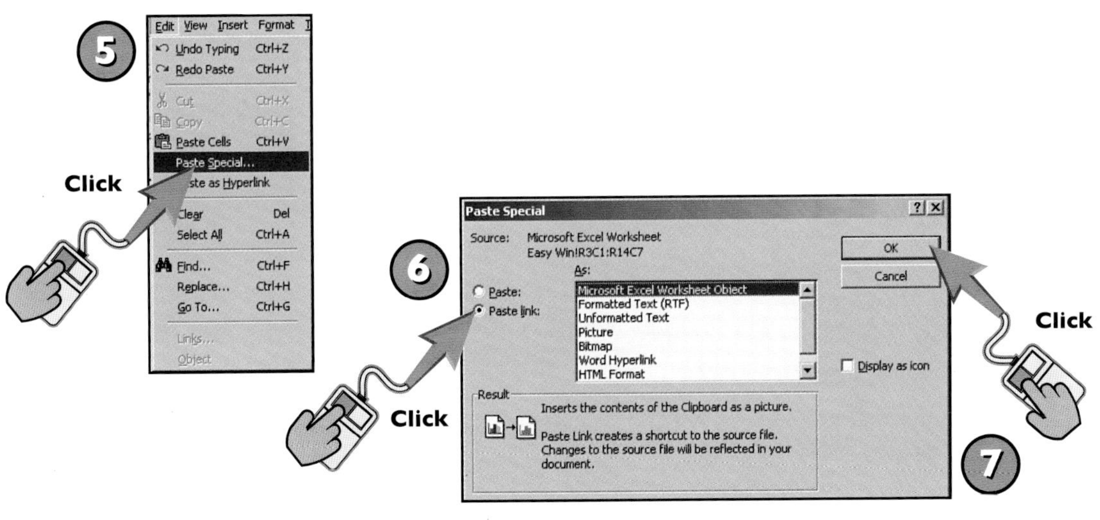

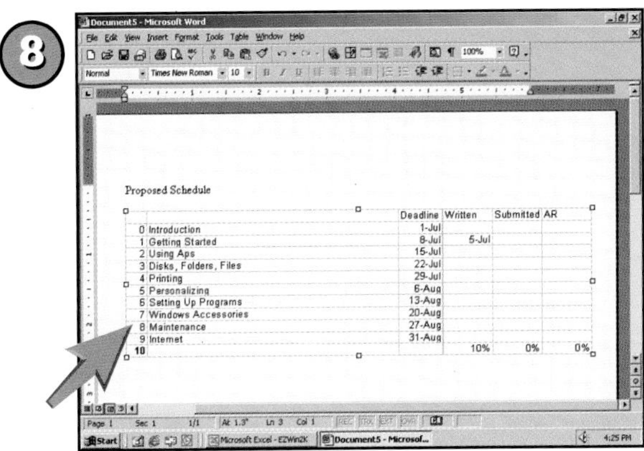

5 Click **Edit** and then click the **Paste Special** command.

6 Select the **Paste Link** radio button and then select the format you want to paste from the **As** list box.

7 Click the **OK** button.

8 Windows inserts the data with a link between the destination and the source files.

What Formats Are Listed?
The available formats depend on the type of data you're pasting and control how the data is inserted into the document.

PART 3

Working with Disks, Folders, and Files

One part of working with Windows is learning how to work with the documents you save and store on your system. Think of your computer's hard drive as a filing cabinet. To keep your files organized, you can set up folders. Folders on the hard drive represent drawers in the filing cabinet, and each folder can hold files or other folders. (In previous versions of Windows, folders were called ***directories***.) You can open and close folders, view a folder's contents, copy and move folders, and create or delete folders.

The more you work on your computer, the more files and folders you'll add. After a while, your computer will become cluttered, and you'll need a way to keep these files organized. Windows provides features that can help you find, organize, and manage your files. You can copy files, move files, delete unnecessary files, and more. For working with files and folders, you can use either My Computer or Windows Explorer, as covered in this section.

Tasks

Task 1: Opening Folders

Folders contain files, programs, or other items that you can use to do work in Windows. You can display the contents of a folder to work with the files—move a file, create a shortcut icon, start a program, and so on.

Start Here

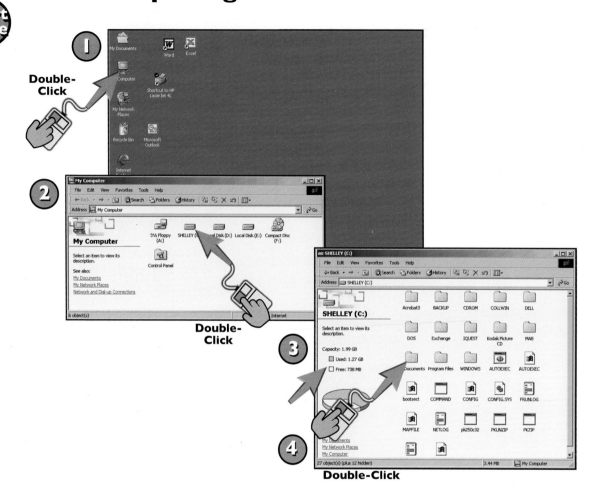

New Window Style
Windows 2000 changes the default way the contents are displayed. You can also select the original style. See Tasks 3, "Changing How the Contents of a Window Are Displayed," and 9, "Changing the View Style," later in this part.

Related Links
Windows 2000 displays related links in the lower-left corner of the window. You can click any of these links to view that folder.

1. Double-click the **My Computer** icon on the desktop.
2. Double-click the icon representing your hard drive (usually **C:**).
3. Review the information about the selected drive (new with Windows 2000).
4. Each folder icon that you see represents a folder on your hard drive. Double-click any of the folders.

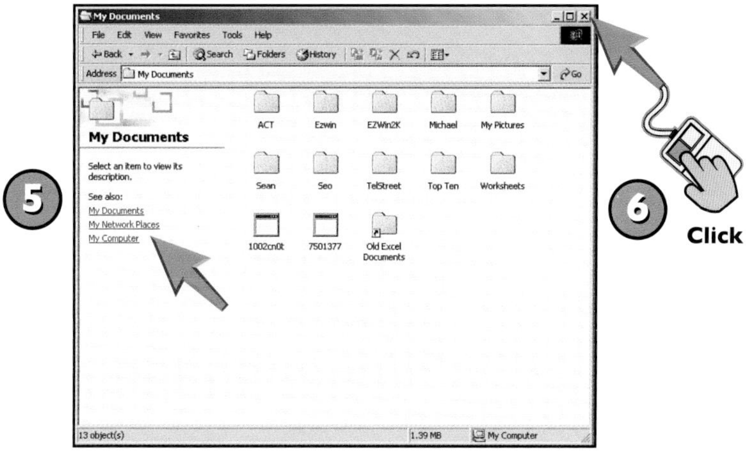

5 Information about the selected folder as well as related links are displayed in the left pane (new with Windows 2000).

6 Click the **Close** (×) button to close the window.

Task 2: Using the Toolbar Buttons in a File Window

Start Here

Each window, whether it's a file or folder window, includes a toolbar that you can use to quickly change drives or directories in the window and to change views of the folder contents.

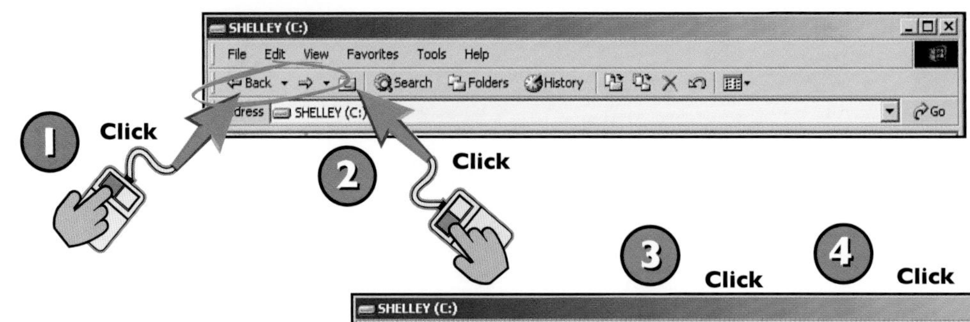

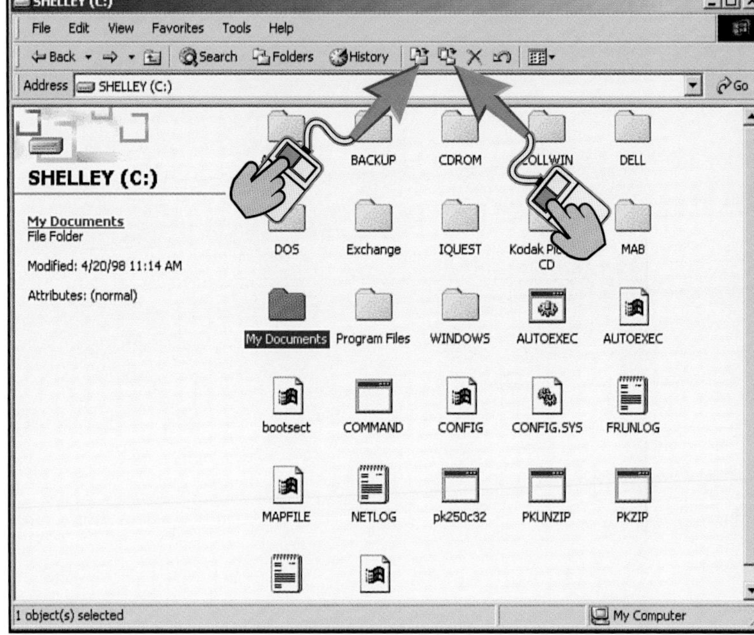

Searching for Files
For information on the Search button, see Task 24, "Finding Files and Folders."

Hiding the Toolbar
You can display other toolbars or hide the toolbar(s). Click **View**, **Toolbars**. Check any toolbars to display them. Uncheck a toolbar to hide it.

1. Click the **Back** button to go back to a previously viewed page or the **Forward** button to go forward.
2. Click the **Up** button to display the next level up in the folder structure.
3. Click the **Move To** button to move the selected item (file or folder).
4. Click the **Copy To** button to copy the selected item.

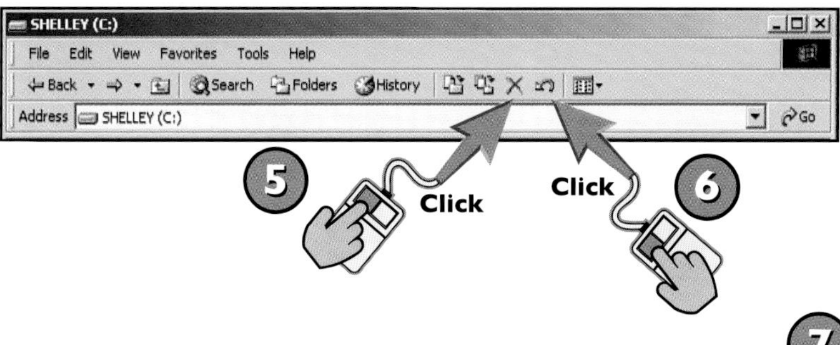

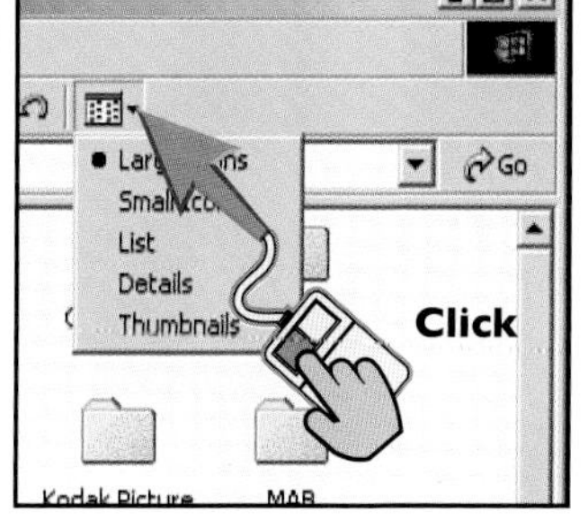

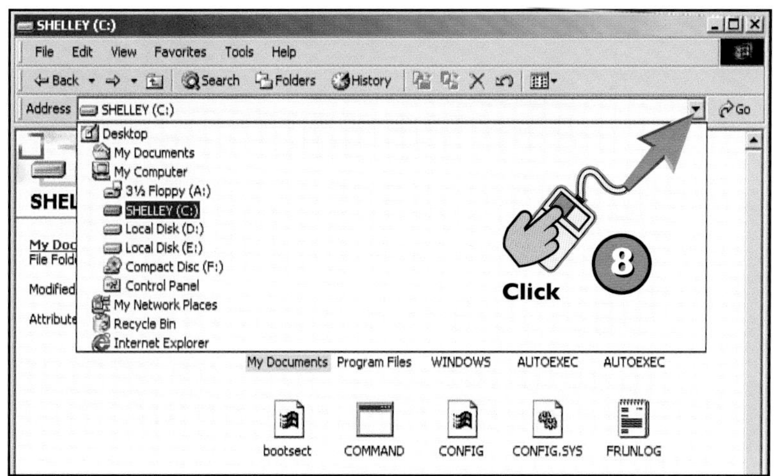

5 Click the **Delete** button to delete the selected item(s).

6 Click the **Undo** button to undo the last action.

7 Click the **Views** button to select a different view.

8 Click the **Address** drop-down list to view another drive or folder.

Task 3: Changing How the Contents of a Window Are Displayed

Start Here

You can view the contents of a window in a variety of ways. By default, Windows uses large icons to display the contents of a window. If you want to see more of a window's contents at one time, you can change the view to Small Icons. You can also display such details about an item as its type, its size, and the date it was last modified. Changing the way a window displays its contents can make it easier to find what you need.

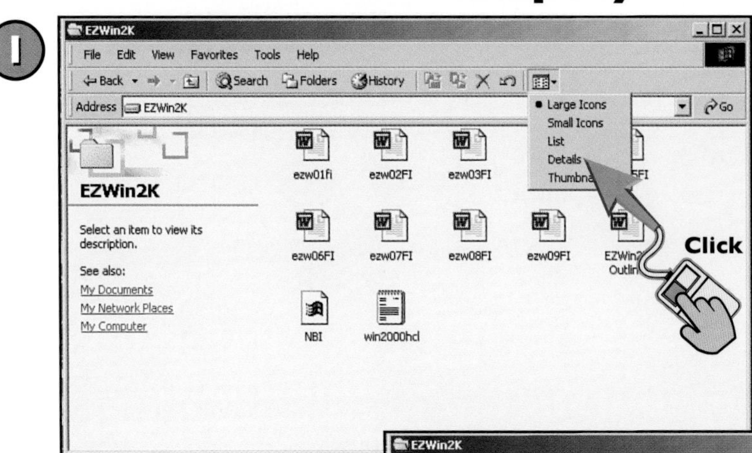

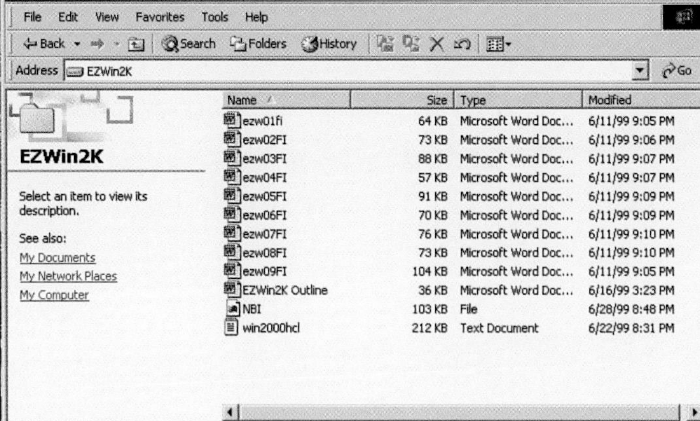

1. In the window you want to change, click the **View** button and then select the view you want.

2. The window displays the contents in that view (in this case, the Details view).

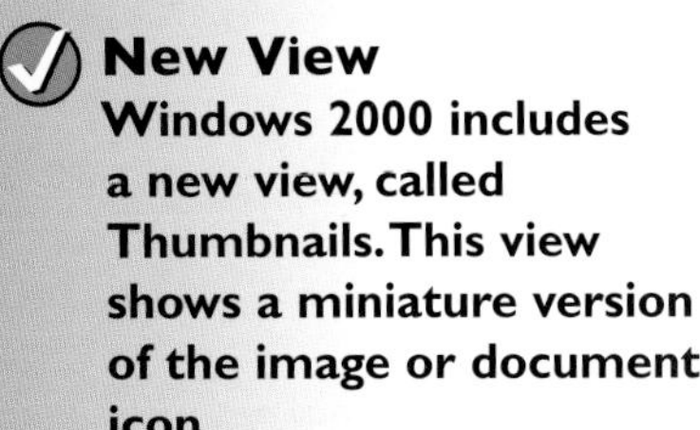

New View
Windows 2000 includes a new view, called Thumbnails. This view shows a miniature version of the image or document icon.

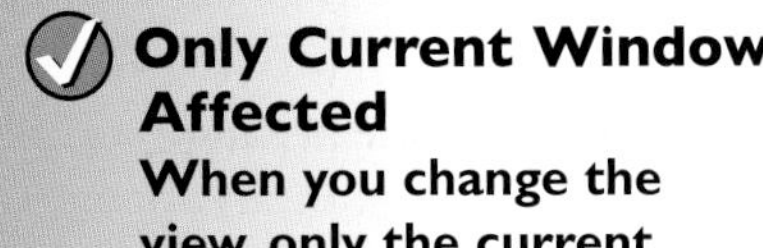

Only Current Window Affected
When you change the view, only the current window is affected.

Task 4: Sorting the Contents of a Window

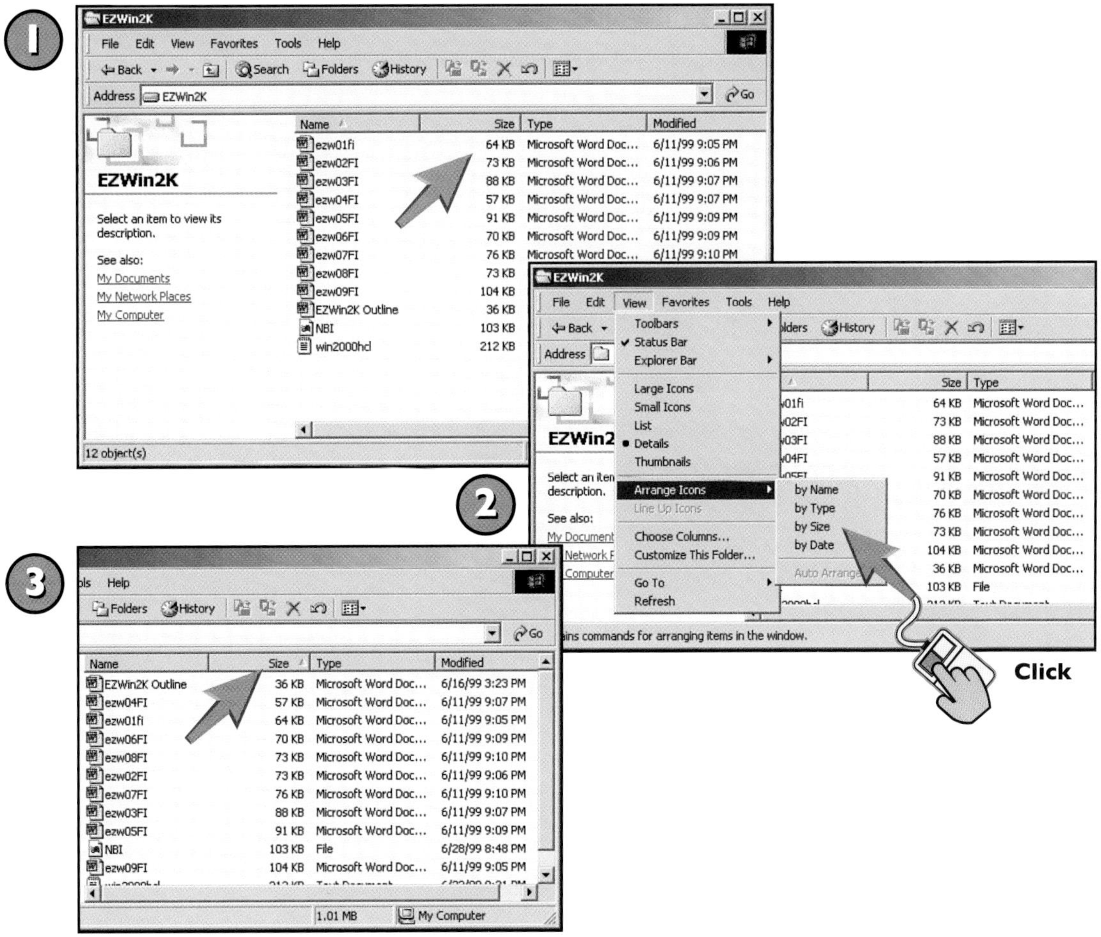

You sort the contents of a window so that you can more easily find the files you want. Windows enables you to arrange the files in a folder by name, type, date, or size. Sorting the files is even easier if you choose to view them by the file details first. You can sort files viewed as large or small icons or as a list.

1. Open the window you want to sort and change to the view you want. In this case, the window is displayed in **Detail** view so that you can see the results of sorting by different columns.

2. Click **View**, select the **Arrange Icons** command, and choose the sort order you want (in this case, **by Size**).

3. Windows sorts the files in the selected order. For instance, this view shows the files sorted by size from the smallest to largest.

Sorting Options

You can also sort by name in alphabetical order, by file type, or by date from oldest to most recent by choosing the appropriate command from the **View**, **Arrange Icons** submenu. You can also click the column header in **Details** view to sort by that column.

Top-Level Sorting

If you are working in the top-level My Computer window, you have different options for arranging the icons. You can arrange by type, size, drive letter, or free space.

Task 5: Displaying a Folder List

When you work with files, you might want to see a hierarchical view of your folders and drives. To do so, you can display folders in the Explorer bar.

1 Click

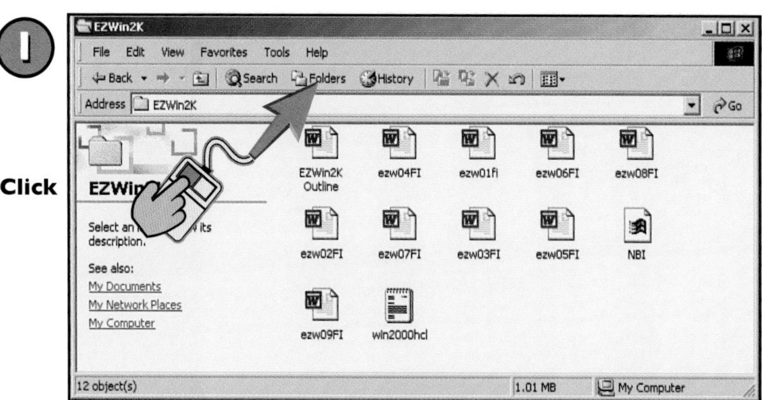

2

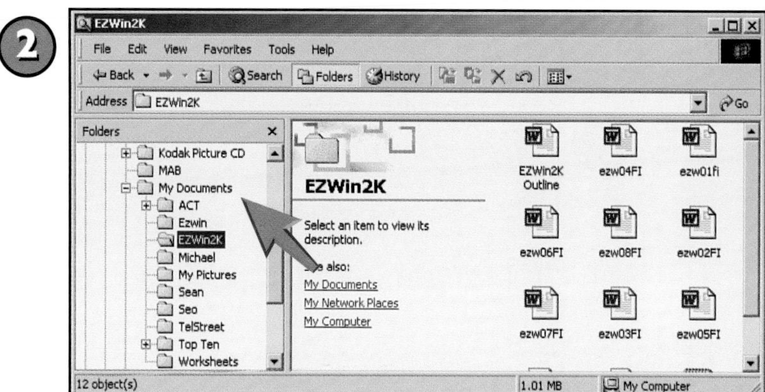

✓ **Hiding the Folders**
Click the button again to hide the folder list.

1. Open the window you want to change and click the **Folders** button.

2. A folder list is displayed in the Explorer bar (left-most pane).

Task 6: Displaying a History List

1 Click

2 Click

3

1 Open the window you want to change and click the **History** button.

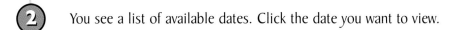

2 You see a list of available dates. Click the date you want to view.

3 Continue clicking folders until you see the list of documents or Web pages you're looking for.

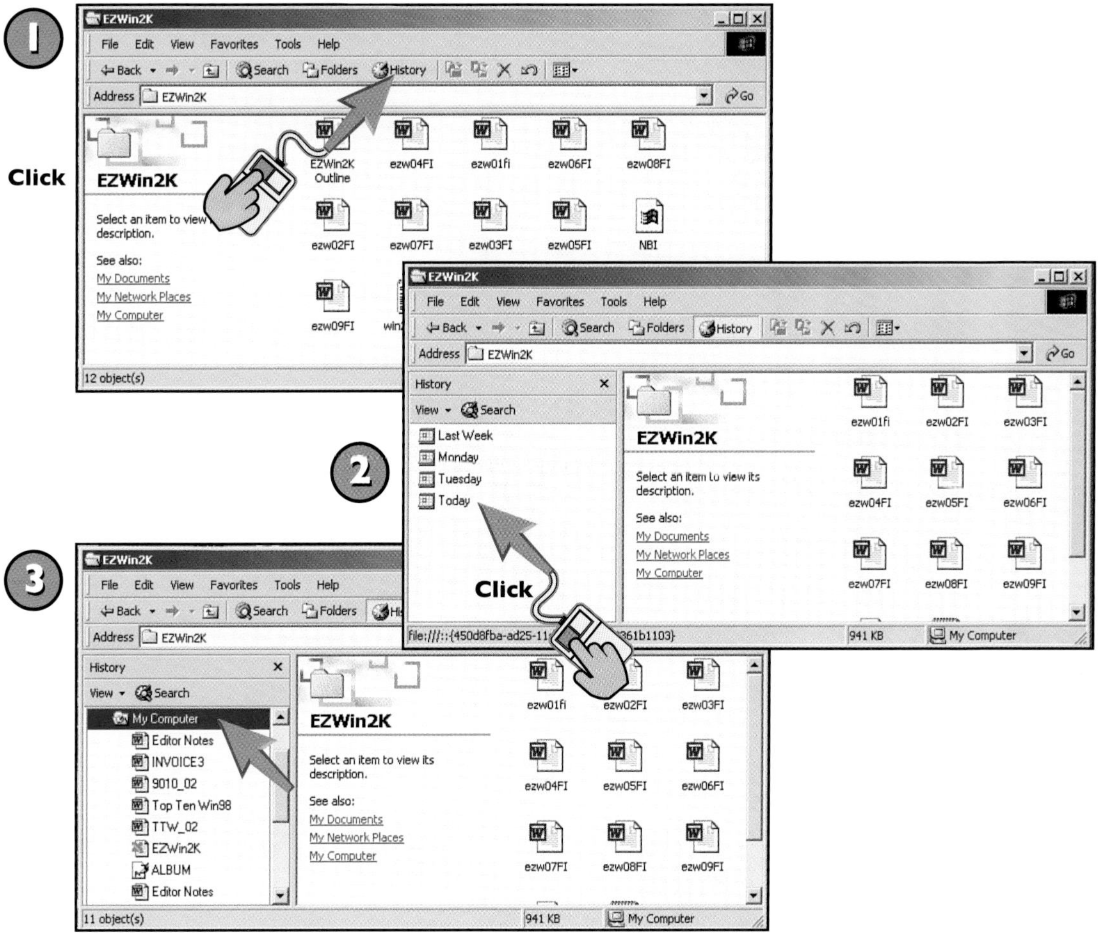

As another option, you can display a history list. This list includes Web pages, folders, and documents you have recently viewed.

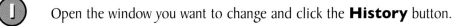

Menu Method
You can also click View, Explorer Bar, History to display this list.

Task 7: Adding a Folder to Your Favorites List

You might find in your work that you use the same folders over and over. To make it easy to view these folders, add them to your Favorites list. You can then quickly select any of the listed folders from the Favorites menu.

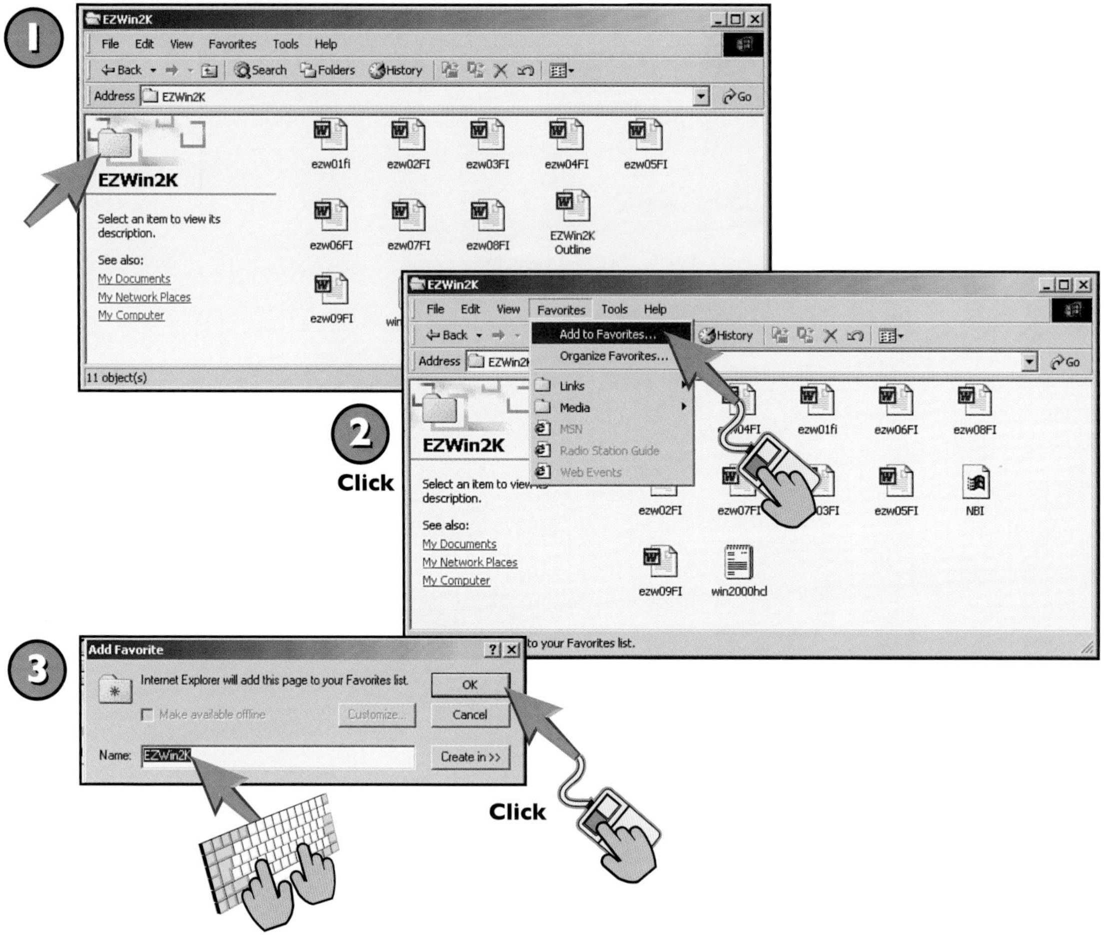

Start Here

1 Display the folder you want to add to your Favorites list.

2 Click **Favorites** and select the **Add to Favorites** command.

3 Edit the name of the folder (if necessary) and click **OK**. The folder is added to your Favorites list.

Also for Web pages
You can also add Web pages to your Favorites list. See Part 9, "Connecting to Online Services and the Internet," for information on this feature.

Task 8: Displaying a Favorites Folder

If you add a folder to your **Favorites** list, you can easily display that folder.

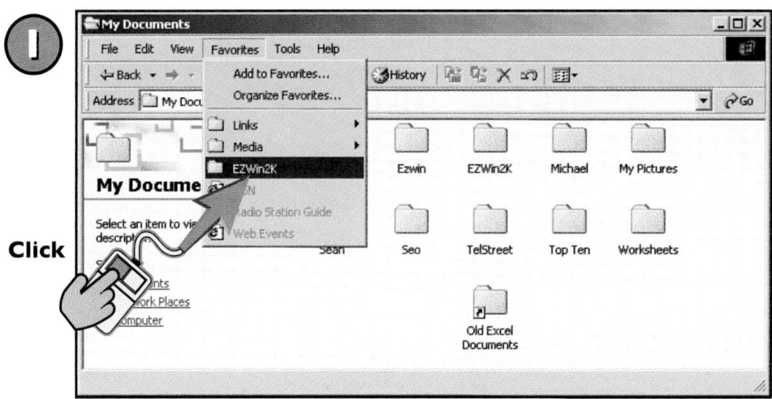

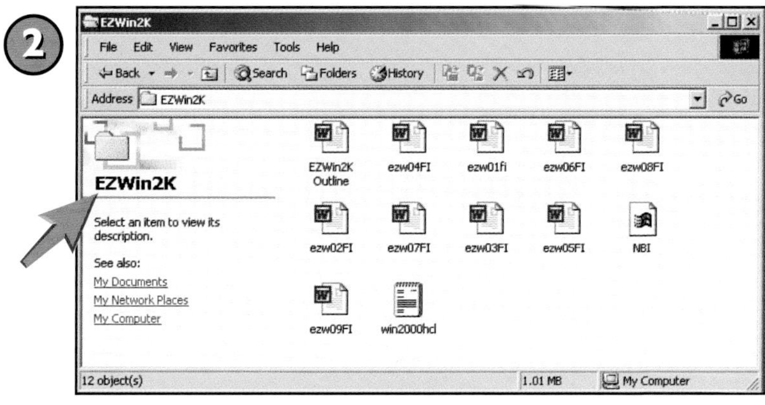

1. Click **Favorites** and select the folder.
2. The folder you selected is displayed.

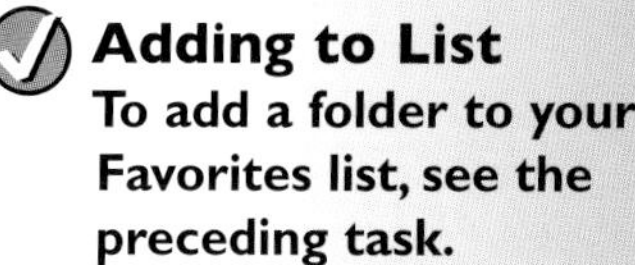

Adding to List
To add a folder to your Favorites list, see the preceding task.

Task 9: Changing the View Style

You can choose to display the contents of a window in the classic style. You can also select whether each folder is opened in its own window and whether you double-click or single-click to open an item.

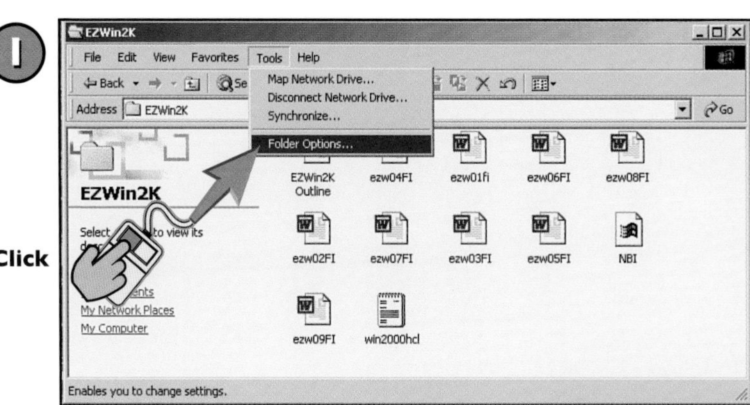

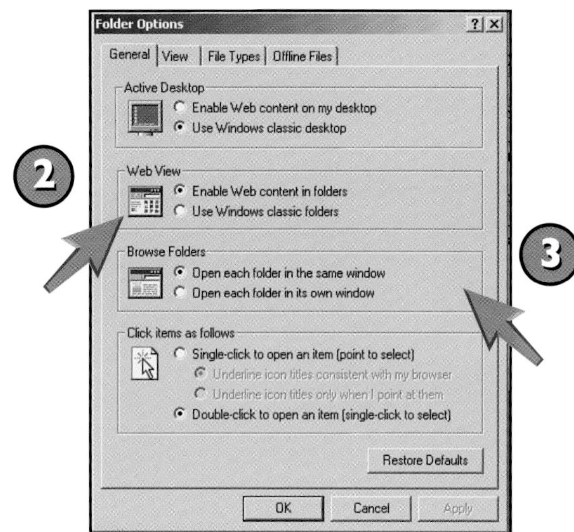

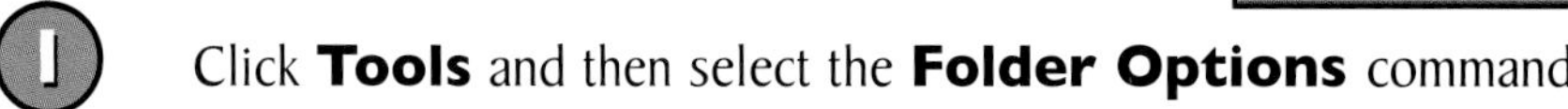

1. Click **Tools** and then select the **Folder Options** command.
2. Click whichever radio button you want under **Web View**.
3. Specify how you want to browse folders.

Active Desktop
For information on using Active Desktop, see Part 5, "Personalizing Windows."

Other Tabs
You can also set more advanced view options by opening the **View** menu, selecting **File Types**, and clicking the **Offline Files** tab.

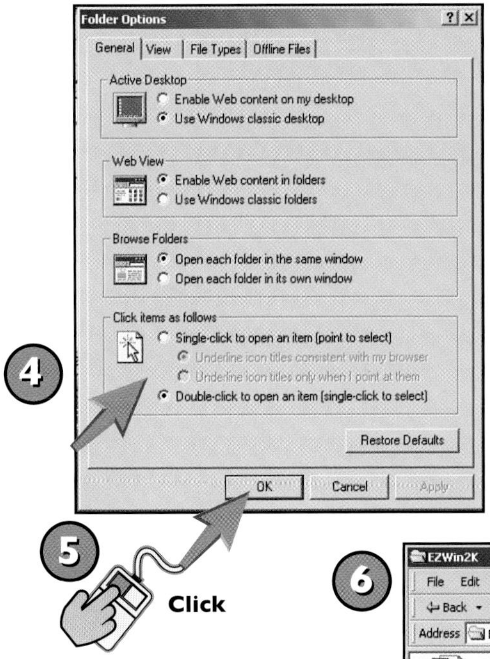

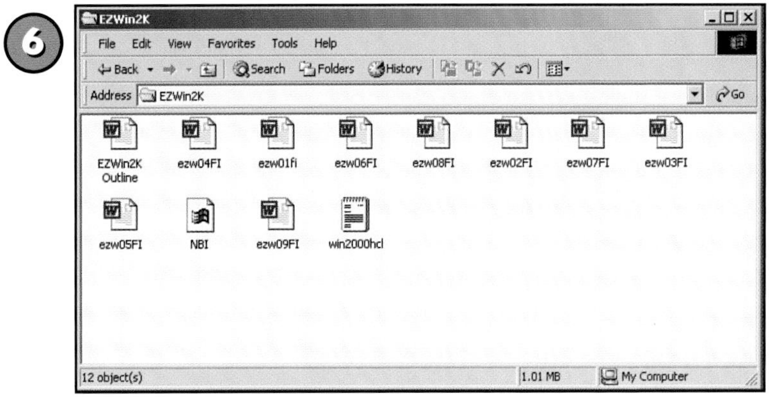

4. Select whether you want to single- or double-click an item to open it.

5. Click **OK**.

6. The contents are displayed with your selections (here in Classic view).

Task 10: Creating a Folder

Working with your files is easier if you group related files into folders. For example, you might want to create a folder in your word-processing program's folder to hold all the documents you create with that program. Creating a folder enables you to keep your documents separated from the program's files so you can easily find your document files.

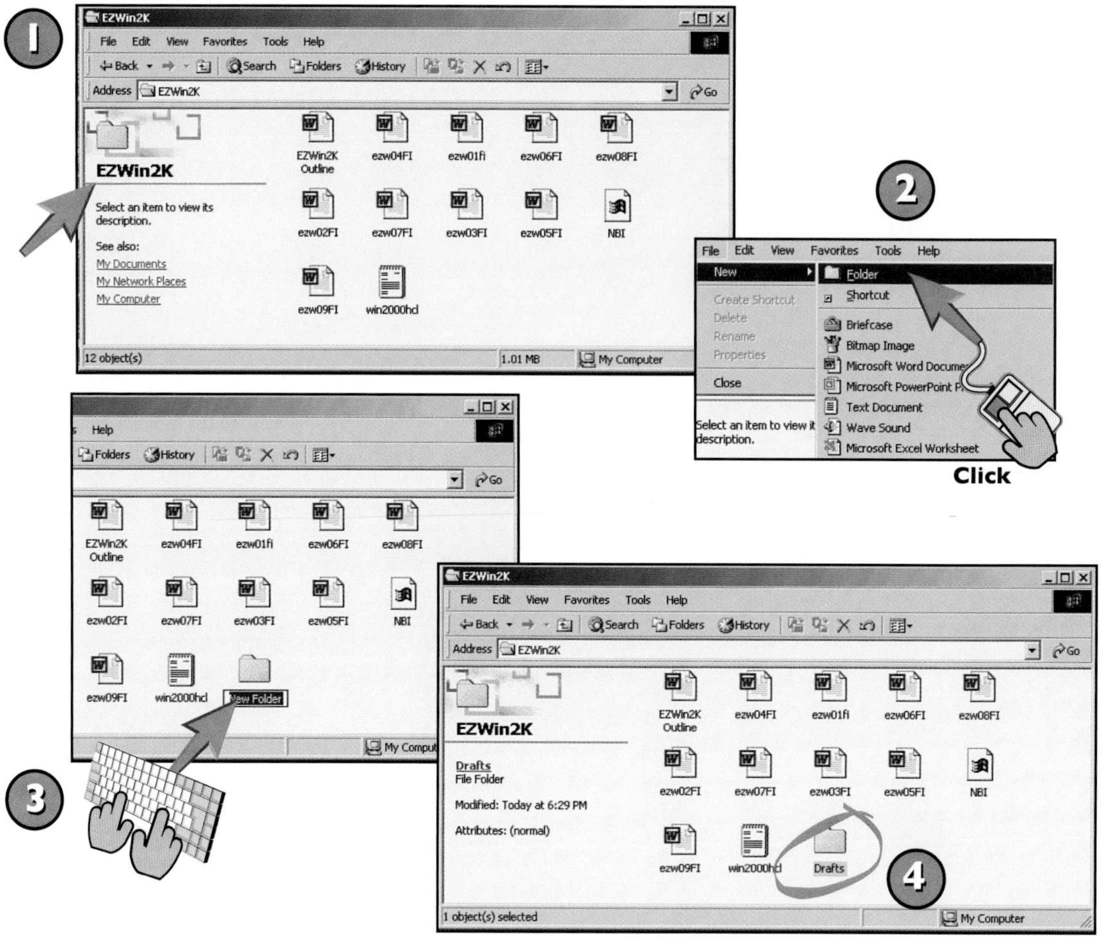

1 Open the window for the folder or disk where you want to create the new folder.

2 Click **File**, select the **New** command, and then click **Folder**.

3 The new folder appears in the window, and the name (**New Folder**) is selected. Type a new name and press **Enter**.

4 The folder is added.

Deleting a Folder

If you change your mind about the new folder, you can always delete it. To delete the folder, select it and then press the **Delete** key on your keyboard. Click the **Yes** button to confirm the deletion.

Folder Name

The folder name can contain as many as 255 characters and can include spaces.

Task 11: Copying Folders

Windows 2000 makes it easy for you to copy a folder and its contents. You can, for example, copy a folder to a floppy disk to use as a backup or to move to another computer. In addition, you can copy a folder and its contents to another location on the hard drive if, for example, you want to revise the original file for a different use.

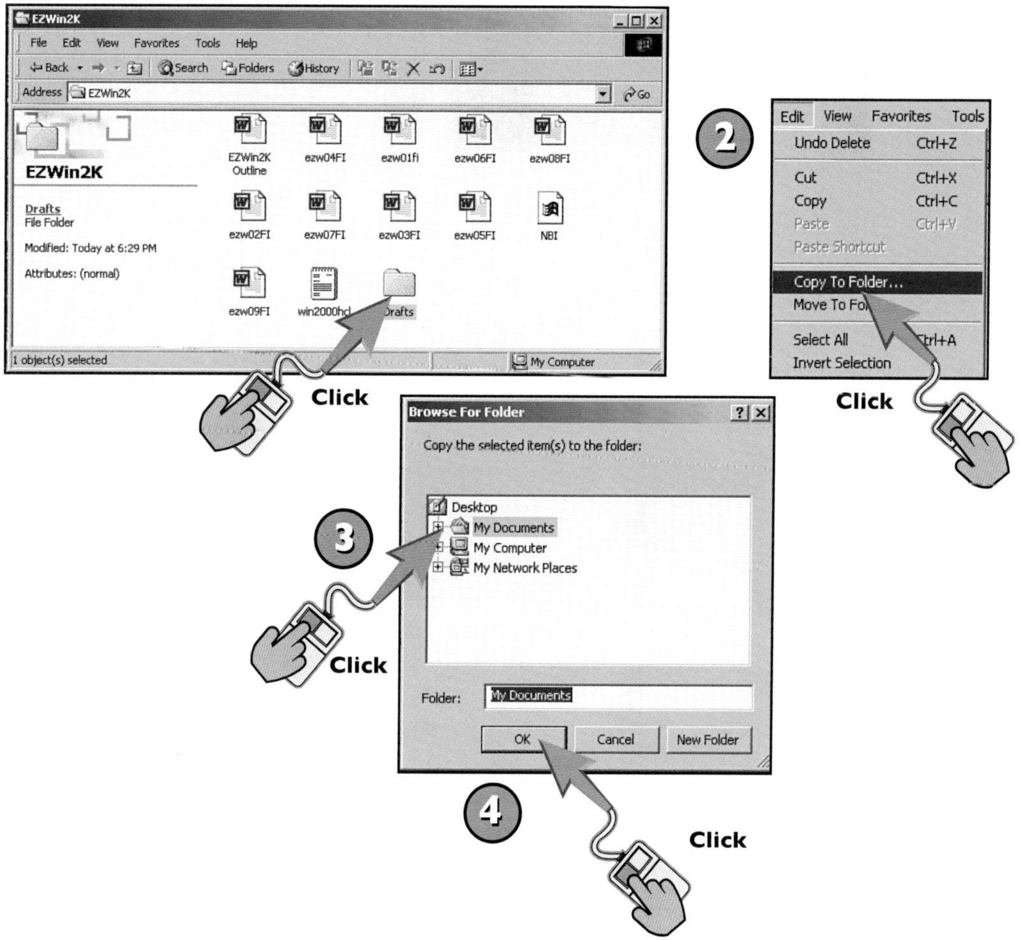

1. Select the folder you want to copy.
2. Click **Edit** and then select the **Copy To Folder** command.
3. Select the folder or drive to where you want to copy the selected folder. You can expand the list by clicking the plus sign next to the drives and folders.
4. Click **OK**. The folder is copied.

Using the Toolbar Button

You can also use the **Copy To** button in the toolbar.

New Method Versus Old Method

Windows 2000 includes new Copy To and Move To commands. If you prefer, you can also use the previous method. Use the **Copy** command to copy the folder. Then use the **Paste** command to paste it in its new location.

Task 12: Moving Folders

You can move a folder and its contents to another folder or to a disk so that you can reorganize your directory structure. For example, you might want to move all related files and folders to the same place on your hard drive so you can find them quickly and easily.

Start Here

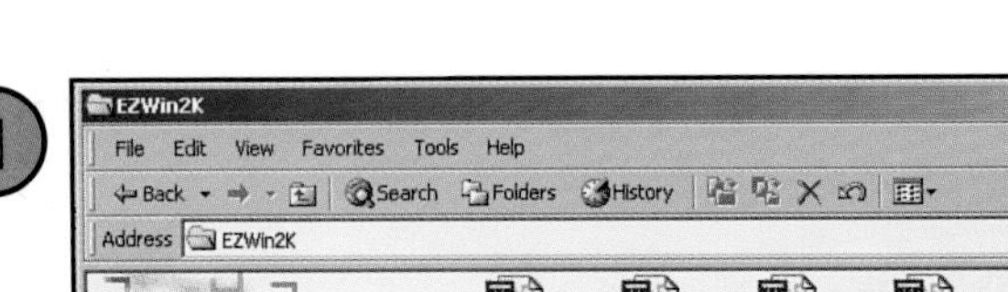

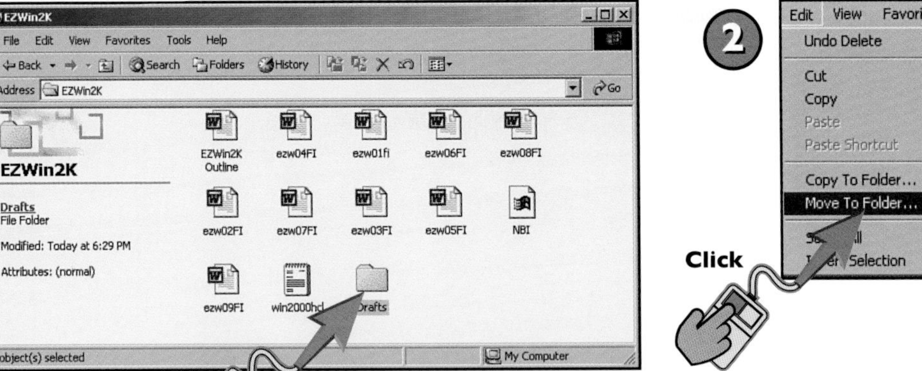

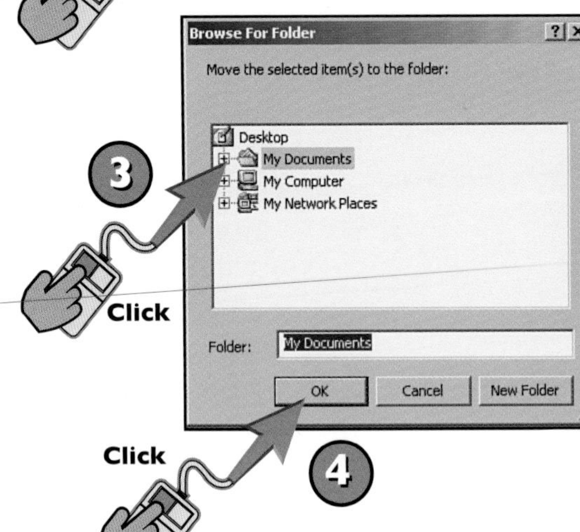

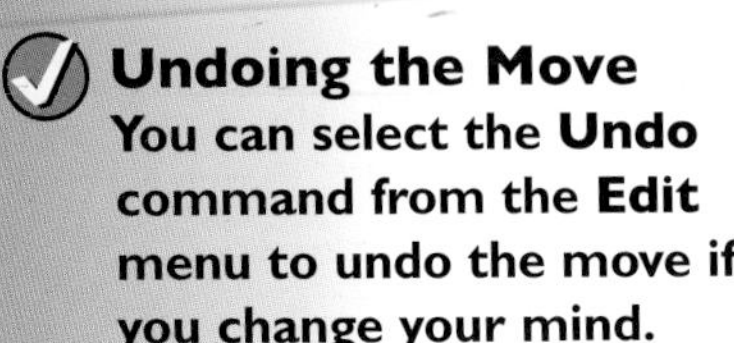

Undoing the Move
You can select the **Undo** command from the **Edit** menu to undo the move if you change your mind.

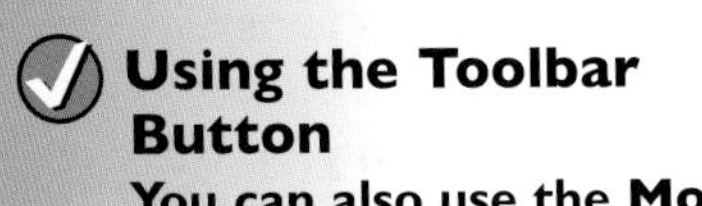

Using the Toolbar Button
You can also use the **Move To** button in the toolbar.

1. Display the folder you want to move.
2. Click **Edit** and then select the **Move To Folder** command.
3. Select the folder or drive where you want to place the selected folder. You can expand the list by clicking the plus sign next to the drives and folders.
4. Click **OK**. The folder is moved.

End Task

Task 13: Renaming Folders

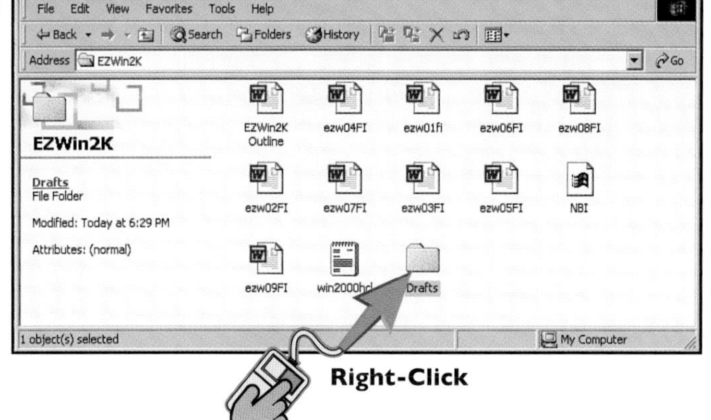

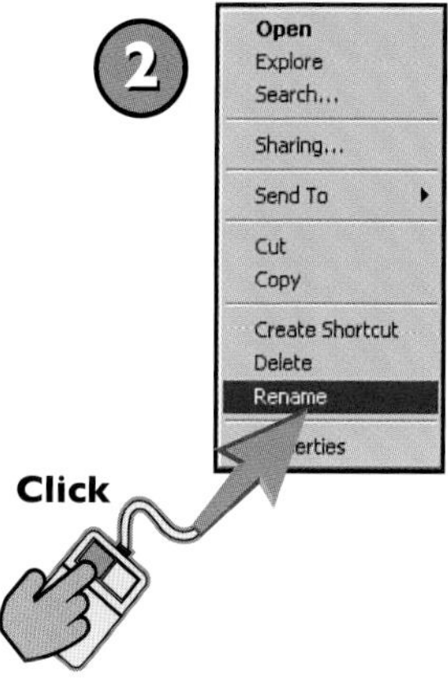

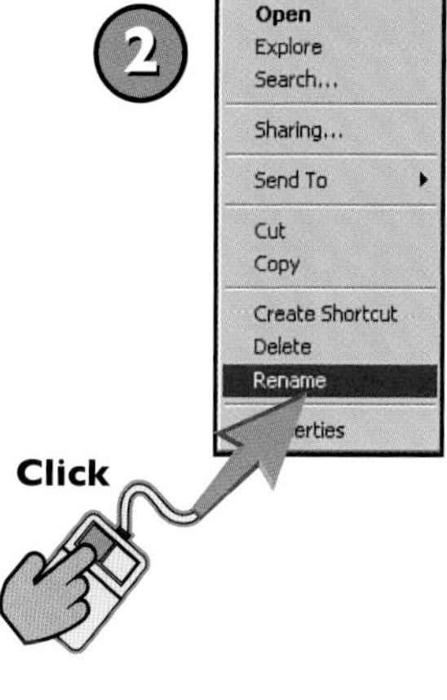

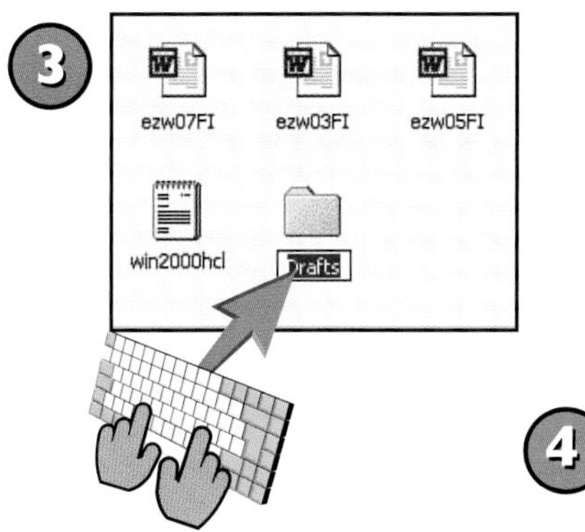

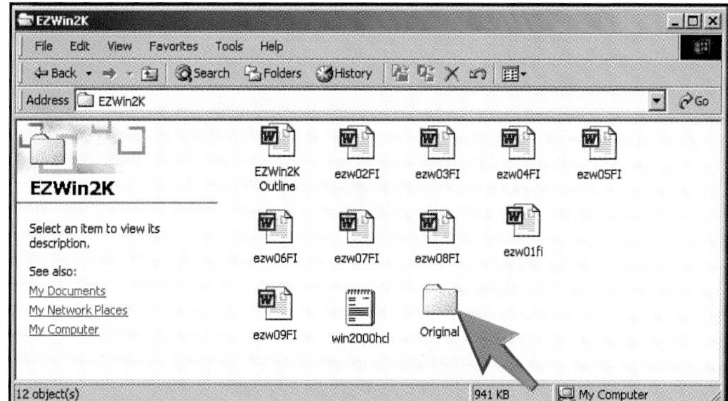

As you add more and more folders and files to your computer, you will eventually need to rearrange and reorganize them. In addition to needing to know how to move folders, you'll need to know how to rename them (for instance, suppose you want to give a folder a more descriptive name). Fortunately, Windows 2000 lets you easily rename folders.

1. Right-click the folder you want to rename.
2. Click the **Rename** command.
3. Type a new name for the folder and press **Enter**.
4. The folder is renamed.

Folder Names
Folder names and filenames can contain as many as 255 characters, including spaces. You also can include letters, numbers, and other symbols on your keyboard, except the following:

| ? / : " * < > \ |

Task 14: Deleting Folders

You can delete folders when you no longer need them. When you delete a folder from your hard drive, you also delete its contents. Windows 2000 places deleted folders in the Recycle Bin. You can restore deleted items from the Recycle Bin if you realize you have placed items there by accident.

Start Here

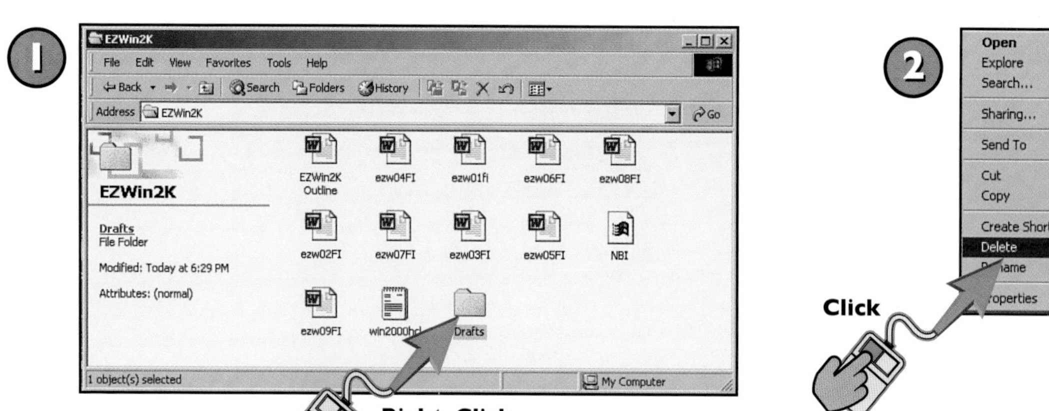

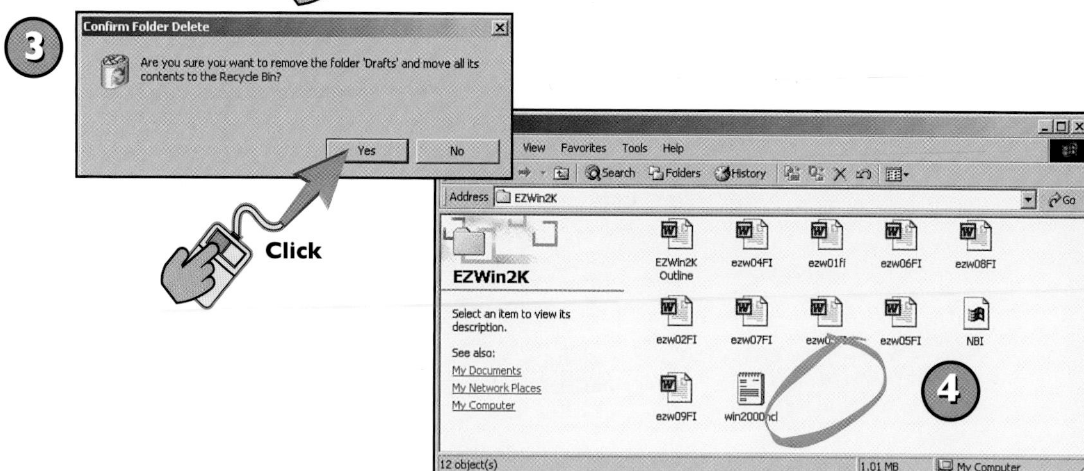

1. Right-click the folder you want to delete.
2. Select the **Delete** command.
3. Click the **Yes** button.
4. The folder is deleted.

Shortcuts

You can also click the Delete button in the toolbar.

Undoing the Deletion

If you change your mind about deleting the folder, click the No button in the Confirm Folder Delete dialog box. The box closes, and you're returned to the intact folder. Alternatively, you can undo the deletion by selecting the Edit Undo command.

End Task

Task 15: Selecting a Single File

When you want to work on files (copy, move, print, delete, and so on), you start by selecting the files you want. Selecting a single file is simple.

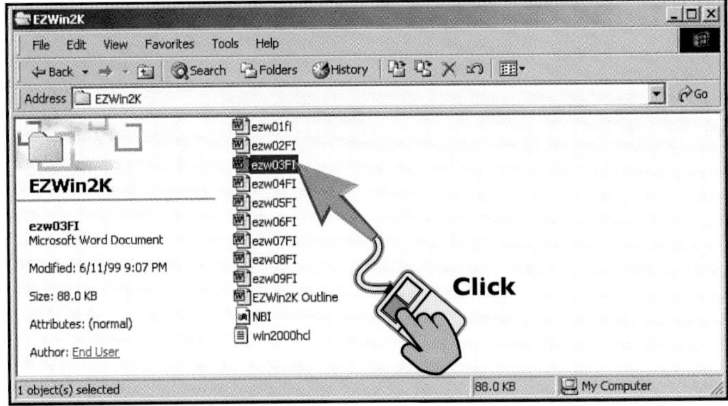

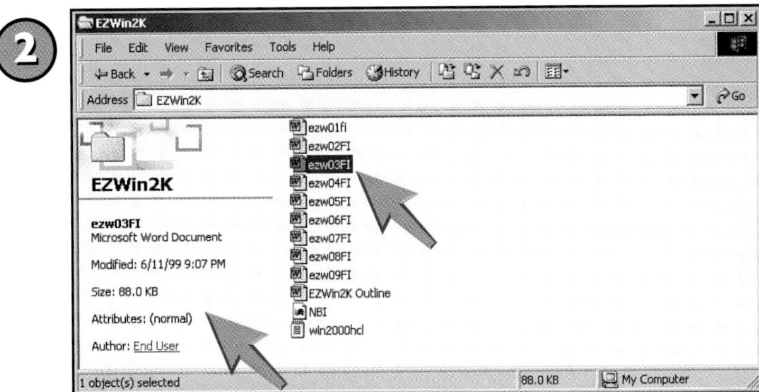

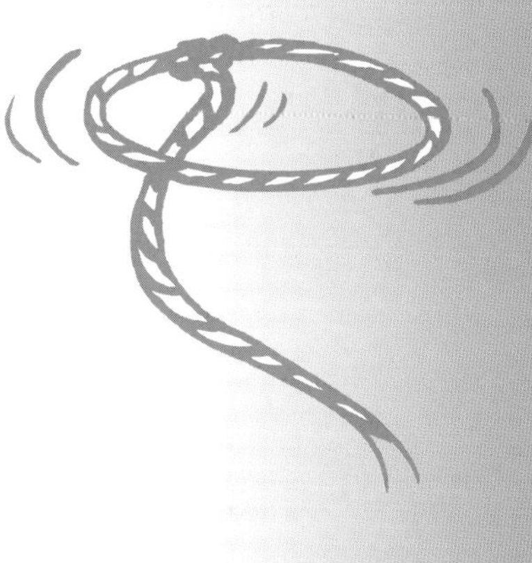

1. Click the file you want to select.

2. That file is selected. You see information about the selected file in the lower-left corner of the folder window.

Deselecting a File
To deselect a file, click outside the selected file list.

Task 16: Selecting Multiple Files That Are Next to Each Other

Windows 2000 enables you to easily select multiple files that are grouped together in the folder.

1

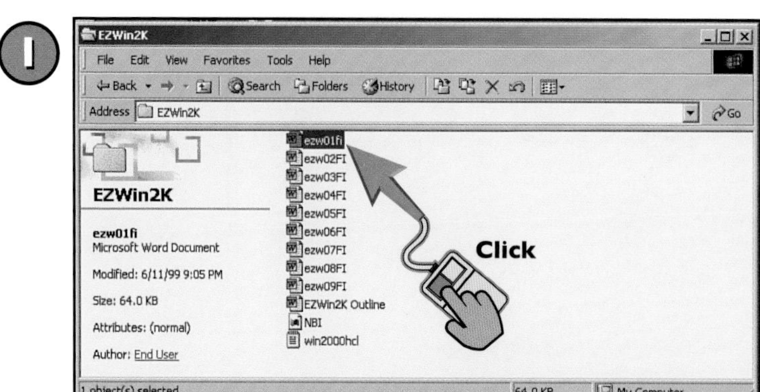

2

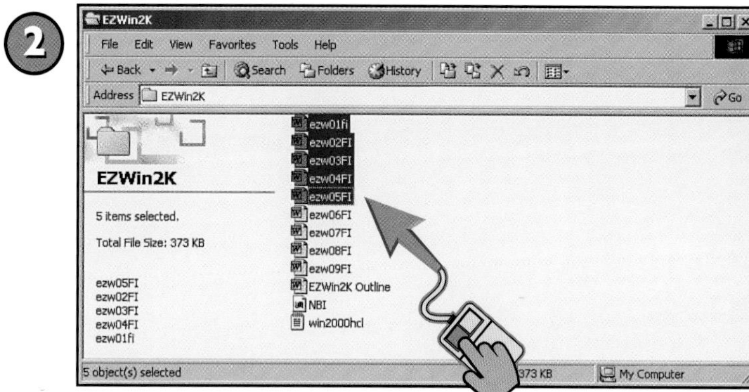

Shift+Click

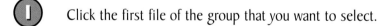

1. Click the first file of the group that you want to select.

2. Press and hold the **Shift** key and click the last file in the group that you want to select. The first and last files, as well as all the files in between, are selected.

Selecting All Files
To select all files, click **Edit** and then click the **Select All** command, or press **Ctrl+A**.

Checking the Window
Check the lower-left corner of the folder window, which lists each selected file, the total number of files selected, and the total file size of all selected files.

Task 17: Selecting Multiple Files That Are Not Next to Each Other

Even if the files you want to select are not grouped together, you can still select them using **Windows 2000**.

1

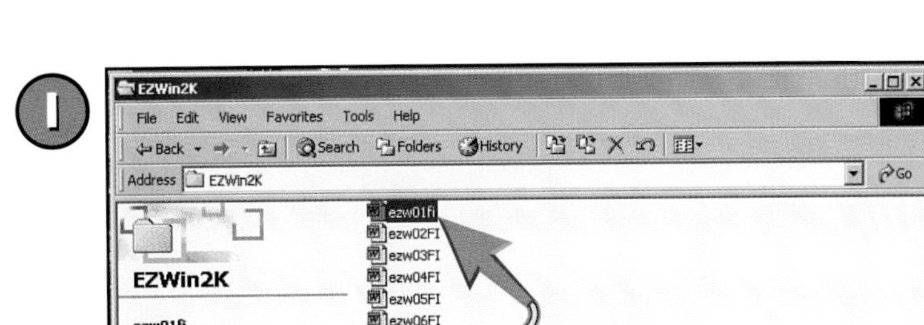

2

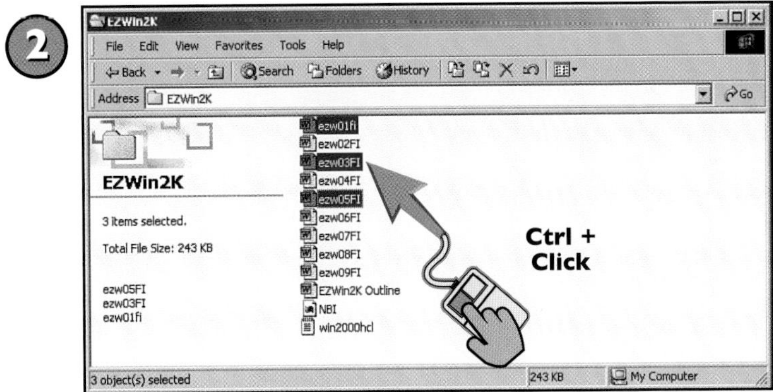

1 Click the first file that you want to select.

2 While holding down the **Ctrl** key, click each file that you want to select. Each file you click remains selected.

Checking the Window

Check the lower-left corner of the folder window, which lists each selected file, the total number of files selected, and the total file size of all selected files.

Task 18: Copying a File to Another Folder

Windows makes it easy to copy files from one folder to another and from one disk to another. You might copy files to create a backup copy or to revise one copy while keeping the original file intact.

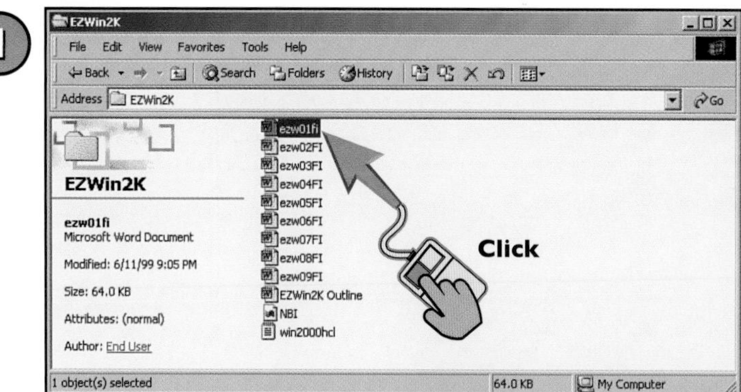

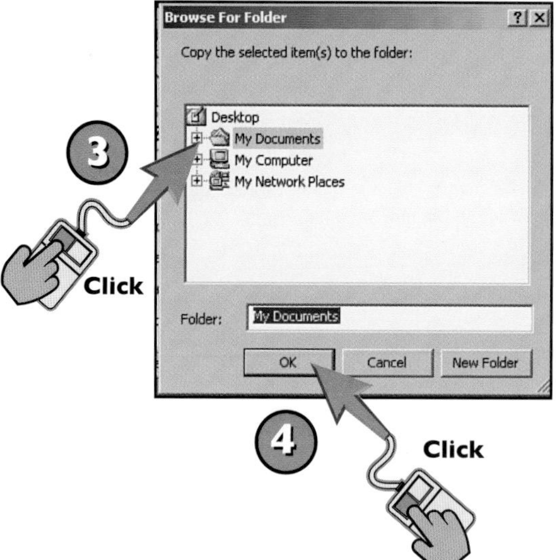

Using the Toolbar Button

You can also use the **Copy To** button in the toolbar.

New Method Versus Old Method

Windows 2000 includes new Copy To and Move To commands. If you prefer, you can also use the previous method. Use the **Copy** command to copy the file. Then use the **Paste** command to paste the file to its new location.

1. Select the file(s) you want to copy.
2. Click **Edit** and then select the **Copy To Folder** command.
3. Select the folder or drive to where you want to copy the selected file(s). You can expand the list by clicking the plus sign next to the drives and folders.
4. Click **OK**. The file(s) is copied.

Task 19: Copying a File to a Floppy Disk

You might want to copy a file to a floppy disk to take the file with you or to make up a backup copy. Windows provides a shortcut (the Send To command) for copying a file to a floppy disk.

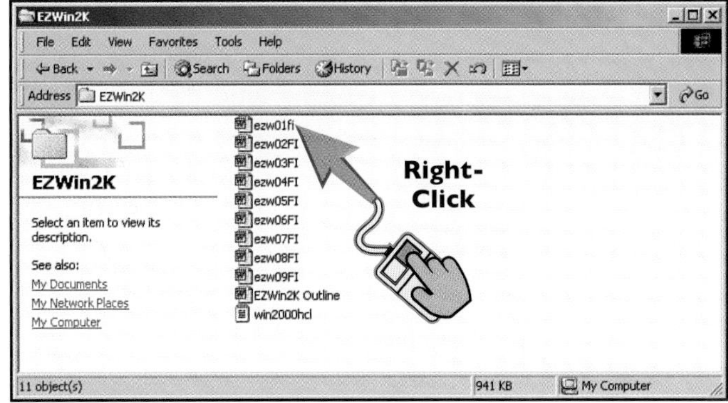

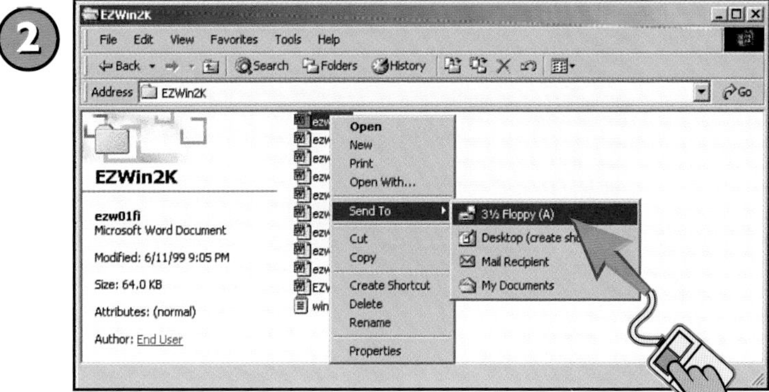

1. After you've inserted a disk into your floppy disk drive, right-click the file(s) you want to copy to the disk.

2. Select the **Send To** command from the shortcut menu and choose the appropriate floppy drive. The file is copied to that disk.

Disk Full?

If the disk is full, you see an error message. Insert a different disk and click the **Retry** button.

Task 20: Moving a File

You might need to move files from one folder or drive to another (for example, to reorganize folders by putting similar files together in the same folder). You might also move a file that you accidentally saved in the wrong folder.

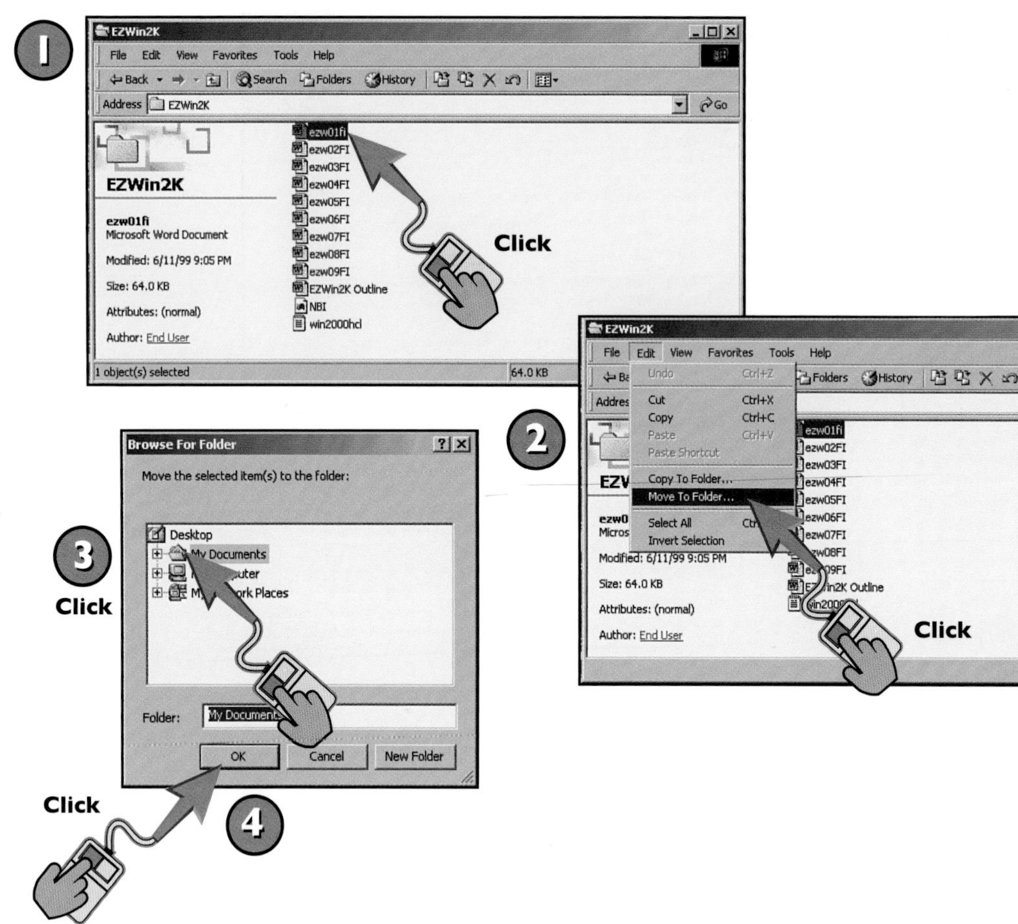

1. Select the file(s) you want to move.
2. Click **Edit** and then select the **Move To Folder** command.
3. Select the folder or drive where you want to place the selected file(s). You can expand the list by clicking the plus sign next to the drives and folders.
4. Click **OK**. The file(s) is moved.

Undoing the Move
If you make a mistake, you can undo the move by selecting the **Undo** command from the **Edit** menu.

Using the Toolbar Button
You can also use the **Move To** button in the toolbar.

Task 21: Deleting a File

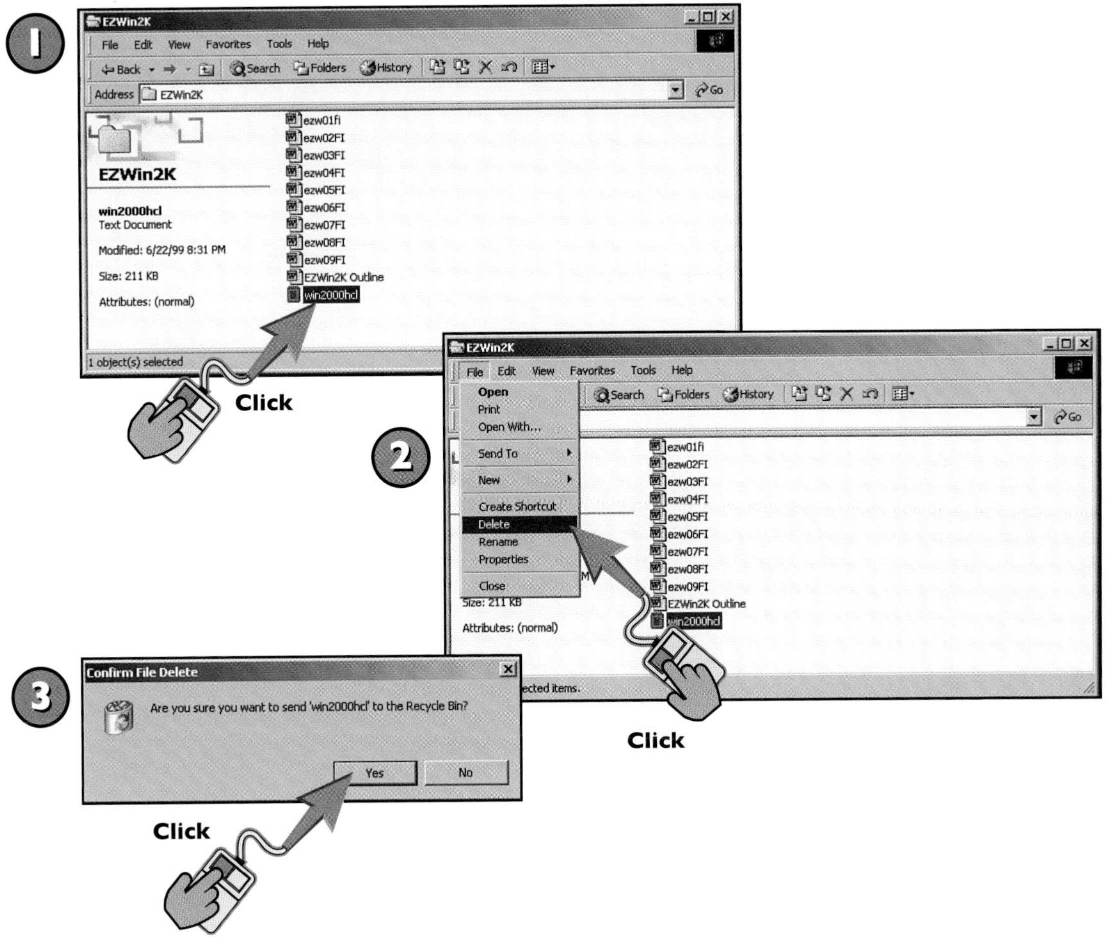

Eventually, your computer will become full of files, and you'll have a hard time organizing and storing them all. You can copy necessary files to floppy disks, tapes, and so on and then delete the files from your hard drive to make room for new files. In addition, you will sometimes want to delete files you no longer need.

1 Select the file(s) you want to delete.

2 Click **File** and then select the **Delete** command.

3 Click **Yes** to delete the file(s). Windows removes the file(s), placing it in the **Recycle Bin**.

Undoing the Deletion
You can undo a deletion by selecting the **Undo** command from the **Edit** menu. Or, you can retrieve the deleted item from the **Recycle Bin**, as covered in the next task.

Other Methods
Other alternatives for deleting files and folders include clicking the **Delete** button, right-clicking the folder or file and choosing **Delete** from the shortcut menu, and pressing the **Delete** key on your keyboard.

Task 22: Undeleting a File or Folder

Sometimes you will delete a file or folder by mistake. You can retrieve the file or folder from the Recycle Bin (as long as the Recycle Bin has not been emptied) and return it to its original location.

Emptying the Recycle Bin

If you want to be permanently rid of the files in the Recycle Bin, you can empty it. Double-click the **Recycle Bin** icon and make sure that it doesn't contain anything you need to save. Then click the **Empty Recycle Bin** button. Click **Yes** to empty the Recycle Bin.

1. Double-click the **Recycle Bin** icon.
2. In the Recycle Bin window, you see all the files, programs, and folders you have deleted. Click the file(s) or folder(s) you want to undelete.
3. Click the **Restore** button. The file(s) or folder(s) is moved from the Recycle Bin to its original location.

Task 23: Creating a Shortcut to a File or Folder

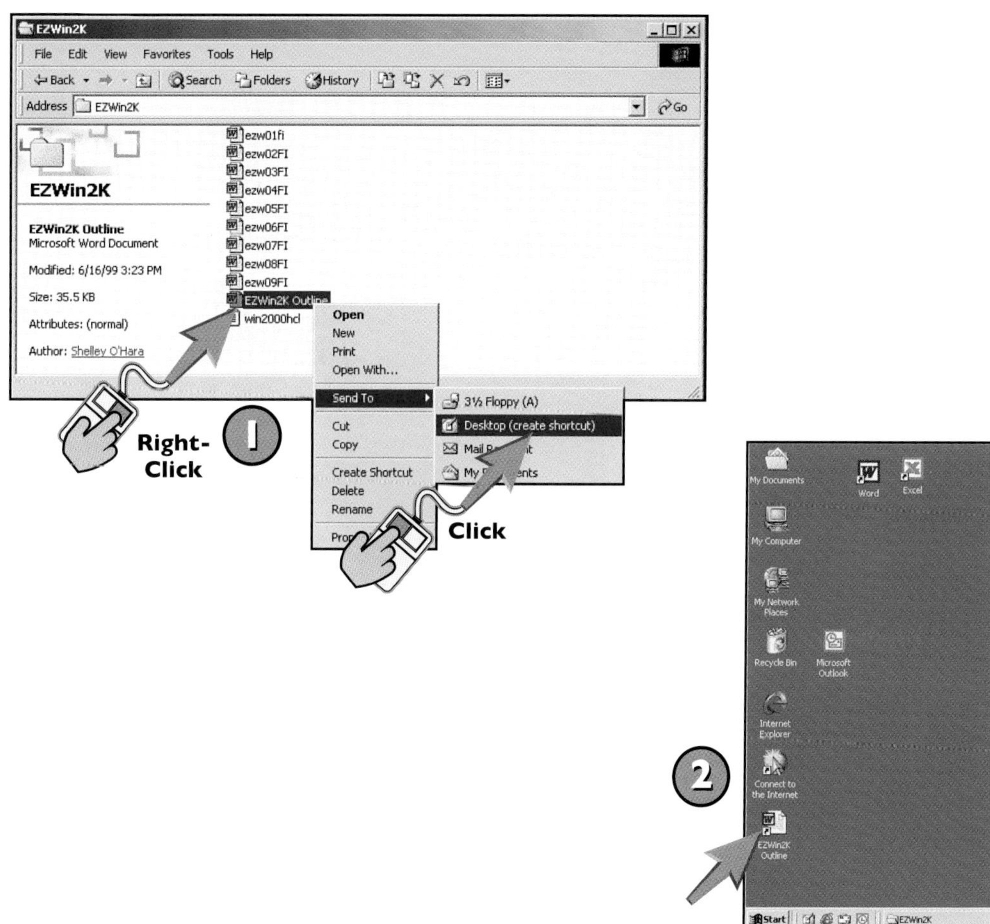

1 Right-click the file or folder for which you want to create a shortcut icon, click **Send To**, and then click **Desktop (Create Shortcut)**.

2 Windows adds a shortcut icon to your desktop. (You can close the other windows to better see the shortcut icon, as I've done here.)

If you often use the same file or folder, you might want fast access to it. If so, you can create a shortcut icon for the file or folder on the desktop. Double-clicking a shortcut icon to a file opens the file in the program you used to create the file. Double-clicking a folder displays the contents of the folder in a window.

Dragging with the Right Button

You can also drag the icon from the window to the desktop and select the **Create Shortcut(s) Here** command.

Deleting the Shortcut Icon

To delete the shortcut icon, right-click it and then choose **Delete** or drag the icon to the **Recycle Bin** icon on your desktop.

Renaming the Icon

To rename the shortcut icon, right-click it and then choose **Rename.** Type a new name and press **Enter.**

Task 24: Finding Files and Folders

After you've worked for months with your applications, your computer will become filled with various folders and files, which can make it nearly impossible for you to know where everything is. Luckily, Windows includes a command that helps you locate specific files or folders by name, file type, location, and so on.

Start Here

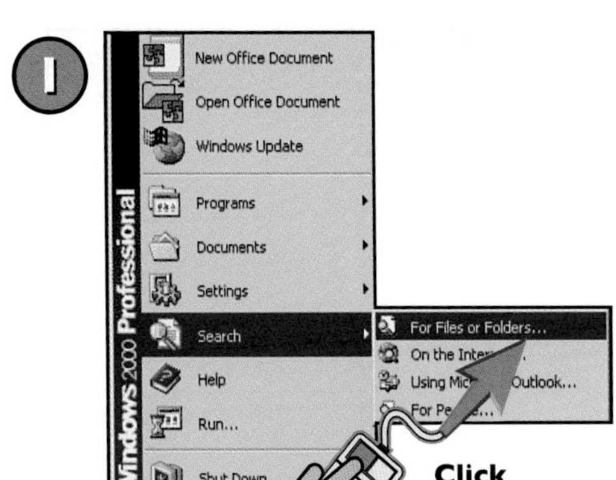

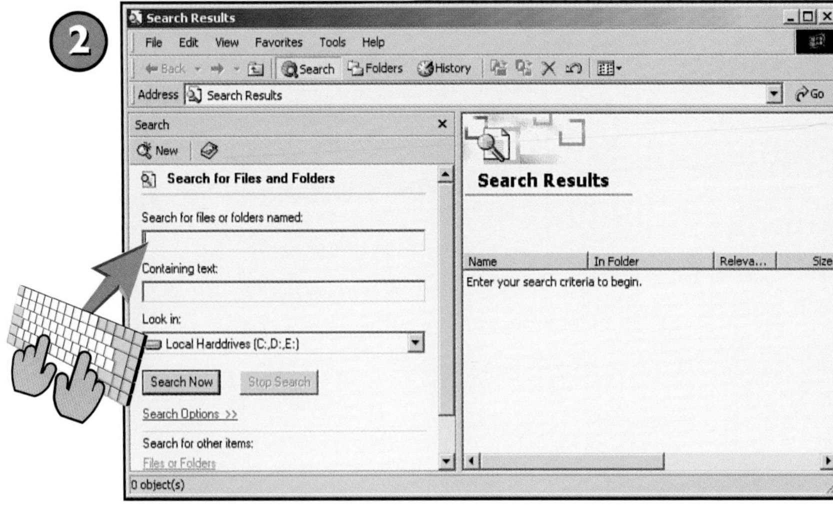

1. Click the **Start** button, select the **Search** command, and then choose **For Files or Folders**.

2. Enter the name of the file or folder you want to find.

Searching by Content
You can also search for a file or folder based on content. To do so, type the text in the **Containing Text** field.

Starting from Content Window
You can also start a search from a content window. To do so, click the **Search** button.

Next Step

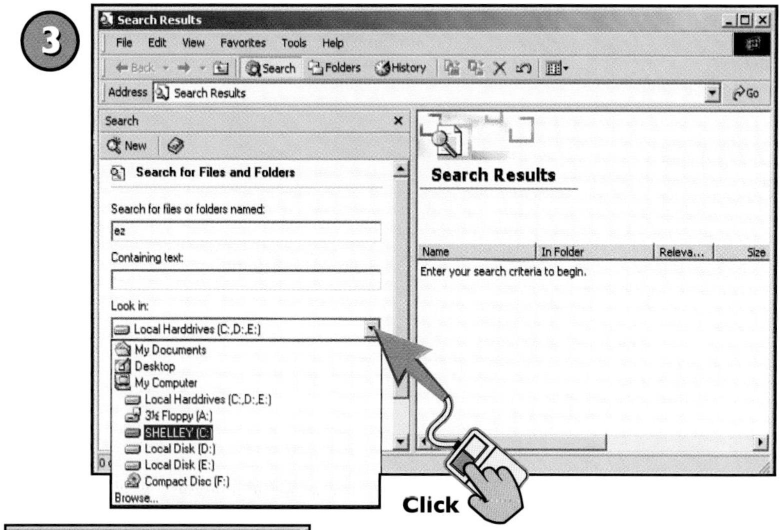

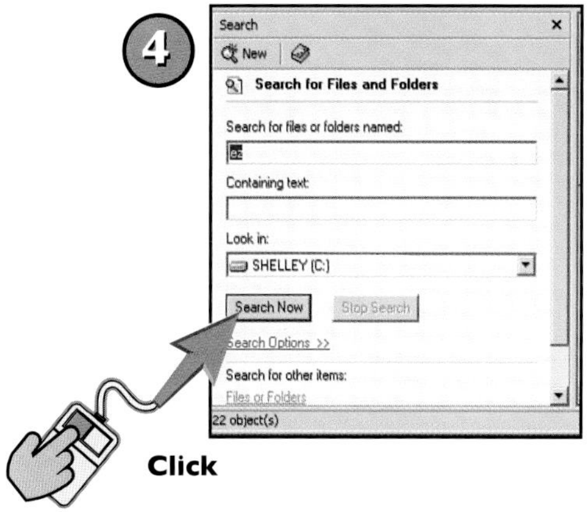

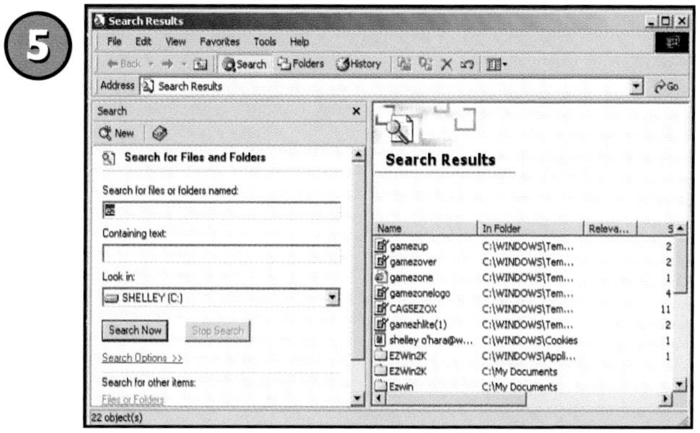

Click

Click

3 Display the **Look In** list box and choose the drive(s) or folder(s) you want to search.

4 Click the **Search Now** button.

5 Windows searches the selected drive(s) and folder(s) and displays a list of found files. You can double-click any of the listed files or folders to go to that file or folder.

More Options
For more options on searching, click the Search Options link.

Closing the Search Bar
Click the Search button again or click the Close (×) button in the Search bar to close this pane.

Task 25: Using Windows Explorer

You can use Windows Explorer in much the same way you use My Computer: to copy and move folders, create and rename folders, view details, and so on. Basically, Windows Explorer is the content window with the folder list displayed in the Explorer bar. That is, selecting the program is the same as clicking folders in a content window. You might simply prefer to see the hierarchical view shown in Windows Explorer.

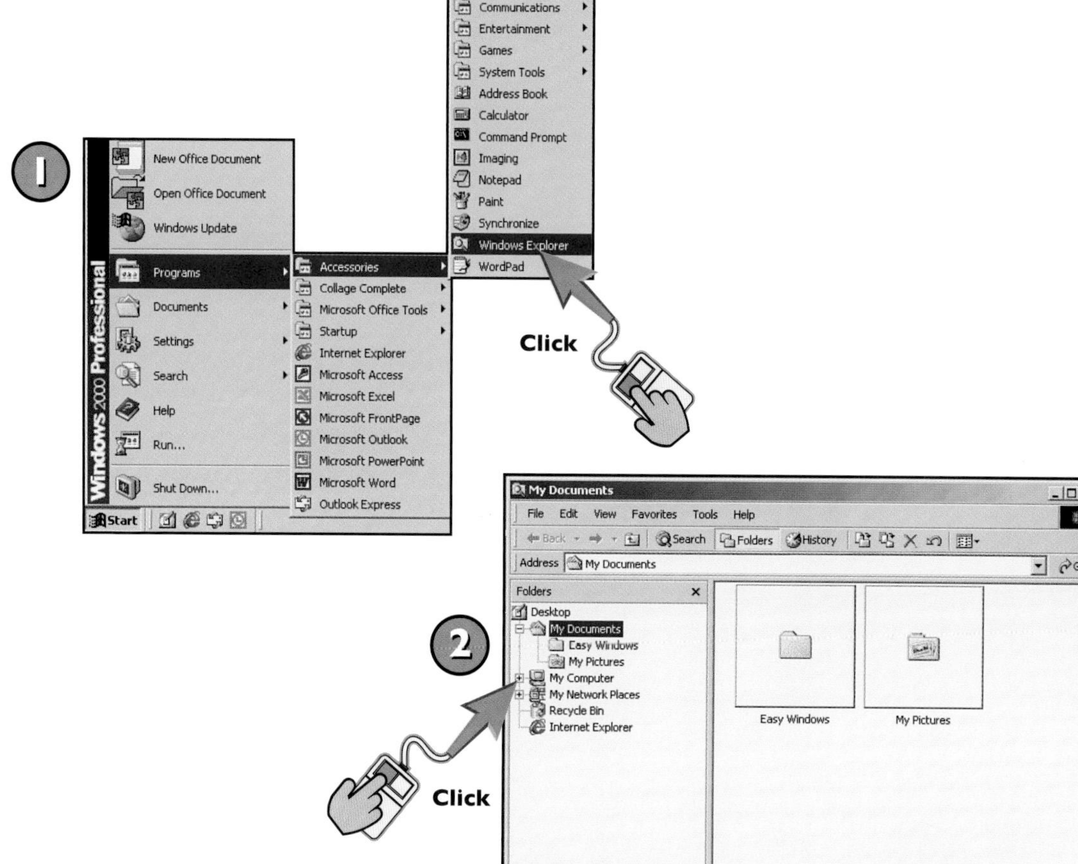

Click the **Start** button, select the **Programs** command, select **Accessories**, and then click **Windows Explorer**.

You see the folders list in the Explorer bar. To display folders within a drive or folder, click the plus sign.

Closing Windows Explorer

Close Windows Explorer just like you do any other window: Click the Close (×) button in the program's title bar.

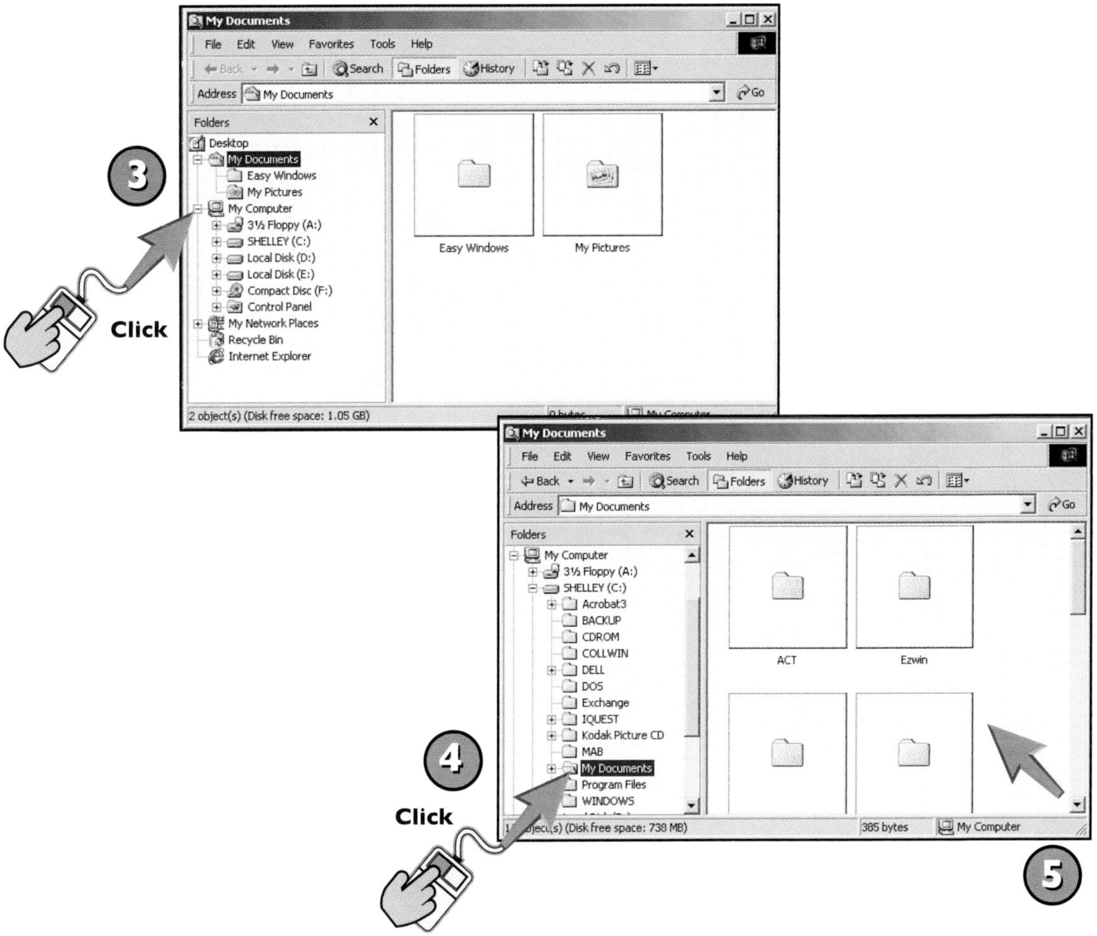

3 The list expands to show other folders. A minus sign appears next to the drive or folder name. To hide the contents, click the minus sign.

4 To display a drive or folder's contents, click the folder in the list in the left pane.

5 The folder's contents appear on the right side of the Explorer window.

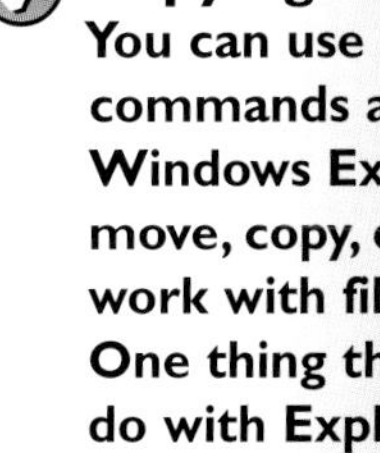

Copying and Deleting

You can use any of the commands and features of Windows Explorer to move, copy, delete, and work with files and folders. One thing that is easy to do with Explorer is to copy and move files by dragging. Drag a file from the right side of the Explorer window to the left side and drop it on top of the folder you want to copy or move it to. When you drag a file to another drive, Windows copies the file; when you drag the file to another folder, Windows moves it.

PART

Printing with Windows

All Windows applications use the same setup for your printer, which saves time and ensures that you can print from any Windows application without resetting for each program. When you first install Windows, it sets up your printer. If needed, you can set up more than one printer in Windows and choose the printer you want to use at any given time. In addition, you can easily manage printing for all of your applications through Windows.

You print a document from the application in which you created it. When you send a file to the printer, the file first goes to a ***print queue***, or holding area. The print queue can contain one or many files at any time, and you can make changes to this print queue. While a file is in the print queue, you can pause, restart, and even cancel the printing. This part shows you how to control and manage printing in Windows.

Tasks

Task 1: Previewing a Document

In most applications, you can preview a document to check the margins, heads, graphic placement, and so on before you print.

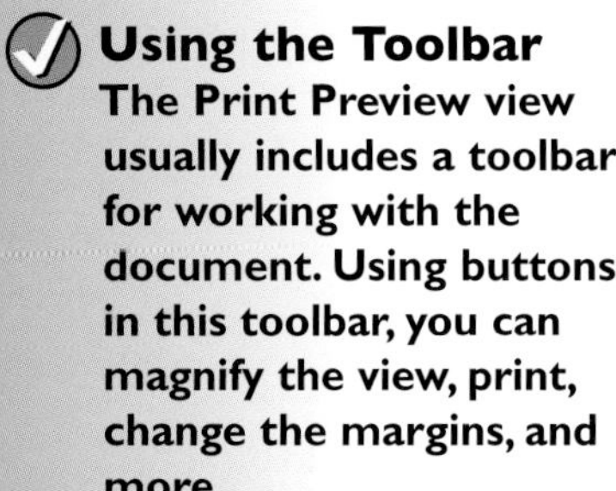

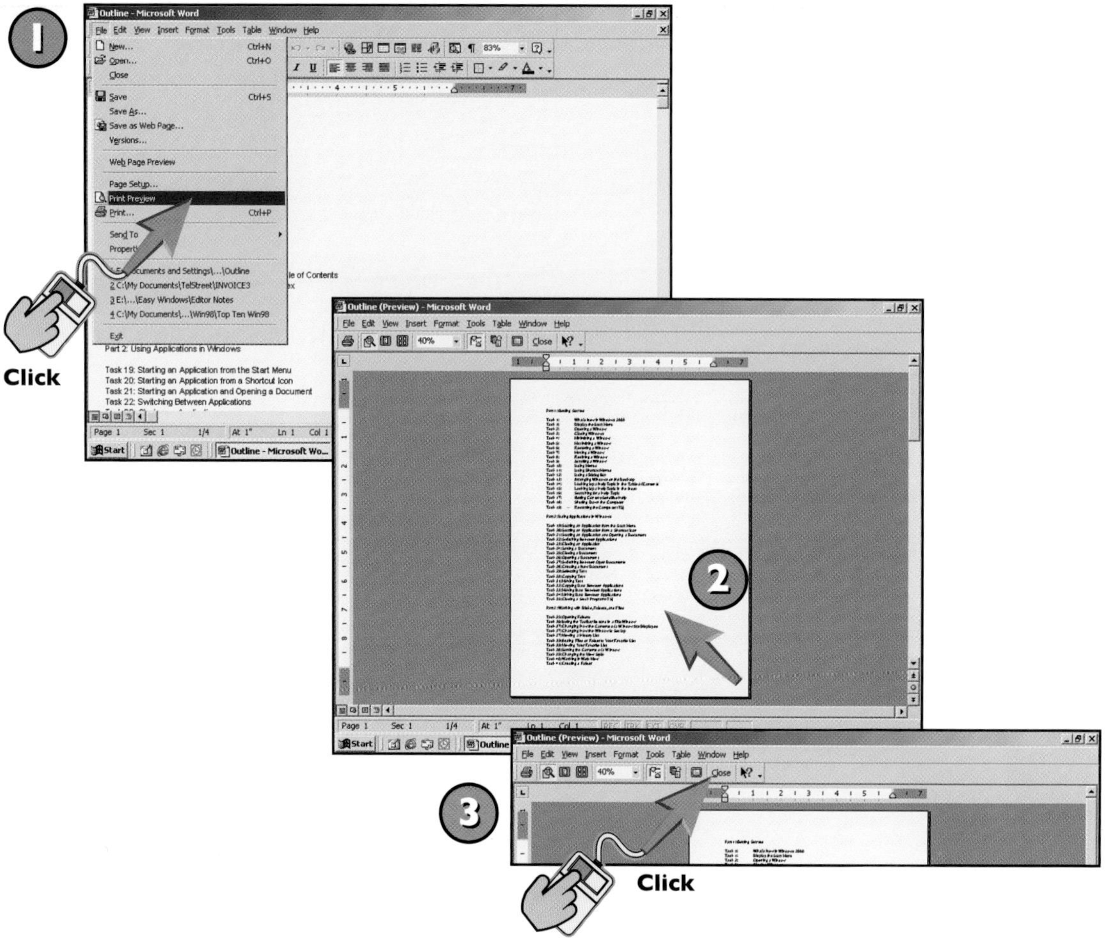

Using the Toolbar
The Print Preview view usually includes a toolbar for working with the document. Using buttons in this toolbar, you can magnify the view, print, change the margins, and more.

No Preview?
Most programs have a preview option, but if you don't see this command listed in your program, it might not be available. You have to print the document to see how it looks.

1. In an open document, click **File** and then select the **Print Preview** command.
2. You see a preview of the document.
3. After you finish viewing the preview, click the **Close** button in the toolbar (not for the window).

Task 2: Printing a Document

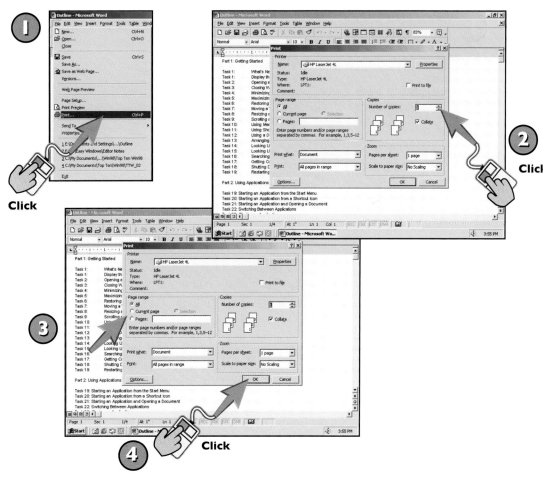

You can print documents from any application. When you first install Windows, it sets up a default printer, and you can print from any application using this printer. Printing your documents gives you a paper copy you can proofread, use in reports, give to co-workers, and so on.

1 Click **File** and then click the **Print** command.

2 Using the spin box, specify the number of copies you want printed (or type a number in the field).

3 Specify a page range.

4 Click the **OK** button.

Shortcut

As a shortcut, look for a **Print** button in your toolbar. Alternatively, you can use a keyboard shortcut (usually **Ctrl+P**) to print.

Nothing Prints?

If nothing prints, make sure that your printer is plugged in, online, and has paper.

Using a Different Printer

If you want to use a printer other than the default, choose the printer you want to use from the **Name** drop-down list in the Print dialog box.

Task 3: Viewing the Print Queue

The print queue lists the documents that have been set to a printer, and it shows how far along the printing is. Using the print queue, you can pause, restart, or cancel print jobs. This task shows how to view the print queue.

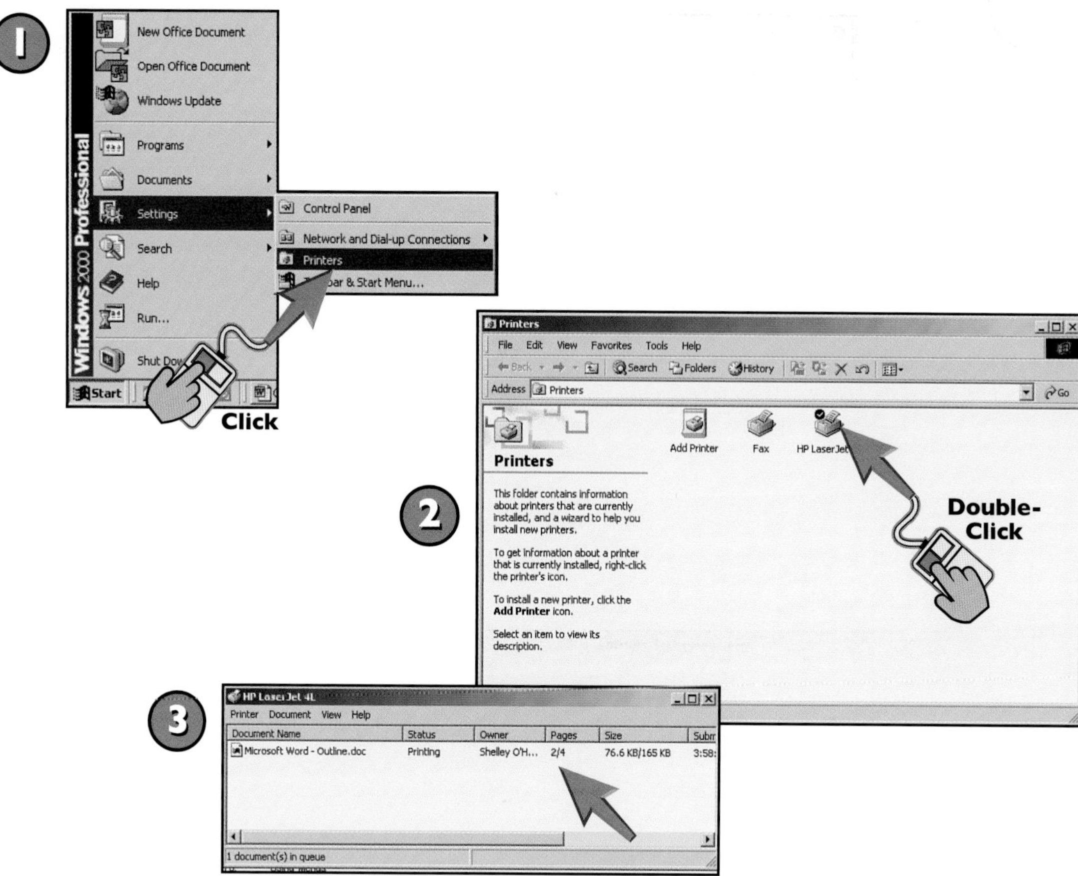

Closing the Window

To close the print queue, click the **Close** (×) button.

Double-clicking the Printer Icon

You can display the print queue by double-clicking the **Printer** icon in the taskbar. This icon appears whenever you are printing something.

Queue Empty?

If the print queue window is empty, it means there is nothing in the print queue. If you just sent a job to the printer and the print queue window is empty, it means the job has already been printed.

1. Click the **Start** button, click the **Settings** command, and then choose **Printers**.
2. Double-click the printer whose print queue you want to view.
3. The printer window displays a list of the documents in the queue as well as statistics about the documents being printed.

Task 4: Pausing and Restarting the Printer

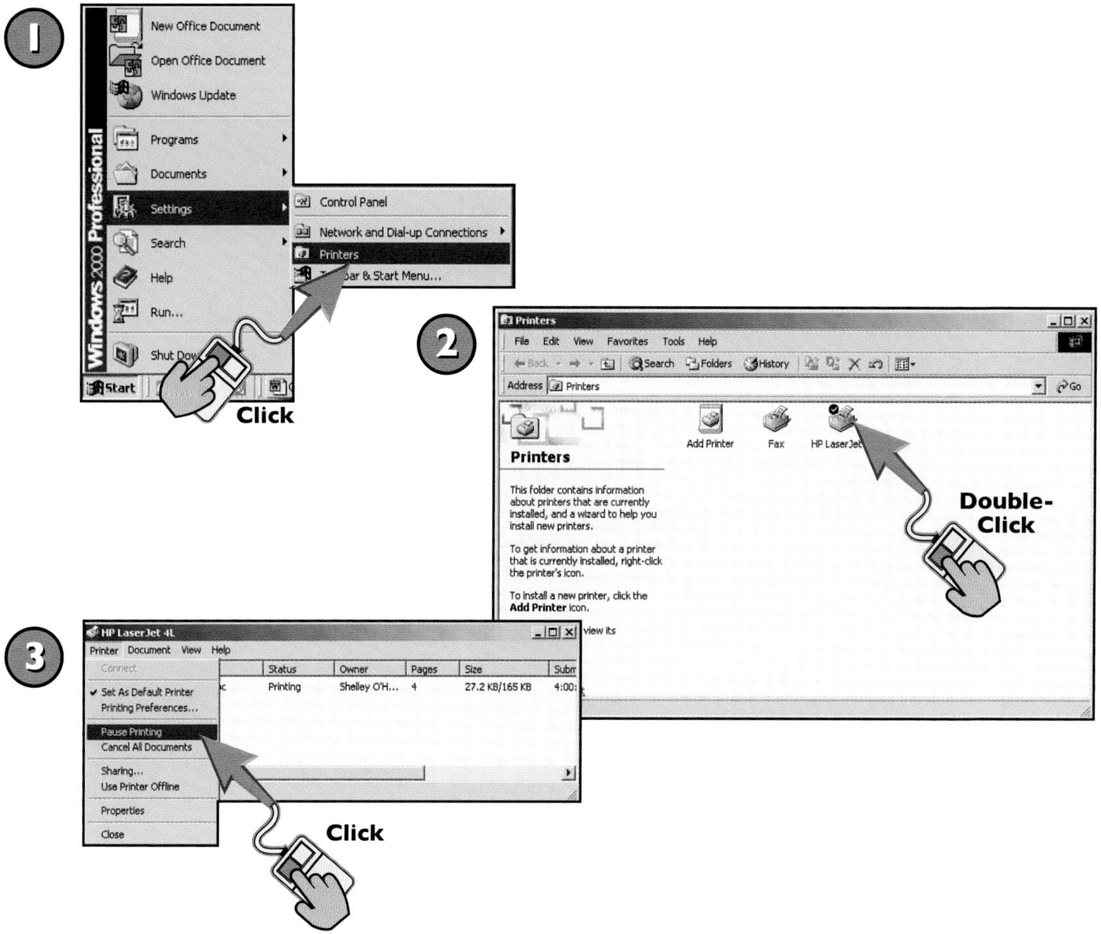

You might want to pause printing when you have a change to make in the text or when you want to load a different paper type, for example. You can easily stop the printing from the Printers folder and can restart it at any time.

1. Click the **Start** button, click the **Settings** command, and then choose **Printers**.

2. Double-click the printer whose print queue you want to view.

3. Click **Printer** and then select the **Pause Printing** command.

Be Quick!

You have to be quick to pause or stop a short print job. If nothing appears, it probably means that the entire print job has already been sent to the printer.

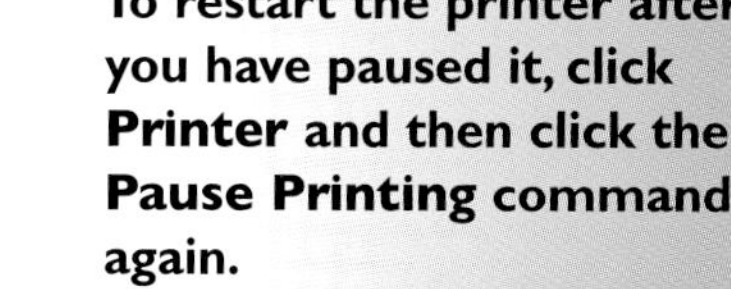

Restarting Printing

To restart the printer after you have paused it, click **Printer** and then click the **Pause Printing** command again.

Task 5: Canceling Printing

If you discover an error in the job you are printing or if you decide that you need to add something to it, you can cancel the print job. Canceling the print job prevents you from wasting time and paper.

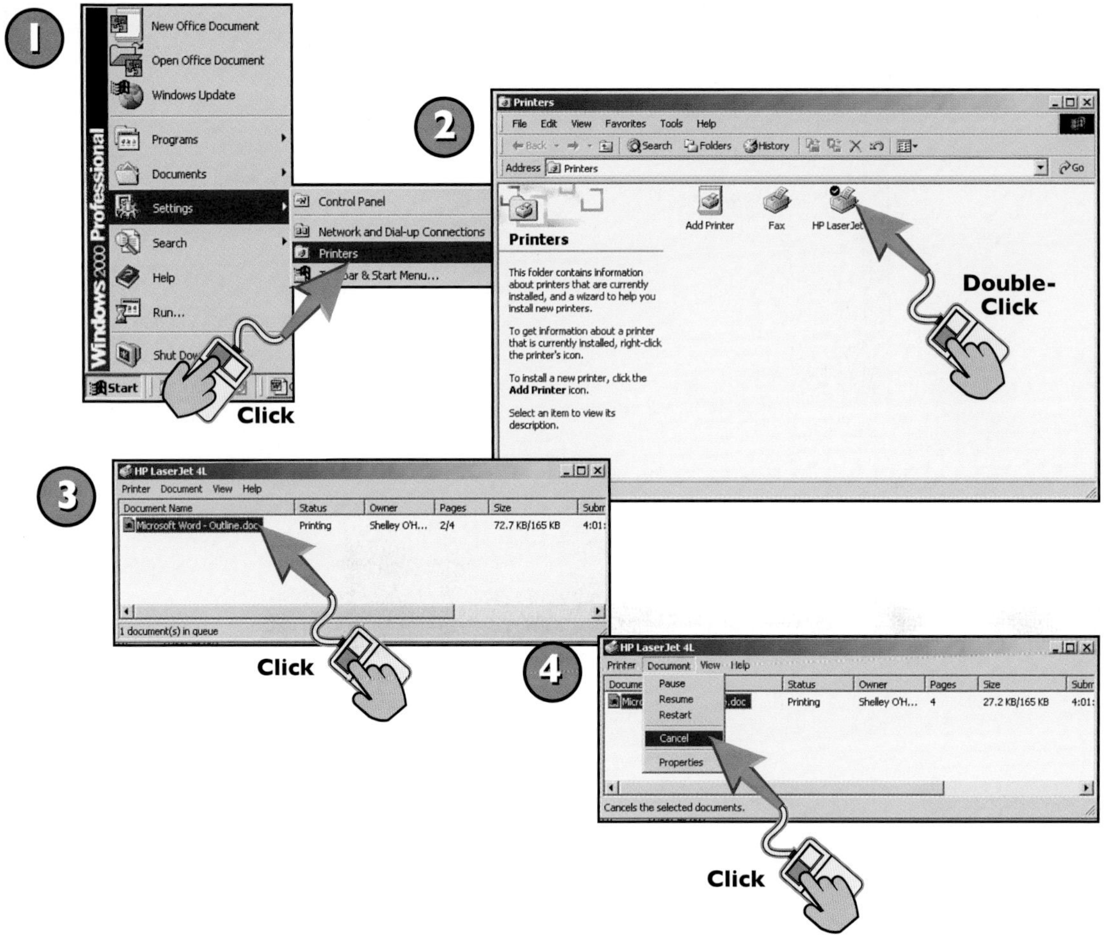

1. Click the **Start** button, click the **Settings** command, and then select **Printers**.
2. Double-click the printer whose print queue you want to view.
3. In the print queue, select the print job you want to cancel.
4. Click **Document** and then select the **Cancel** command.

Job Not Listed?

Depending on your computer and your printer, the print job might be listed in the print queue for only a few seconds before it is sent to the printer. You might not be able to cancel it.

Canceling All Jobs

To cancel all jobs, open the **Printer** menu and select **Cancel All Documents**.

Task 6: Setting the Default Printer

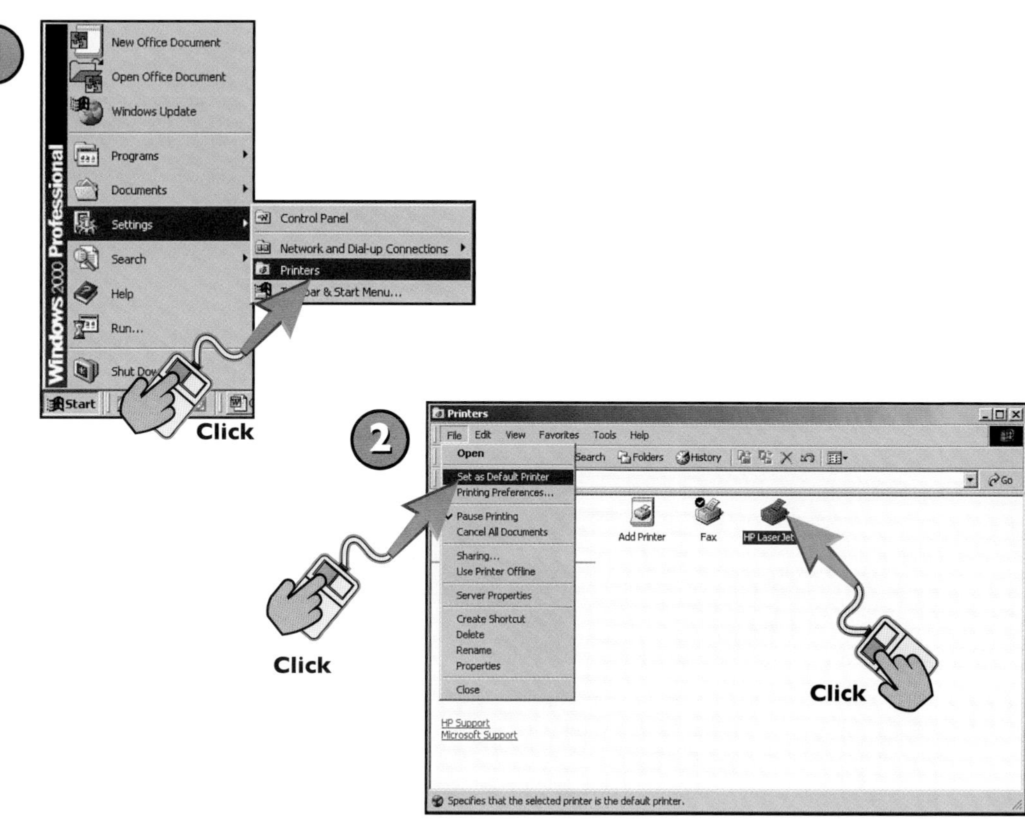

If you have more than one printer connected, you must select one as the default. The default printer you set in Windows is the printer your applications automatically use when you choose to print. The default printer is the one you want most of your documents printed on.

1 Click the **Start** button, click **Settings**, and then select the **Printers** command.

2 After you select the printer you want to choose as the default, click **File**, and then select the **Set as Default Printer** command.

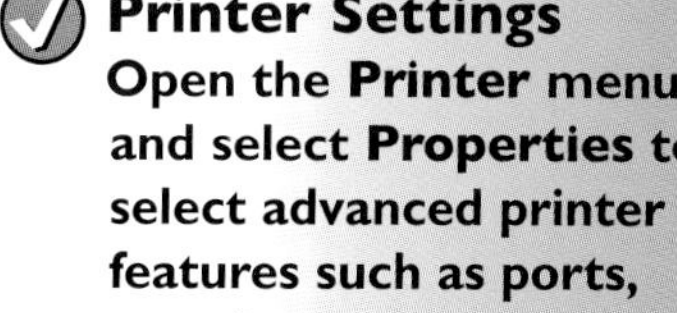

Printer Settings
Open the Printer menu and select Properties to select advanced printer features such as ports, security, and device settings.

Task 7: Changing Printer Preferences

You can change printer settings, such as the orientation (direction the page is printed), page order, paper size, and more. To make these changes, view the Printing Preferences dialog box.

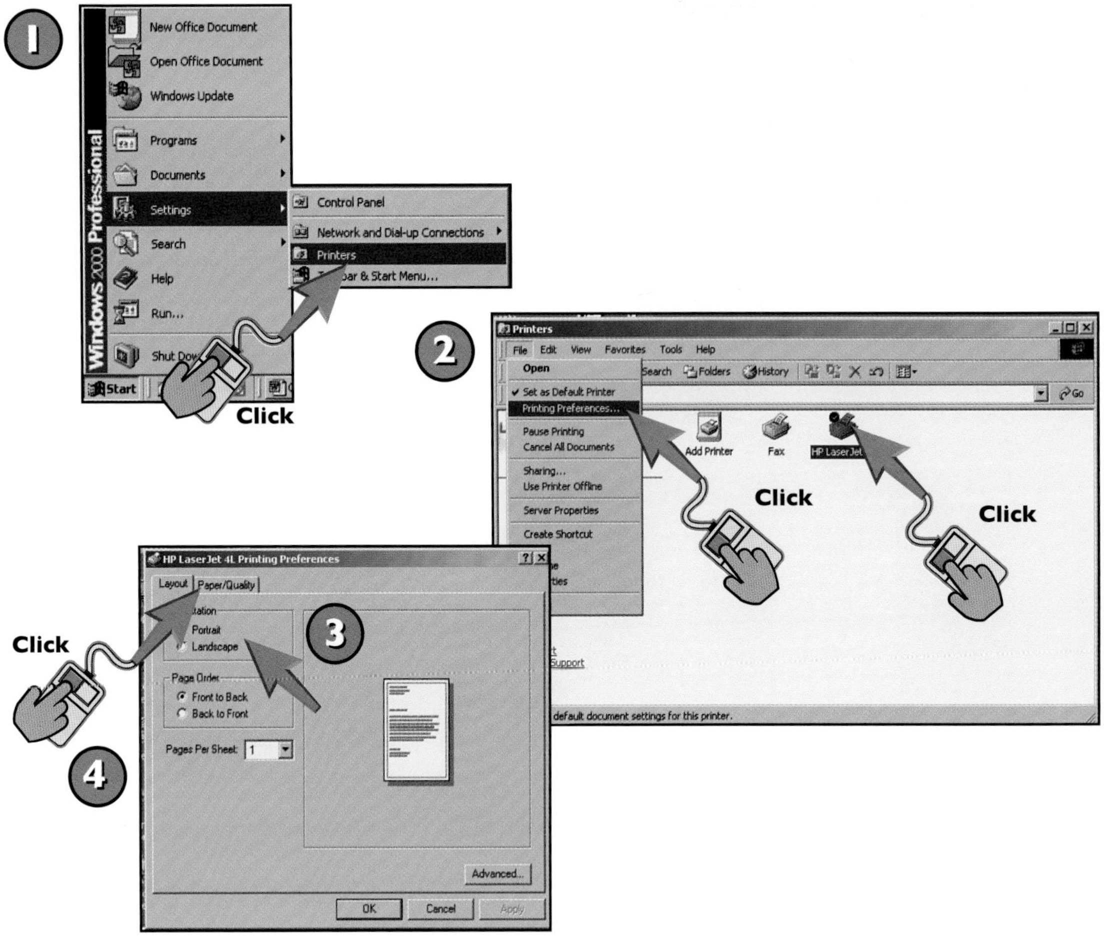

Changing Settings for a Single Document
Changing the printer's properties changes them for all documents you print on this printer. If you want to change properties for just one document, use the **Page Settings** or **Print Setup** command in the particular program.

Landscape Versus Portrait
In portrait orientation, the program prints down the long side of the page. In landscape, the program prints across the long side of the page.

1. Click the **Start** button, click the **Settings** command, and then choose **Printers**.
2. After you select the printer whose settings you want to modify, click **File**, and then select the **Printing Preferences** command.
3. On the **Layout** tab, select the default orientation and page order.
4. Click the **Paper/Quality** tab.

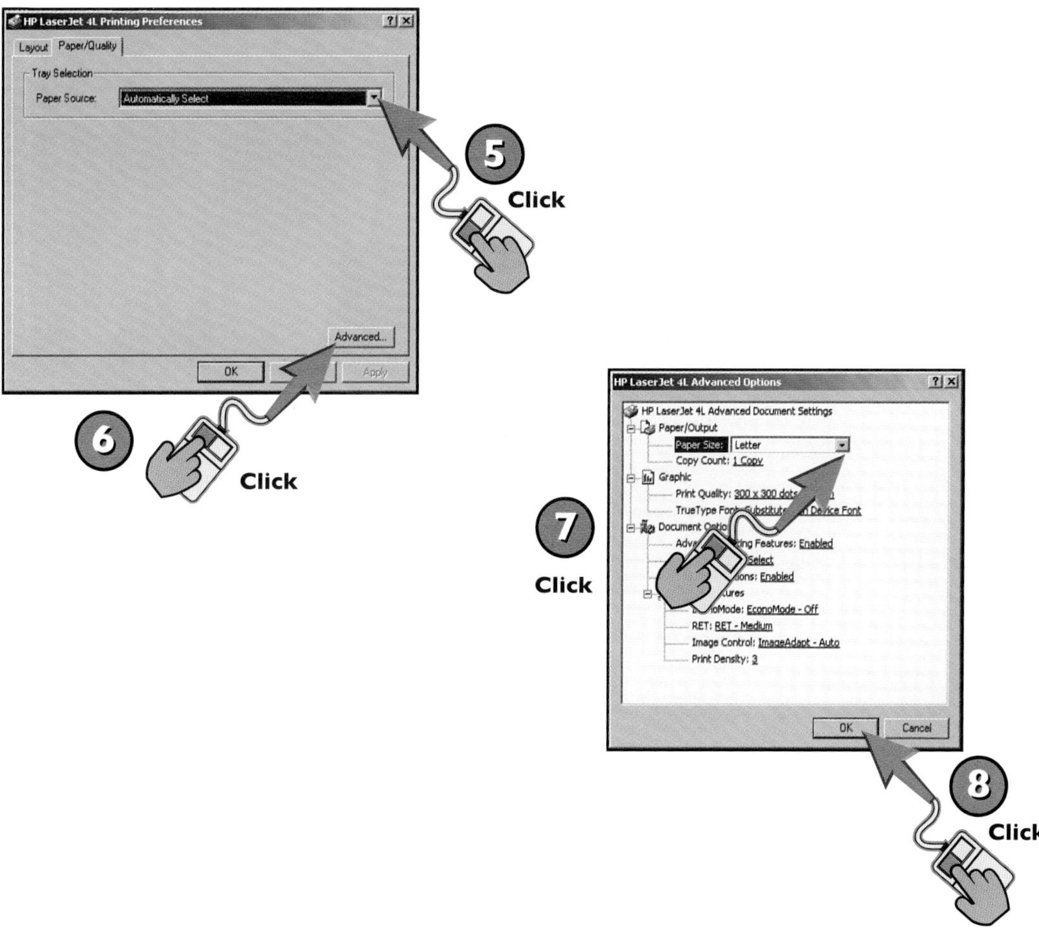

1. **5** Display the **Paper Source** drop-down list and select the paper source.
2. **6** To change the paper size, click the **Advanced** button.
3. **7** Display the **Paper Size** drop-down list and select the paper size.
4. **8** Click the **OK** button.

Other Advanced Options

You can also make changes in the Advanced Options dialog box. Be sure you know what each feature does. Otherwise, just keep the defaults.

Task 8: Adding a Printer

You can add a new printer to your Windows setup using a step-by-step guide called a *wizard* that Windows provides. Use the wizard any time you get a new printer or change printers.

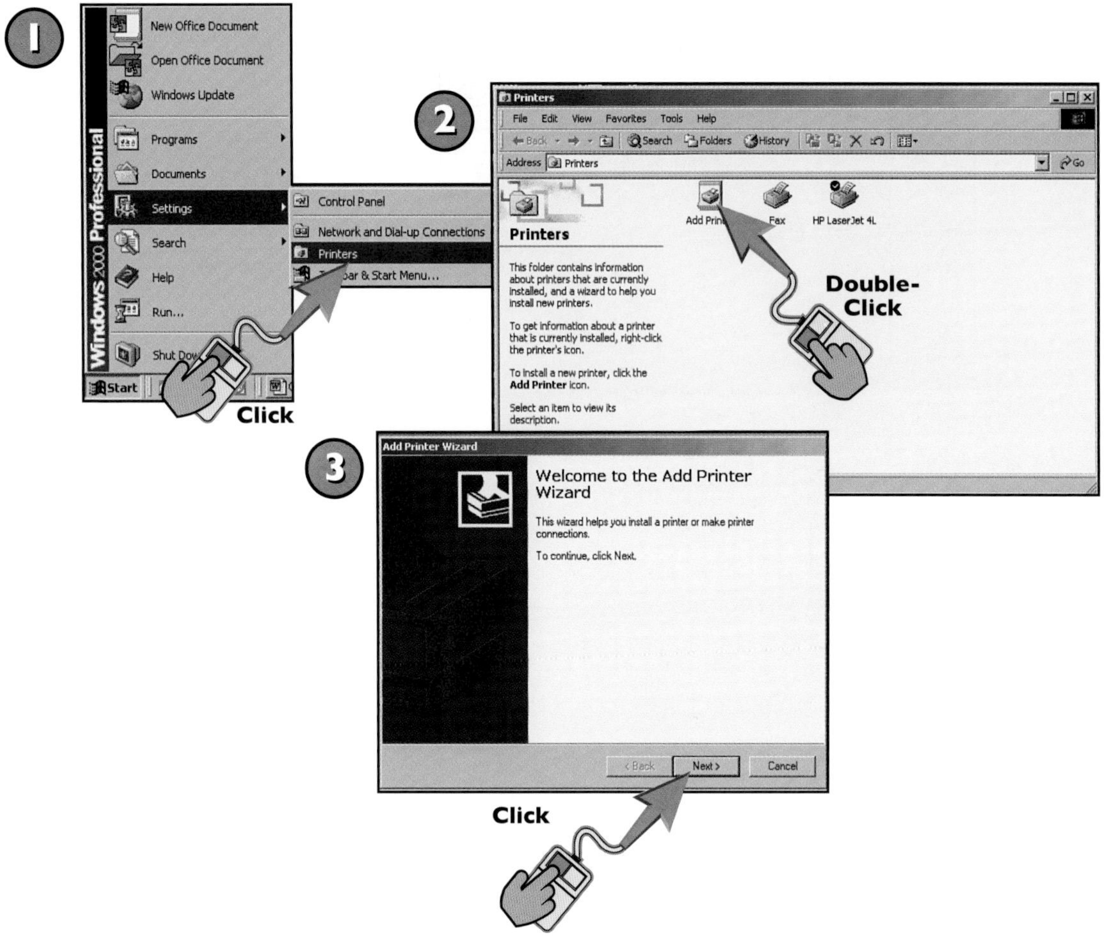

Canceling the Wizard
You can cancel this process at any time by clicking the **Cancel** button in any of the wizard dialog boxes.

Local Versus Network
If the printer is actually connected to your PC, it is a local printer. If you are connected to a printer through a network, it is a network printer.

1. Click the **Start** button, click the **Settings** command, and then select **Printers**.
2. Double-click the **Add Printer** icon.
3. Click the **Next** button to continue with the installation.

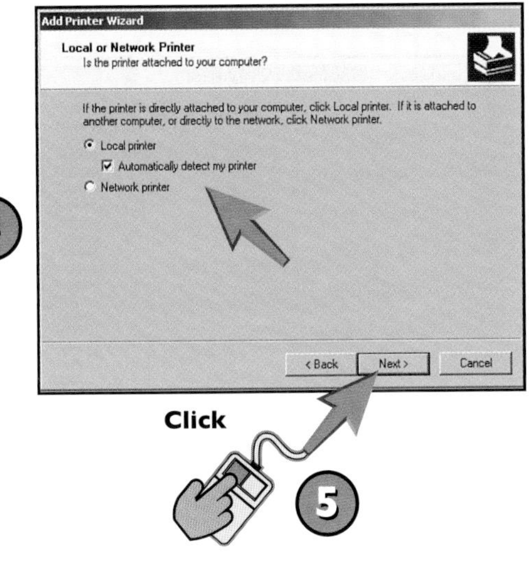

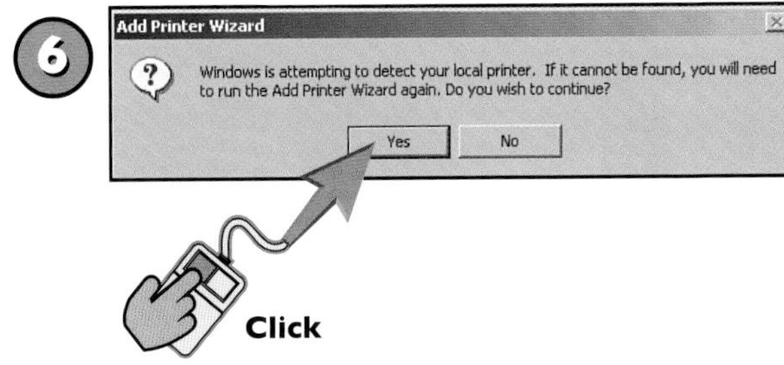

4 Select whether the printer is local or on a network. If local, select whether you want Windows to automatically detect the printer.

5 Click the **Next** button.

6 Click the **Yes** button to continue. Follow the onscreen instructions. Windows adds the new printer's icon to the Printers folder.

Printer Not Detected?
If the printer was not detected, rerun the wizard and uncheck Automatically Detect My Printer. Follow the onscreen instructions. You will be prompted to select the port, select the manufacturer and printer name, type a name for the printer, select whether to use this printer as the default, select whether to share the printer, and select whether to print a test page. Click Next after making each selection and Finish to complete the wizard.

Task 9: Deleting a Printer

If you get a new printer, you can delete the setup for the old printer so that you don't get confused about which printer is which. Deleting a printer removes it from the available list of printers.

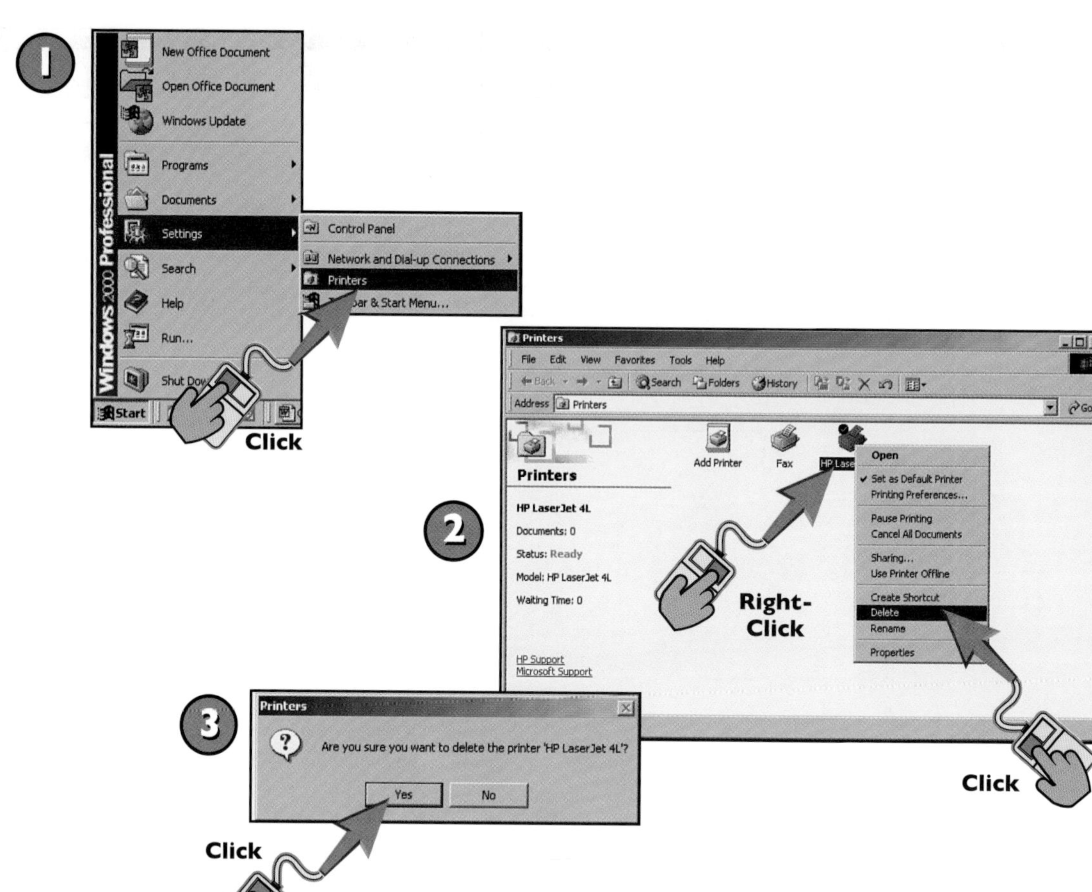

1. Click the **Start** button, click the **Settings** command, and then select **Printers**.
2. Right-click the printer you want to delete and select the **Delete** command from the shortcut menu.
3. Click the **Yes** button to confirm the deletion.

Undoing a Deletion

If you delete a printer by mistake, you can always add it back using the Add Printer Wizard (refer to the preceding task).

Task 10: Adding a Printer Icon on the Desktop

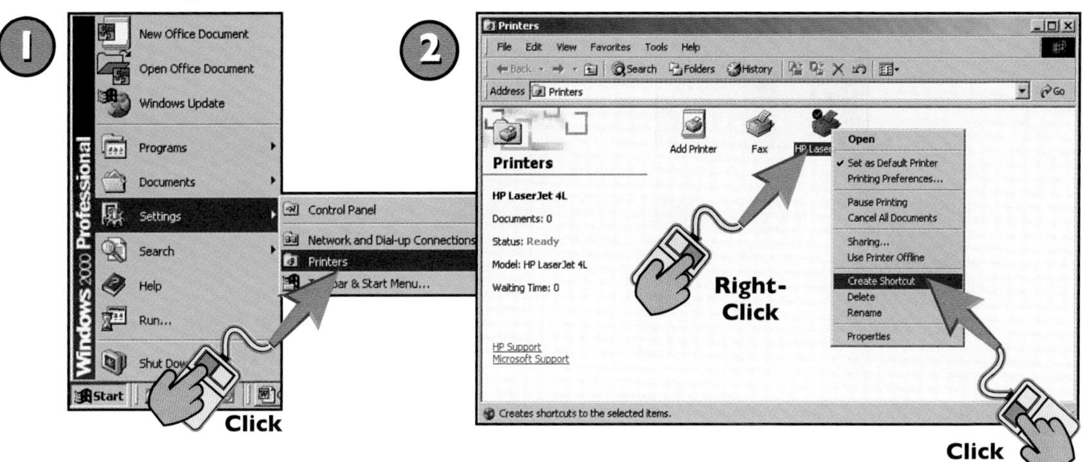

For fast access to your printer, you can add a printer icon to your desktop. You can then double-click this icon to view the print queue. You can also drag documents from a file window to the printer icon to print the documents.

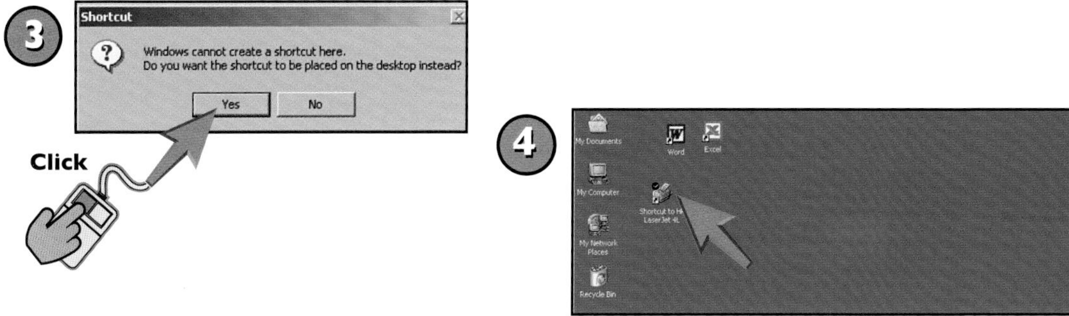

1. Click the **Start** button, click the **Settings** command, and then select **Printers**.
2. Right-click the printer and select the **Create Shortcut** command.
3. When prompted whether you want to place the shortcut on the desktop, click **Yes**.
4. The printer shortcut is added to your desktop.

Deleting the Printer Shortcut Icon

To delete the shortcut icon, right-click it and then select **Delete** from the shortcut menu. When prompted to confirm the deletion, click the **Yes** button.

PART 5

Personalizing Windows

To make Windows most suited to how you work, Microsoft has made it easy for you to customize the program. You can adjust the colors used for onscreen elements such as the title bar. You can change how the mouse works, when sounds are played, and more. Windows 2000 includes many options for setting up your work environment just the way you want. This part shows you how to customize Windows.

Tasks

Task 1: Showing and Hiding the Taskbar

Start Here

The default for Windows is to show the taskbar at all times on the desktop. You can, however, hide the taskbar so that you have more room on the desktop for other windows, folders, and programs. When you hide the taskbar, it disappears while you are working in a window and then reappears when you move the mouse to the bottom of the screen.

Undoing the Change
To undo this change, open the **Start** menu, click the **Settings** command, and then click the **Taskbar & Start Menu** command. Click the **Auto Hide** option to remove the check mark. Then click **OK**.

Right-clicking Taskbar
You can right-click a blank area of the taskbar and select **Properties** to make a change.

Other Options
You can select to display small icons and to enable or disable the clock.

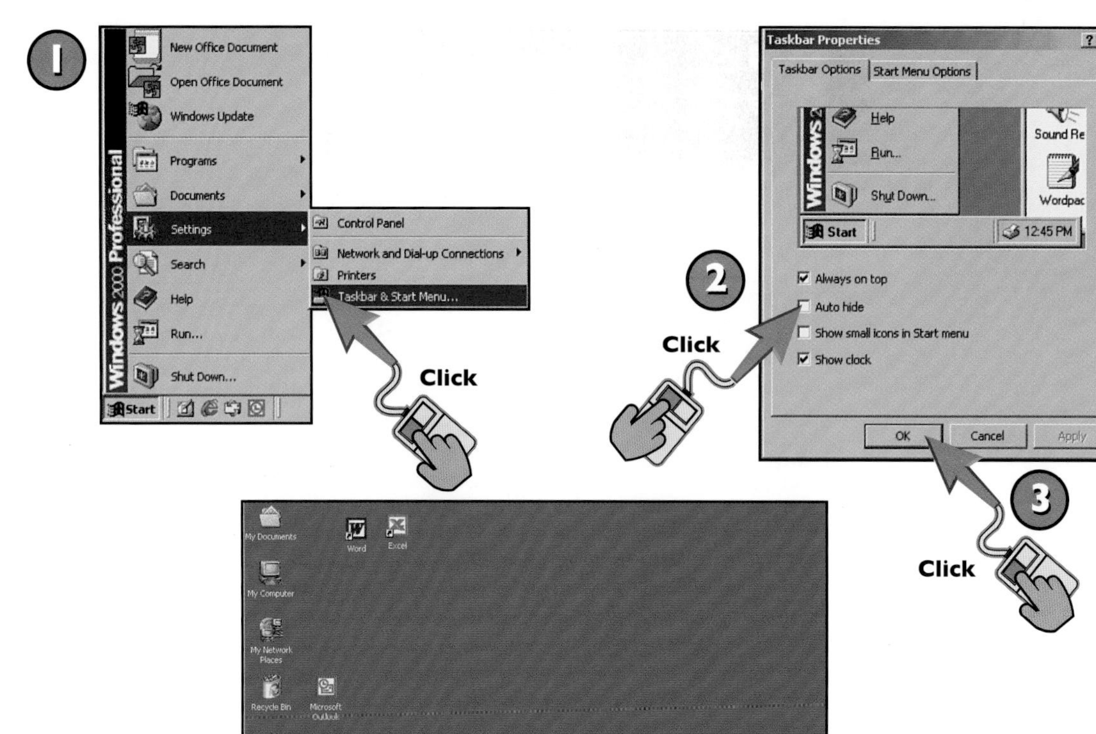

1. Click **Start**, click the **Settings** command, and then select **Taskbar & Start Menu**.
2. Click the **Auto Hide** check box to select it.
3. Click the **OK** button.
4. The window closes, and the taskbar disappears.

Task 2: Moving the Taskbar

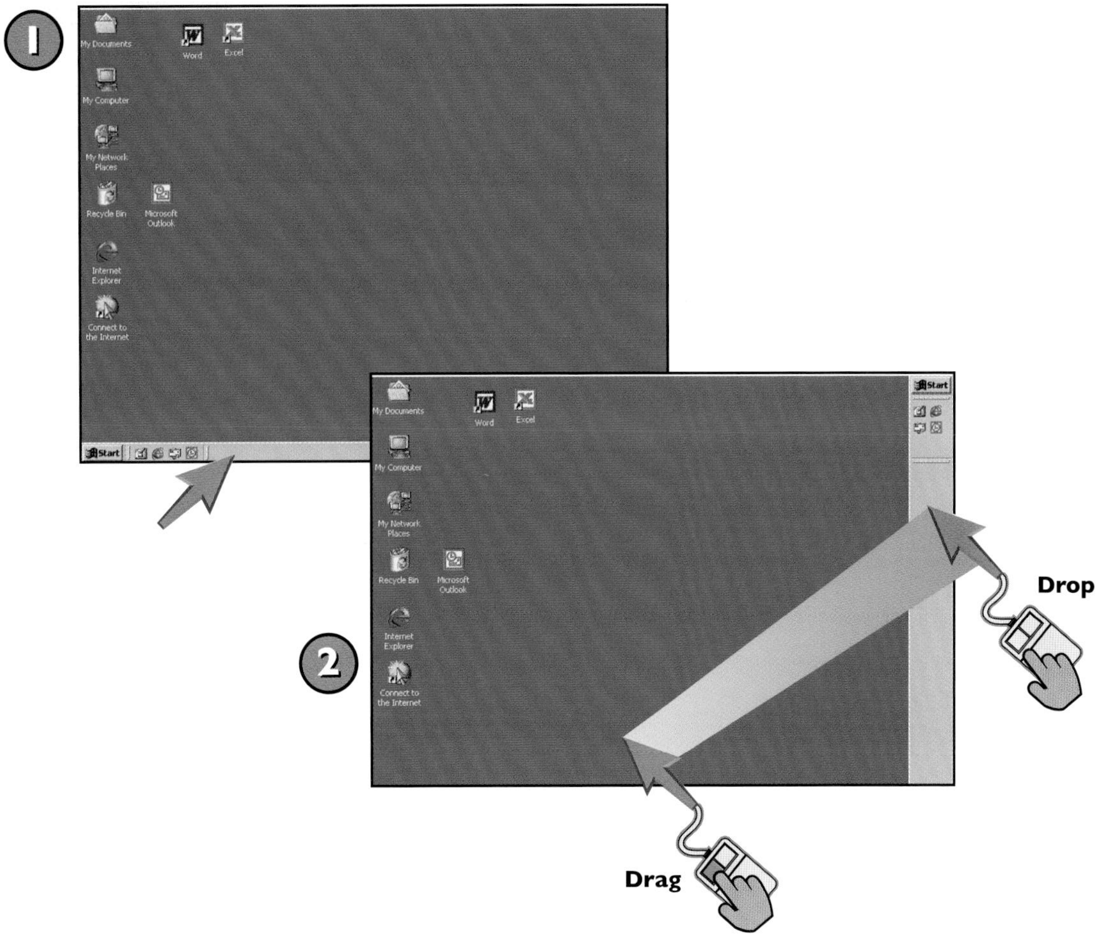

Windows enables you to place the taskbar in the top, left, right, or bottom of the screen so that the desktop is set up how you like it. Try moving the taskbar to various areas on the screen and then choose the area you like best.

Position the mouse pointer anywhere on the taskbar except on a button or the clock.

Press and hold the left mouse button and drag the taskbar to the location you want. When you release the mouse button, the taskbar jumps to the new location.

Resizing the Taskbar

You can also resize the taskbar by putting the pointer on the taskbar border and dragging it.

Task 3: Changing the System Date and Time

Start Here

Windows displays the current time in the taskbar. You can place the pointer over the time to display the current date. If your system clock is wrong, you can correct it; you should do so because Windows places a time and date stamp on every file you save, identifying it for later use.

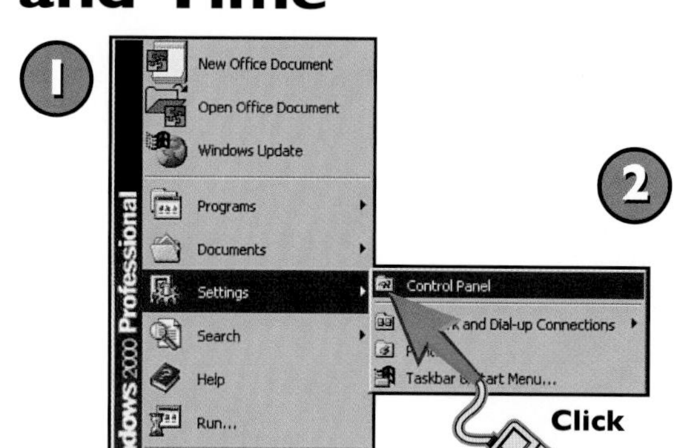

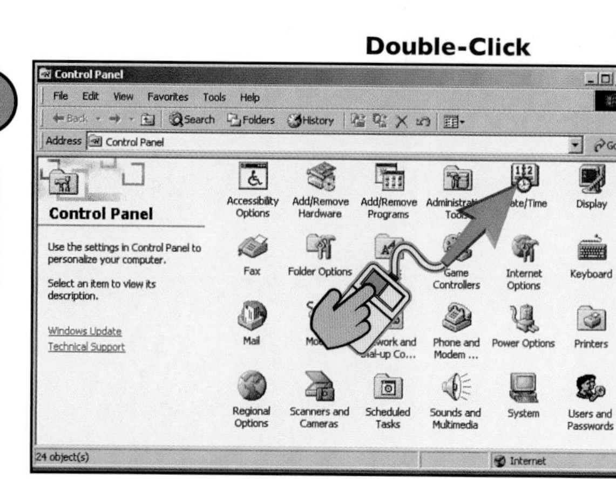

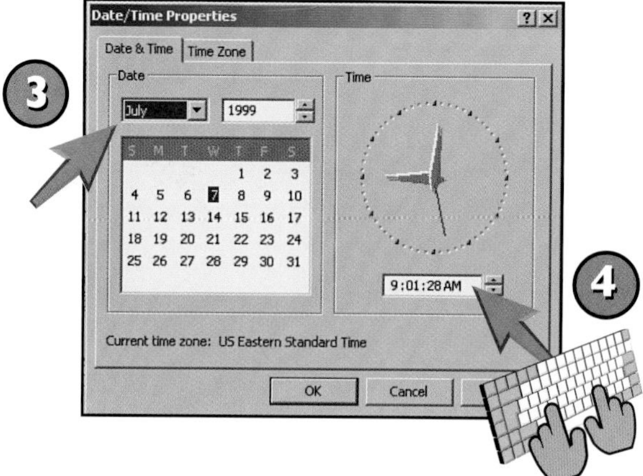

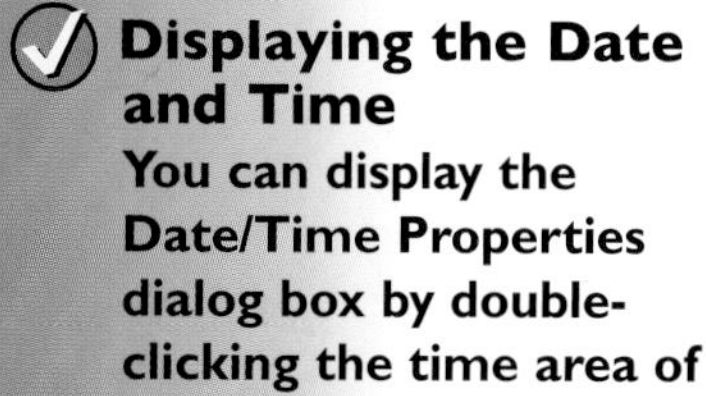

Displaying the Date and Time
You can display the Date/Time Properties dialog box by double-clicking the time area of the taskbar.

Entering the Time Zone
Use the **Time Zone** tab to select the correct time zone for your area.

1. Click the **Start** menu, click **Settings**, and select **Control Panel**.
2. Double-click the **Date/Time** icon.
3. Select the correct month from the drop-down list, click the date in the calendar, and type the correct year in the spin box.
4. Enter the correct time in this format: ***hour:minutes:seconds*** and **AM** or **PM**. Click **OK**.

End Task

Task 4: Using Wallpaper for the Desktop

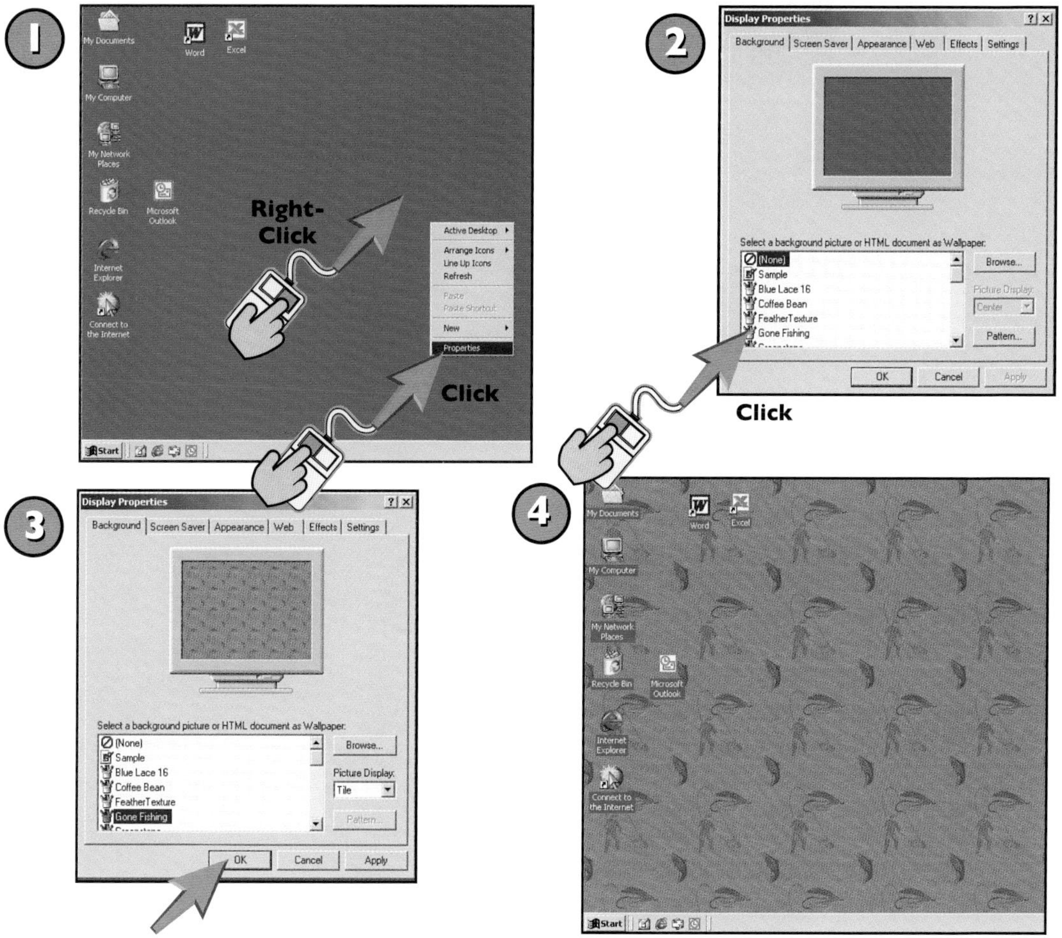

You can personalize your desktop in Windows by adding wallpaper. Windows offers many colorful wallpaper options, including Blue Lace, Gone Fishing, Coffee Bean, Soap Bubbles, and more.

1 Right-click any blank area of the desktop and then click **Properties**.

2 In the **Background** tab, select the wallpaper you want displayed on your desktop.

3 The selected wallpaper appears on the sample monitor. Click the **OK** button.

4 The wallpaper is added to your desktop background.

Adding a Pattern

Alternatively, you can add a pattern to the desktop, as covered in the next task.

Undoing the Wallpaper

To revert to a plain background, follow these steps, but select **(None)** from the Wallpaper list.

Only Centered Wallpaper?

If you see only one small image in the center of your screen when selecting wallpaper, click the **Picture Display** drop-down list and choose **Tile**. Click **Apply**, and then click **OK** to accept the changes. Doing so will repeat this image on the page.

Task 5: Using a Pattern for the Desktop

If you don't like the wallpaper selections, you might want to experiment with a pattern. Windows offers paisley, tulip, waffle, and box background patterns (among others).

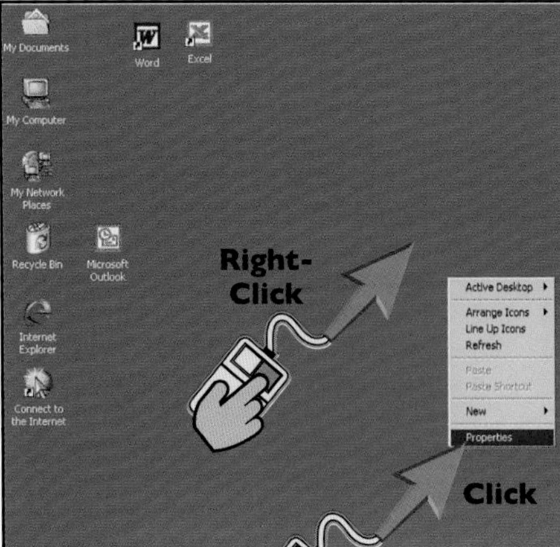

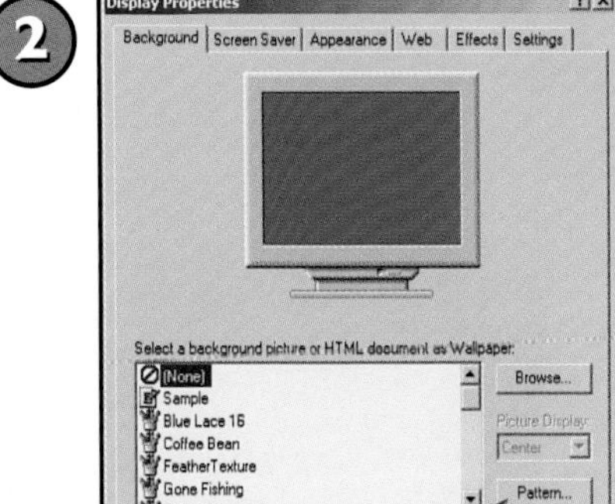

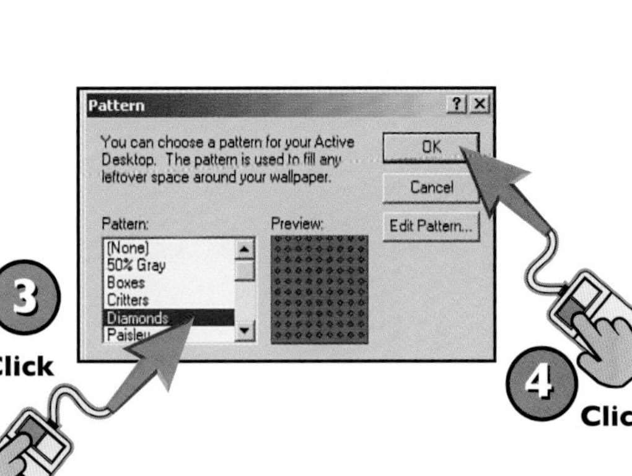

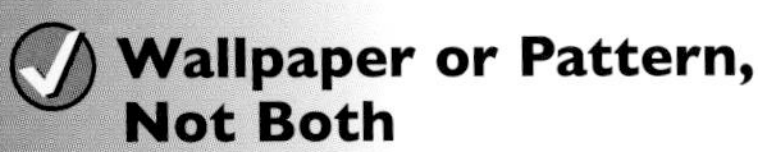

Wallpaper or Pattern, Not Both
You cannot use both wallpaper and a pattern. If you select wallpaper, the **Pattern** button is dimmed. If you want to use a pattern, select **(None)** from the Wallpaper list.

Right-click any blank area of the desktop and then click **Properties**.

Click the **Pattern** button.

Select the pattern you want displayed on your desktop. The selected pattern appears in the Preview area.

Click **OK** to close the Pattern dialog box.

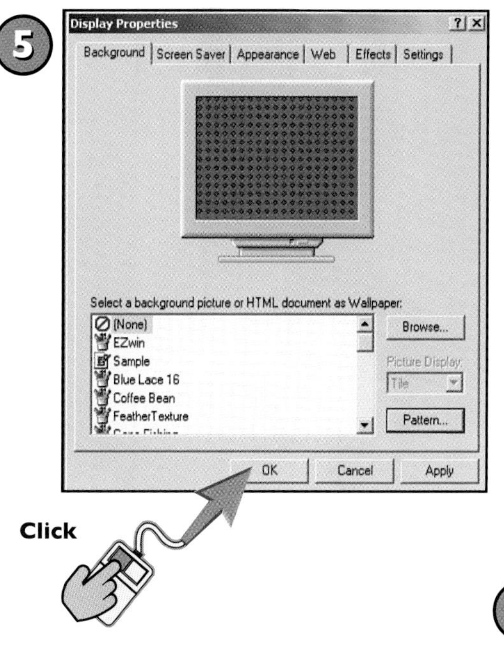

5 Click the **OK** button in the Display Properties dialog box.

6 Windows uses the selected pattern on your desktop.

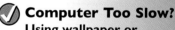

Computer Too Slow?
Using wallpaper or patterns generally slows the speed of your computer and taxes its memory. If your applications seem too slow or if you decide you don't want a pattern or wallpaper, return to the Display Properties dialog box, click the Pattern button, and choose (None).

Task 6: Changing the Colors Windows Uses

Windows enables you to change the sets of colors used for certain onscreen elements such as the title bar, background, and so on. These sets of colors are called ***schemes***, and you can select colors that work best for you and your monitor. Lighter colors might, for example, make working in some Windows applications easier on your eyes. On the other hand, you might prefer bright and lively colors.

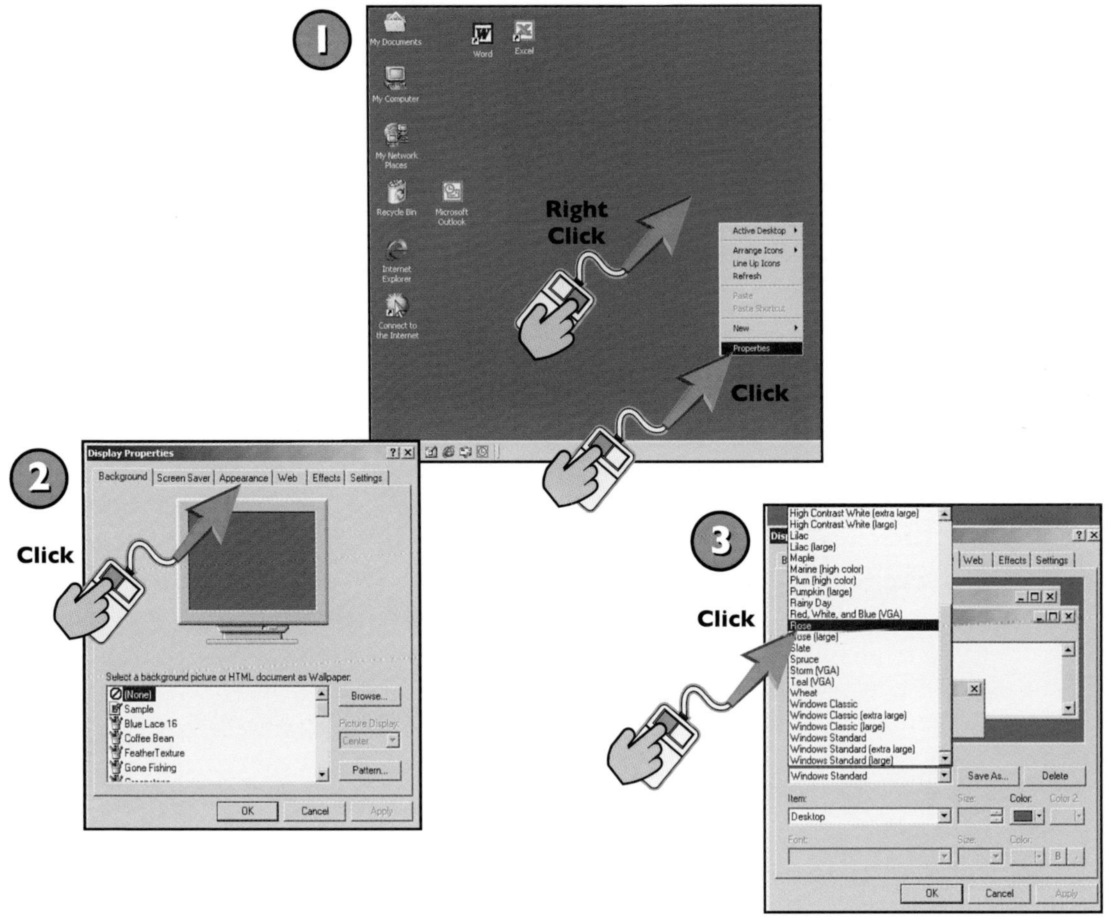

1 Right Click

Click

2 Click

3 Click

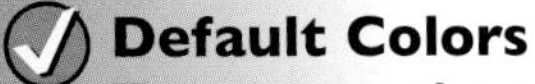

Default Colors
To revert to the original colors, click **Cancel** instead of **OK**. If you have already closed the Properties dialog box, you can revert to the **Windows Standard** scheme by selecting it from the list.

1. Right-click any blank area of the desktop and then click **Properties**.
2. Click the **Appearance** tab.
3. From the **Scheme** drop-down list, select any of the available schemes. (I've selected **Rose**.)

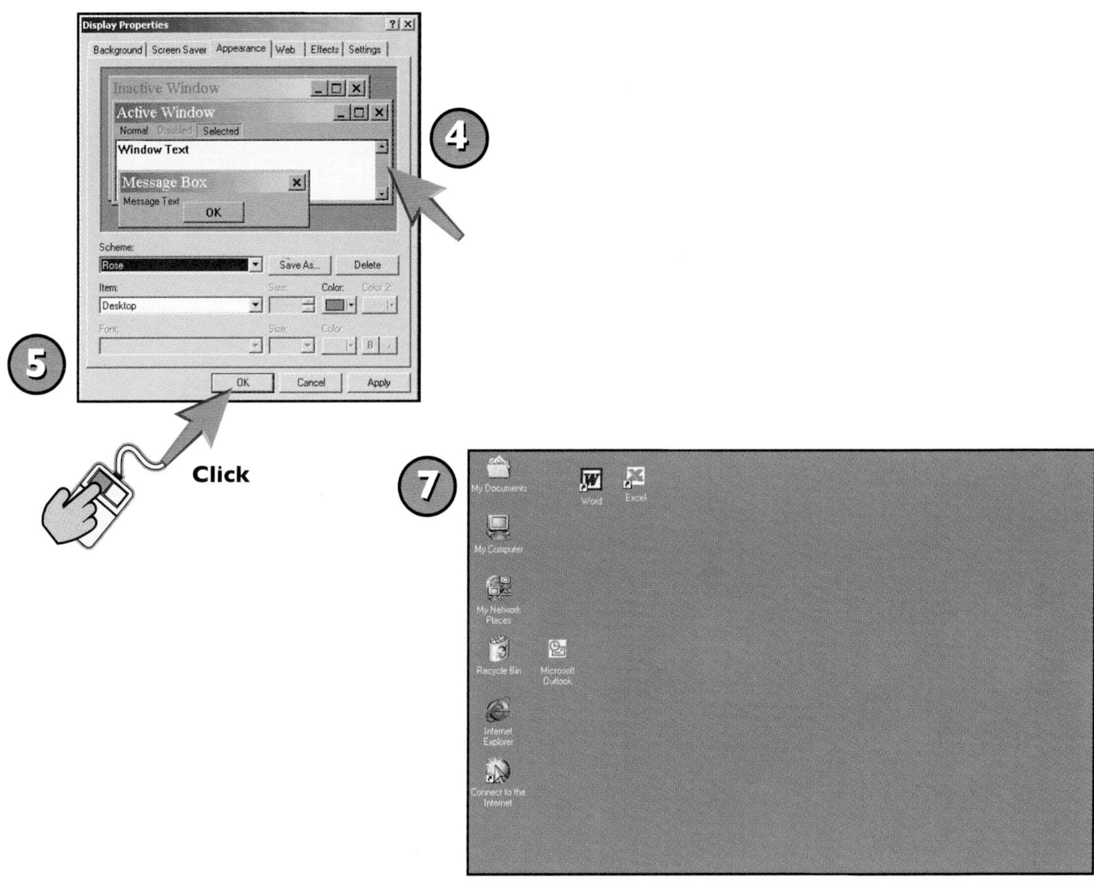

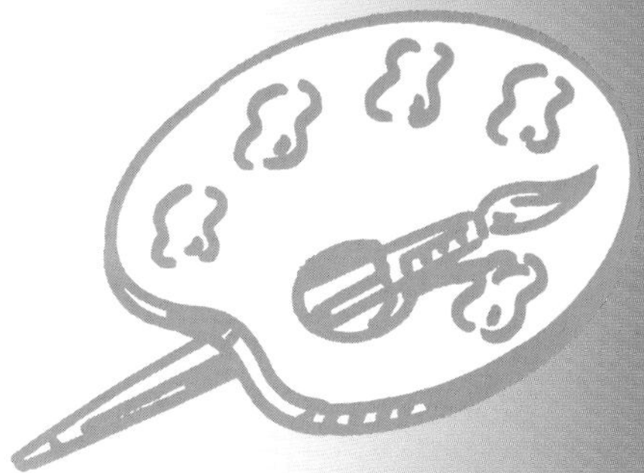

4. The color scheme you selected (in this case, **Rose**) appears in the sample box.

5. Click the **OK** button to accept the changes.

6. Windows uses the new set of colors you selected.

Changing Individual Colors

When you see a preview of the color scheme, you can change any individual item's color by clicking the item and then selecting a different color from the Color list. When you're satisfied with your changes, click OK to accept the changes.

Task 7: Using a Screen Saver

In the past, when you used Windows or Windows applications, the concentration of bright or white colors on older monitors would, over time, burn into the screen (commonly called ***burn-in***). When this happened, you saw a "ghost" of the Windows screen on your display after you turned off your computer. A screen saver (a moving pattern of dark and light colors or images) helped protect your screen from burn-in by displaying a moving pattern whenever the computer was on but inactive. Even though burn-in is not a problem with most modern monitors, screen savers are still around; these days, however, they're used mostly for fun.

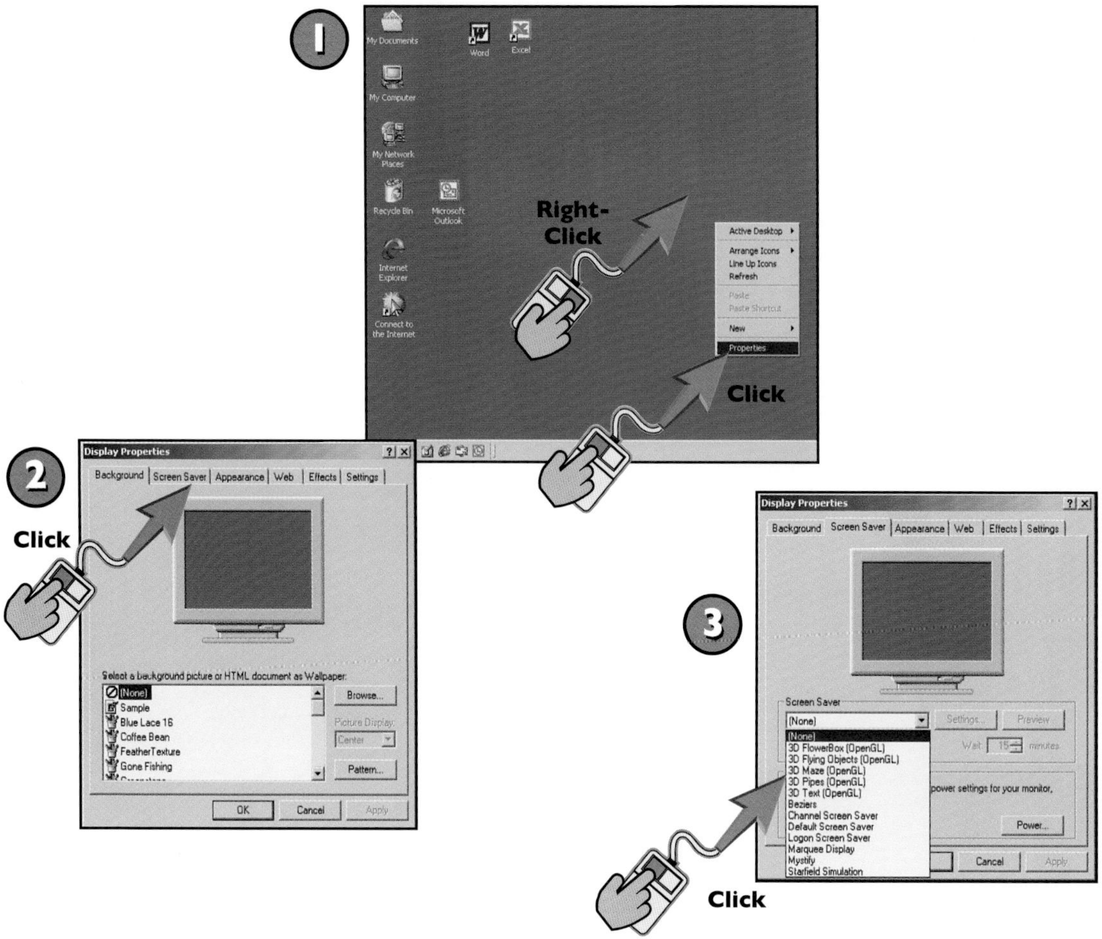

1. Right-click any blank area of the desktop and then click **Properties**.
2. Click the **Screen Saver** tab.
3. Click the **Screen Saver** drop-down list box arrow to display the list of available screen savers and then select the screen saver you want to use.

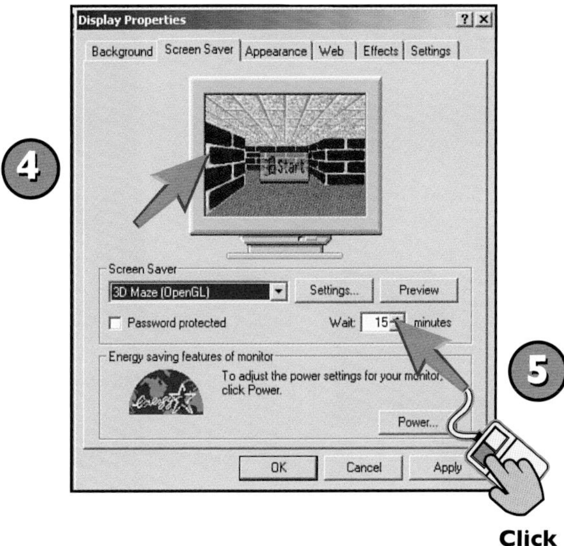

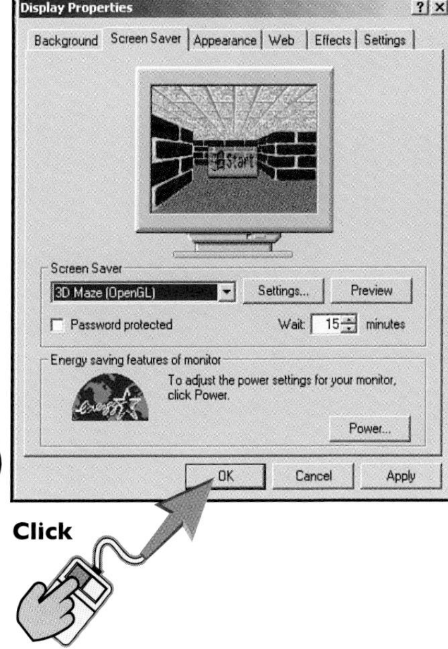

4 The screen saver you selected appears on the sample monitor.

5 When satisfied with the screen saver you have chosen, specify the number of minutes (using the **Wait** spin box) your system should be idle before the screen saver begins.

6 Click the **OK** button.

Previewing the Screen Saver

To see what the screen saver will look like on the full screen, click the **Preview** button. Click the mouse button or press the spacebar to return to the Display Properties dialog box.

Pressing the Spacebar

When the screen saver is displayed, move the mouse or press the spacebar to return to the normal view.

Turning Off Screen Saver

To turn off the screen saver, invoke the Display Properties dialog box, click the **Screen Saver** tab, and select **(None)**. Click the **OK** button.

Setting Screen Saver Options

Click the **Settings** button to select options for how the screen saver is displayed; these options vary depending on the screen saver. Make your choices and click the **OK** button.

Task 8: Changing How Your Monitor Works

Many monitors allow you to select certain options about how they operate—such as the number of colors it displays or its resolution. (*Resolution* measures the number of pixels or picture elements displayed. An example of a common resolution is 800×600.) You might need to change your monitor's display properties if you get a new monitor, want to update your monitor driver, or want to change how the monitor looks.

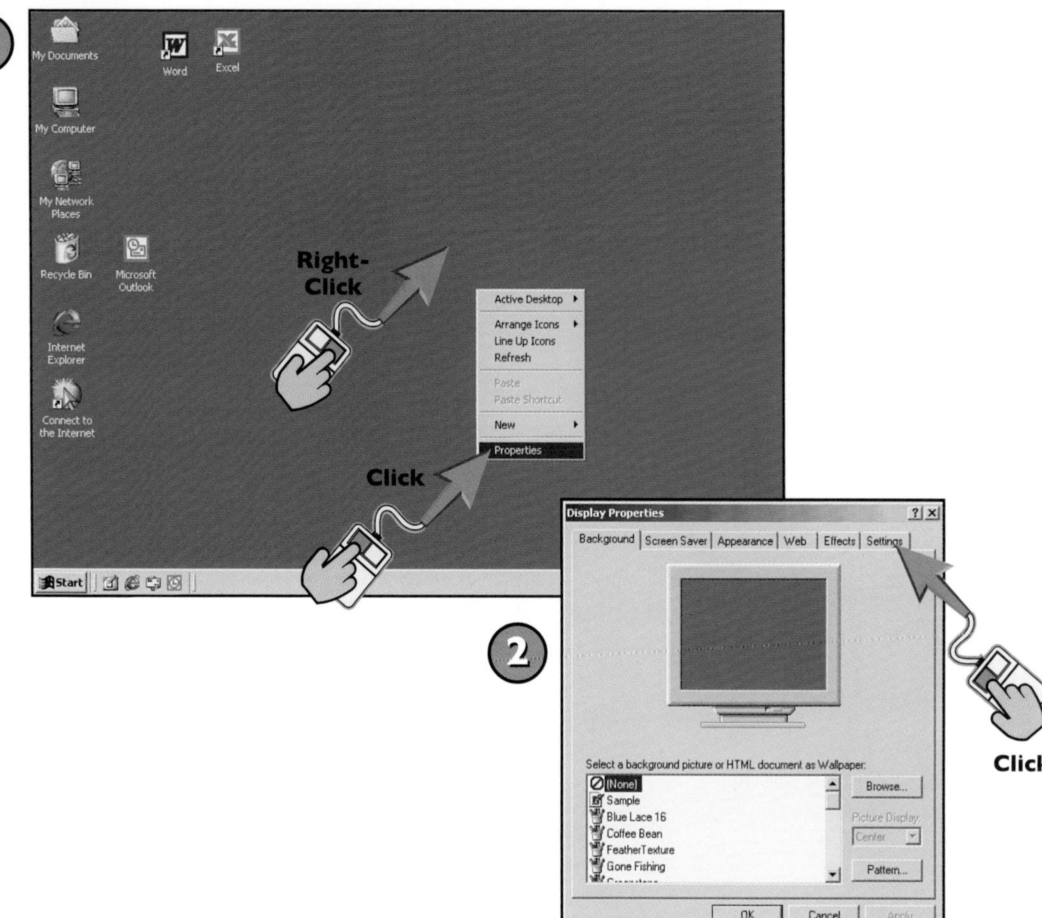

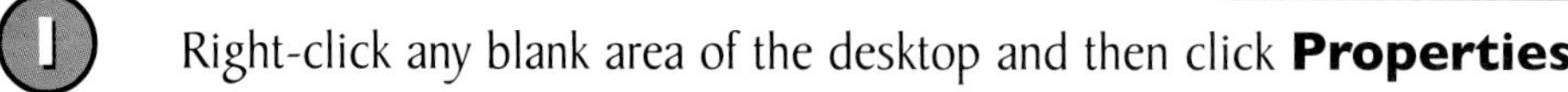

1. Right-click any blank area of the desktop and then click **Properties**.
2. Click the **Settings** tab.

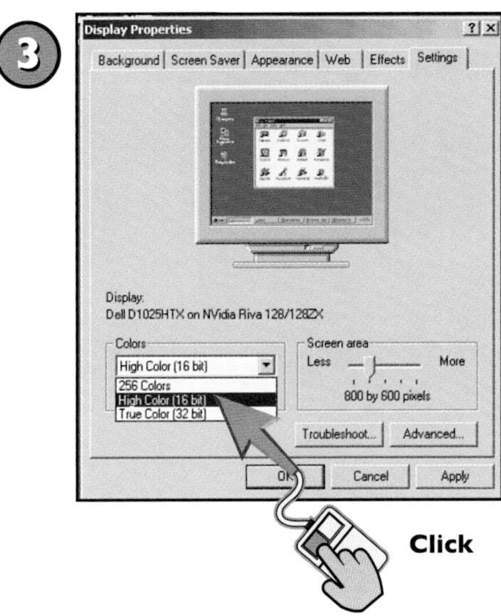

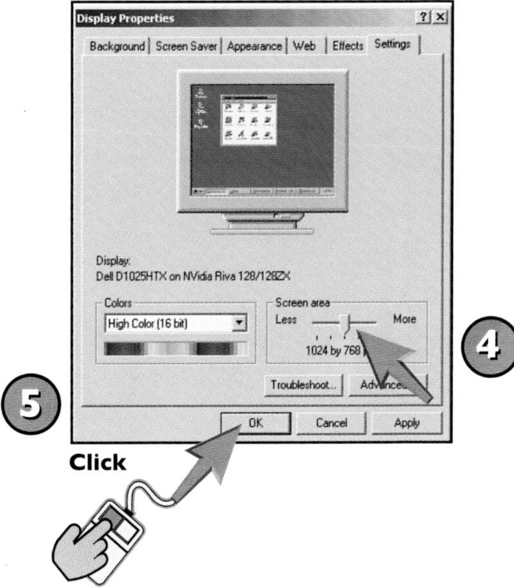

3 To change the number of colors used for the display, display the **Colors** drop-down list and choose the option you want.

4 To change the resolution, drag the **Screen Area** bar to the desired setting.

5 Click the **OK** button.

Updating a Monitor or Adapter

To update a monitor or adapter, click the Advanced button on the Settings tab and then select either the Adapter or Monitor tab. Click the Change button and follow the wizard's instructions for installing a new monitor or adapter.

Troubleshooting Monitor Problems

If you are having problems with your monitor, click the Troubleshoot button (new with Windows 2000) and use Windows online help to apply the Display Troubleshooter.

Task 9: Changing How the Desktop Icons Look

Another way to experiment with the appearance of the desktop is to change how the icons are displayed. You can select a different picture for any of the default icons. Windows 2000 comes with several icons to choose from. You can also select the size and colors used for icons on the desktop.

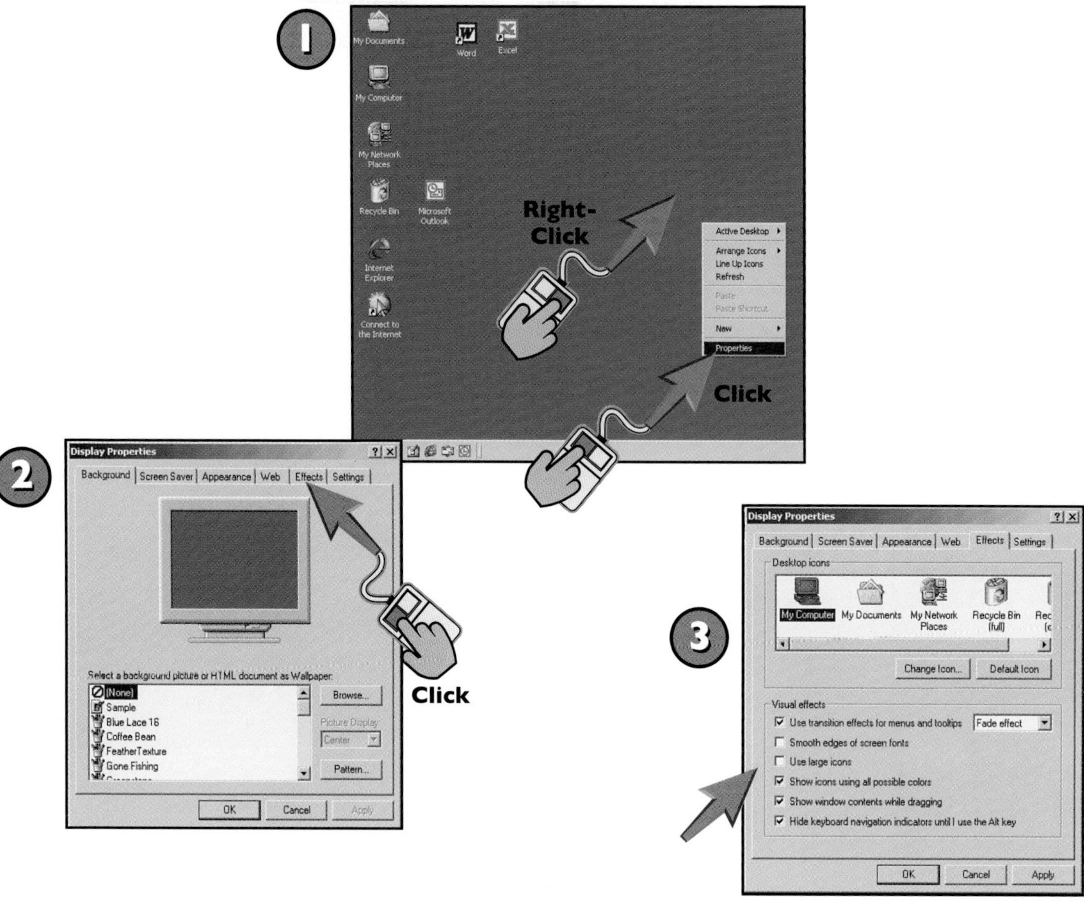

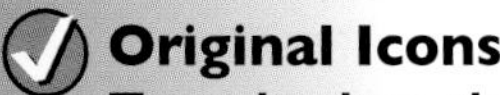

Original Icons

To go back to the original icon, display the Effects tab and select the icon. Click the Default Icon button and then click the OK button.

1. Right-click any blank area of the desktop and then click **Properties**.
2. Click the **Effects** tab.
3. Click to place check marks next to the visual effects you want to use in the Visual Effects section of the tab. (If an option is unchecked, it is not in effect.)

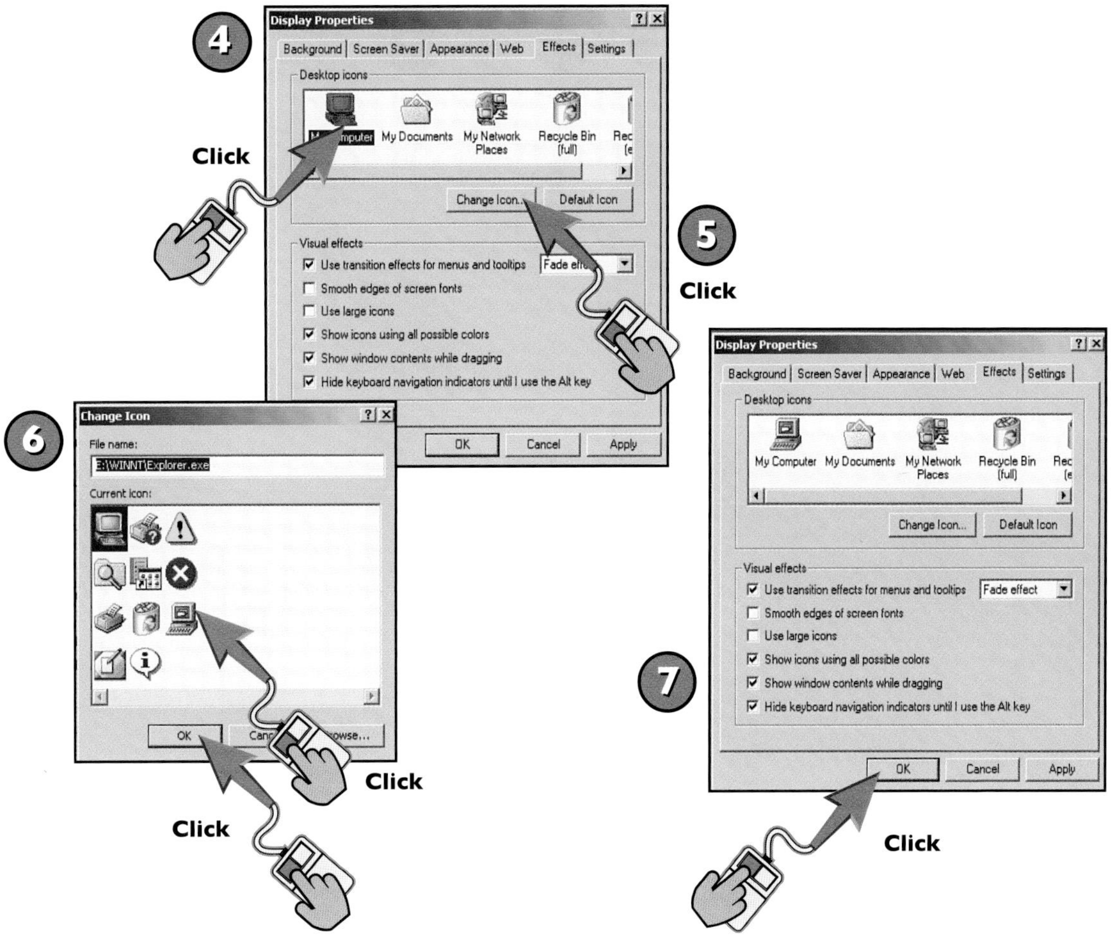

4. To use a different icon, select the icon you want to change.

5. Click the **Change Icon** button.

6. Click the icon you want to use instead and click **OK**.

7. The new icon appears in the Desktop Icons area. Click **OK** to close the Display Properties dialog box.

Browsing for Other Icons

Other icons are available. To browse for these icons, click the Browse button and then select the file that contains the icons.

Task 10: Viewing the Desktop as a Web Page

If you have used the Internet, you might be comfortable with the methods used on it for viewing content. For example, when you browse the Internet, you can click a link to display its contents. You can set up your desktop to browse its contents just like you browse a page on the Internet. You also can display your Internet home page as part of the desktop. (For more information about browsing the Internet, see Part 9, "Connecting to Online Services and the Internet.")

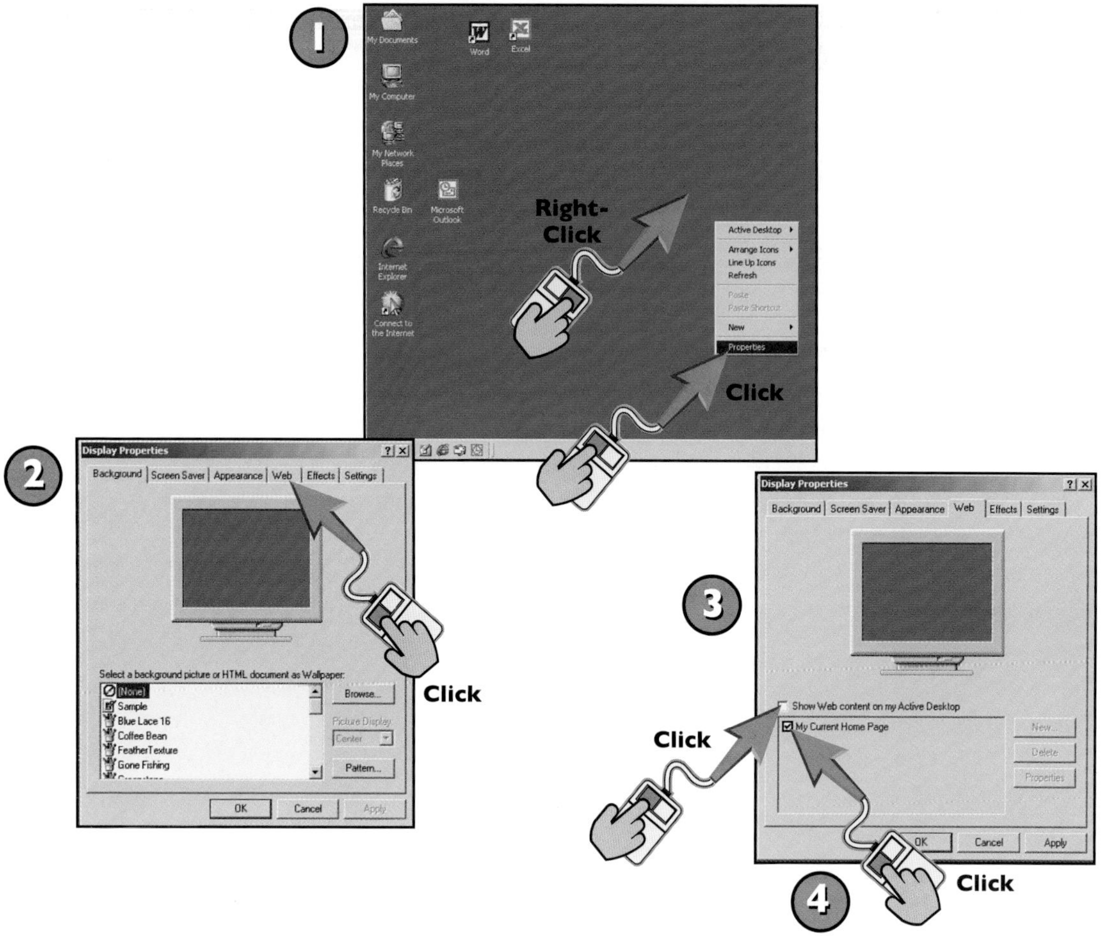

1. Right-click any blank area of the desktop and then click **Properties**.
2. Click the **Web** tab.
3. Check the **Show Web Content on My Active Desktop** check box.
4. To display your home page, check the **My Current Home Page** check box.

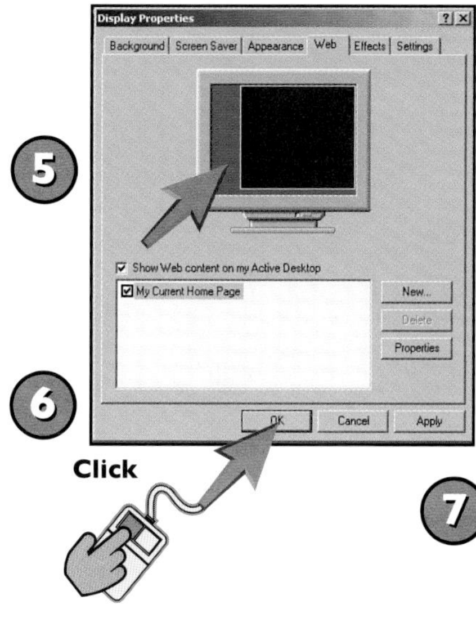

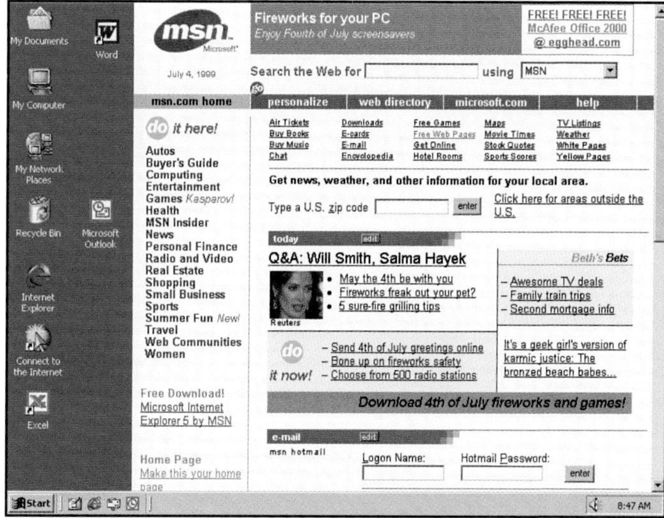

5 The area that will be used to display the Web content appears in the preview.

6 Click the **OK** button.

7 The desktop is displayed as a Web page.

Turning Off Active Desktop
To revert to the regular desktop, right-click a blank area of the desktop, choose **Active Desktop**, and uncheck **Show Web Content**.

Showing Icons or Home Page
When Web content is displayed, you can select whether the icons and your home page are displayed. Right-click the desktop and select **Active Desktop**. Uncheck **Show Desktop Icons** or **My Current Home Page** to hide these items.

PART 5

Task 11: Adding Web Content to the Desktop

In addition to your home page (or instead of your home page), you can select other Web content for display on your desktop. You can display other Web pages or select a Web picture or document to view on the desktop.

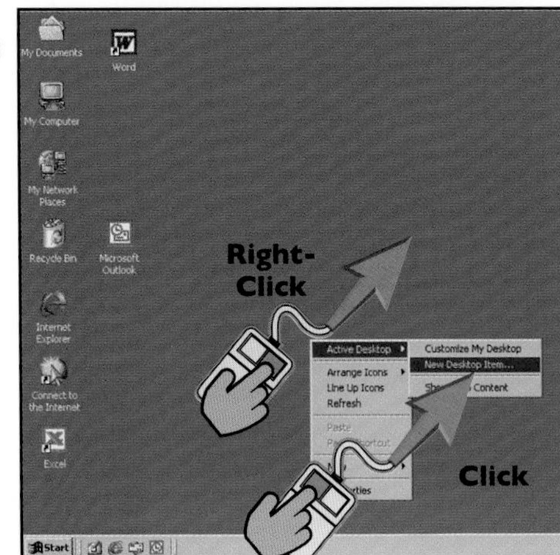

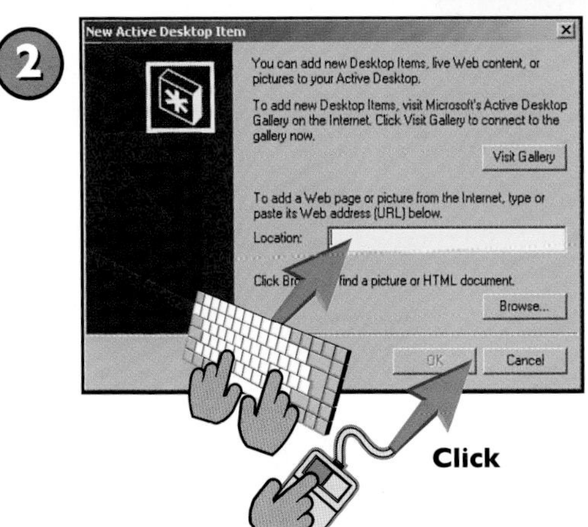

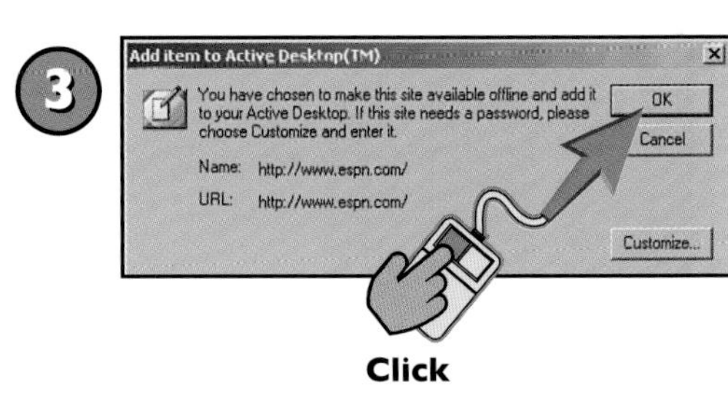

1 Right-click the desktop, select **Active Desktop**, and then click **New Desktop Item**.

2 Type the address to the Web page you want to view and click the **OK** button.

3 The page is set up for offline viewing. Click **OK**.

Checking the Gallery
You can add items from Microsoft's Gallery on the Internet. Click the **Visit Gallery** button to connect and select content.

Browsing for a Picture
To browse for a picture or Web document, click the **Browse** button and select the file you want to use.

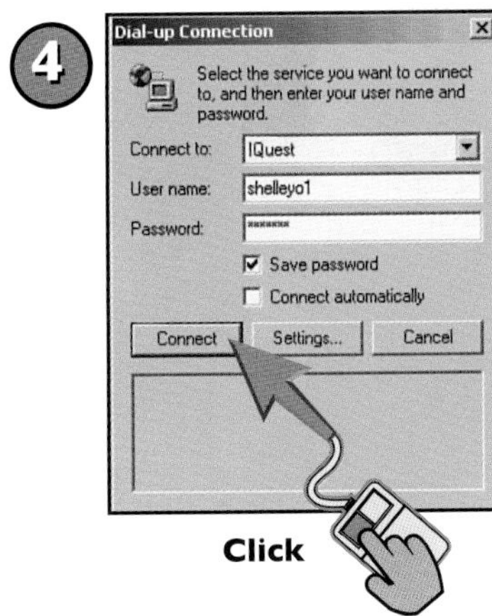

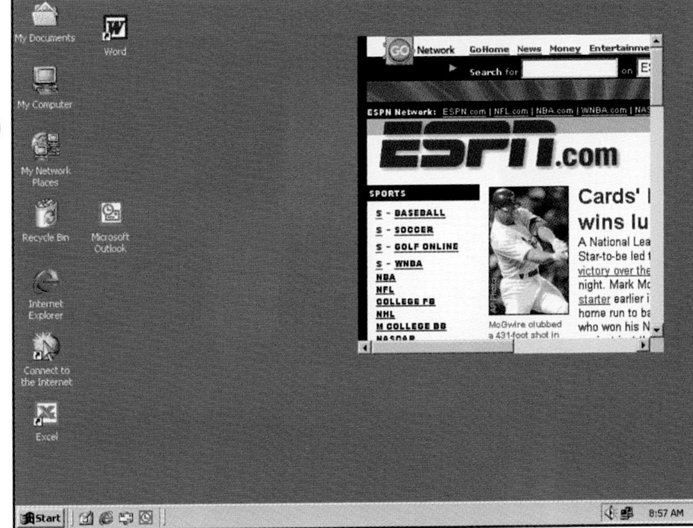

4 When prompted to connect to your Internet service provider, click **Connect** to do so.

5 The content is displayed on your desktop.

Password Required?
If you need a password to access the site, click the Customize button and enter the password.

Getting Rid of Item
If you no longer want the desktop item displayed, right-click the desktop, select Active Desktop, and then uncheck the item you added.

Task 12: Changing How the Mouse Works

You can adjust the mouse buttons and double-click speed to make using the mouse more comfortable for you. Suppose, for example, that you are left-handed; switching the left and right mouse buttons can make your work much easier. Likewise, if you are having trouble getting the double-click correct, you can change the double-click speed on the mouse.

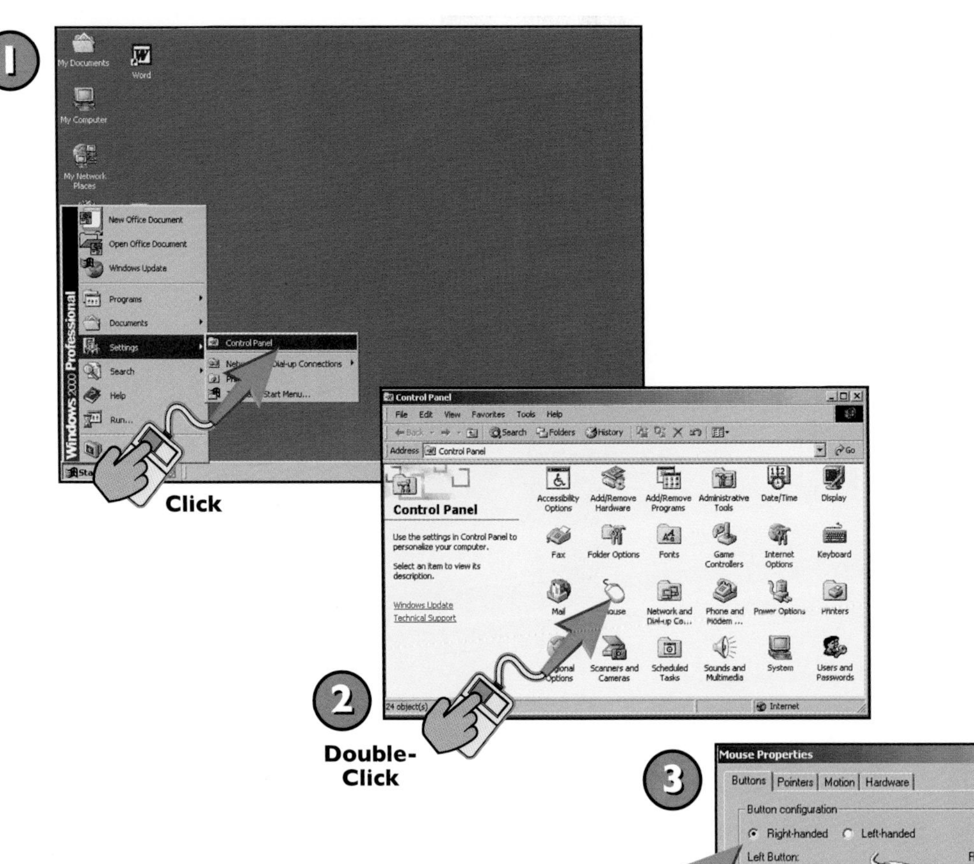

1. Click the **Start** menu, click **Settings**, and select **Control Panel**.

2. Double-click the **Mouse** icon.

3. Select left- or right-handed button configuration.

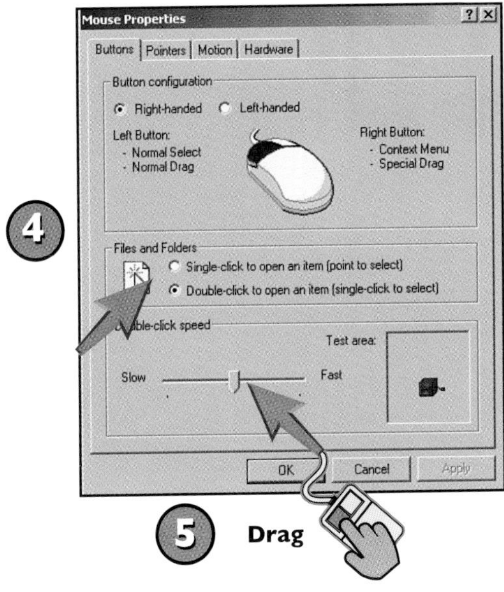

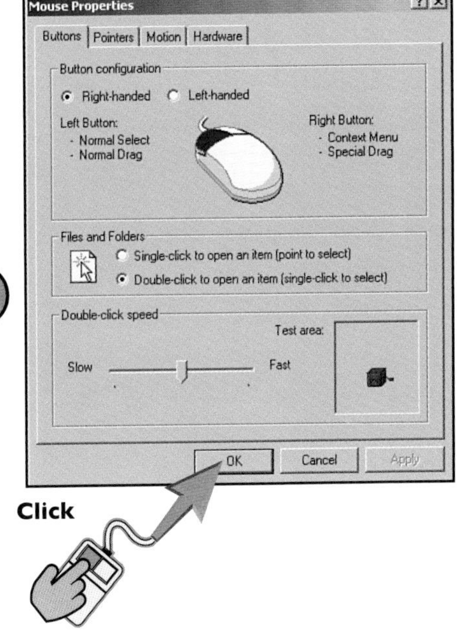

4 Select single- or double-click to open a folder.

5 To change the double-click speed, drag the **Double-Click Speed** lever between **Slow** and **Fast**.

6 Click the **OK** button.

Motion Tab
Click the Motion tab to make changes to the pointer speed and acceleration. You can also have Windows automatically move the pointer to the default button in dialog buttons (new with Windows 2000).

Testing the Double-Click Speed
You can test the double-click speed by double-clicking in the Test box. When you double-click correctly, a Jack-in-the-box pops out. Double-click again, and Jack goes back into the box.

Task 13: Changing How the Mouse Pointers Look

Start Here

Another mouse change you can make is the way the pointer appears onscreen. Depending on the action, the pointer takes several different shapes. For instance, when Windows is busy, you see an hourglass. You can select a different set of shapes (called a *scheme*) if you prefer.

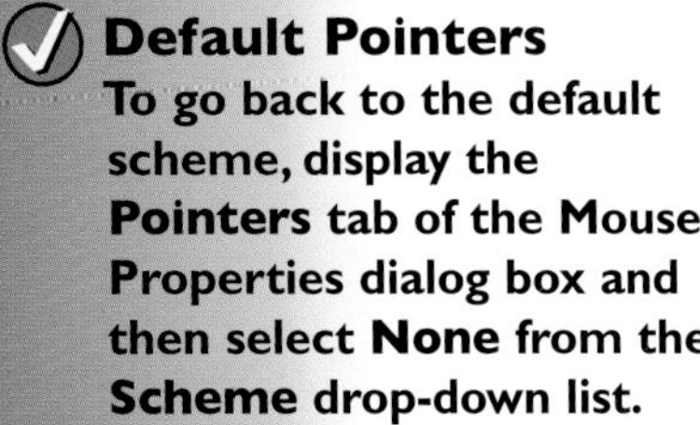

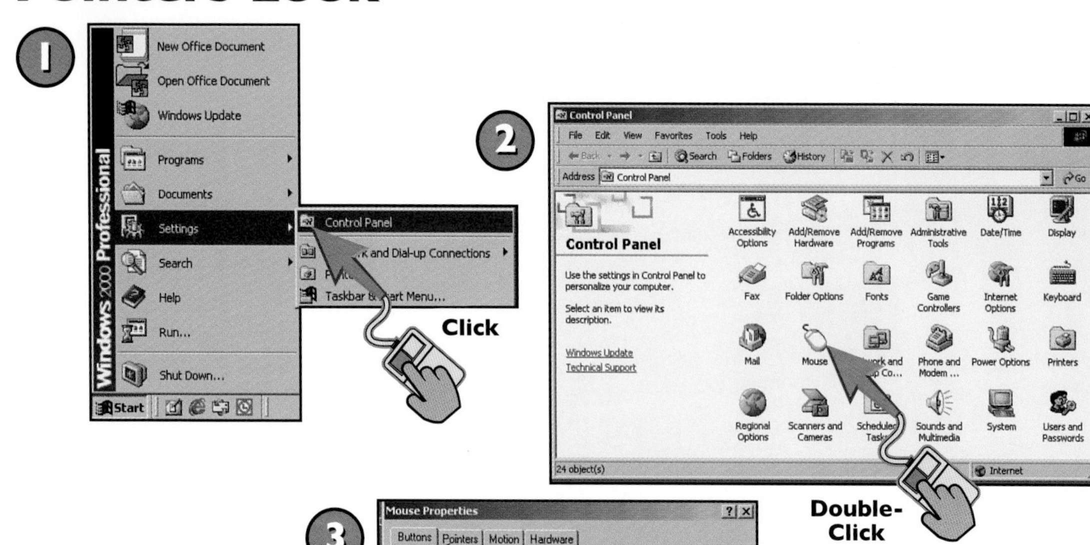

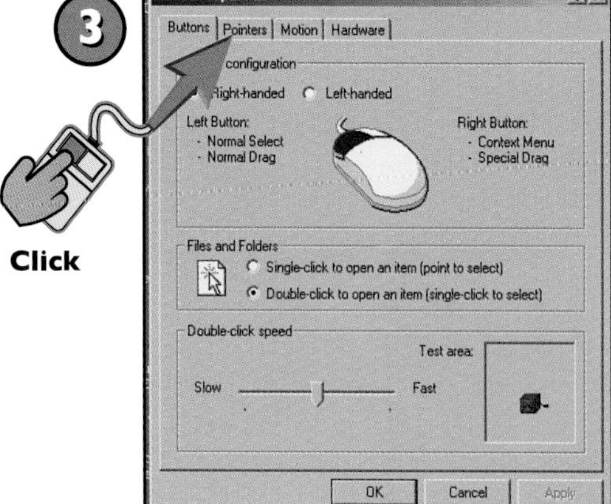

Default Pointers
To go back to the default scheme, display the Pointers tab of the Mouse Properties dialog box and then select None from the Scheme drop-down list.

Mouse Hardware
You can review or update the mouse hardware by clicking the Hardware tab. Click the Troubleshoot button to troubleshoot any problems you are having with the mouse.

1. Click the **Start** menu, click **Settings**, and select **Control Panel**.
2. Double-click the **Mouse** icon.
3. Click the **Pointers** tab.

Next Step

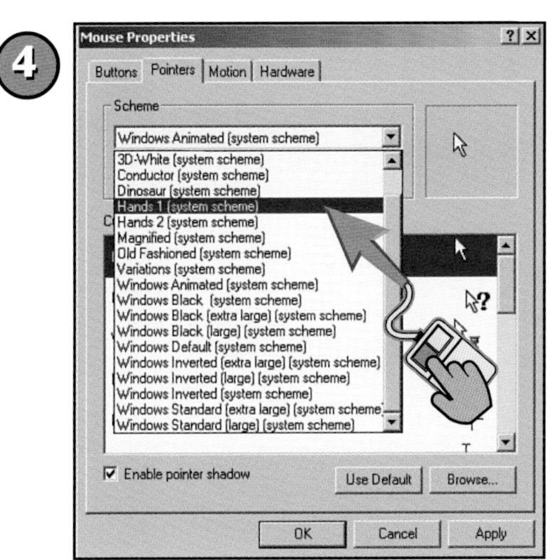

Click

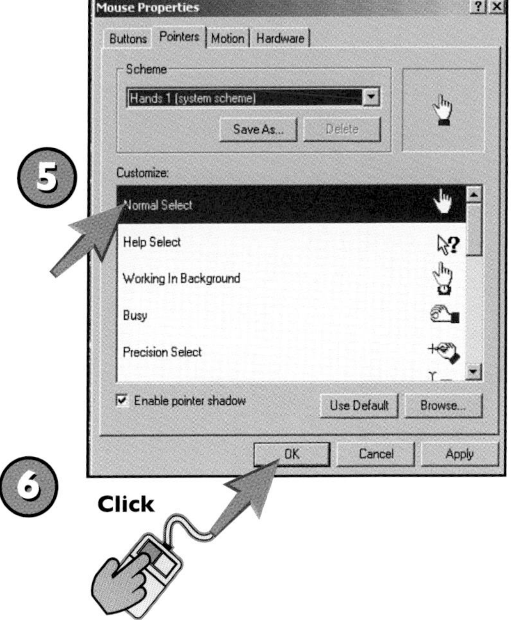

Click

4. Display the **Scheme** drop-down list and choose the scheme you want to use.

5. A preview of each pointer in the chosen scheme is displayed.

6. Click **OK** to accept the changes and to close the dialog box.

Customizing Individual Pointers

You can select which pointer to use for each individual pointer. Simply select the pointer you want to change, click the Browse button, choose the pointer you want to use, and click Open. Do this for each pointer you want to change and then click the OK button.

Task 14: Playing Sounds for Certain Windows Actions

When you perform certain actions in Windows 2000, you might hear a sound. For instance, you hear a sound when Windows 2000 is started; you might also hear a sound when an alert box is displayed. You can stick with the default sounds, or you can select a different sound to use for each key Windows event.

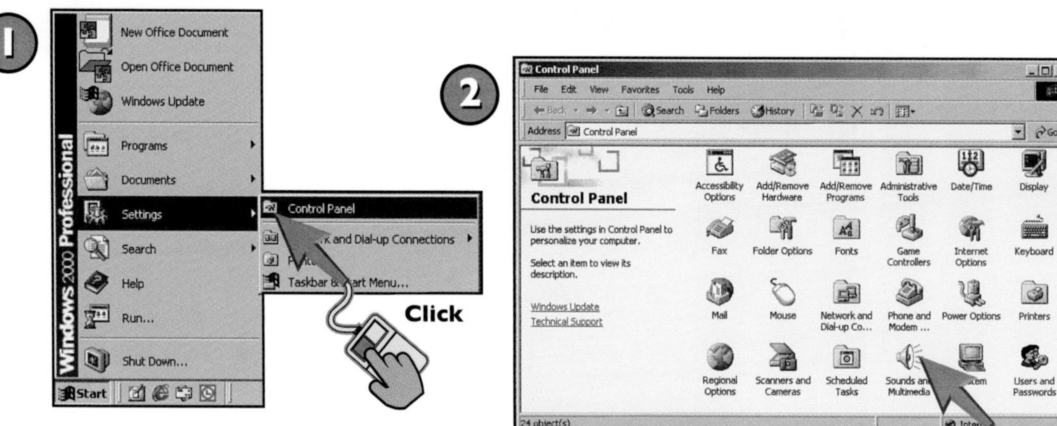

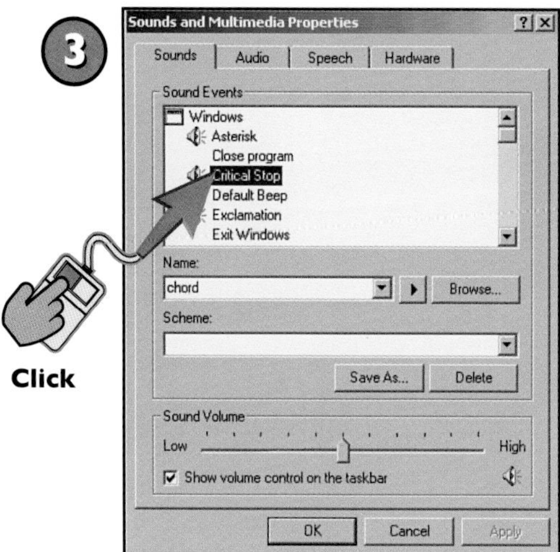

1. Click the **Start** menu, click **Settings**, and select **Control Panel**.
2. Double-click the **Sounds and Multimedia** icon.
3. Select the sound event you want to change.

See a Speaker?
Events that have sounds associated with them are displayed with a speaker icon.

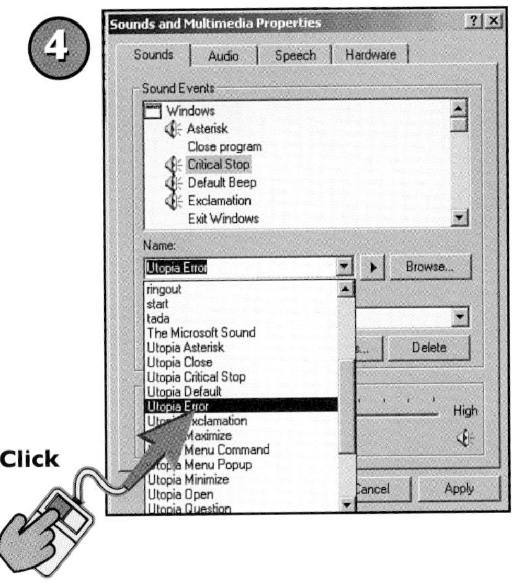

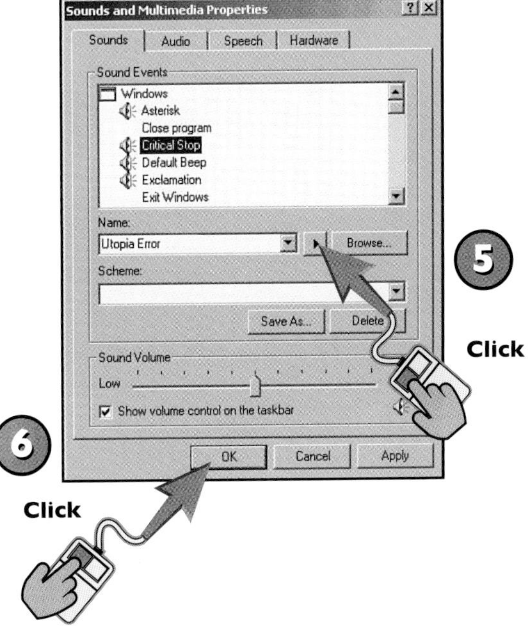

No Sound?

If you don't want a sound played for an event, select that event and choose **(None)** from the **Name** list.

Using a Scheme

If you have sound schemes, you can select a set of sounds by displaying the **Schemes** drop-down list in the Sound and Multimedia Properties dialog box. Select the scheme you want and then click **OK**.

Setting Up Multimedia

You can use the **Audio** tab to set up your audio devices. Click the **Speech** tab to set up any speech recognition devices you might have. Click **Hardware** to review or make changes to your hardware settings for your multimedia devices.

4. Display the **Name** drop-down list to select the sound that you want to assign.
5. To hear a preview of the sound, click the **Play** button.
6. Click **OK** to accept the changes and to close the dialog box.

Task 15: Setting Up Windows for the Impaired

Start Here

If you are physically impaired, you can apply certain features of Windows 2000 to make it easier to use. You can select different settings for the keyboard, sounds, display, and mouse.

Using the Accessibility Programs

You can also use the several Accessibility programs included with Windows 2000. Click **Start**, select **Accessories**, click **Accessibility**, and then select the program you want to run. You can select **Accessibility Wizard**, **Magnifier**, **Narrator**, **On-Screen Keyboard**, or **Utility Manager**.

Keyboard Options

Check the **Use StickyKeys** option to press one key at a time for key combinations. Check **Use FilterKeys** to ignore brief repeated keystrokes. Check **Use ToggleKeys** to play a tone when you have pressed **Caps Lock**, **Num Lock**, or **Scroll Lock**.

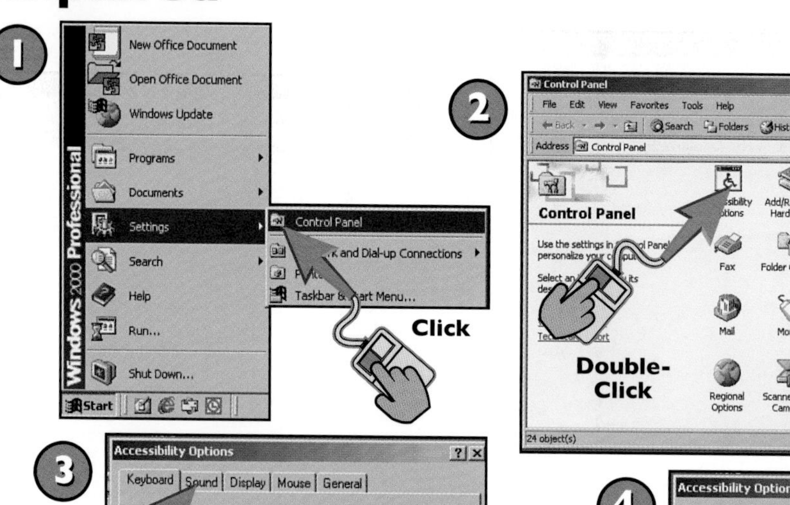

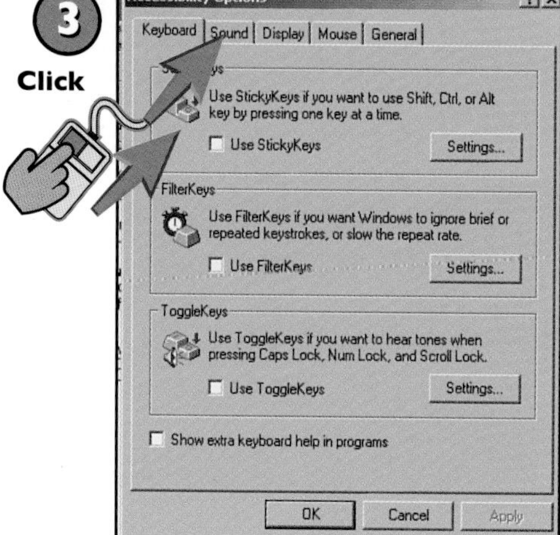

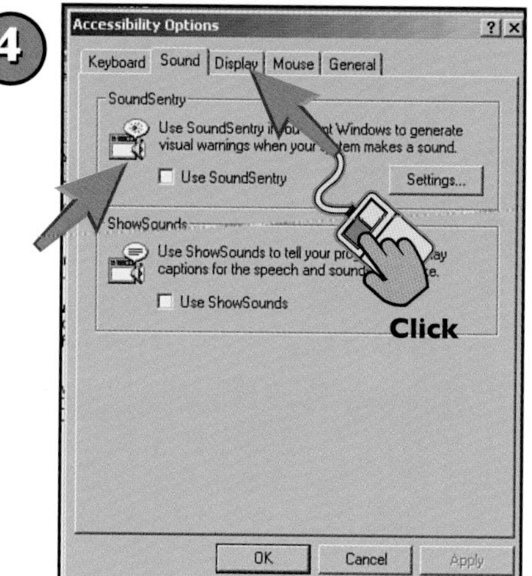

1. Click the **Start** menu, click **Settings**, and select **Control Panel**.
2. Double-click the **Accessibility Options** icon.
3. Enable any keyboard features by checking the appropriate check box. After you finish, click the **Sound** tab.
4. Select to display visual warnings and/or captions for alert messages and then click the **Display** tab.

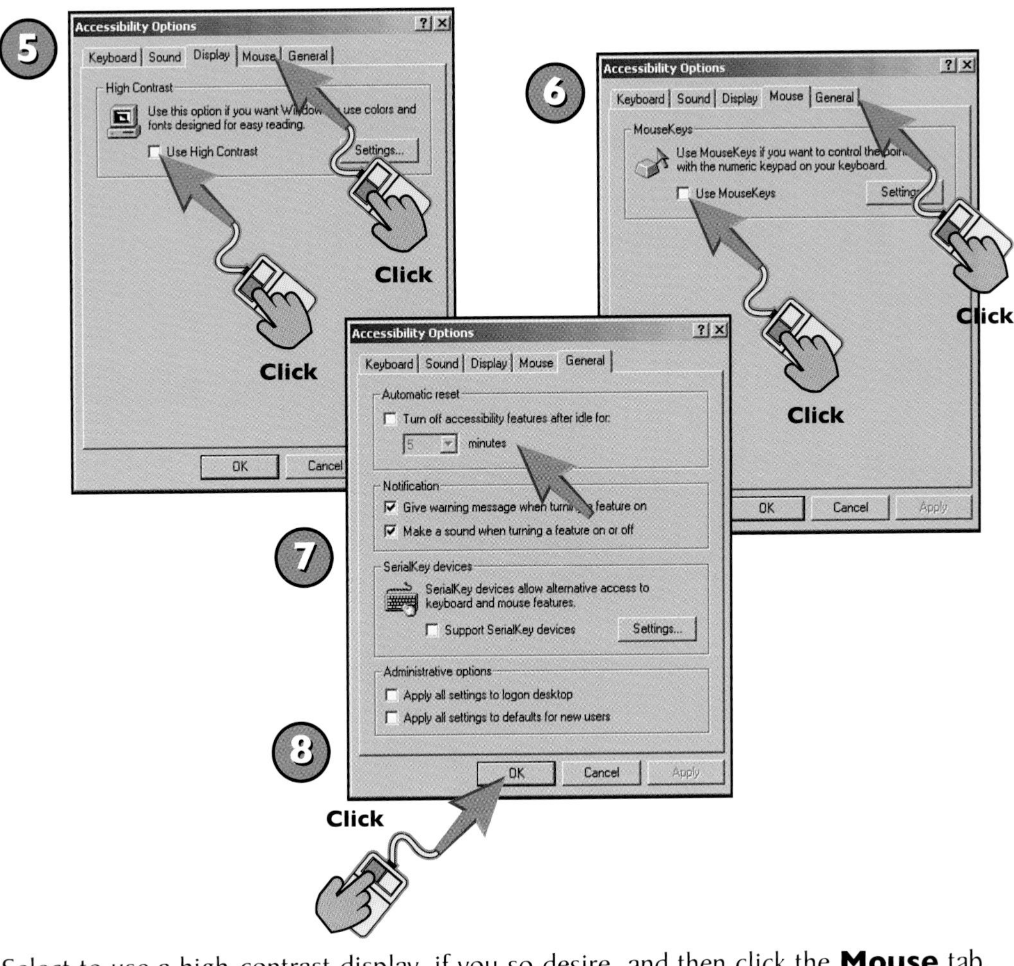

5. Select to use a high-contrast display, if you so desire, and then click the **Mouse** tab.

6. Select to use the numeric keypad to control the mouse and then click the **General** tab.

7. Make changes as needed to the reset and notification options.

8. Click the **OK** button.

PART

Setting Up Programs

Most of the time you spend on your computer will be spent using some application. (The terms application and program mean the same thing, and I've used them interchangeably here.) To make it as easy as possible, Windows 2000 enables you to set up several ways for starting programs. You can create a shortcut to a program and place the shortcut on the desktop to make it more accessible. You can rearrange the programs on the Start menu so that they are more suited to how you work. You can install new programs and remove programs you no longer use. This part shows you how to accomplish all of these setup tasks and more.

Tasks

Task 1: Installing Applications

Start Here

When you bought your computer, it might have come with certain programs already installed. If you want to add to these, you can purchase more programs and then add them to your system. Installing a new program basically copies the program files to a folder on your system and then adds a program icon for starting that program. The program's installation might also make changes to other files or programs on your system.

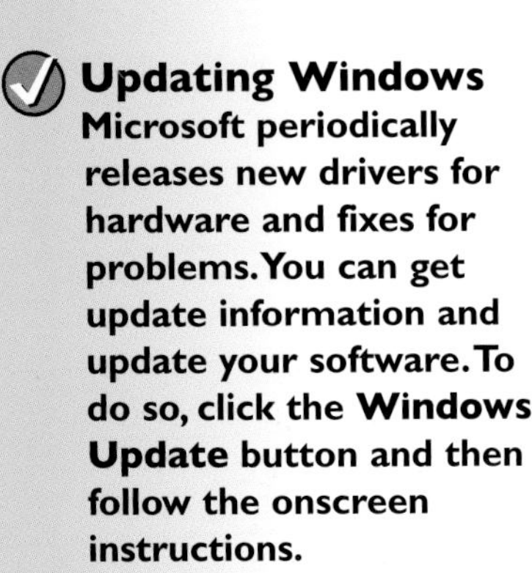

Updating Windows

Microsoft periodically releases new drivers for hardware and fixes for problems. You can get update information and update your software. To do so, click the **Windows Update** button and then follow the onscreen instructions.

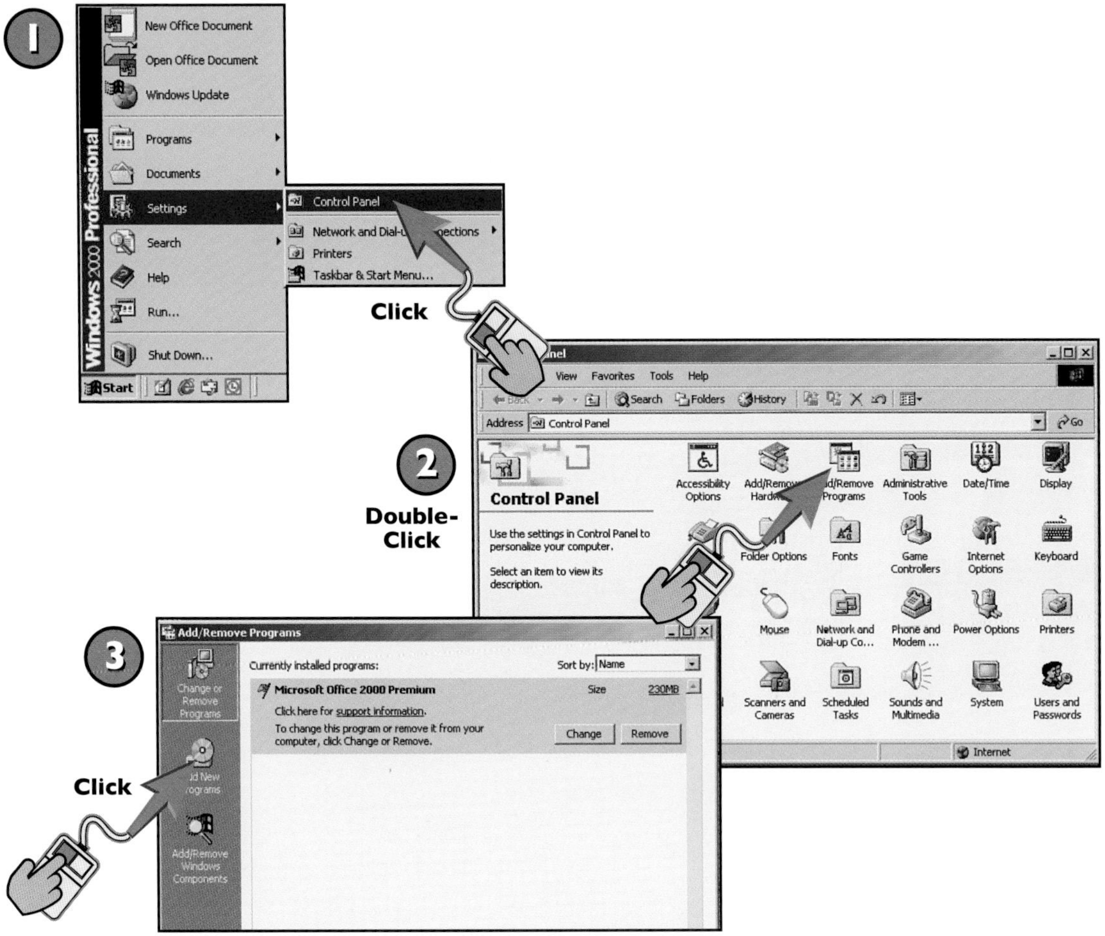

1. Click **Start**, select **Settings**, and click **Control Panel**.
2. Double-click the **Add/Remove Programs** icon.
3. Click the **Add New Programs** button.

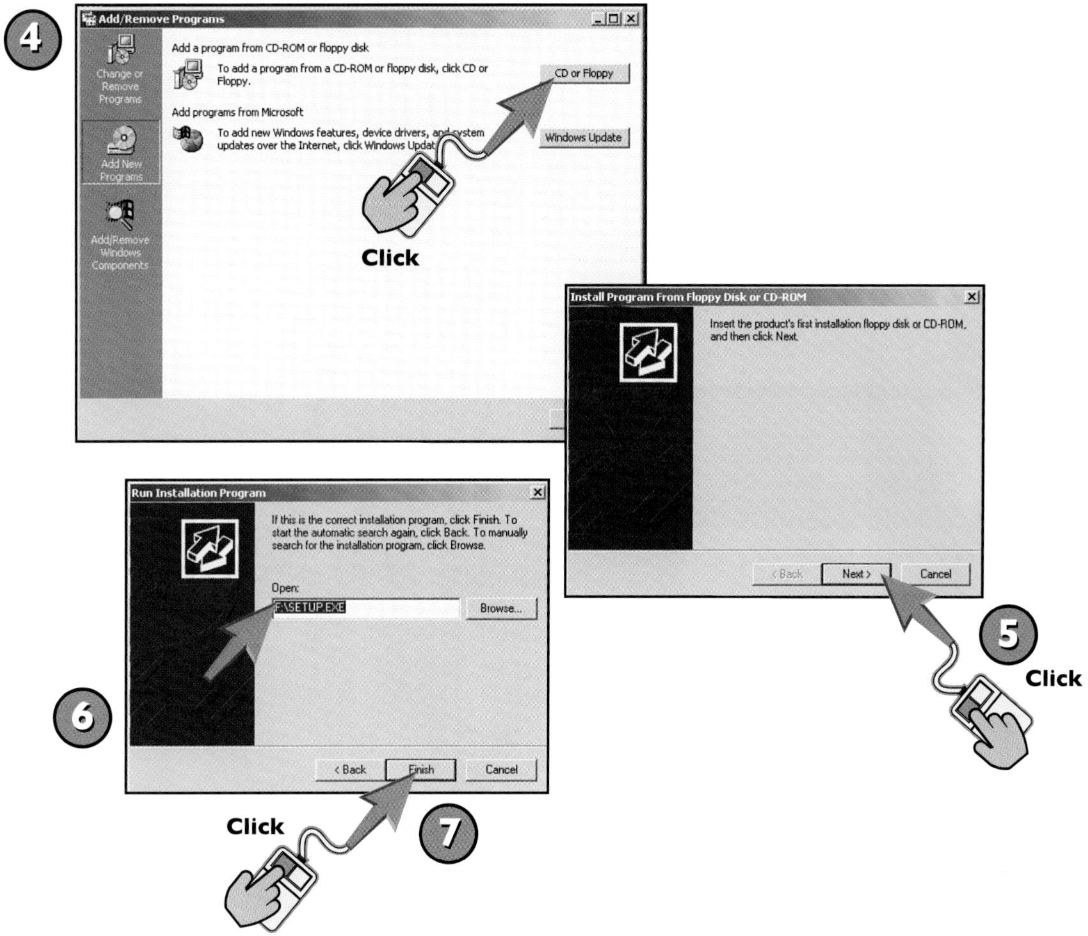

4. Click the **CD or Floppy** button.

5. Insert the CD-ROM or floppy disk for the program you want to install and then click the **Next** button.

6. When Windows has detected the installation program, it displays the name in the Run Installation Program dialog box.

7. Click the **Finish** button and then follow the onscreen instructions for your particular program.

Using the Run Command

If the procedure in this task does not work, you can use the Run command to run the installation program. Insert the CD-ROM or disk into the appropriate drive and then click the Start button and choose Run. Enter the disk drive and command for the installation program (check the program instructions for this command). Click OK and then follow the onscreen instructions.

Uninstalling a Program

Use the Change or Remove Programs link to change or remove an installed program (see Task 11, "Uninstalling Applications").

Task 2: Installing Windows Components

Start Here

If you have a new PC, it probably came with Windows already installed. As a result, you might not know which components are installed and which are not. Likewise, if you have upgraded to Windows 2000, you might not have installed all the components when you performed the installation. If you want to add other components or simply view what else might be available, you can do so.

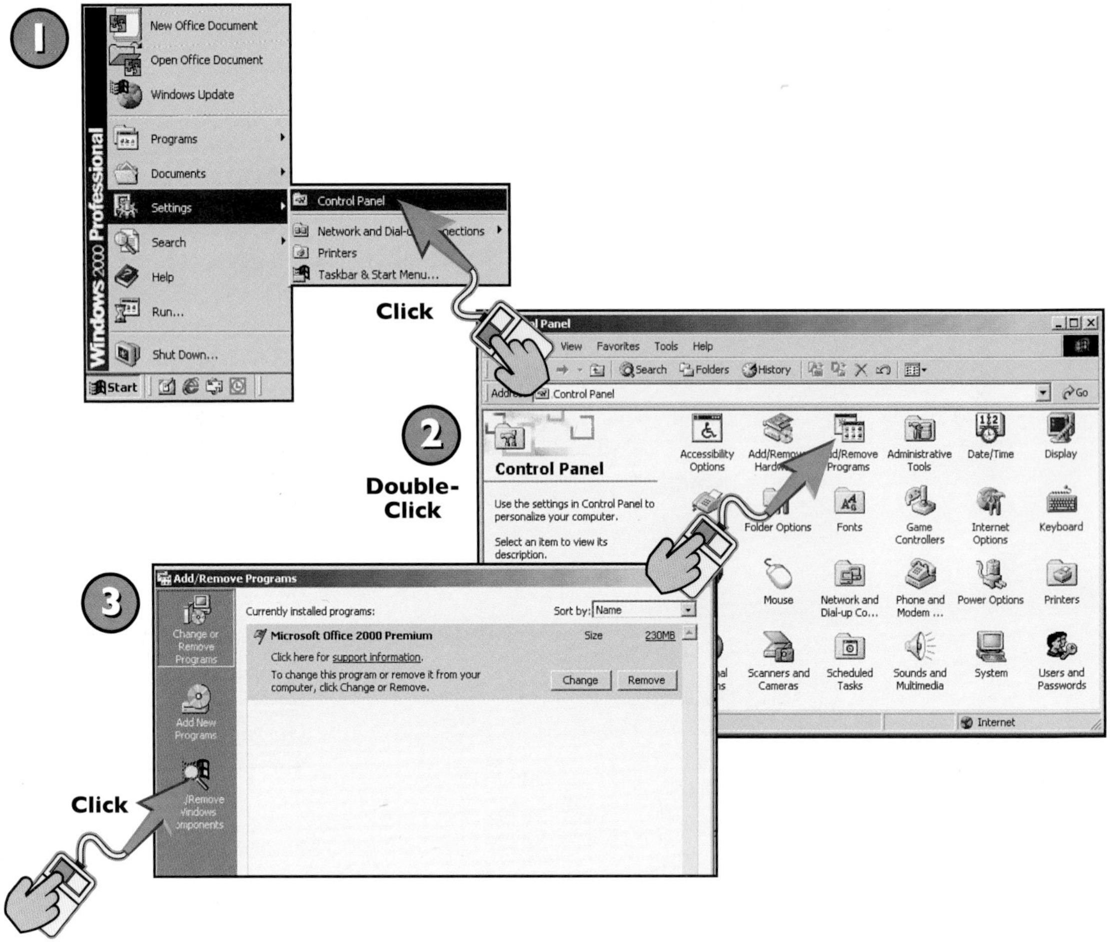

Click

Double-Click

Click

Shaded Check Box?
If a check box is shaded, only some components are installed. To see a list, select that item and click the **Details** button.

1. Click **Start**, select **Settings**, and click **Control Panel**.
2. Double-click the **Add/Remove Programs** icon.
3. Click the **Add/Remove Windows Components** button.

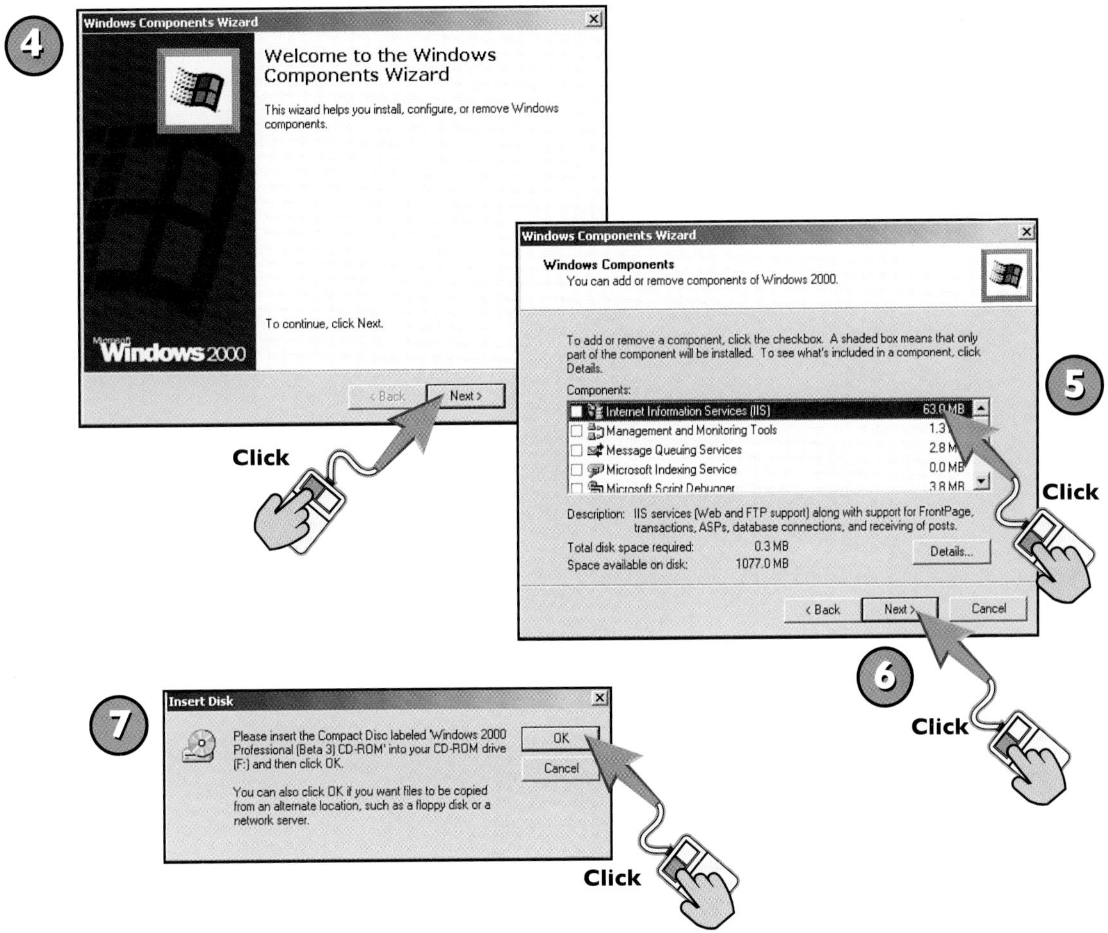

4. Click the **Next** button to start the Windows Components Wizard.
5. Select the feature you want to change or check.
6. Click the **Next** button.
7. Insert your Windows CD-ROM and click the **OK** button. The necessary files are copied to your system, and the desired component is available for you to use.

Checked or Not Checked

If an item is checked, it is installed. Items that are gray and checked have some of the components installed.

Task 3: Adding Programs to the Start Menu

When you install most programs, they are added automatically to the Start menu. If a program is not added during installation, you can add it yourself.

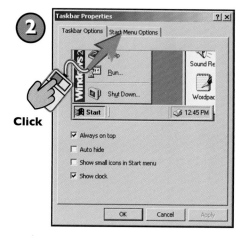

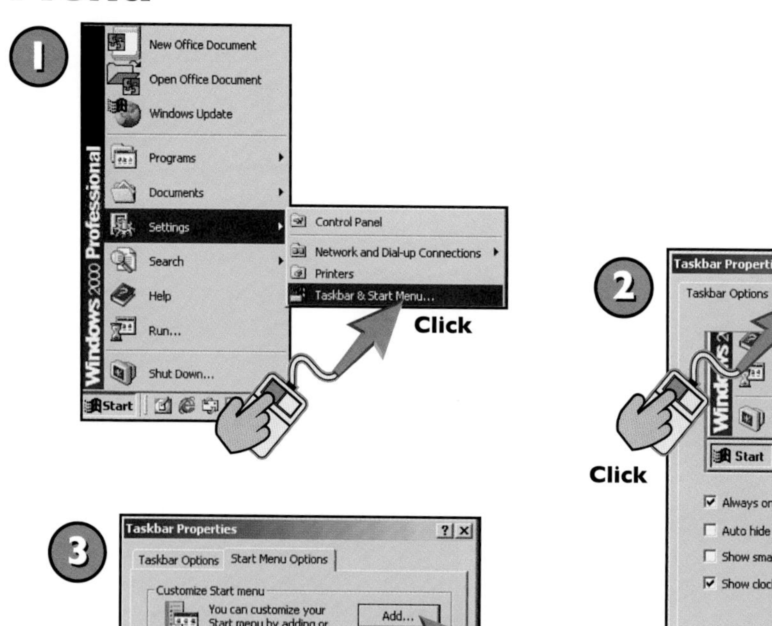

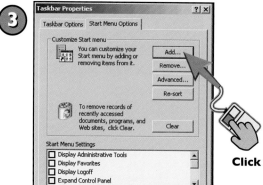

Removing a Program
To remove a program from the Start menu, see the next task.

1. Click **Start**, select the **Settings** command, and then click the **Taskbar & Start Menu** command.
2. Click the **Start Menu Options** tab.
3. Click the **Add** button.

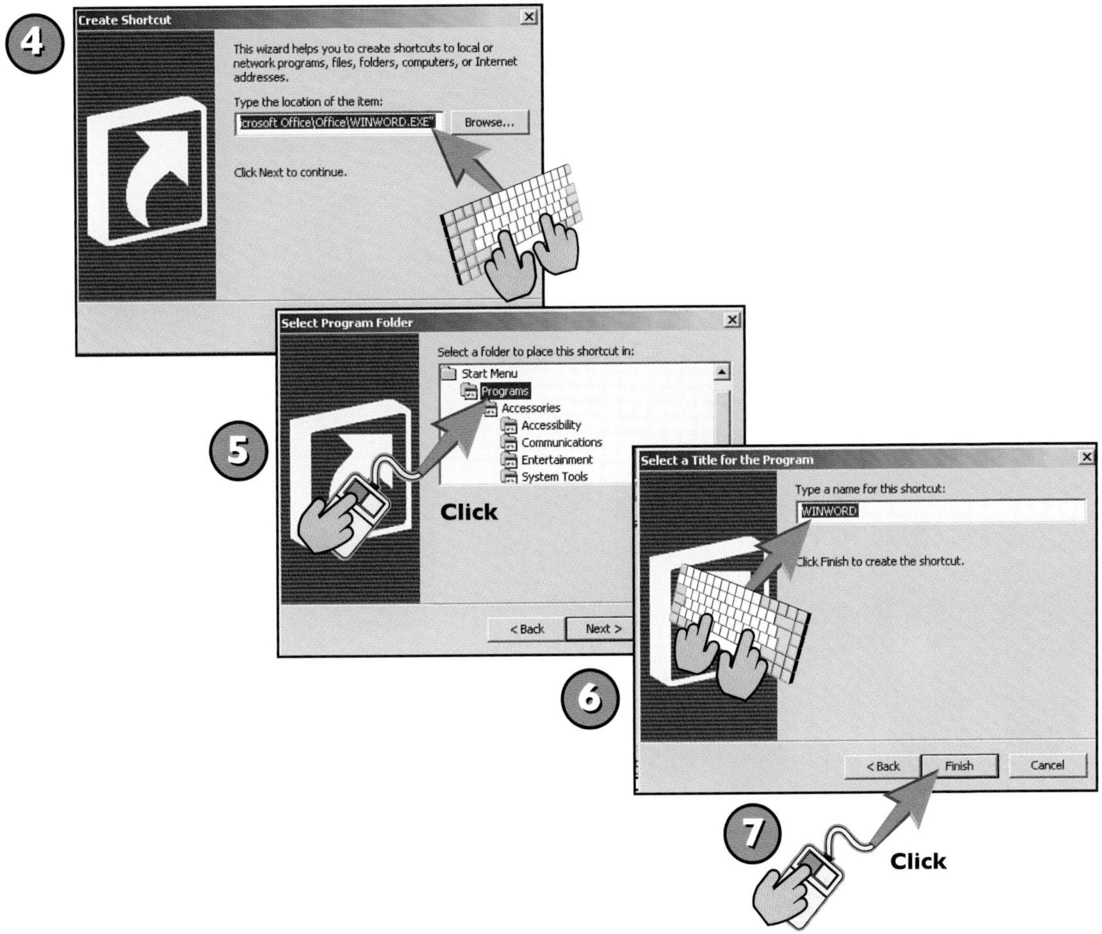

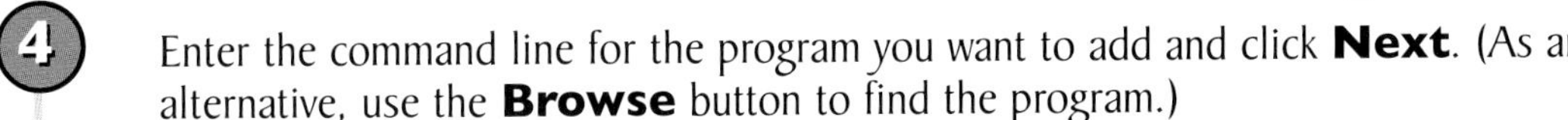

4 Enter the command line for the program you want to add and click **Next**. (As an alternative, use the **Browse** button to find the program.)

5 Select the folder in which you want to place the program and click **Next**.

6 Enter a name in the text box or accept the one Windows displays.

7 Click the **Finish** button to add the new program.

Browsing for the Program
If you don't know the command line, click the Browse button, and then select the folder and the program name from the Browse dialog box.

Creating a New Folder
You can click the New Folder button to add a new folder (also see Task 5, "Adding Folders to the Start Menu").

Task 4: Deleting Programs from the Start Menu

Start Here

When you first get your computer, you might go a little crazy and add all kinds of icons to the Start menu. But after you use the computer more and more, you might want to streamline the Start menu and weed out programs that you don't really use. If your Start menu becomes cluttered, you can delete icons for programs that you don't use.

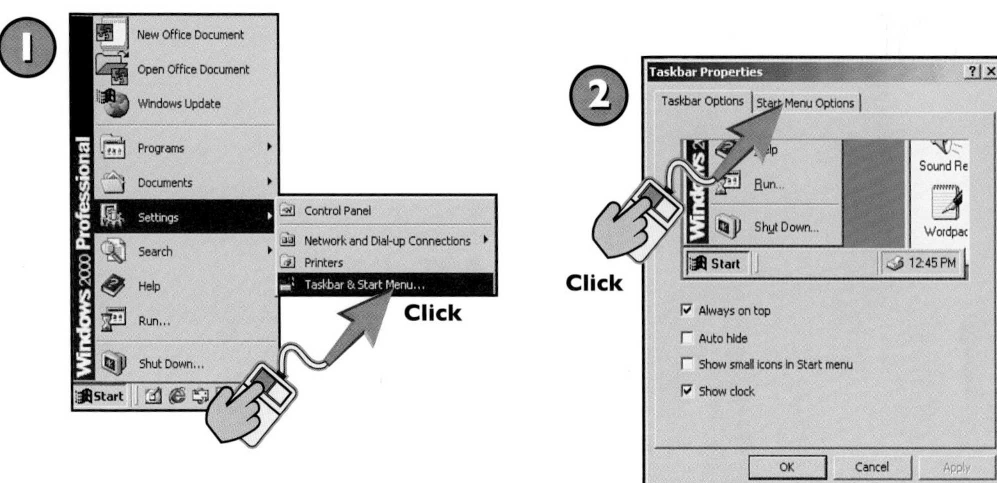

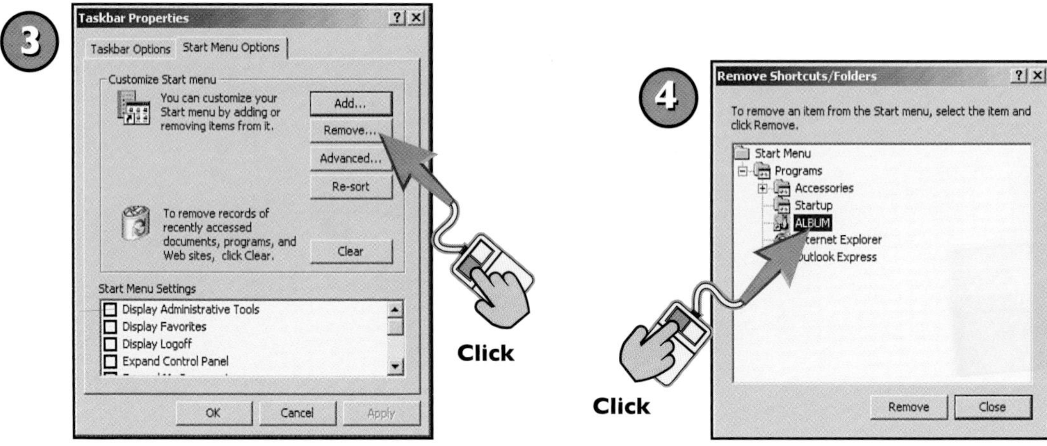

1. Click **Start**, select the **Settings** command, and then click the **Taskbar & Start Menu** command.
2. Click the **Start Menu Options** tab.
3. Click the **Remove** button.
4. Click the program you want to remove to select it.

Removing a Folder
You can follow this procedure to remove a folder from the Start menu. Simply select the folder and then click the **Remove** button. You are prompted to confirm the removal; click **Yes**. The folder and all its contents are removed.

5 Click the **Remove** button.

6 Click the **Yes** button to confirm the removal.

7 The program is removed from the menu.

8 Click the **Close** button to close the Remove Shortcuts/Folders dialog box and then click **OK** to close the Taskbar Properties dialog box.

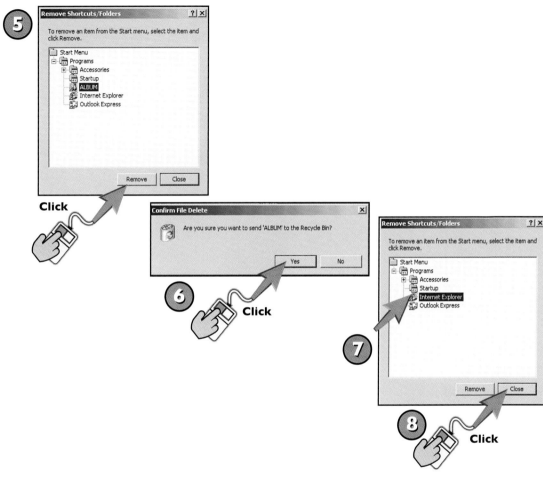

Program Files Not Removed

Keep in mind that removing a program from the Start menu does not remove the program and its files from your hard disk. To do this, you must *uninstall* the program or manually delete it and its related folders and files (see Task 11).

Expanding the Start Menu List

To display and select the program you want to remove, you might need to expand the folder listings. Click the plus sign next to the folder that contains the desired program.

Task 5: Adding Folders to the Start Menu

Start Here

When you install a new program, that program's installation sets up program folders and icons for itself. If you don't like the arrangement of the folders and icons, you can change it. For instance, if more than one person uses your PC, you might set up folders for each person and then add the programs that a certain person uses to his or her folder.

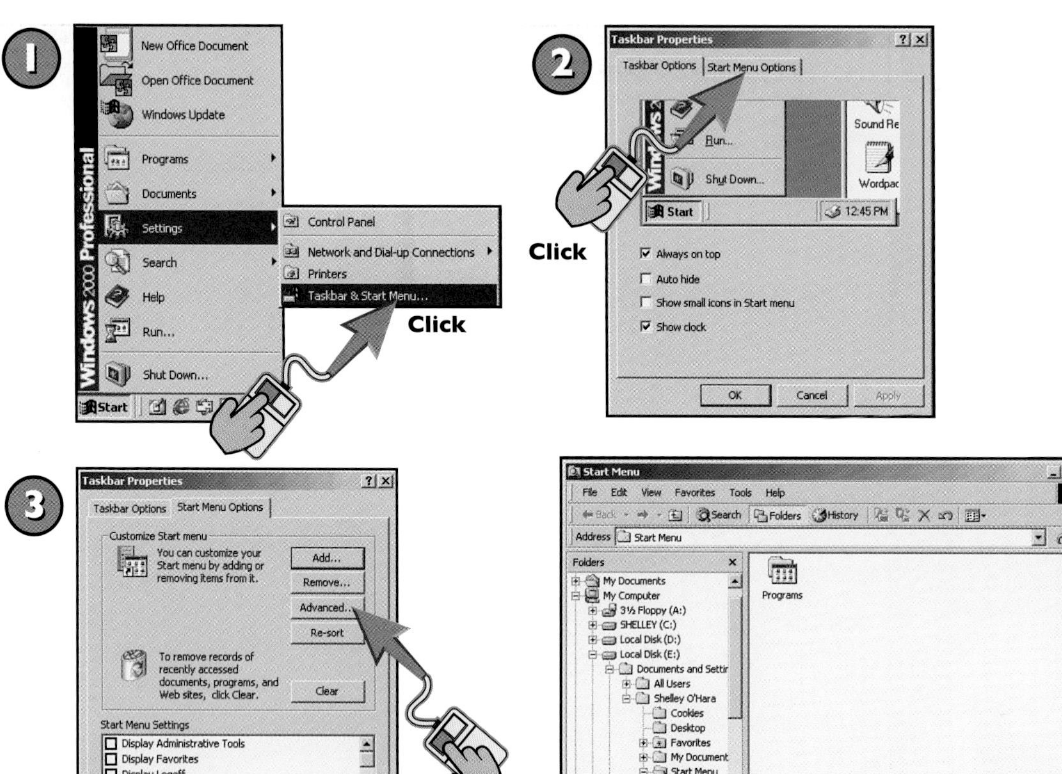

1 Click **Start**, select the **Settings** command, and then click the **Taskbar & Start Menu** command.

2 Click the **Start Menu Options** tab.

3 Click the **Advanced** button.

4 The contents of your system is displayed in a content window, with the Start menu selected. Double-click the **Programs** folder to select this folder.

Deleting a Folder

You can delete folders. To do so, simply right-click the folder and select the **Delete** command from the shortcut menu. Click **Yes** to confirm the deletion.

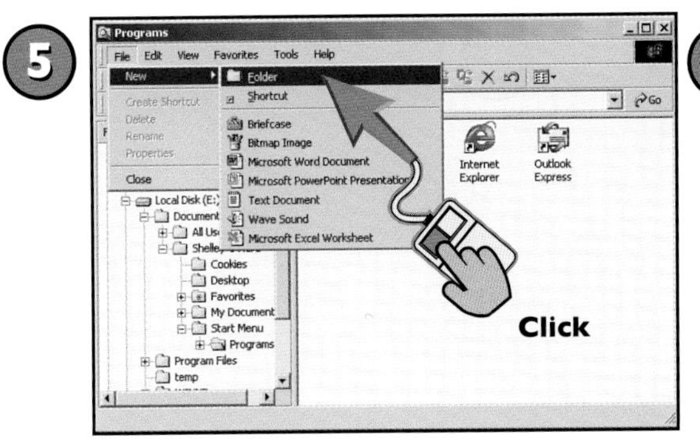

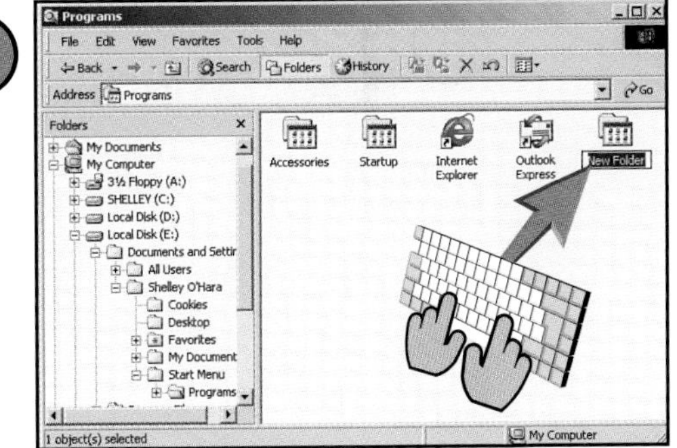

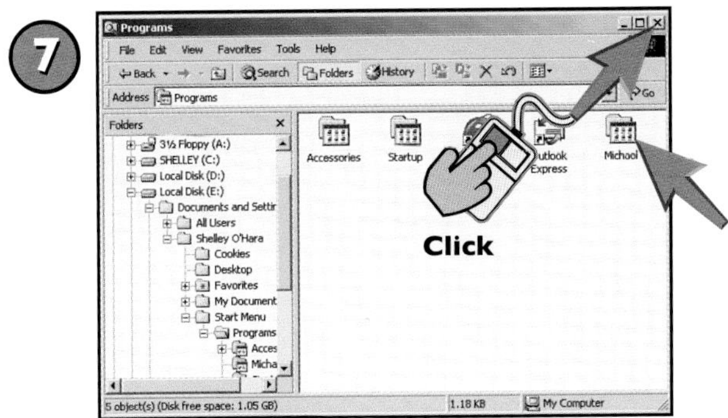

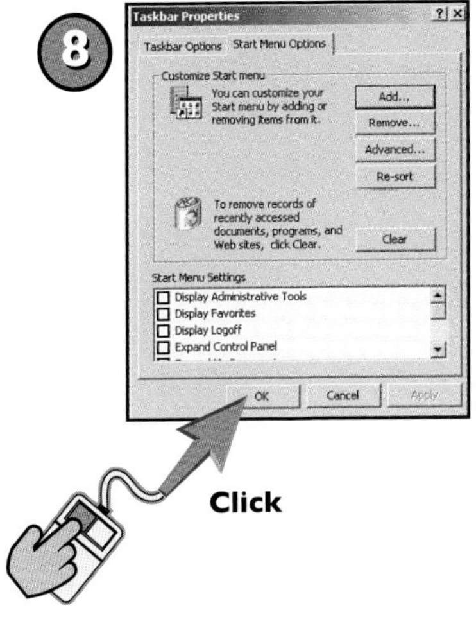

Just Like Working with a Folder

If you follow the steps in this task, you'll see the Programs folder in a content window. You can use any of the commands and features in the content window to work with the contents of your Programs folder.

Folders Within Folders

You can place folders within folders. To do so, simply open the folder in which you want to place the new one. This example places the new folder within the top-level Programs folder.

5 The folders within the Programs folder are displayed. Click **File**, select **New**, and then click **Folder**.

6 Type the name for the folder and then press **Enter**.

7 The folder is added. Click the **Close** (×) button.

8 Click the **OK** button in the Taskbar Properties dialog box.

Task 6: Rearranging the Start Menu

After you set up folders, you can organize your Start menu, putting the program icons in the folder and order you want.

Start Here

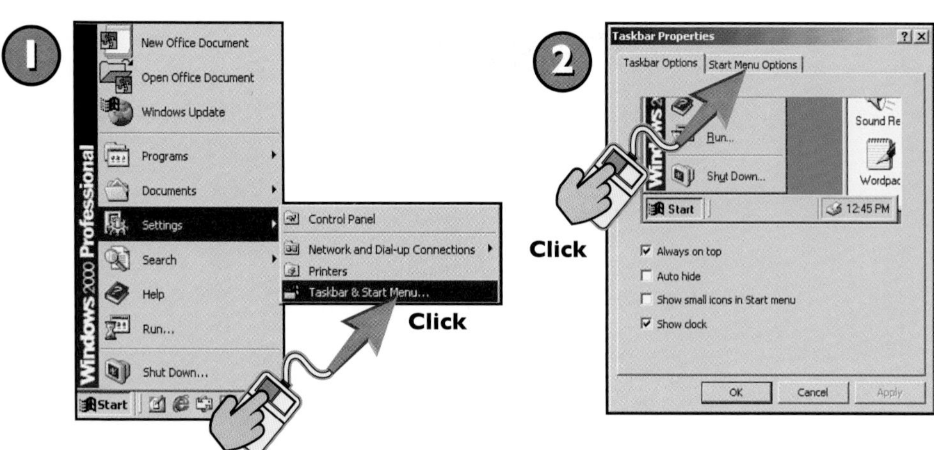

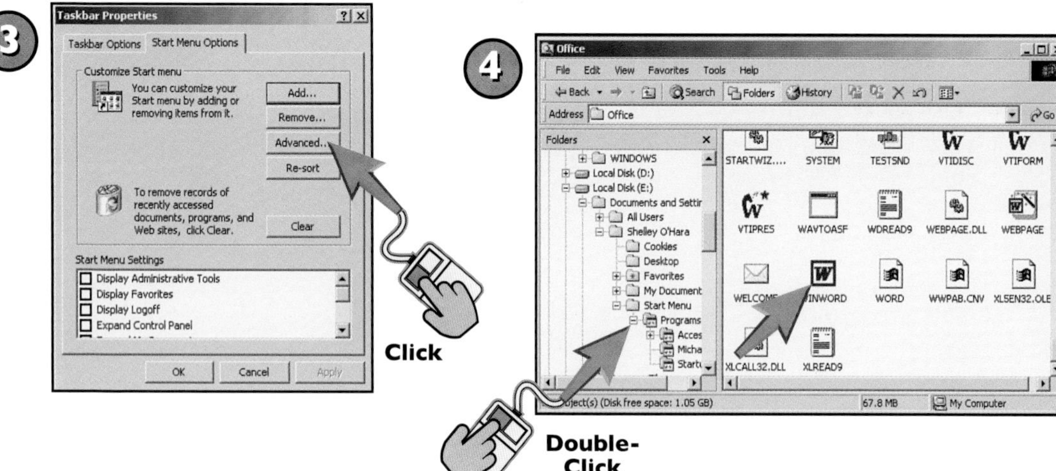

1. Click **Start**, select the **Settings** command, and then click the **Taskbar & Start Menu** command.

2. Click the **Start Menu Options** tab.

3. Click the **Advanced** button.

4. Double-click the folders/drives in the Folders list until the file for the program you want to add to the Start menu is displayed in the pane on the right.

Re-sorting the Menu
Click the Re-sort button in the Start Menu Options tab to re-sort the programs back to the default order.

Starting Menu Settings
You can check any of the check boxes in the Start Menu Options tab's Start Menu Settings area to turn on these features. If you aren't sure what a feature does, right-click it and then select What's This for an explanation.

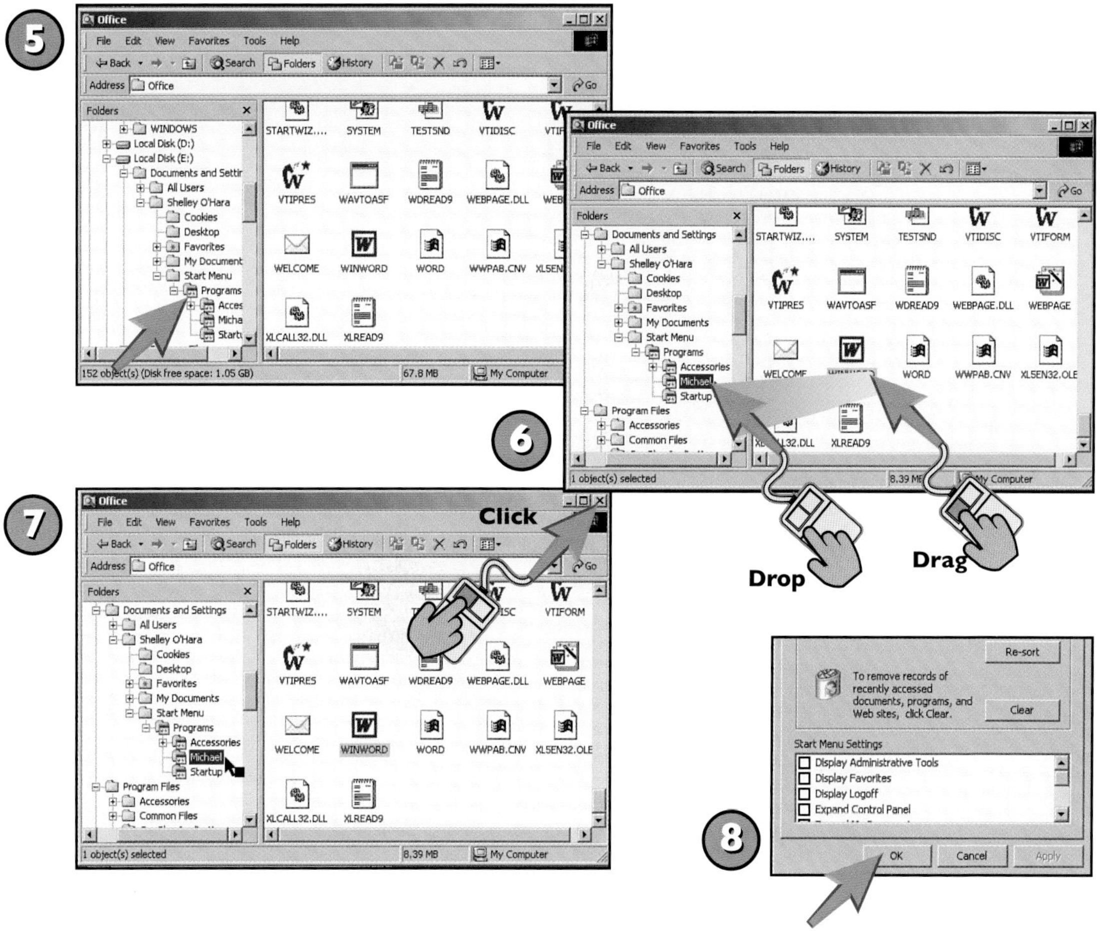

5. Be sure the Programs folder under the Start Menu entry is displayed in the Folders list on the left.

6. Drag the program in the right pane to the folder to which you want to add it (I've dragged **WINWORD** to the Michael folder under Programs).

7. Click the **Close** (×) button.

8. Click the **OK** button in the Taskbar Properties dialog box.

Task 7: Starting an Application When You Start Windows

Start Here

You can configure Windows to automatically start one or more programs at the same time that you start Windows by turning your computer on. Applications you might want to open automatically include those that you use every day or those that you use first thing every morning.

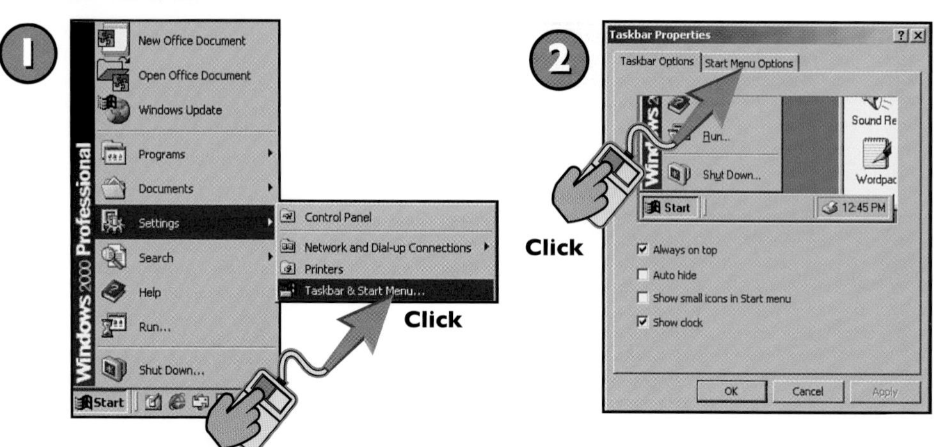

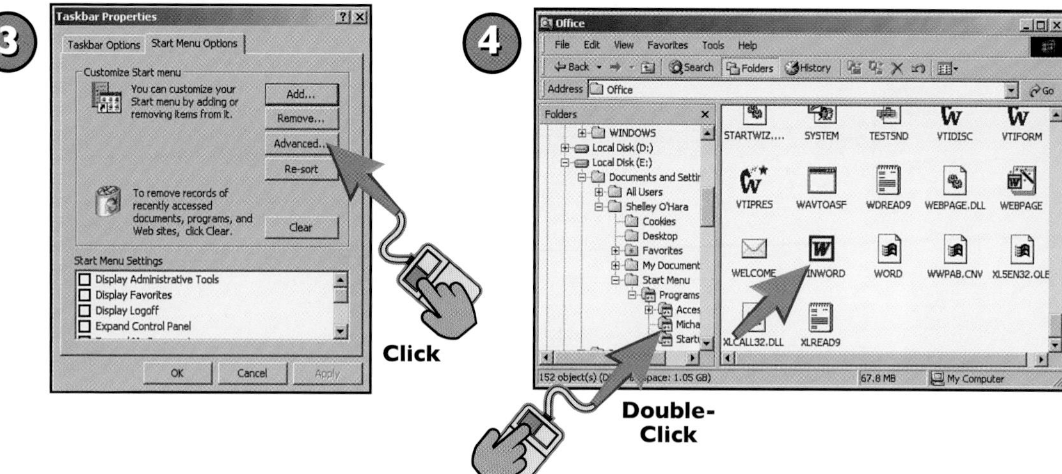

Only Starts When You Start PC

If you don't turn off your computer each night and then turn it on again when you begin work, these programs will not be started each morning. They are started only when you start Windows.

1. Click **Start**, select the **Settings** command, and then click the **Taskbar & Start Menu** command.
2. Click the **Start Menu Options** tab.
3. Click the **Advanced** button.
4. Double-click the folders/drives in the Folders list until the file for the program you want to start automatically when you start Windows is displayed in the pane on the right.

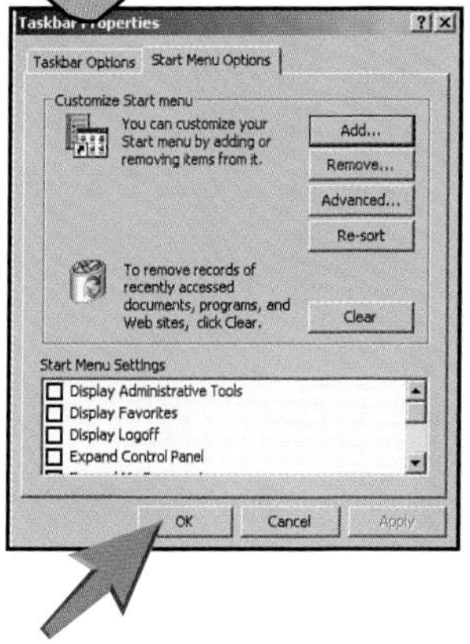

5 Be sure the Programs folder under the Start Menu entry is displayed in the Folders list on the left.

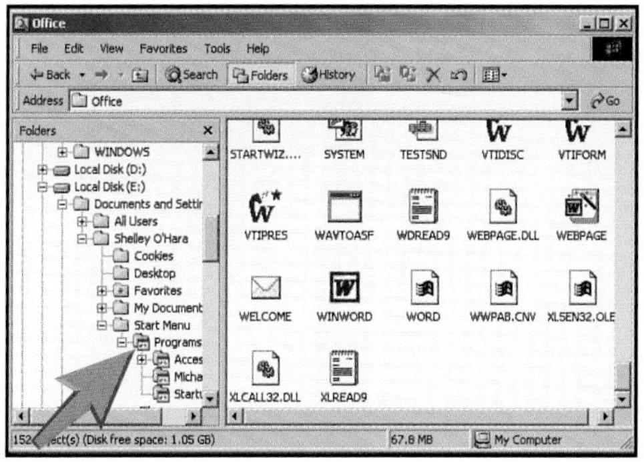

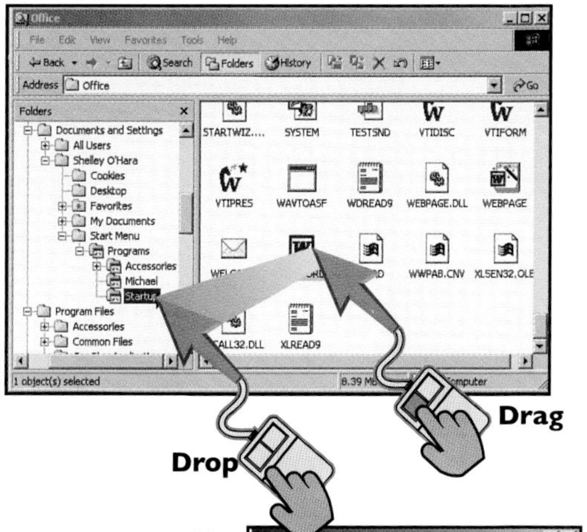

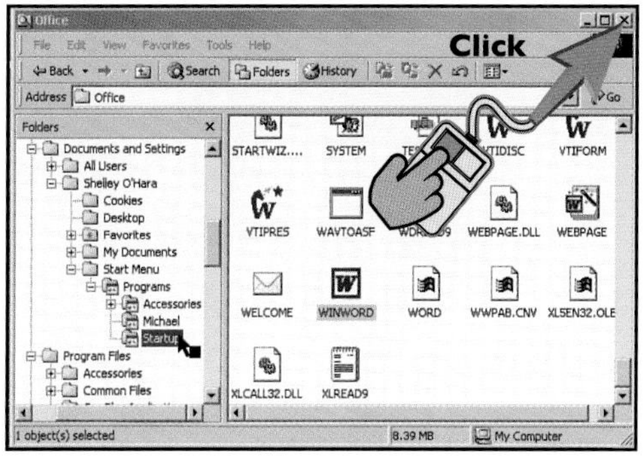

6 Drag the program in the right pane (in this example, the **WINWORD** program) to the Startup folder under Programs.

7 Click the **Close** (×) button.

8 Click the **OK** button in the Taskbar Properties dialog box.

Removing a Program

To remove an icon from the Startup folder, click the Remove button in the Start Menu Options tab of the Taskbar Properties dialog box. Then choose the item you want to remove from the menu and click the Remove button. Close the Remove Shortcuts/Folders dialog box and then click OK.

Task 8: Adding Shortcuts

Start Here

You can create shortcuts to your programs and place them on the desktop to provide quick access to programs. You then double-click a shortcut to quickly start that program—without having to open menus and folders.

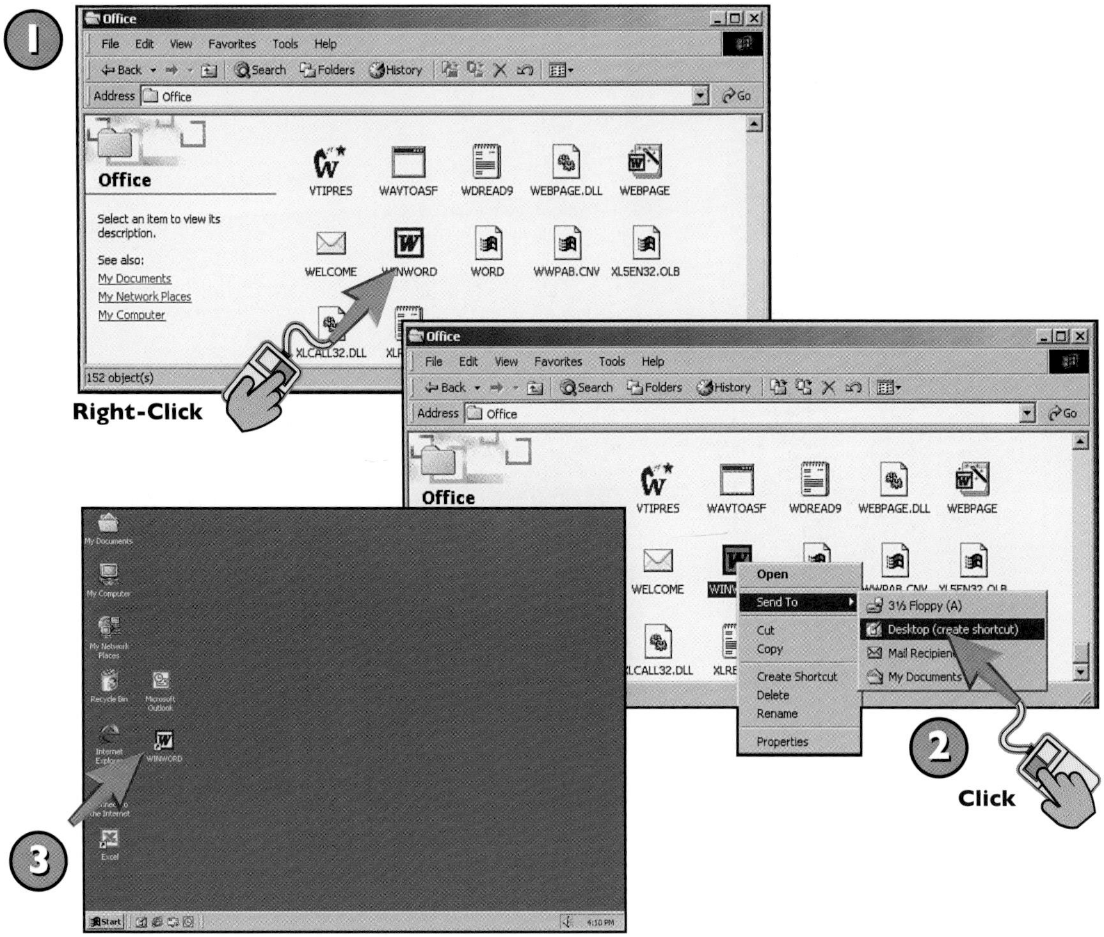

Right-Click

Click

Shortcuts to Files and Folders

You can also create shortcut icons to files or folders (Task 23, "Creating a Shortcut to a File or Folder," in Part 3, "Working with Disks, Folders, and Files") or to your printer (Task 10, "Adding a Printer Icon on the Desktop," in Part 4, "Printing with Windows").

Can't Find the Program?

If you can't find the program file, try searching for it. Finding a particular file is covered in Task 24, "Finding Files and Folders," in Part 3.

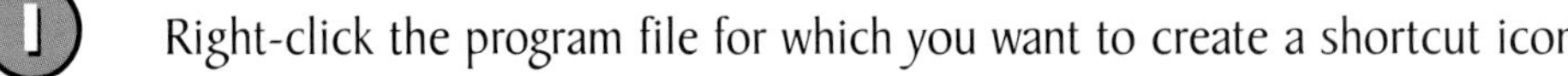

1. Right-click the program file for which you want to create a shortcut icon.
2. In the pop-up menu that appears, select **Send To** and then click **Desktop (Create Shortcut)**.
3. Windows adds the shortcut to your desktop.

End Task

Task 9: Renaming Shortcuts

When you create a shortcut, Windows 2000 assigns a name to the icon, but you might want to use a different name. For instance, rather than the name **WINWORD** (the program filename), you might prefer **Word.** You can rename any of the shortcut icons on your desktop.

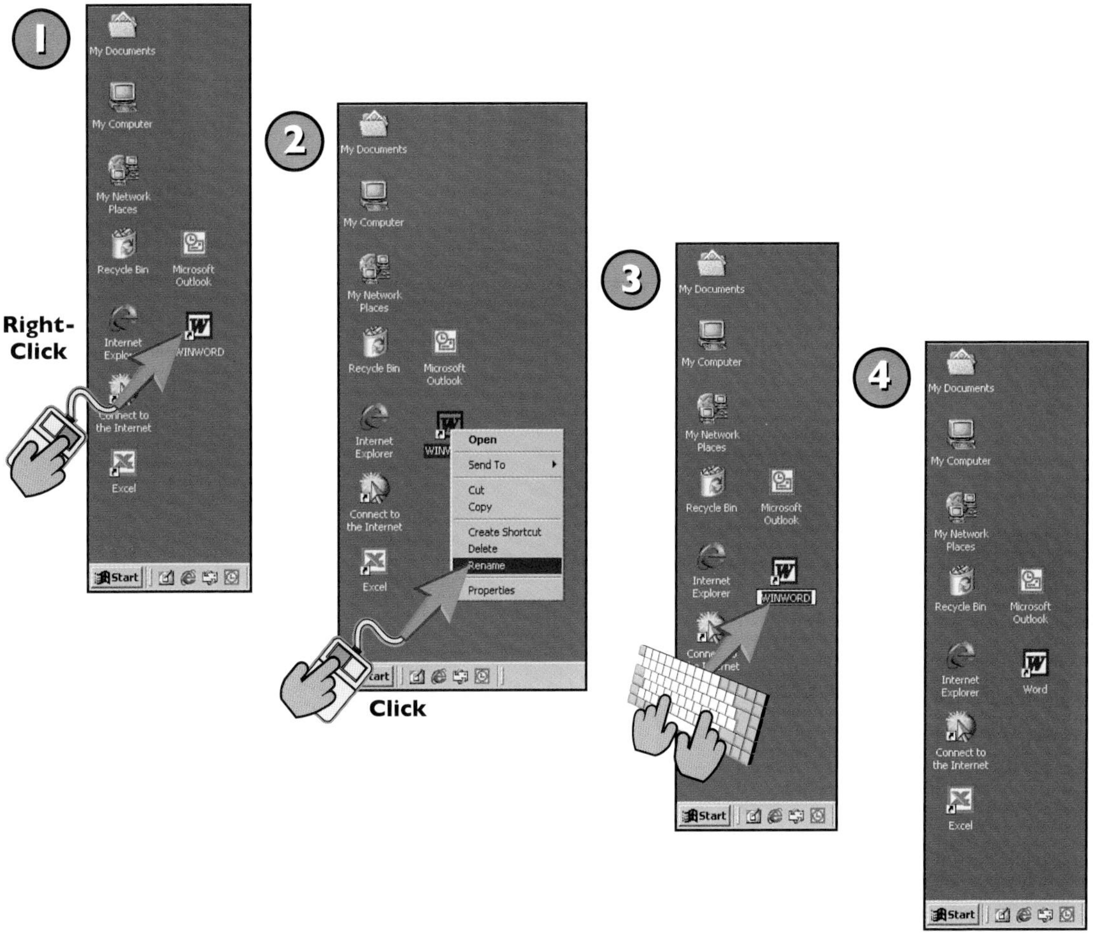

1. Right-click the icon that you want to rename.
2. In the pop-up menu that appears, click the **Rename** command.
3. Type the new shortcut name (in my example, I've typed `Word`) and press **Enter**.
4. The icon is renamed.

Task 10: Deleting Shortcuts

You can use shortcuts to quickly open the program you need. Just as you can create new shortcuts as you add new programs, you can delete shortcuts you no longer use.

Program Is Not Deleted
Deleting a shortcut does not delete that program from your hard drive. To delete the program, you must uninstall it or delete the program and its related folders and files. You can use the Add/Remove Programs link in the Confirm Shortcut Delete dialog box to do so.

Restoring the Shortcut
In case you change your mind about deleting the shortcut, you can restore it. To do so, double-click the **Recycle Bin**. In the Recycle Bin window, click the item you want to restore and click the **Restore** button. The item returns to its original location.

Start Here

1
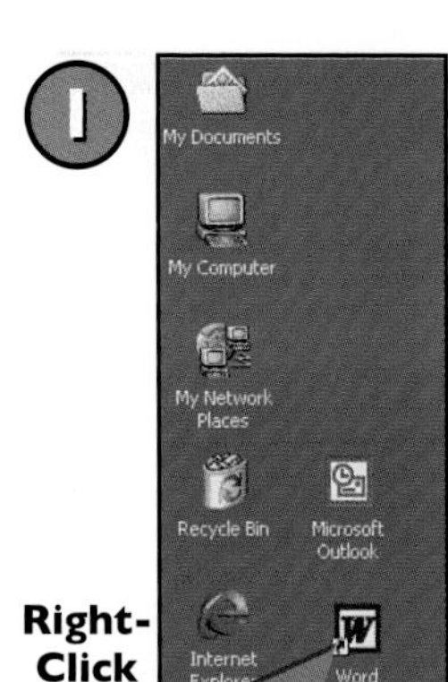

2

3
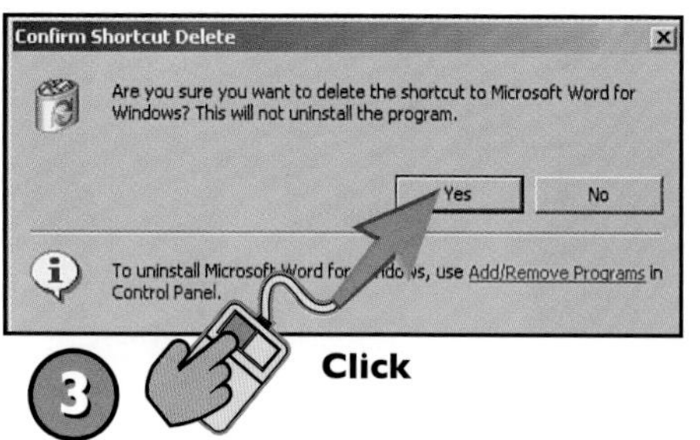

4
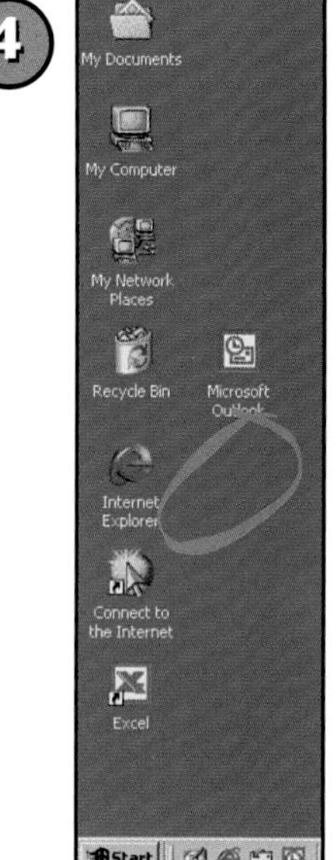

1. Right-click the icon that you want to delete.
2. In the pop-up menu that appears, click the **Delete** command.
3. In the Confirm Shortcut Delete dialog box, click **Yes** to delete the shortcut.
4. The shortcut icon is deleted.

End Task

Task 11: Uninstalling Applications

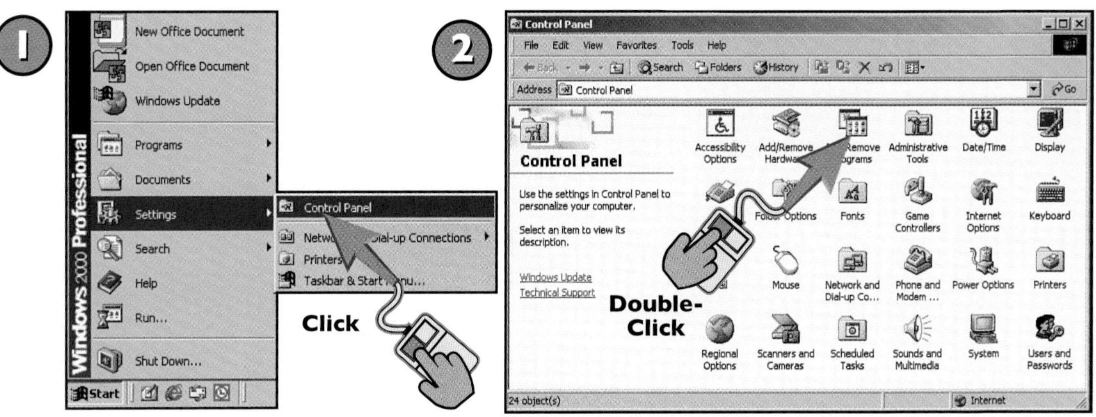

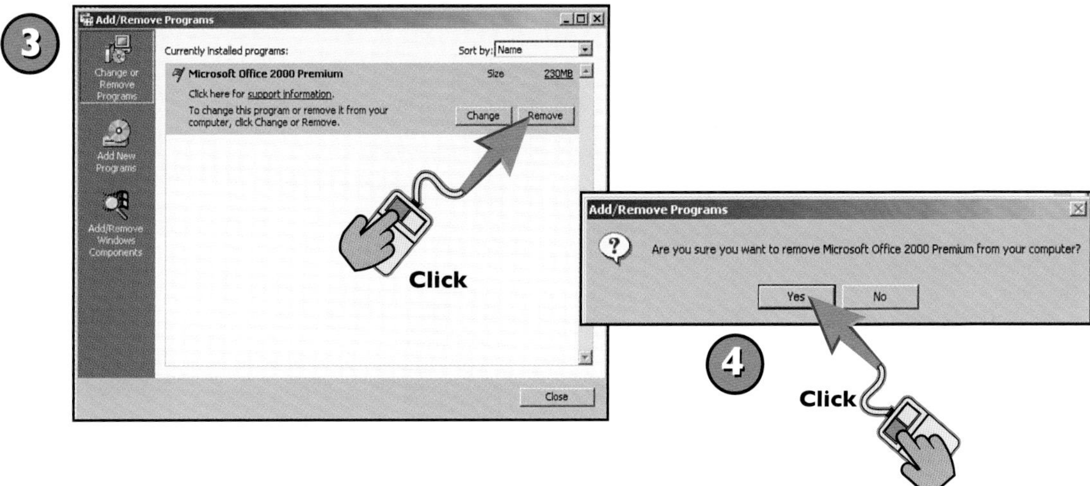

You can easily remove a shortcut icon or item from the Start menu, but doing so leaves that program on your hard disk. Uninstalling a program removes the program and all its related files and folders from your hard disk. Keep in mind that you should move any data files from your program folders if, for example, you plan to use them in another program.

Program Not Listed?

If your program is not listed in the Add/Remove Programs window, you must use a different procedure. Check your program documentation for specific instructions.

Changing Features Installed

You can add new features or components for an installed program. To do so, click the **Change** button next to the listed program in the Add/Remove Programs window.

1. Click **Start**, select **Settings**, and click **Control Panel**.
2. Double-click the **Add/Remove Programs** icon.
3. Next to the program you want to remove, click the **Remove** button.
4. Confirm the removal by clicking **Yes**. The program is removed.

PART

Using Windows Accessories

Windows 2000 provides several ***accessories*** that you can use to help you in your work. These accessories are not full-blown programs, but they are useful for specific jobs in the Windows environment. Accessories include a calculator, games, a painting program, an imaging program, a word processor, an address book, a text editor, system tools, and Internet applications. (The Internet applications and fax program are discussed in Part 9, "Connecting to Online Services and the Internet." System tools are covered in Part 8, "Maintaining Your System.") Windows 2000 also includes some multimedia tools for playing CDs and for recording and playing back sounds. This part covers the basic applications included with Windows 2000.

Tasks

Task 1: Playing Games

Windows provides several games that you can play to break up your workday with a little entertainment. Use any of the games to fill a lunch hour or coffee break and to ease the tensions of the day. Playing games is also a good way to help you get the hang of using the mouse. For instance, playing Solitaire can help you practice such mouse skills as clicking, dragging, and so on.

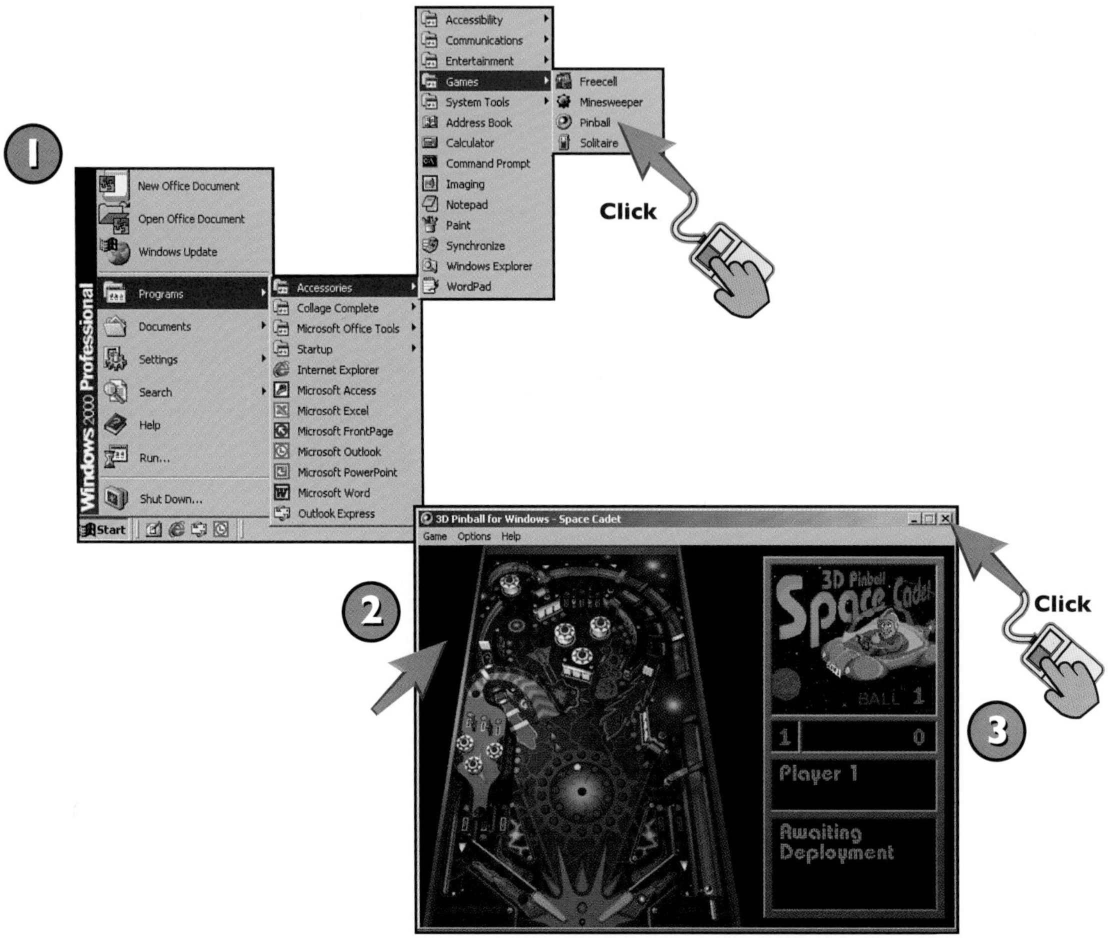

Games Not Listed?

If you don't see any games listed, they might not have been installed. You can easily add these Windows components to your system (refer to Task 2, "Installing Windows Components," in Part 6 "Setting Up Pragrams,"of this book).

Getting Help

If you aren't sure how to play a game, you can get instructions using the online help. Simply open the **Help** menu and select **How To Play**.

1. Click **Start**, select **Programs**, choose **Accessories**, select **Games**, and then click the name of the game you want to open (in this case, **Pinball**).
2. Play the game.
3. When you are finished, click the **Close** (×) button to exit.

Task 2: Using Calculator

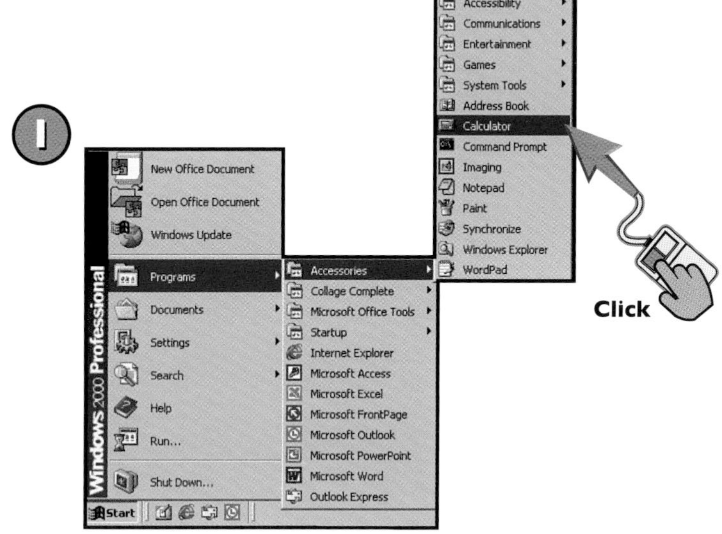

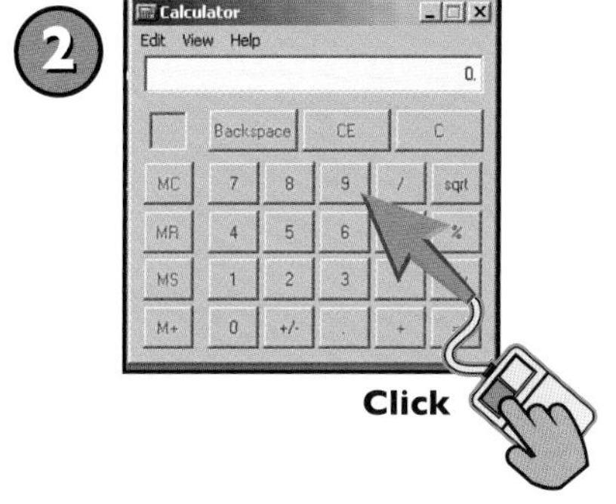

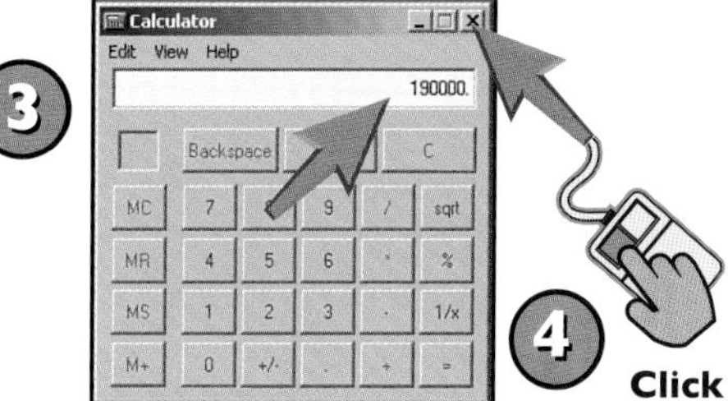

If you need to perform a quick calculation, use the Calculator program included with Windows 2000. You can add, subtract, multiply, divide, figure percentages, and more with this handy tool.

1. Click **Start**, select the **Programs** command, choose the **Accessories** folder, and then click **Calculator**.
2. Click the buttons on the calculator, or use the number pad on your keyboard, to enter an equation.
3. You see the results of the calculation.
4. When you are finished, click the **Close** (×) button.

Scientific Calculator

To use a more complex scientific calculator, click the calculator's **View** menu and then click **Scientific**.

Copying Results

You can copy the results of a calculation into a document. To do so, select the results, click **Edit**, and then choose **Copy**. Then move to the document where you want to paste the results, click **Edit**, and then choose **Paste**.

Using Numeric Keypad

To use the numeric keypad to enter numbers, press the **Num Lock** button. Then type the equation using the keys on the numeric keypad.

Task 3: Using the Command Prompt

There will be times when you'll want to access the DOS prompt from Windows. For example, you might want to run a DOS application or use such DOS commands as CD, DIR, and so on. Alternatively, you might have programs (especially games) that run in DOS. You can run any program by typing the appropriate DOS command. Windows provides a command prompt window that you can open while working in Windows.

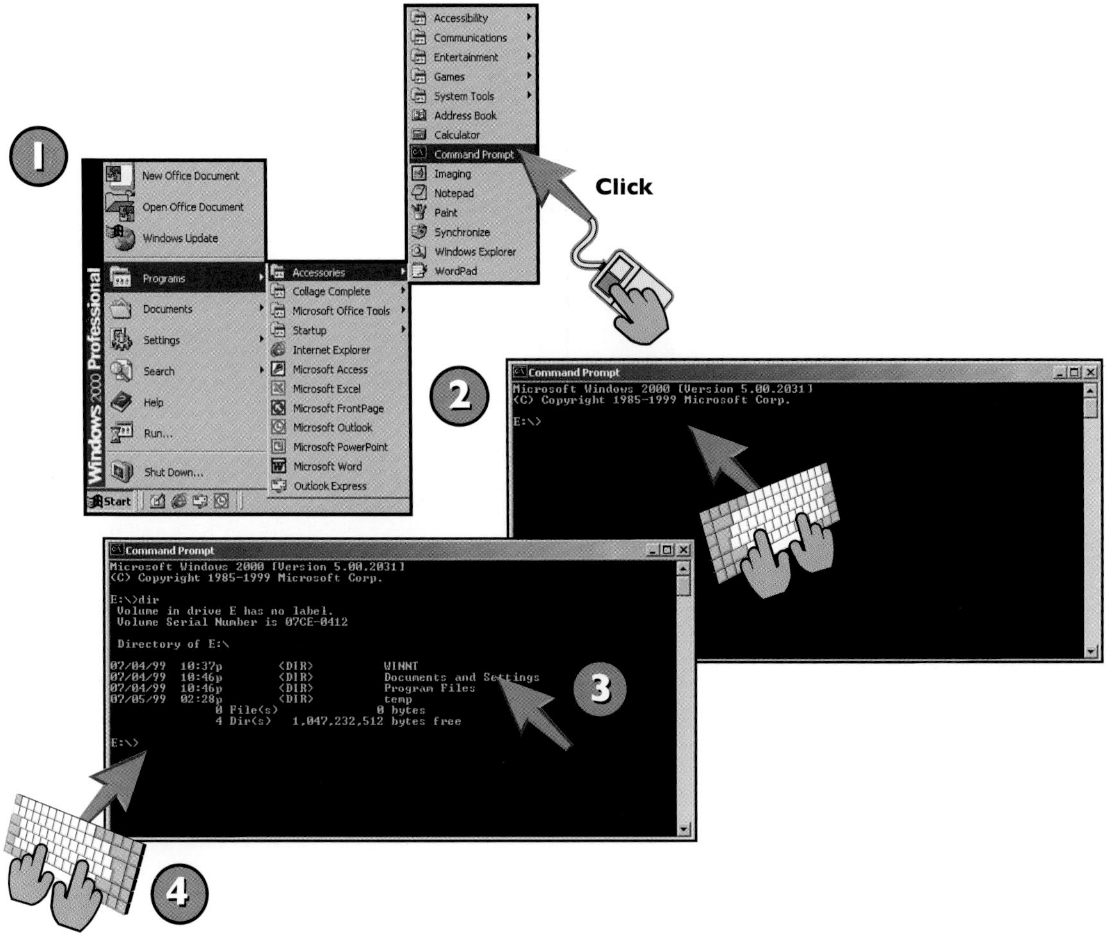

1. Click **Start**, select **Programs**, click **Accessories**, and then click **Command Prompt**.
2. Type the desired command and press **Enter**.
3. You can see the results of the command you typed.
4. Type **`exit`** and press **Enter** to close the command prompt window.

Maximizing the Window
Press Alt+Enter to enlarge the command prompt window to full screen. Press Alt+Enter again to restore the DOS window to its original size.

End Task

Task 4: Using Notepad

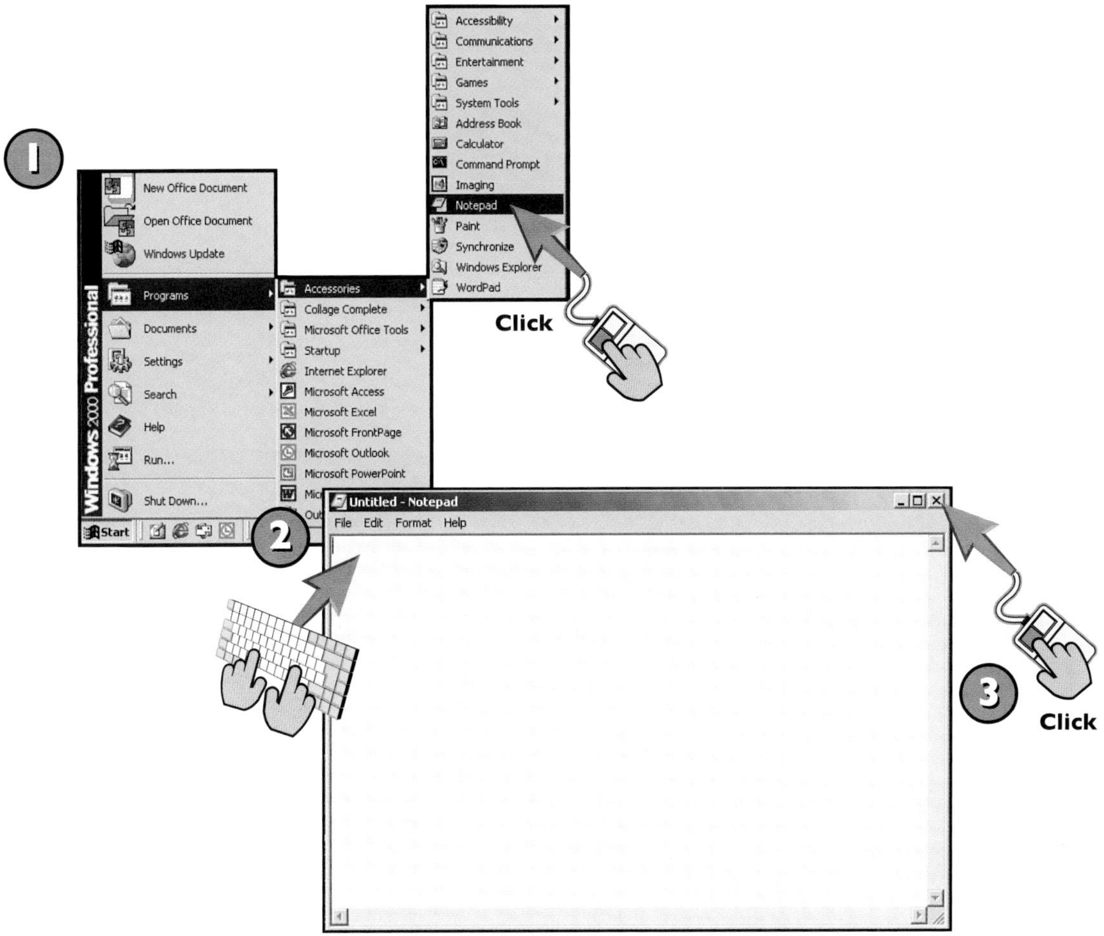

The most common type of simple file is a *text file*. You can find instructions on how to install a program, beta notes, and other information in text files. Some configuration files are also text files. To edit and work with this type of file, you can use Notepad, a simple text editor provided with Windows 2000.

1. Click **Start**, select the **Programs** command, click the **Accessories** folder, and then choose **Notepad**.
2. Type in the text file or open and edit an existing file.
3. To exit Notepad, click the **Close** (×) button.

Be Careful!
Be careful when making changes to any configuration text file. Be sure you know exactly what you are doing.

Opening a File
You can open a text file using the **File**, **Open** command. You can save an edited text file by clicking **File** and then choosing **Save**.

Task 5: Starting WordPad

Use WordPad to edit text files or to create simple documents such as notes, memos, fax sheets, and so on. WordPad saves files in Word for Windows format by default, but you can choose to save in a text-only format.

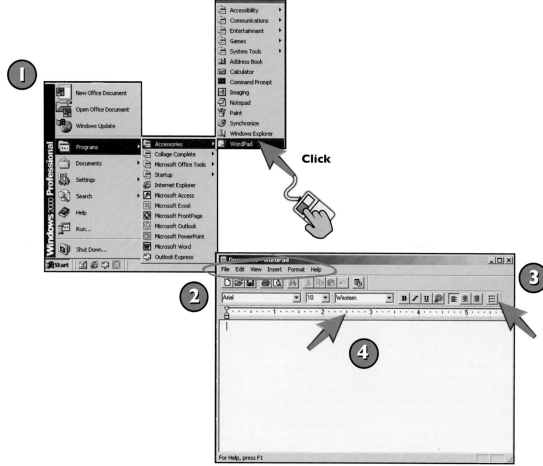

Maximizing the Window

You can click the **Maximize** button to enlarge the WordPad window and make it easier to work in.

Hiding Program Elements

To hide any of the screen elements in WordPad, open the **View** menu and click the tool you want to hide. A check mark indicates that the tool is showing; no check mark indicates that it is hidden.

1. Click **Start**, select the **Programs** command, click the **Accessories** folder, and select **WordPad**.
2. Use the menu bar to select commands.
3. Use the toolbar to select buttons for frequently used commands. Use the format bar to make changes to the appearance of the text.
4. Use the ruler for setting tabs and indents.

Task 6: Adding and Deleting Text

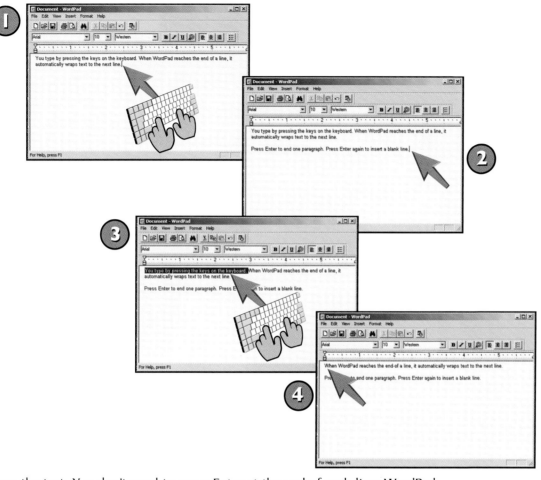

One of the greatest things about using a word-processing program, even a simple program like WordPad, is how easily you can make changes. You can add text, delete text, and more. You can also polish the content of your document, making whatever changes are necessary.

1. Type the text. You don't need to press Enter at the end of each line; WordPad automatically wraps the lines within a paragraph.
2. To end a paragraph and start a new one, press **Enter**. The insertion point moves to the next line.
3. To delete text, select the text you want to delete and then press the **Delete** key on your keyboard.
4. The text is deleted.

Make a Mistake?
If you make a mistake while typing, press the **Backspace** key to delete one character at a time. Then retype the text. You can also undo your last action, such as an accidental deletion, by clicking the **Edit** menu and choosing **Undo**.

Saving Your Work
Be sure to periodically save your document. See Task 8, "Saving a Document," in Part 2, "Using Applications in Windows 2000."

Task 7: Formatting Text

You can easily make simple changes to the appearance of the text. For example, you can change the font or font size, and you can make text bold, italic, or underlined. This task touches on just a few of the formatting changes you can make. Experiment to try out some of the other available formatting features.

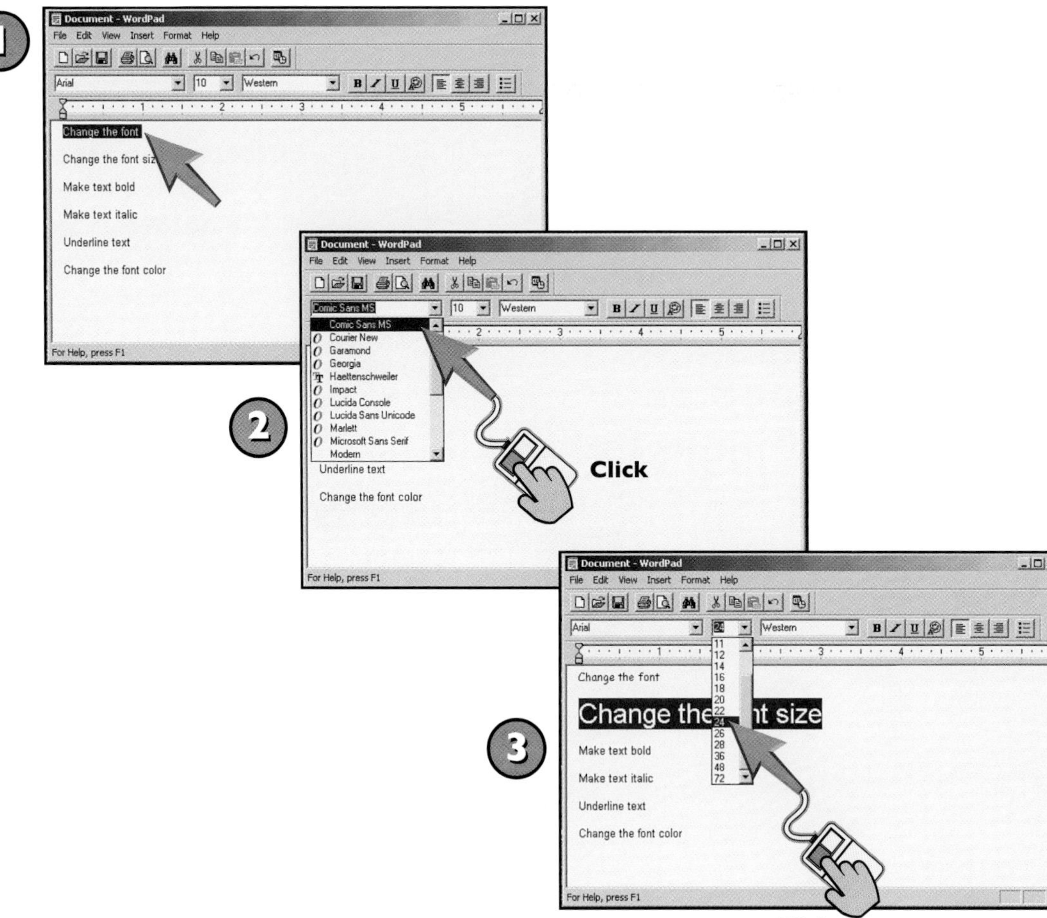

1. Select the text you want to change.
2. To use a different font, click the **Font** drop-down arrow and click the font you want.
3. To use a different font size, select the text you want to change, click the **Font Size** drop-down arrow, and click the size you want to use.

Formatting Paragraphs

You can use toolbar buttons to change many features of the paragraph. For example, use the **Alignment** buttons to change the alignment of the paragraph. Add bullets by clicking the **Bullets** button. To undo a change, click the **Undo** button.

Formatting Text This Way in Other Programs

Most other Windows programs work in a similar fashion. You can make formatting changes (font, font size, font style, color) using the same toolbar methods.

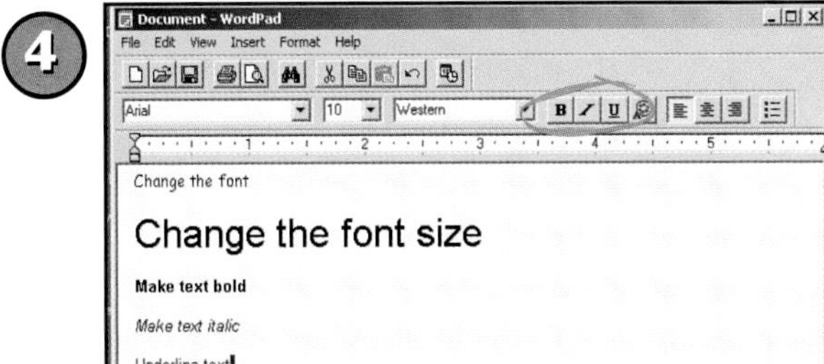

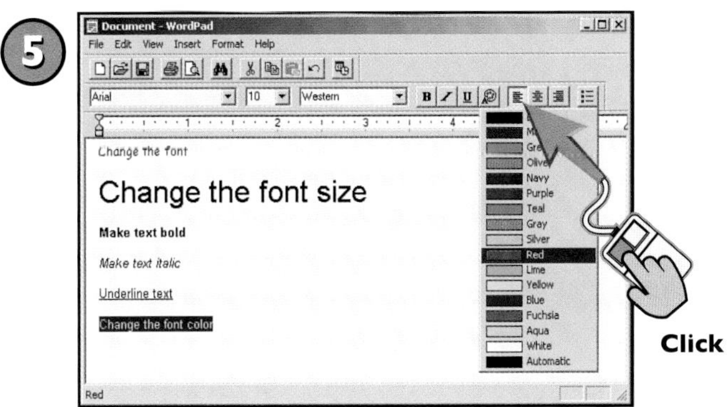

4 To make text bold, italic, or underlined, select the text, and then click the appropriate button in the format bar.

5 To change the font color, select the text you want to change, click the **Font Color** button, and then click the color you want.

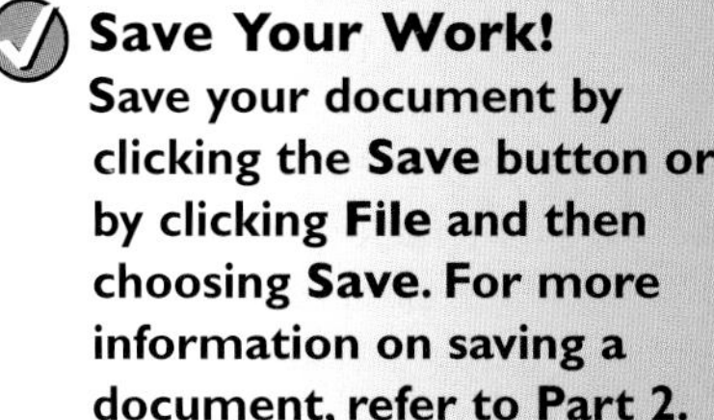

Save Your Work!
Save your document by clicking the Save button or by clicking File and then choosing Save. For more information on saving a document, refer to Part 2.

Task 8: Using Paint

Use Paint to create art and edit graphics such as clip art, scanned art, and art files from other programs. You can add lines, shapes, and colors, as well as alter the original components.

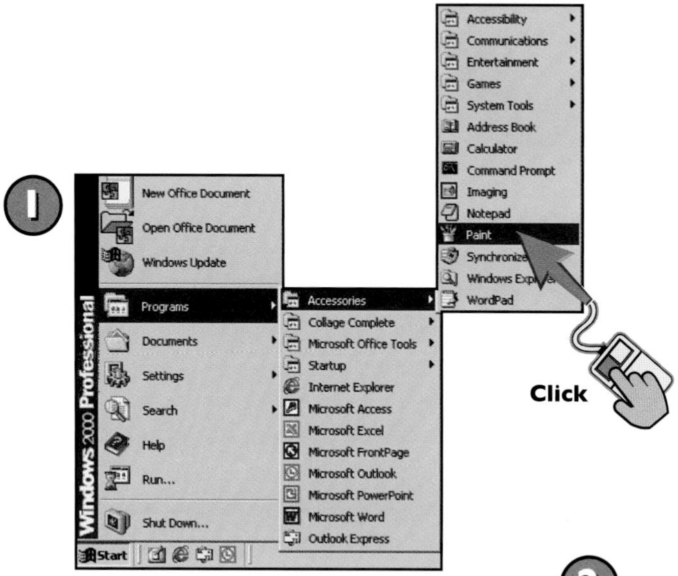

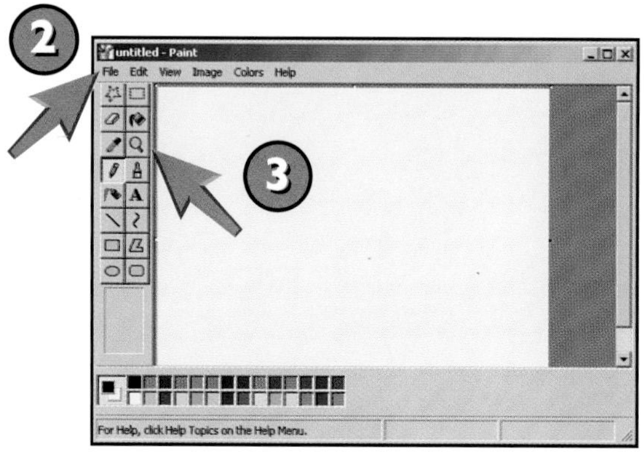

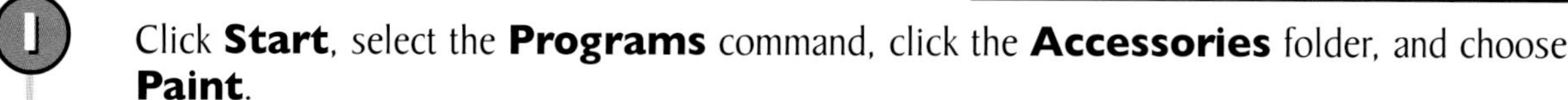

1. Click **Start**, select the **Programs** command, click the **Accessories** folder, and choose **Paint**.
2. Use the menu bar to select commands.
3. Use the toolbox to select the drawing tool you want to work with.

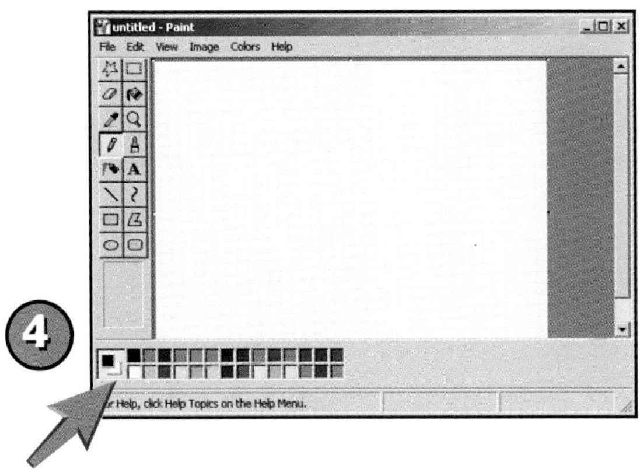

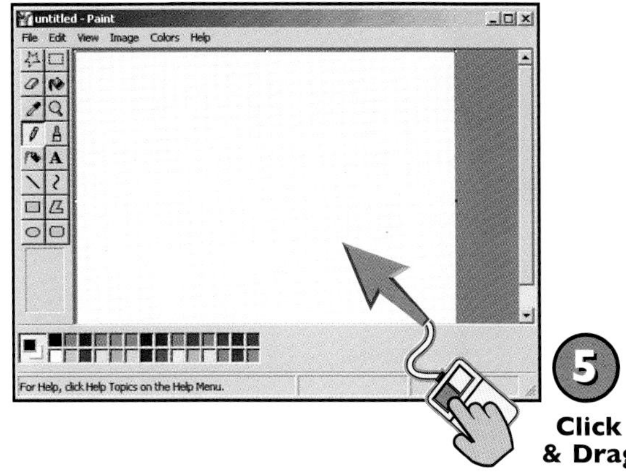

4 Use the color box to select colors for the lines and fills of the objects you draw.

5 Draw in the drawing area.

Experiment!
You can learn more about Paint by experimenting. Also, use the online help system to look up topics.

Not Sure What a Tool Does?
Put your pointer on the tool, and the tool name will pop up.

Save Your Work!
If you want to keep a copy of your artwork, be sure to save the document. Refer to Task 8 in Part 2 for more help on saving a file.

Task 9: Drawing a Shape in Paint

Start Here

You can create many different types of shapes, including lines, curves, rectangles, polygons, ovals, circles, and rounded rectangles.

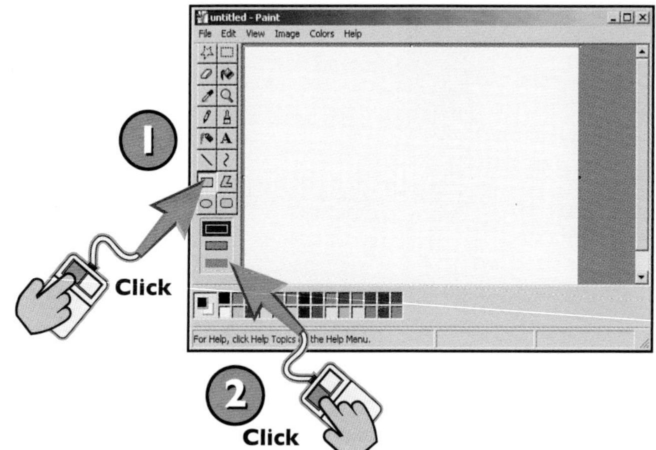

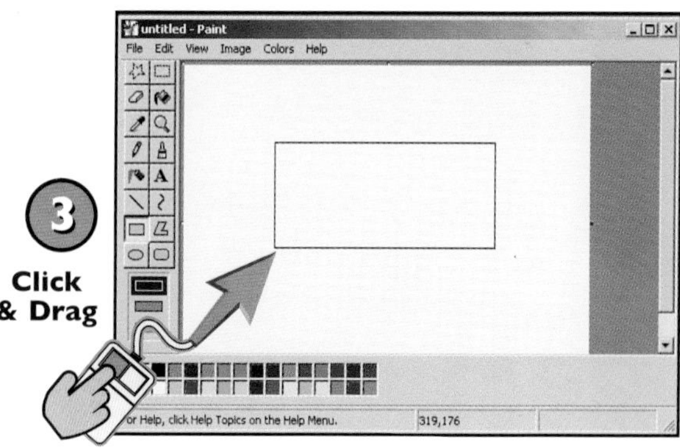

Selecting a Color

You can click in the color bar at the bottom of the Paint window to choose a color. Click the color you want to use for the lines and borders. To select a fill color, right-click the color you want to use.

Undoing a Mistake

If at any time you do not like what you've drawn, open the **Edit** menu and choose **Undo** to undo the last action.

Erasing

If you make a mistake, you can use the Eraser tool. Simply click the **Eraser** tool in the toolbox, select the size of the eraser, and hold down the mouse button and drag across the part you want to erase. To clear everything on the page, click **Image** and then choose **Clear Image**.

1. Click the tool you want to draw with (in this case, the **Rectangle** tool).

2. The toolbox displays options for drawing with the selected tool. In this case, specify whether you want to draw an empty rectangle; a filled, bordered rectangle; or a filled rectangle without a border.

3. Move the pointer into the drawing area, and click and drag to draw. The object is drawn in the document.

End Task

Task 10: Adding Text to a Paint Document

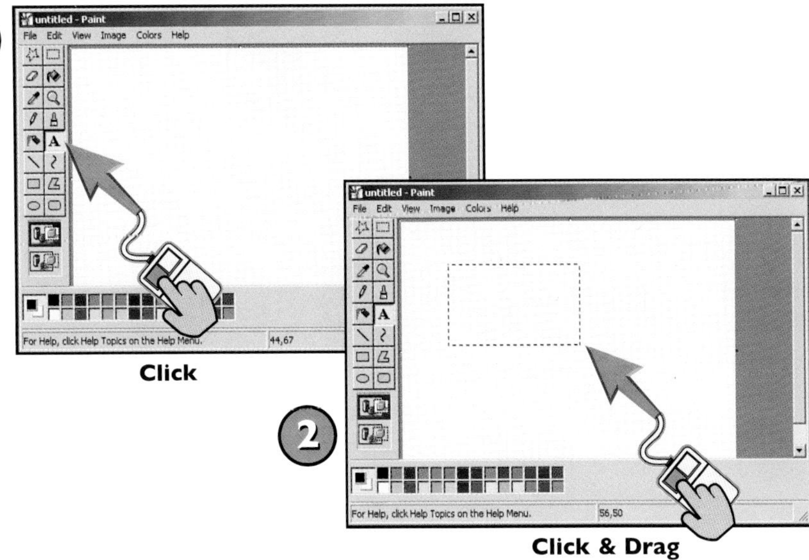

Click

Click & Drag

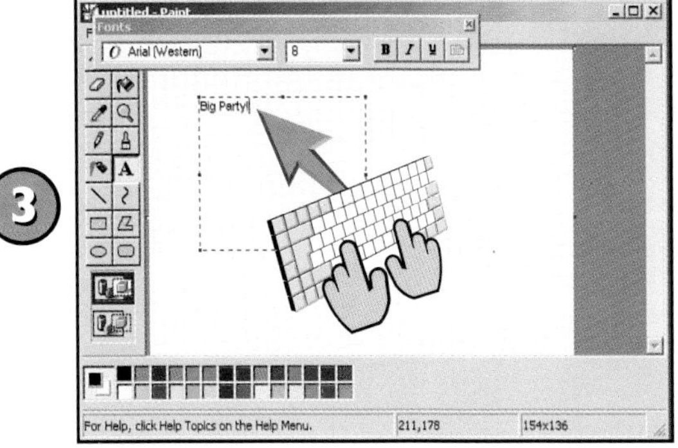

You can include text as part of your drawing. To do so, draw a text box and then type the text you want to include.

Click the **Text** tool.

Move the pointer into the drawing area and drag to draw a text box.

Type the text you want to add. The text is added to the text box.

Formatting Text

Use the Fonts toolbar to make changes to the font, font size, and font style when you are typing the text.

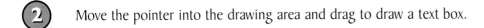

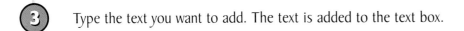

Task 11: Using the Brush Tool in Paint

You can draw on the page using a paintbrush. To do so, use the **Brush** tool. You can select the brush size and style (slant, for instance).

Drawing Freehand
You can also use the **Pencil** tool to draw on the page.

Spraying Paint on the Page
Click the **Airbrush** tool, select a splatter size, and drag to spray paint on the page.

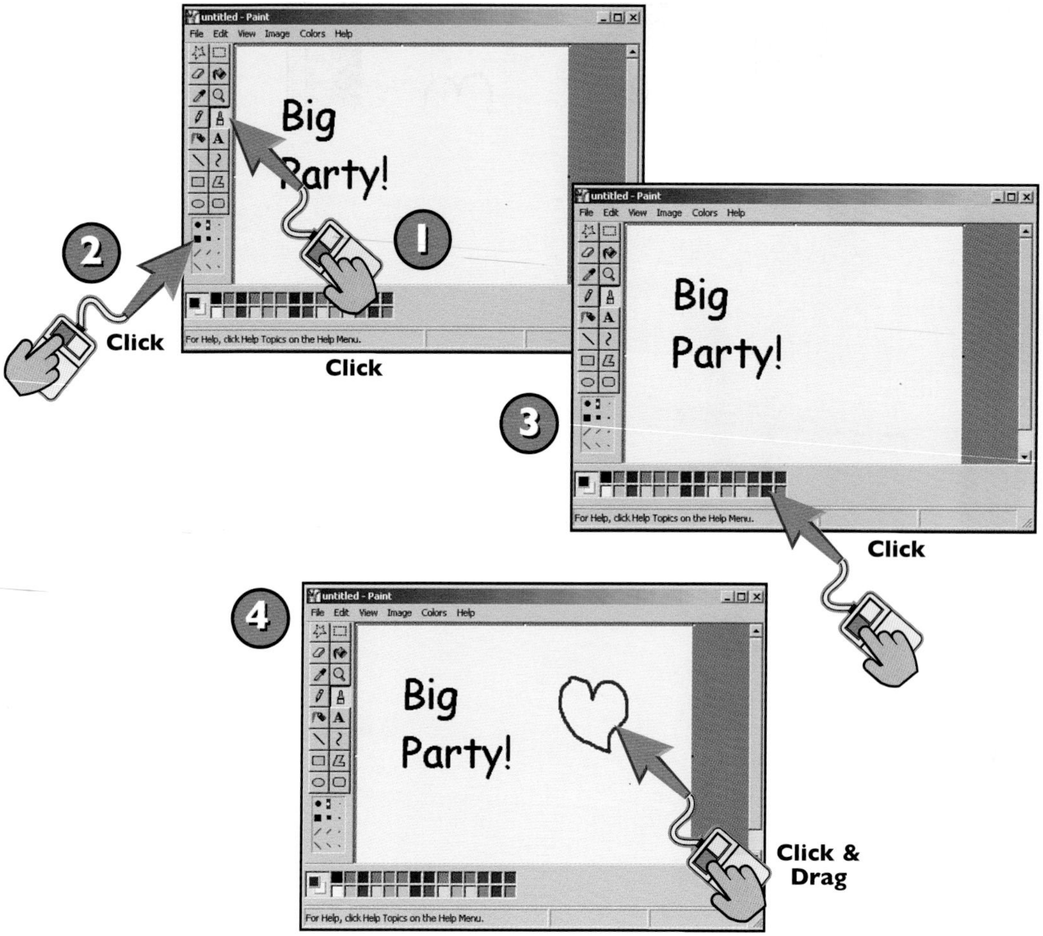

1. Click the **Brush** tool.
2. Click the brush size and shape.
3. Click the color you want to use in the color box.
4. Hold down the mouse button and drag across the page to "paint" with the brush.

Task 12: Filling an Object in Paint

You can use the **Fill with Color** tool to fill an object or drawing area with color. For instance, you can fill a rectangle or circle with any of the colors available in the color palette.

1. Click the **Fill with Color** tool.

2. Click the color you want to use.

3. Click inside the area you want to paint. That area is filled with the color you selected.

Color Spilling Out?
If color spills outside the area you intended to fill, that probably means you tried to fill an area that was not closed. Be sure that you are filling an area that is completely bordered.

Task 13: Using the Imaging Program

For more complex imaging tasks, you can use the Imaging program. You can open most types of graphics files—including TIFF, BMP, and JPG—and then edit, print, or annotate these images.

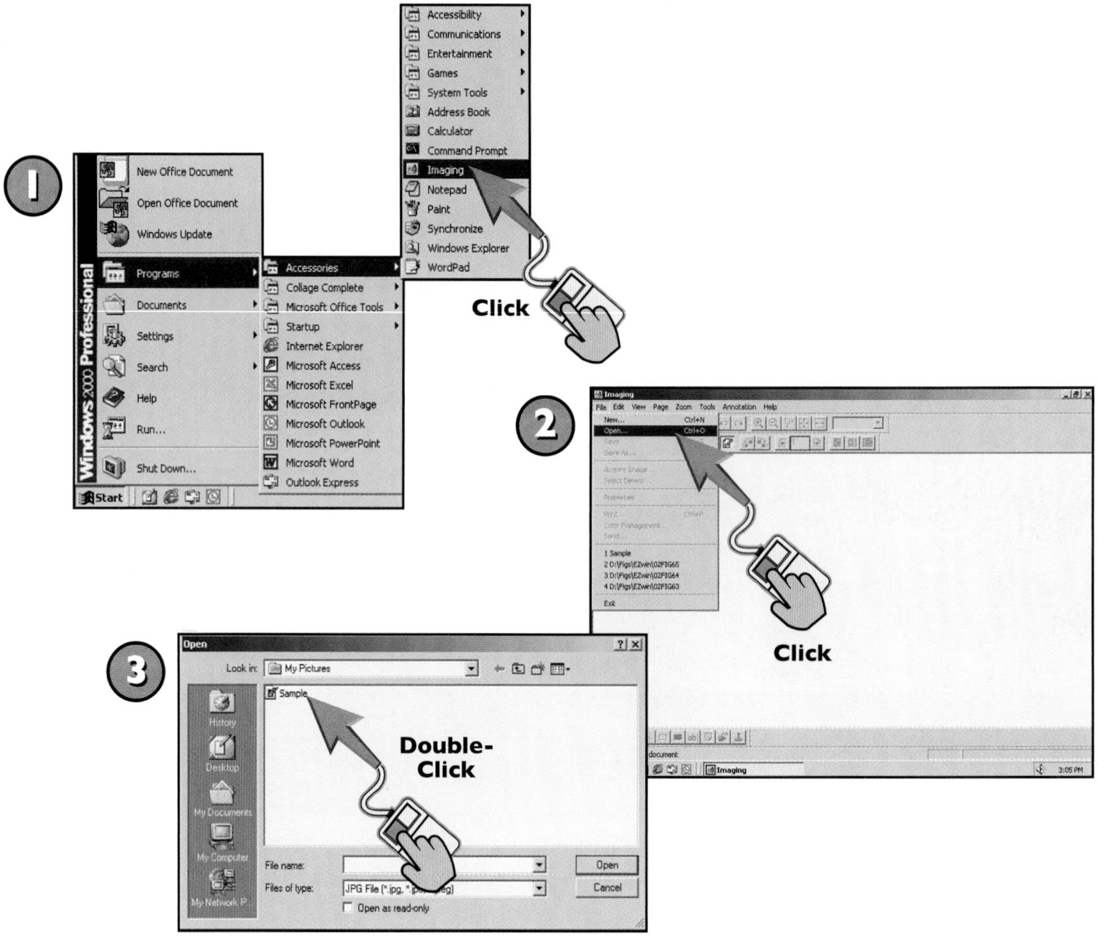

Start Here

1 Click **Start**, select **Programs**, click **Accessories**, and then click **Imaging**.

2 You see the **Imaging** program window. To open a file, click **File** and then choose **Open**.

3 Double-click the file you want to open. (You might have to change to the drive and folder that contain the image.)

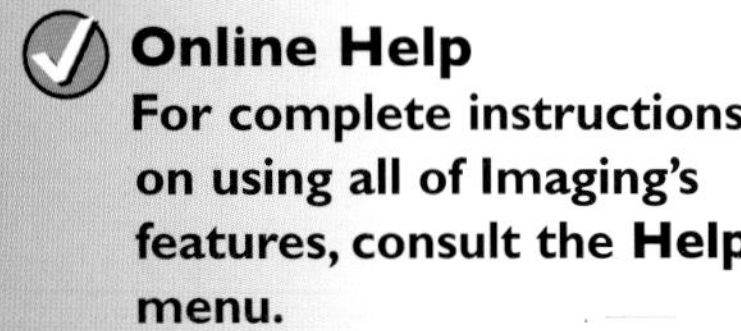

Online Help
For complete instructions on using all of Imaging's features, consult the Help menu.

4 The image is displayed onscreen. Use the buttons in the Standard toolbar to print, save, or zoom the view.

5 Use the Annotation toolbar buttons to add annotations—shapes, text boxes, arrows, and so on.

6 When you are finished viewing or editing the image, click the **Close** (×) button to close the program.

Finding a File
For information on opening a document, see Task 9, "Opening a Document," in Part 2. Remember that you can use the Look In drop-down list to display another drive or folder. Click the Up One Level button to move up in the folder structure.

Save Your Work!
If you edit an image and want to save the changes, click File and then Save.

Printing the Image
To print the image, click the Print button or click File and then Print. Click OK in the Print dialog box.

Task 14: Playing a Sound with Sound Recorder

You can use various Windows multimedia devices, such as the Sound Recorder, to add to the presentations or documents you create in Windows. Use Sound Recorder to record your own sounds and insert the sound files into your documents for clarification or interest. To use the multimedia features of Windows 2000, you need a sound card and speakers.

Start Here

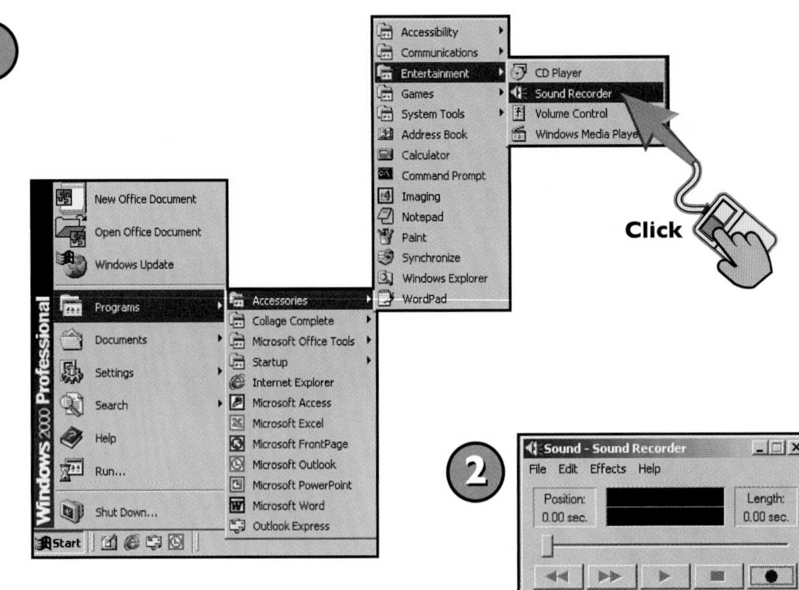

Recording Sounds
You can record sounds using Sound Recorder. To do so, you must have an audio input device (microphone) attached to your PC. Click **File**, choose **New**, and then click the **Record** button and record your sound. To stop recording, click the **Stop** button. To save your sound, click **File** and then choose **Save As**.

1. Click **Start**, select the **Programs** command, choose the **Accessories** folder, click the **Entertainment** folder, and select **Sound Recorder**.
2. The **Sound Recorder** window appears.
3. Click the **File** menu and then choose **Open**.

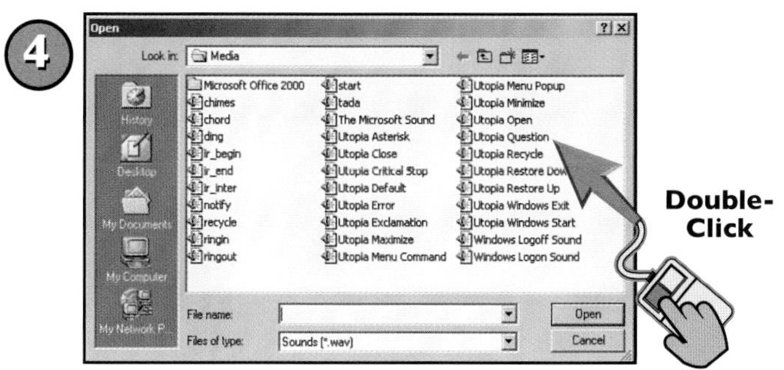

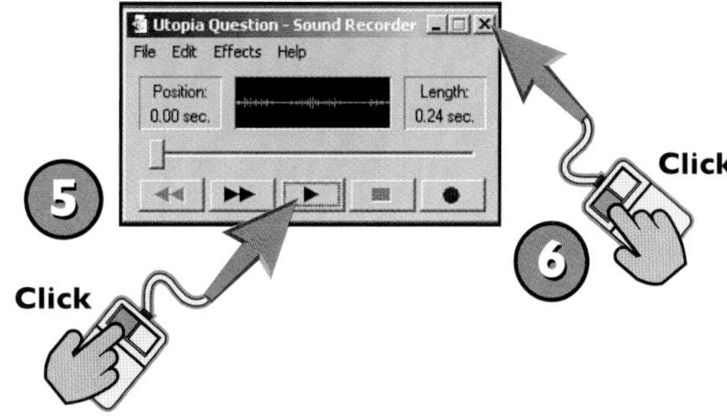

4 Double-click the sound file you want to play. (You might need to change to the drive and folder that contain the sound.)

5 Click the **Play** button.

6 Click the **Close** (×) button to close the **Sound Recorder** window.

Nothing Plays?
If you cannot hear the sound, adjust the volume on your speakers.

Adjusting the Volume
Use the Volume program to adjust the volume and balance. Click **Start**, **Programs**, **Accessories**, **Entertainment**, and **Volume Control**. Make any changes and click **OK**.

Task 15: Playing an Audio CD

In addition to being able to play back sound files, you can play audio CDs using CD Player, enabling you to listen to the background music of your choice as you work. Note that to use the multimedia features of Windows 2000, you need a sound card and speakers.

Some CDs Play Automatically

If you insert a CD, CD Player might start automatically. (It depends on whether your CD player has an auto-play feature.)

Listening to Music on the Internet

The Internet includes many, many music sites; CD Player makes it easy to sample music from some of these sites. To do so, click the **Internet** button in the CD Player window, choose **Internet Music Sites**, and then select the site to visit. When prompted, connect to your Internet provider. Note: To use this feature, you must have an Internet connection.

Start Here

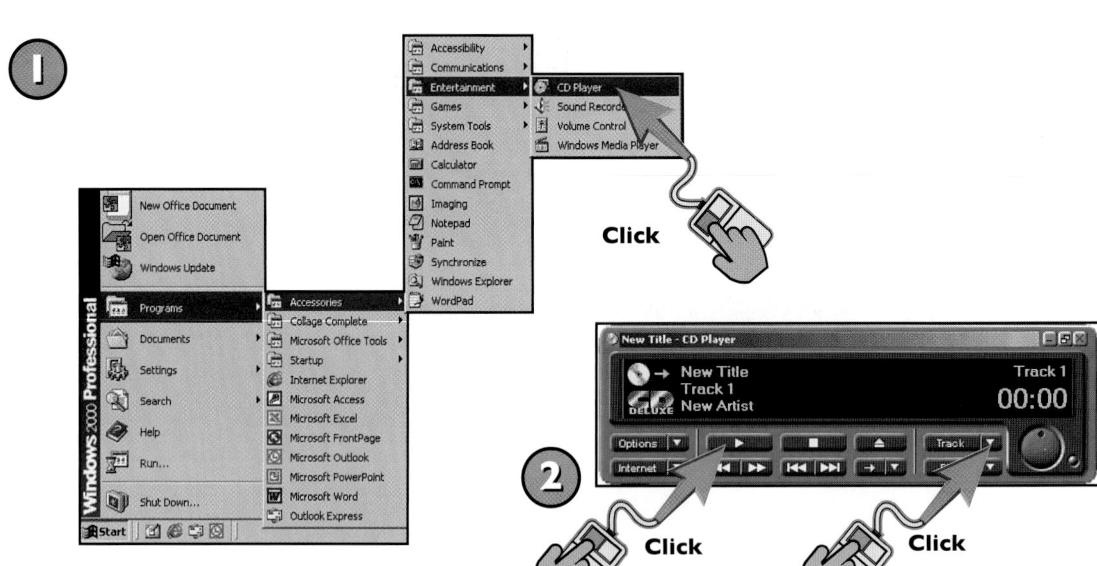

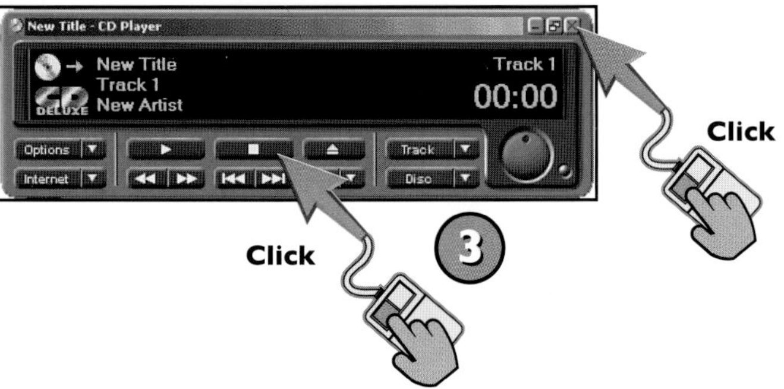

1 Click **Start**, select the **Programs** command, choose the **Accessories** folder, click the **Entertainment** folder, and choose **CD Player**.

2 After you insert your CD into your CD drive, click the **Play** button in the CD Player window. To play a different track, display the **Track** drop-down list and select the track you want to play.

3 To stop playing, click the **Stop** button. To close the CD Player window and exit CD Player, click the **Close** (×) button.

Task 16: Playing a Media File

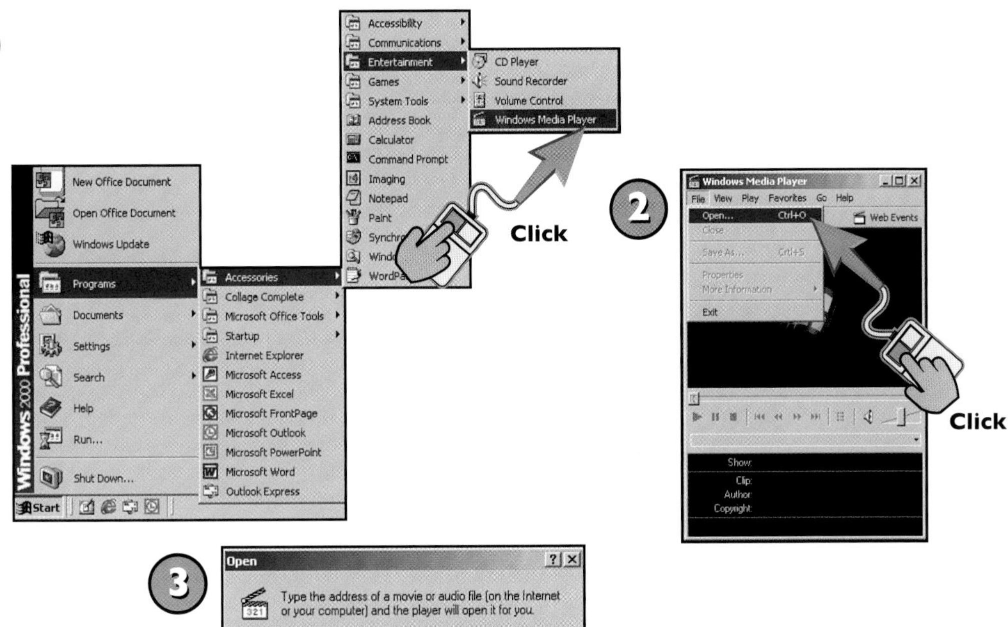

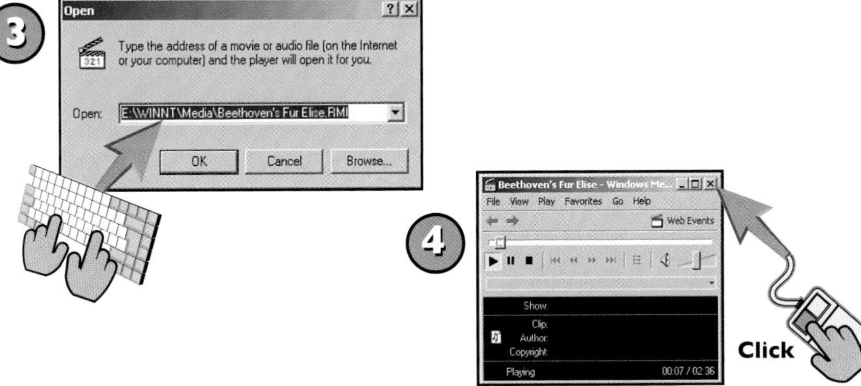

Media files are a combination of text, graphics, sounds, video, and animations. As computers take more and more advantage of the multimedia features of your PC, you will find more media files for your use. For instance, Windows 2000 comes with some sample media files. To play these presentations, you can use Media Player.

More Information on the Internet

The Internet includes many types of media files. For information on browsing the Internet, see Part 9.

Browsing to Find the File

If you don't know the exact path to the file or address of the Web page, you can browse for it. Click the **Browse** button and then browse through the drives and folders to find the file.

1. Click **Start**, select the **Programs** command, choose the **Accessories** folder, click the **Entertainment** folder, and select **Windows Media Player**.
2. In the Windows Media Player window, click **File** and then choose **Open**.
3. Type the path of file you want to play and click **OK**.
4. The file is played. To close Media Player, click the **Close** (×) button.

PART 8

Maintaining Your System

This part of the book introduces some techniques that are useful for maintaining your system: defragmenting a disk, backing up data files, scanning a disk for damage, and others.

To safeguard your data files, you should periodically make an extra copy, called a ***backup***. You can use the backup program included with Windows 2000 to make backup easy. You can also install and troubleshoot hardware problems, as covered in this section.

Tasks

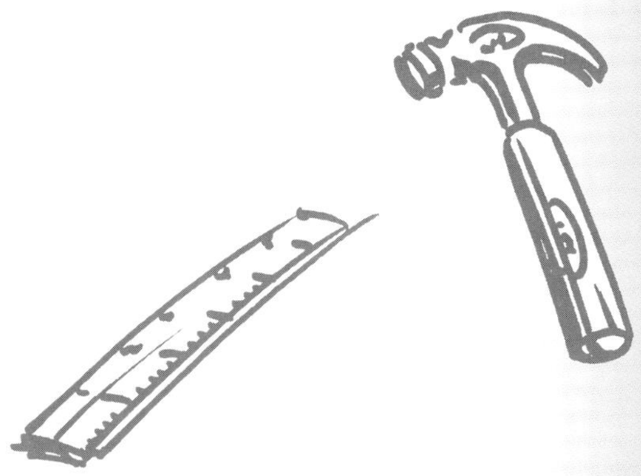

Task 1: Displaying Disk Information

You can display information about your disks, such as the size, amount of space taken, and amount of free space. You can also enter a label for a disk; this label is used in file windows to identify the disk.

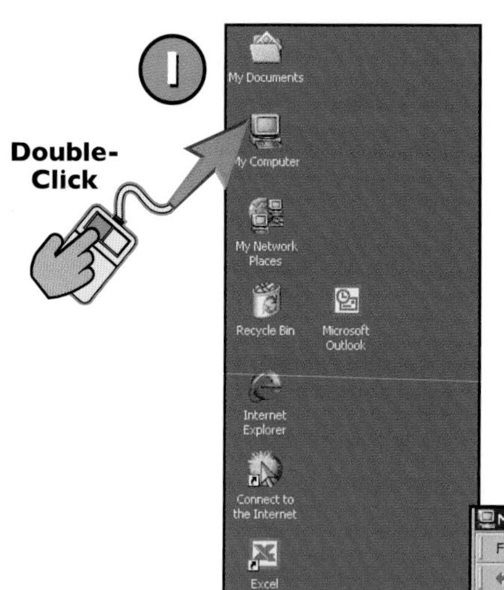

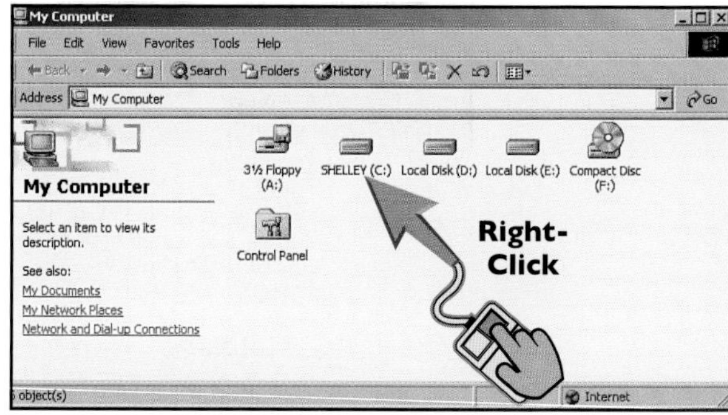

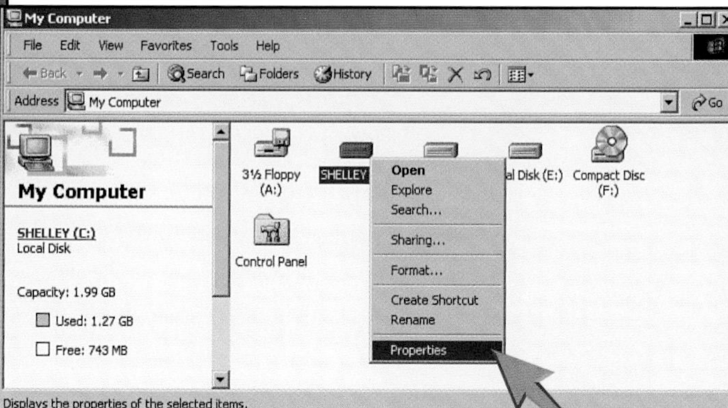

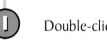

Checking Out the Disk Window
The lower-left corner of the window displays information about the selected drive, including the capacity, used space, and free space.

1. Double-click the **My Computer** icon.

2. In the **My Computer** window, right-click the disk for which you want information.

3. Click **Properties**.

Next Step

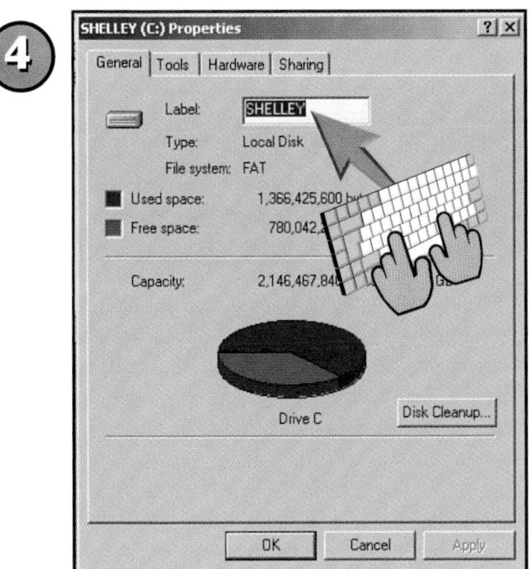

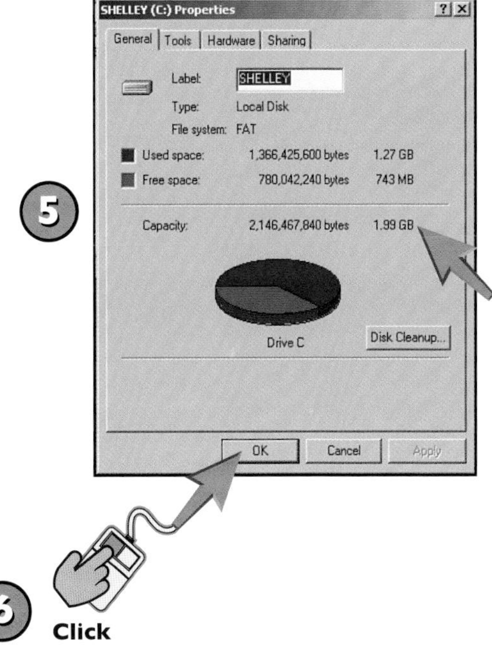

4 If you want, enter a disk label in the **Label** field.

5 View information about used and free space.

6 Click the **OK** button to close the dialog box.

Other Tabs

Use the Tools tab to select different programs for maintaining your system (covered later in this part). For information about the particular drive, click the Hardware tab.

Task 2: Scanning Your Disk for Errors

Start Here

Sometimes parts of your hard disk get damaged. You might see an error message when you try to open or save a file, or you might notice lost or disarrayed data in some of your files. You can use Check Disk to scan the disk for damage and fix any problems. You must also check the disk before you can defragment a hard disk (covered next).

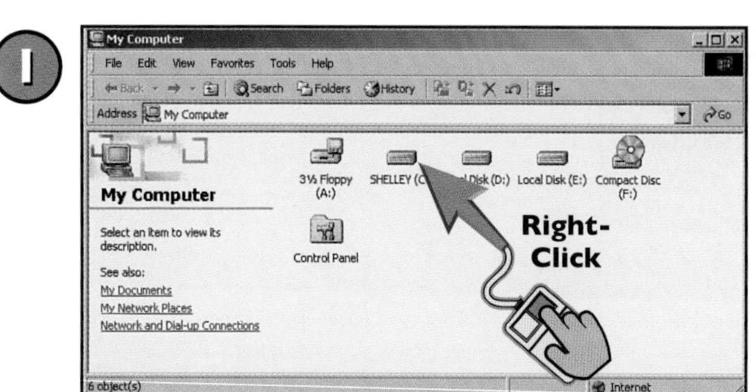

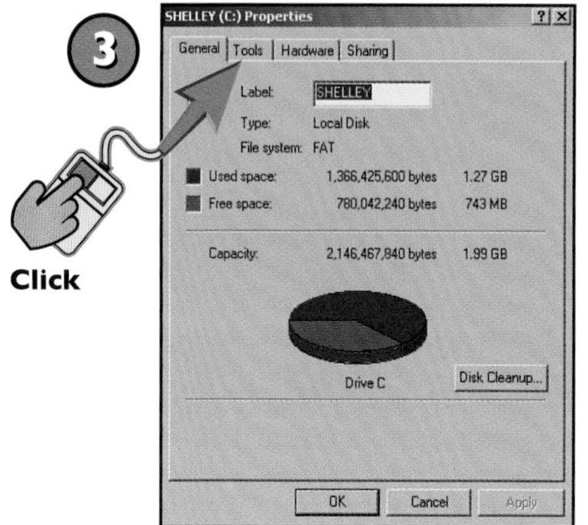

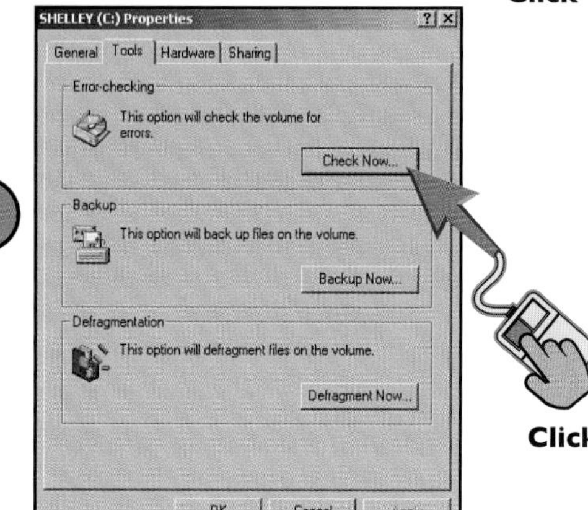

Scanning After Improper Shutdown

If you don't properly shut down Windows, you are prompted to run Check Disk when you reboot. You can then check for errors before your system is restarted.

Start Menu

You can also find most system tools on the Start menu. Click Start, select Programs, and then click Accessories. Open the System Tools folder and click the program you want to run.

1. In the My Computer window, right-click the disk for which you want information.
2. Select **Properties** from the pop-up menu that appears.
3. Click the **Tools** tab.
4. In the Error-Checking area, click the **Check Now** button.

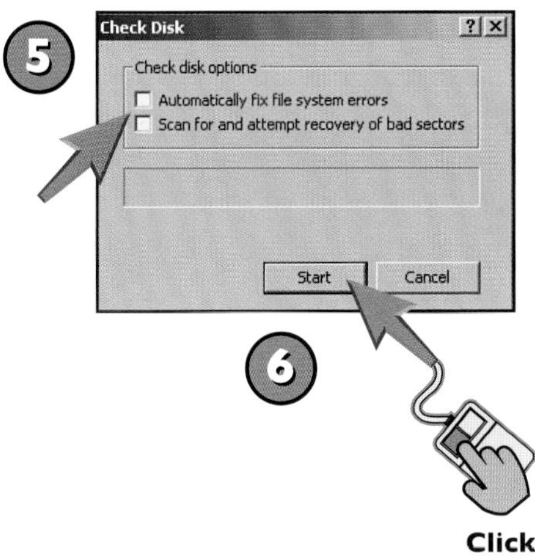

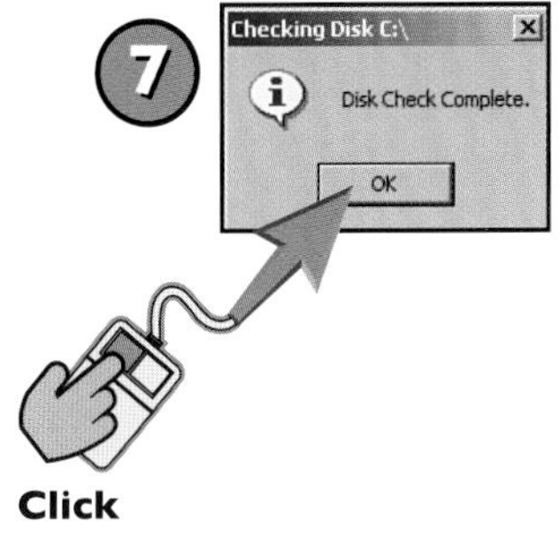

5 Specify whether you want Check Disk to automatically fix errors and decide whether the test should scan for and attempt to recover bad sectors. (This process will increase the test time.)

6 Click the **Start** button.

7 Click the **OK** button when you see a message that the test is complete.

Errors Found?

If an error is found, a dialog box appears explaining the error. Read the error message and choose the option that best suits your needs. Click OK to continue. Do this for each message.

Task 3: Defragmenting a Disk

When a file is stored on your hard drive, Windows places as much of the file as possible in the first available section (called a *cluster*) and then goes to the next cluster to put the next part of the file. Initially, this storage does not cause performance problems, but over time, your disk files become *fragmented*; you might find that it takes a long time to open a file or start a program. To speed access to files and help prevent potential problems with fragmented files, you can defragment your disk, putting files in clusters as close to each other as possible. Defragmenting your disk is a general-maintenance job that you should perform every few months for best results.

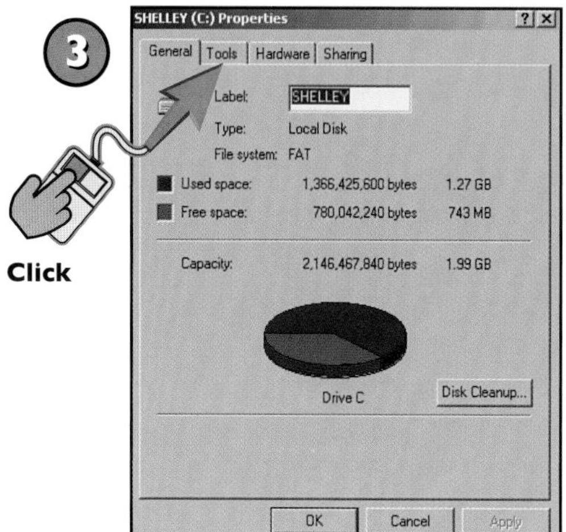

1. In the My Computer window, right-click the disk you want to defragment.
2. Select **Properties** from the pop-up menu that appears.
3. Click the **Tools** tab.

4 Click the **Defragment Now** button.

5 The drive is highlighted. Click the **Defragment** button.

6 When the defragmentation is complete, you see a message. Click **Close**.

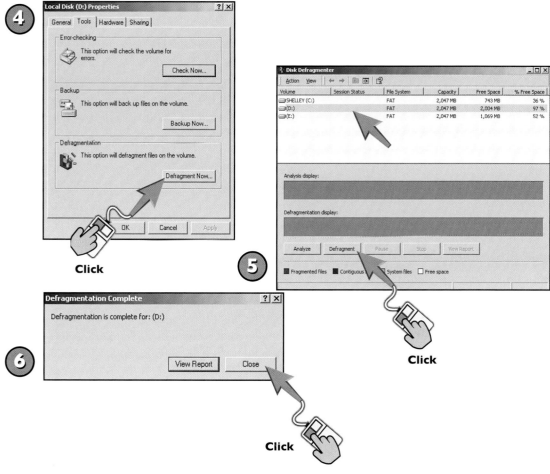

Viewing the Progress
The Defragmenter's progress is indicated by the Defragmentation display. You can stop or pause the defragmenting at any time by clicking the appropriate button.

Analyzing the Disk
You can analyze the disk to see whether disk defragmenting is necessary. To do so, click the Analyze button.

Legend
Use the legend at the bottom to see the contents and organization of files on the drive. Red indicates fragmented files, blue means contiguous files, green shows system files, and white is free space.

Viewing the Report
To view the report of the defragmentation, click the View Report button.

Task 4: Cleaning Up Unnecessary Files

On your system, unnecessary files might be hogging your disk space. For example, programs such as Internet Explorer store temporary files on your system that you can delete. The Recycle Bin also houses files that you have deleted, but that are still kept in case you need them. You can easily get rid of these files and gain some disk space.

Start Here

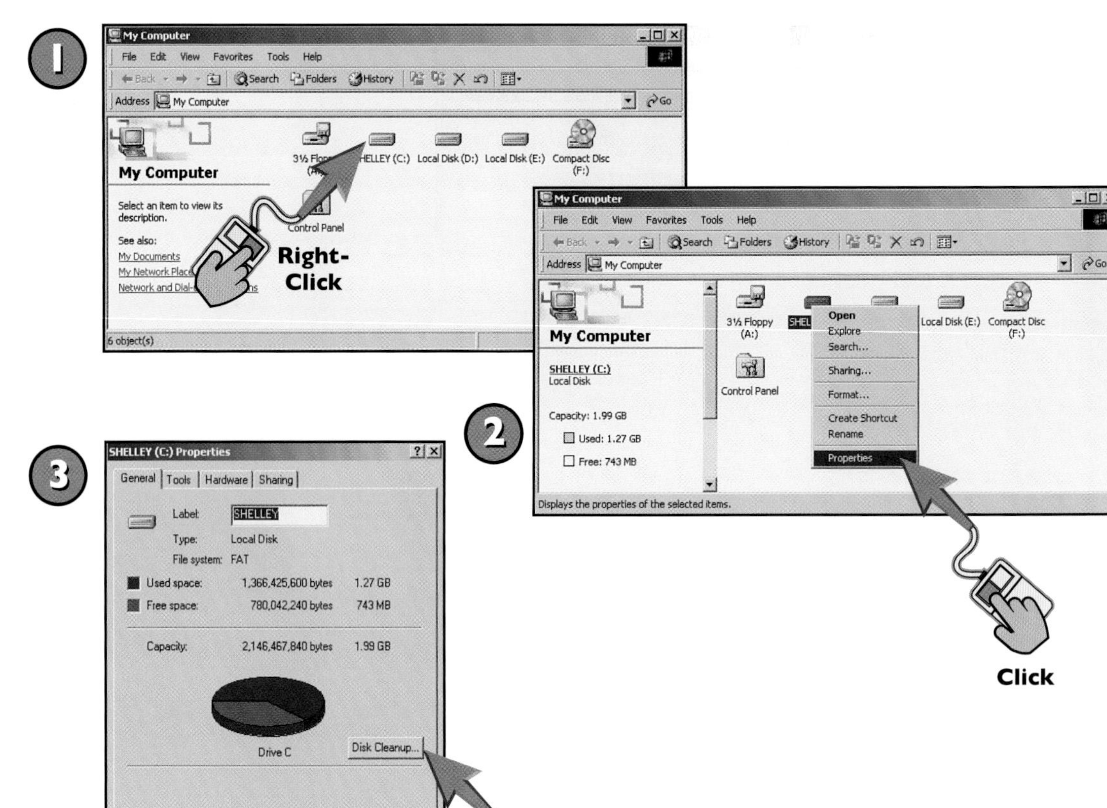

Be Careful!
Be sure you don't need any of these files. After they are removed, you cannot get them back.

1. In the My Computer window, right-click the disk you want to defragment.
2. Select **Properties** from the pop-up menu that appears.
3. Click the **Disk Cleanup** button. Windows calculates the space you can save and displays a list of files recommended for removal.

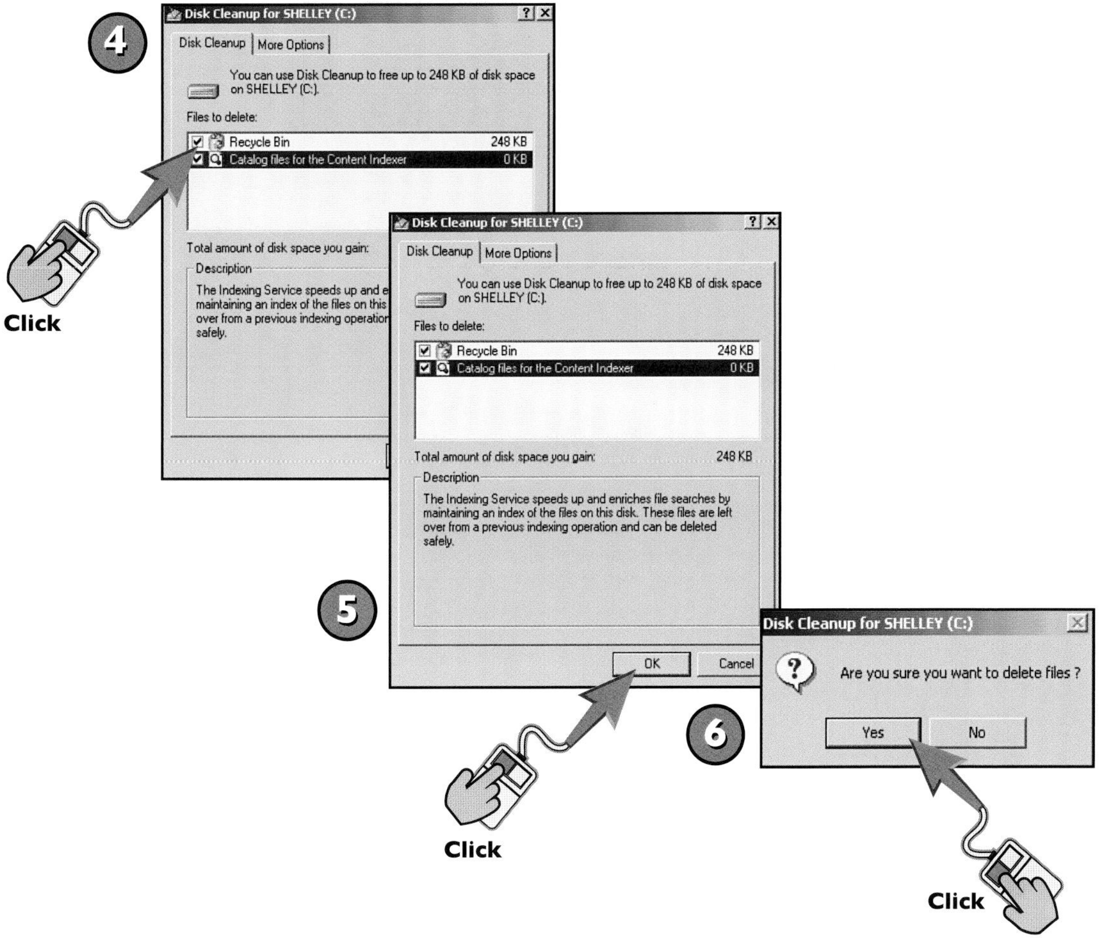

4. Review the list and check any files you want removed. Uncheck any files you don't want removed.

5. Click the **OK** button.

6. When prompted to confirm the removal, click the **Yes** button. Click the **OK** button to close the Disk Properties dialog box.

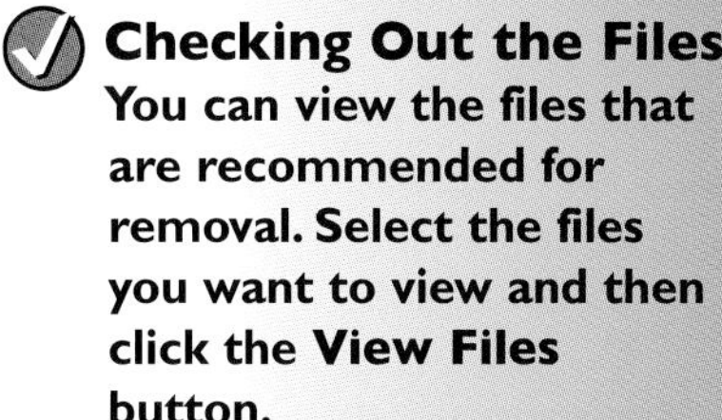

Checking Out the Files
You can view the files that are recommended for removal. Select the files you want to view and then click the View Files button.

Task 5: Backing Up All Files on Your Computer

To safeguard your data, back up the files on your system. That way, if something happens to the original, you can restore with this backup or an extra copy. The first time you do a backup, you might want to back up all the files on your system. After you have a complete backup, you can then back up only selected files. Windows 2000 includes a revised Backup program, including a Backup Wizard. This task covers how to back up all files. The next one covers how to back up selected files.

Using a Tape Backup
If backup is critical to your system, you might want to purchase a tape backup system. This method is faster and more convenient than backing up to floppy disks or to a disk file.

Going Back a Step
You can click the **Back** button to go back and make a change to your selections. Click the **Cancel** button to stop the backup.

Start Here

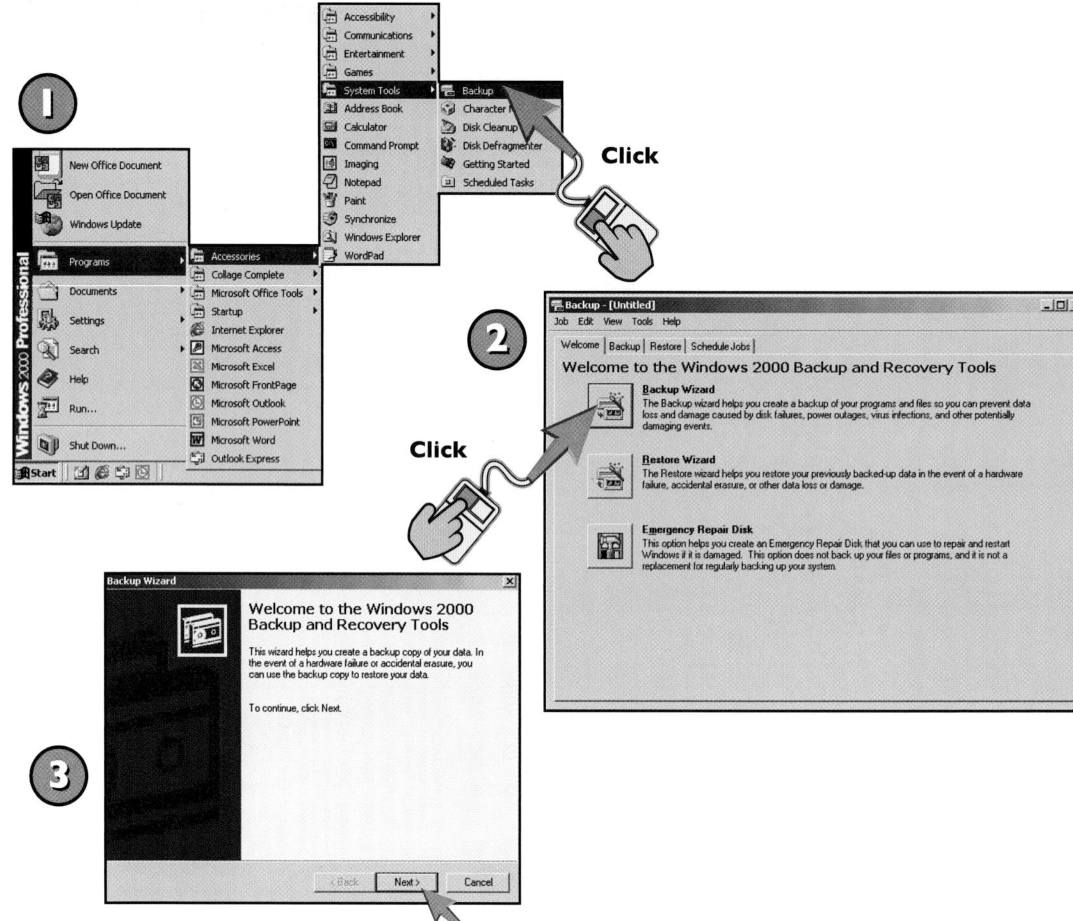

1. Click **Start**, select **Programs**, and then click **Accessories** and **System Tools**. Click **Backup**.
2. Click the **Backup Wizard** button.
3. You see an introduction to the wizard. Click **Next**.

Next Step

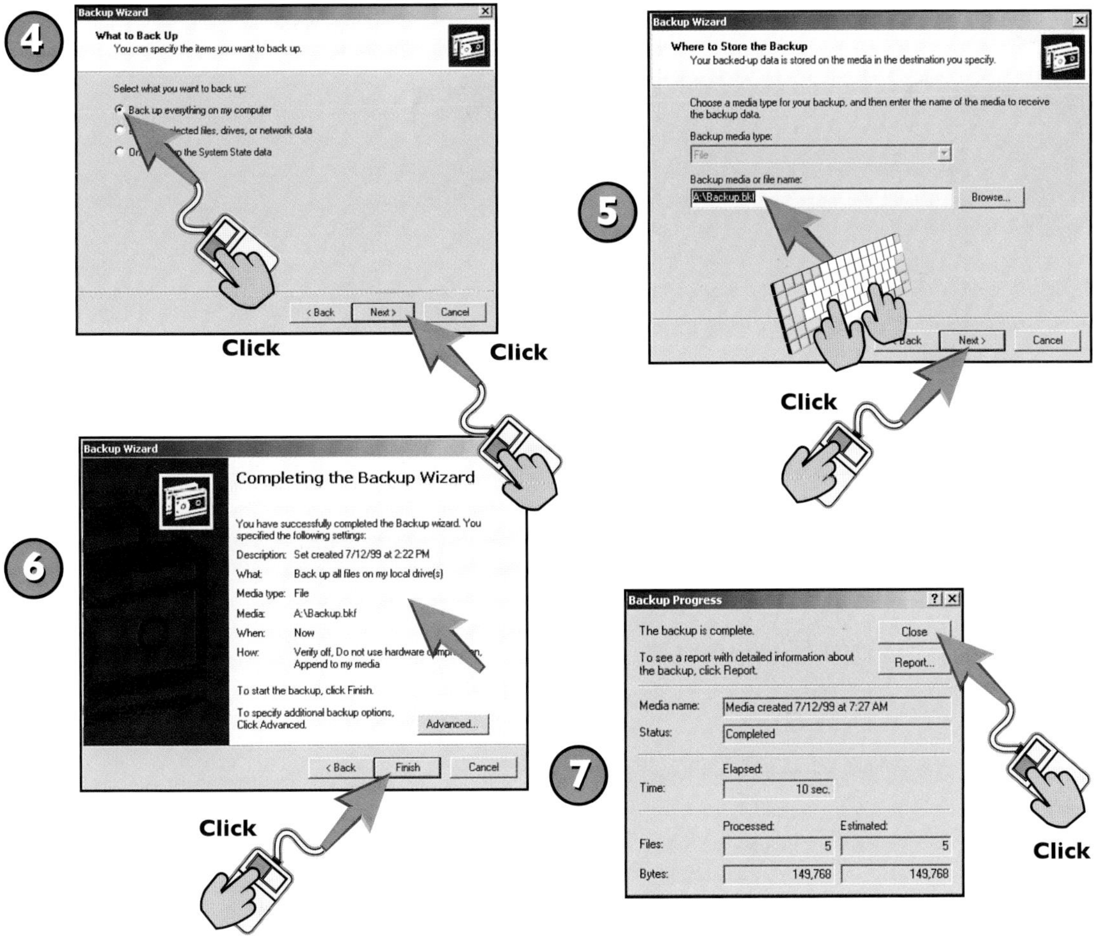

4 Select the **Back Up Everything on My Computer** radio button and then click the **Next** button.

5 Type the backup media or filename and click **Next**.

6 Review the backup information. Click **Finish**.

7 Follow the onscreen prompts, inserting additional disks if needed. After you get a message indicating that the backup is complete, click **Close**.

Advanced Options
To set advanced options, such as whether backup files are compared and verified and whether the backup data is compressed, click the **Advanced** button.

Checking Out the Progress
The Backup Progress dialog box displays the time elapsed, the files processed, and other information.

Browsing
You can click the **Browse** button to select a location for the backup.

Task 6: Backing Up Selected Files

You should set up a backup routine that suits you. You might want to back up daily, weekly, or monthly, depending on how often your data is changed and how difficult it would be to recover that data if it was lost. After you've done a complete backup, you can then back up selected files (all files that have changed, all files in a particular folder, all files of a certain type, and so on). This task explains how to select which files are backed up.

Scheduling Your Backups
You can schedule tasks such as Backup as a reminder to perform them on a regular basis. For information on scheduling tasks, see Task 10, "Scheduling Tasks," later in this part.

Backing Up System Files
To back up system files, select **Only Back Up the System State Data** and then perform the backup.

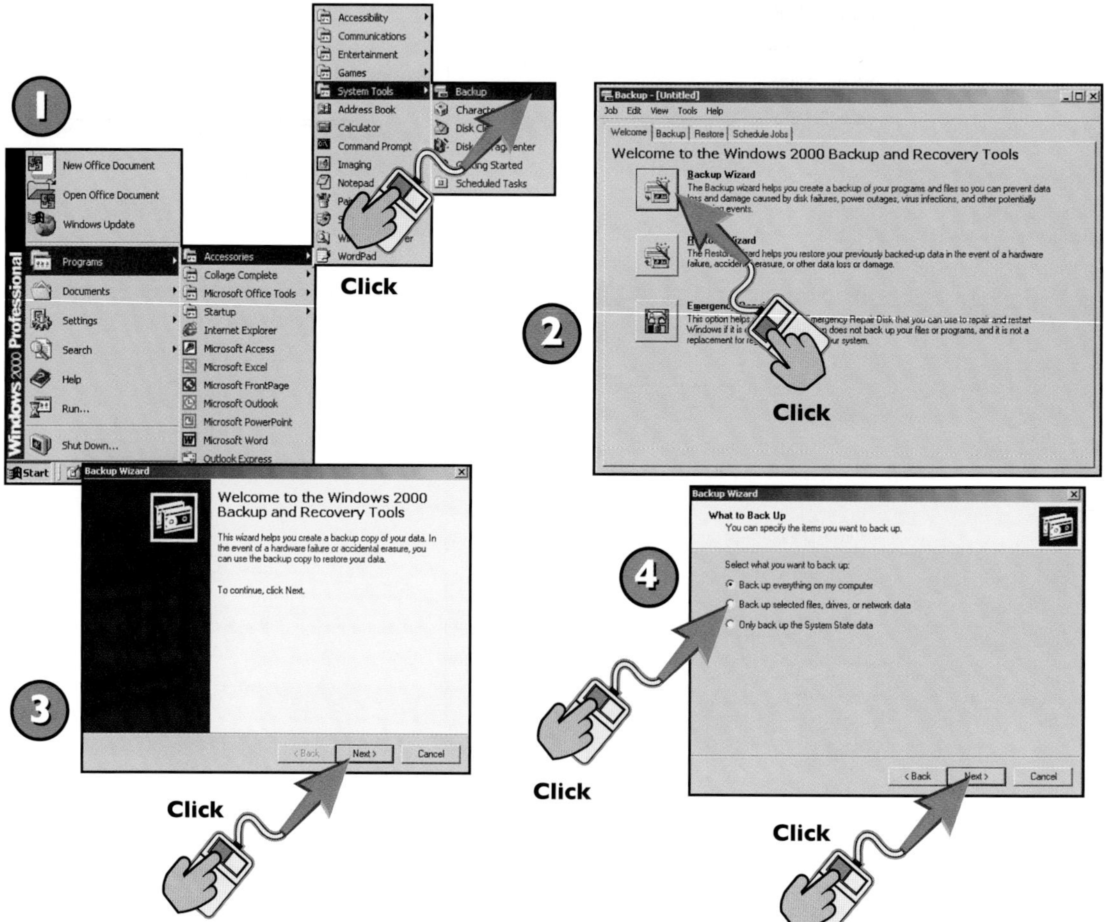

1. Click **Start**, select **Programs**, and then click **Accessories** and **System Tools**. Click **Backup**.
2. Click the **Backup Wizard** button.
3. You see an introduction to the wizard. Click **Next**.
4. Select the **Back Up Selected Files, Drives, or Network Data** radio button and then click **Next**.

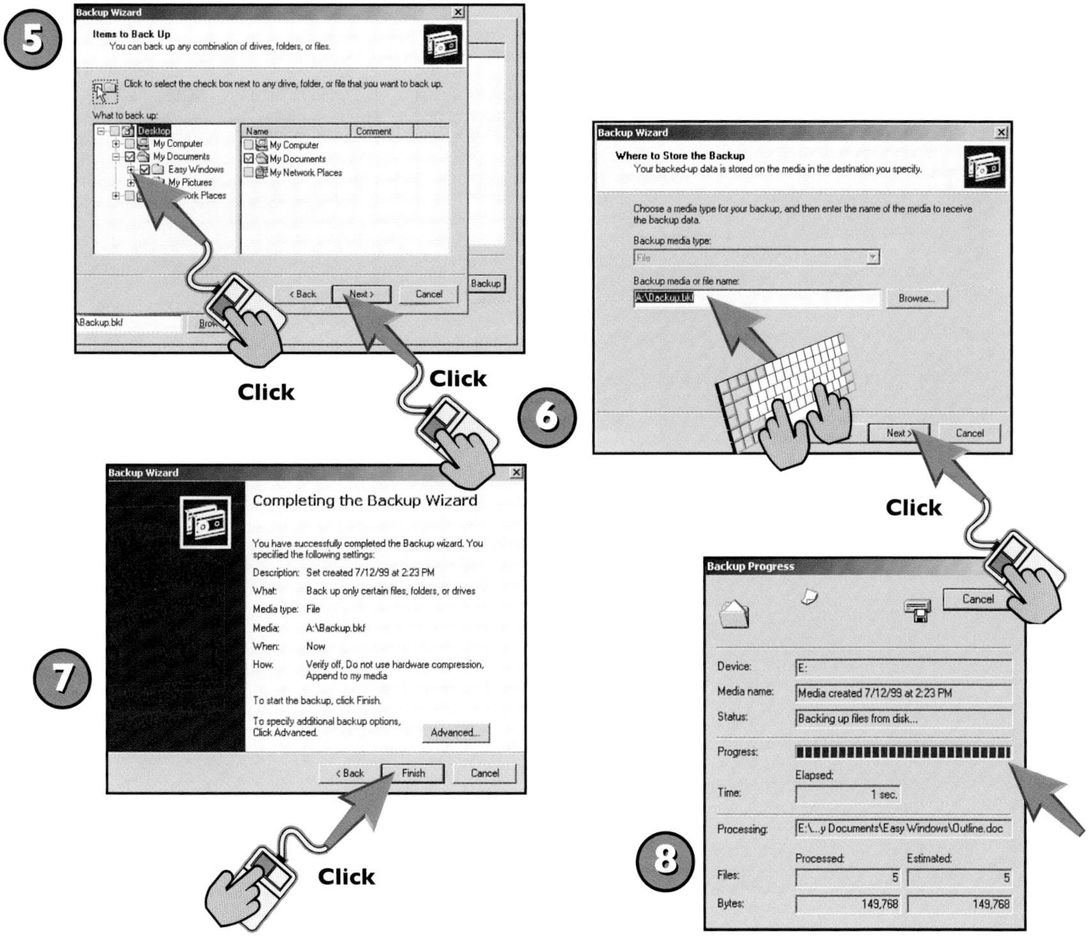

5 Check the items you want to back up and then click the **Next** button.

6 Type the backup media or filename and click **Next**.

7 Click the **Finish** button to start the backup.

8 Watch the backup's progress in the Backup Progress dialog box. After you get a message indicating that the backup is complete, click **OK**.

Expanding the Folder List

If necessary, click the plus signs next to the drive and folders to display the folder(s) you want to back up.

Task 7: Restoring a Backup

Start Here

Backup files are stored in a special format. You can't simply copy these files from the backup disks to your hard disk; you must use a special restore procedure. You can restore any files from any of your backup sets using the Windows 2000 Restore Wizard.

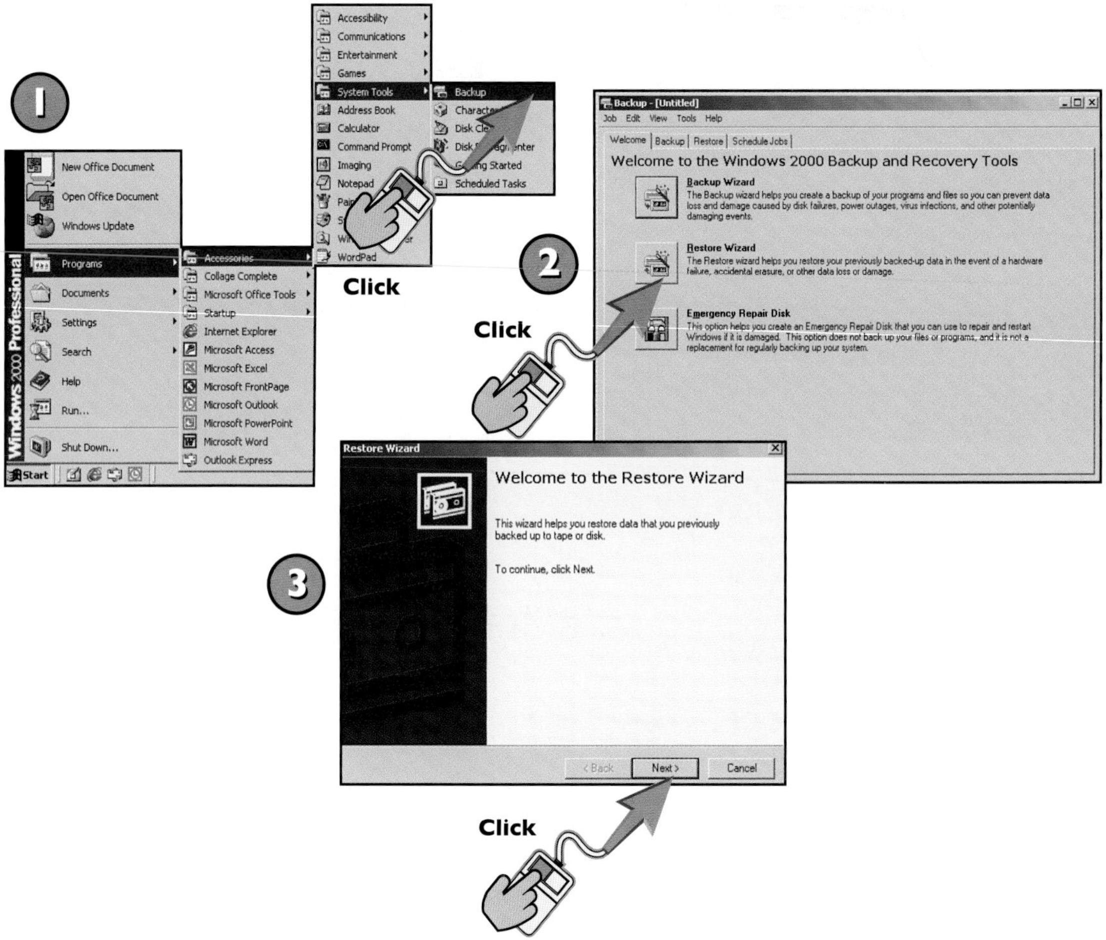

Starting Restore from Tools Tab

You can also start the backup program from the **Tools** tab in the Disk Properties dialog box.

Getting the Disks or Tapes

Before you start a restore, make sure you have the disks or tapes with the backup set.

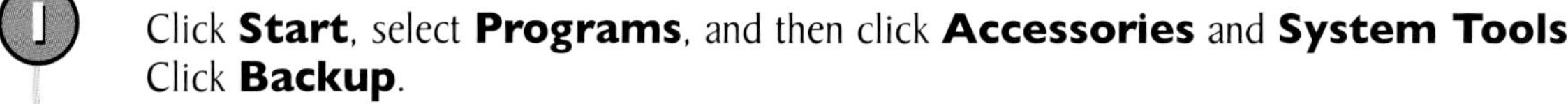

1. Click **Start**, select **Programs**, and then click **Accessories** and **System Tools**. Click **Backup**.

2. Click the **Restore Wizard** button.
3. Click **Next** after reviewing the introduction information.

Next Step

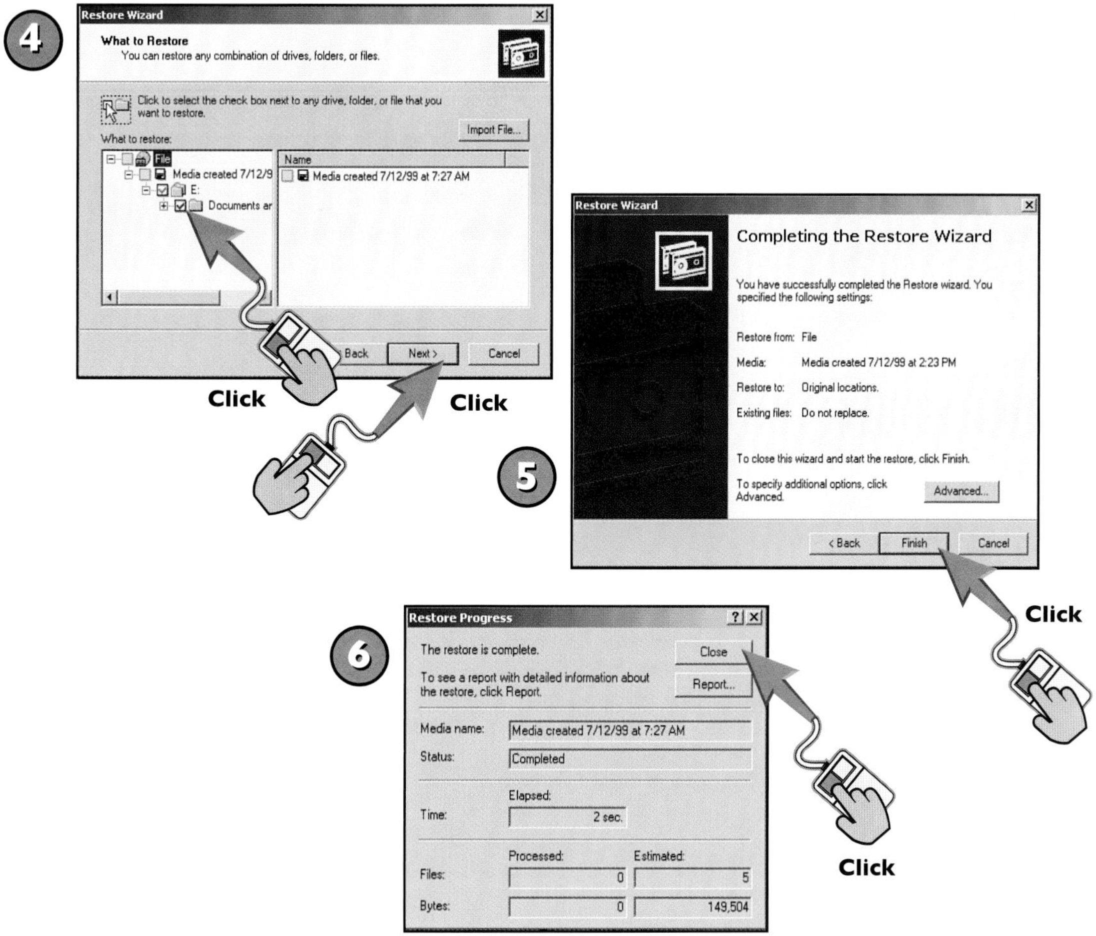

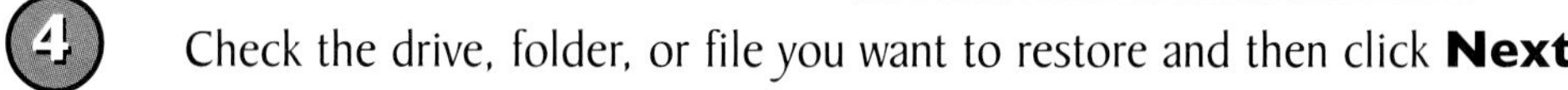

4 Check the drive, folder, or file you want to restore and then click **Next**.

5 Click the **Finish** button.

6 The files are restored; the progress of the restore operation is visible in the Restore Progress dialog box. When it is complete, click **Close**.

Selecting Restore Location

When you restore, you can elect to place the files in the same location or in a different location. Display the Restore Files To drop-down list and select where to restore the files.

Viewing the Progress

The Restore Progress dialog box displays the time elapsed, the files processed, compression statistics, and other information.

Restore Report

When the restore is complete, click the Report button to view a report, a log of the restore displayed as a Notepad file.

Task 8: Formatting a Disk

To be able to use a floppy disk, the disk must be formatted. Many disks sold are already formatted, but if they are not or if you want to reformat a disk, you can do so. Keep in mind that formatting a disk erases all the information on that disk.

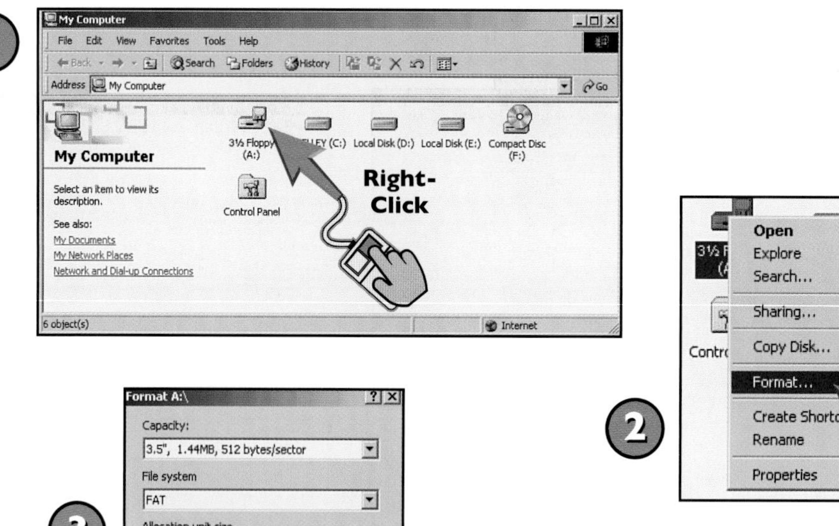

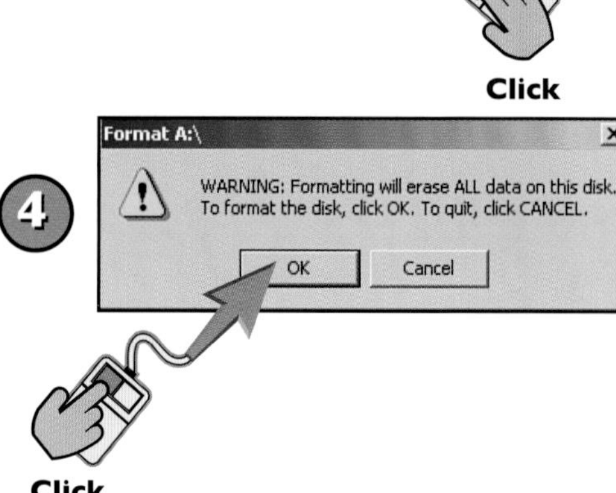

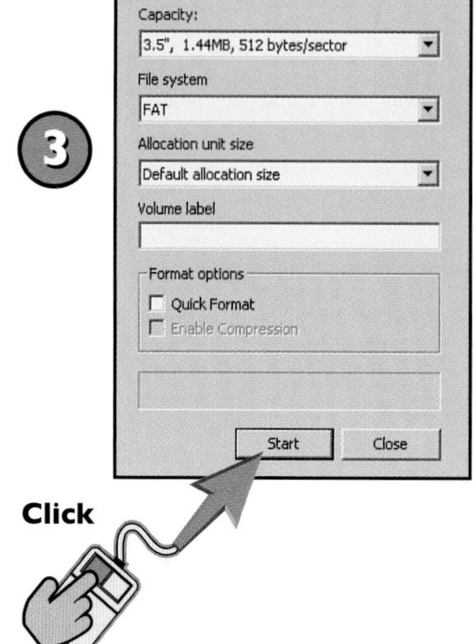

Don't Format Your Hard Drive

You want to format a hard disk only in the most extreme circumstances. Remember that formatting a disk erases all information on that disk. If you format your hard disk, everything on it will be wiped out.

Emergency Disk

For information on creating an emergency startup disk to use to start your system, see the next task.

1. After you've inserted a floppy disk into the drive, open the My Computer window and right-click the floppy disk drive.
2. Choose **Format** from the pop-up menu that appears.
3. Click **Start**.
4. Click the **OK** button to confirm the formatting. When the format is complete, click **OK** again.

Task 9: Creating an Emergency Disk

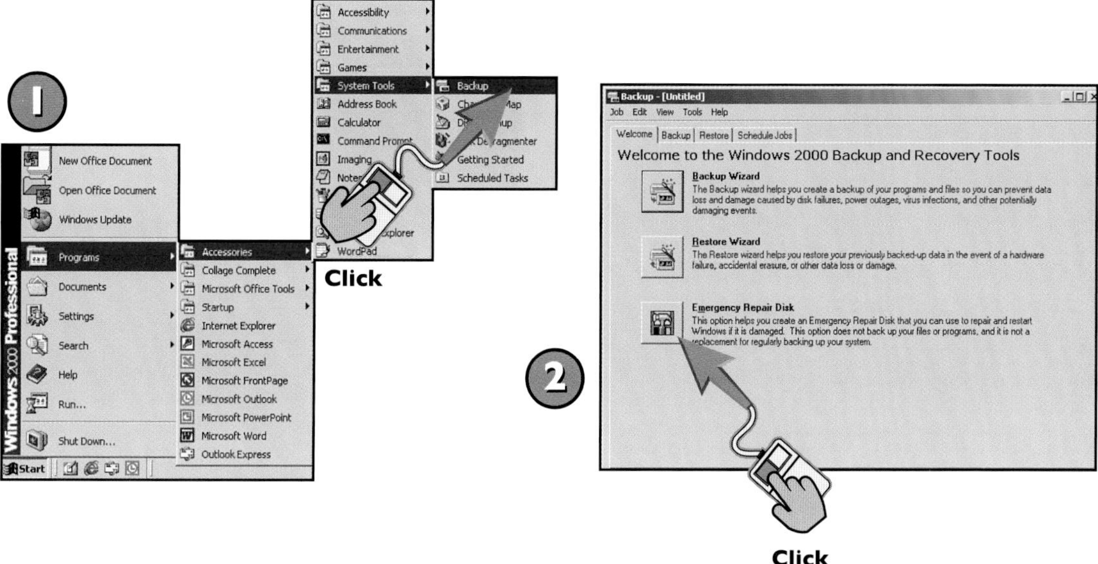

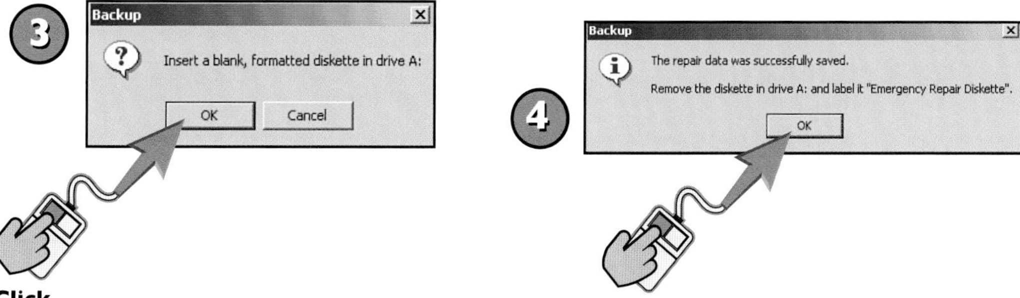

When you start up your system, it looks for the appropriate startup files on the floppy drive and then goes to the hard drive. This startup method ensures that if something is wrong with the hard drive, you can always start from a floppy disk. You can make an Emergency Repair Disk with the necessary files to keep for emergencies.

1. Click **Start**, select **Programs**, and then click **Accessories** and **System Tools**. Click **Backup**.
2. Click the **Emergency Repair Disk** button.
3. Insert a blank, formatted disk into the drive and click **OK**.
4. Click **OK** again when the disk is complete.

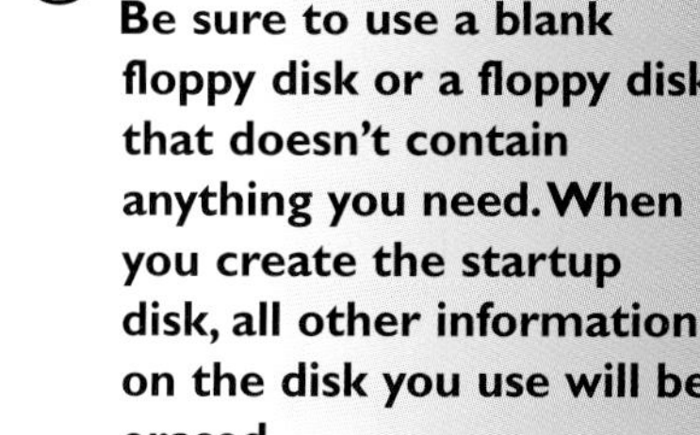

Using a Blank Disk
Be sure to use a blank floppy disk or a floppy disk that doesn't contain anything you need. When you create the startup disk, all other information on the disk you use will be erased.

Task 10: Scheduling Tasks

If you perform the same tasks repeatedly, or if you often forget to perform routine maintenance tasks, you can set up a schedule that instructs Windows to perform these tasks automatically.

Schedule Jobs Tab
You can also schedule jobs from the **Schedule Jobs** tab in the Backup program window.

Removing a Task
To remove a task from the list, display the list. Right-click the item and then choose **Delete.** Confirm the deletion by clicking the **Yes** button.

Changing the Scheduled Activity
To change the settings for the task (the time, interval, name, and so on), display the **Scheduled Task** list. Right-click the item you want to modify and then choose **Properties.** Make any changes to the tabs in the Properties dialog box and then click **OK.**

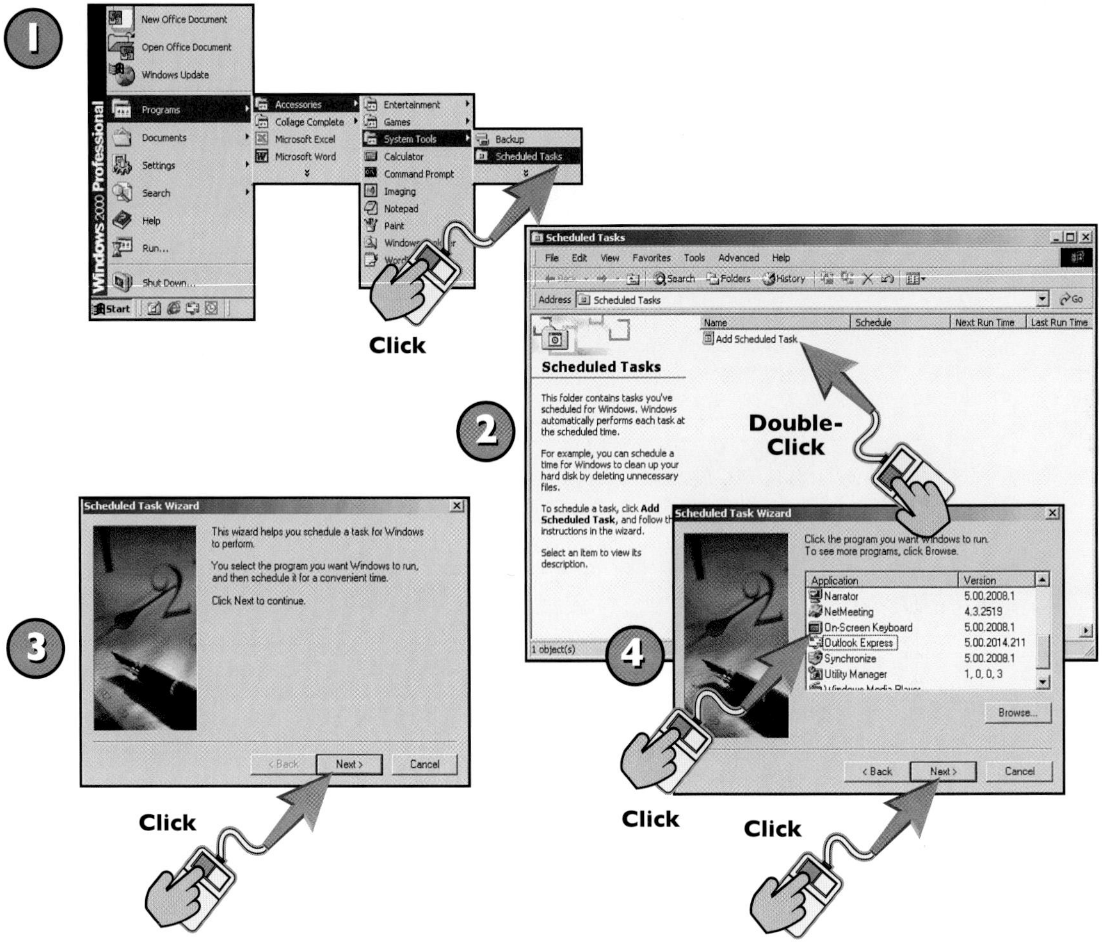

1. Click **Start**, choose **Programs**, select the **Accessories** folder, click **System Tools**, and then choose **Scheduled Tasks**.
2. Double-click the **Add Scheduled Task** list item.
3. Click the **Next** button.
4. Select the name of the program that you want Windows to run and then click the **Next** button.

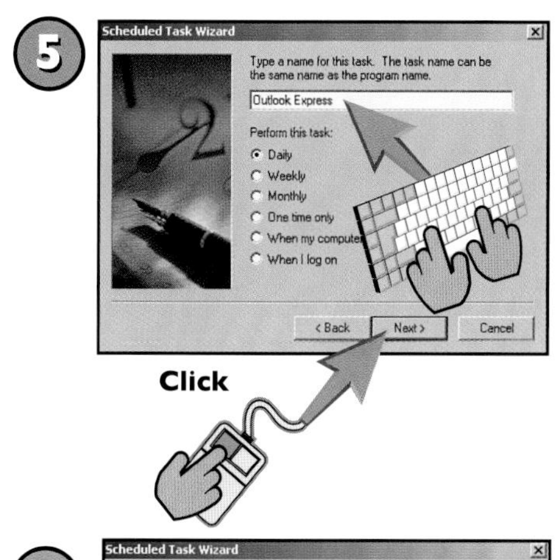

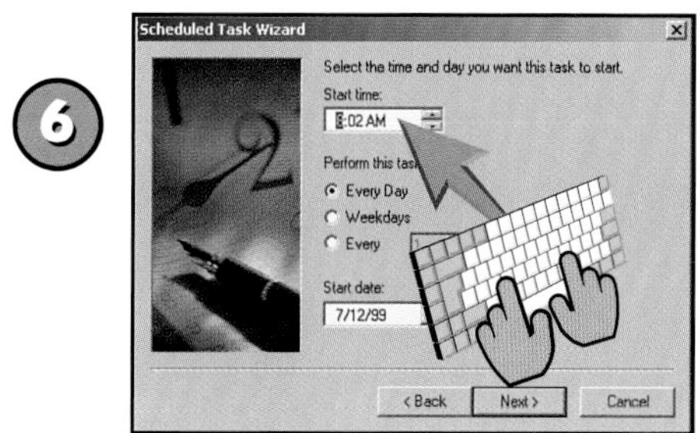

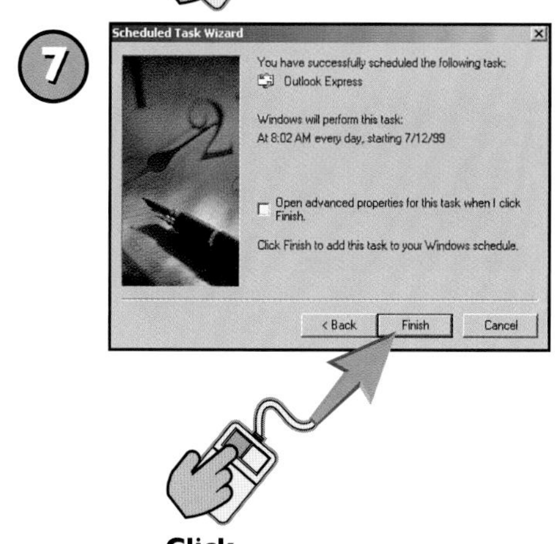

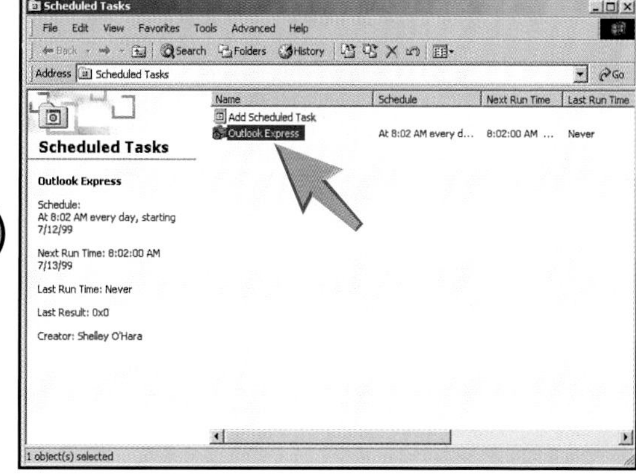

5. Replace or edit the default name. Then select how often to perform this task. Click **Next**.

6. If prompted, enter the time and date to start. (Depending on how often you select to perform this task, you might not have to enter the start time and date.)

7. Click the **Finish** button.

8. The task is added.

Prompted for Password?
You might be prompted to type your username and password for some tasks. If prompted, do so and click Next.

Task 11: Installing New Hardware

You can install a new printer, modem, or other hardware quickly and easily by using the Windows Add/Remove Hardware Wizard feature. Windows guides you through questions about the hardware, and if you do not know the answers, Windows can detect the type of hardware and install it with little input from you. Windows calls this handy feature *plug-and-play*. This task shows you how to install hardware.

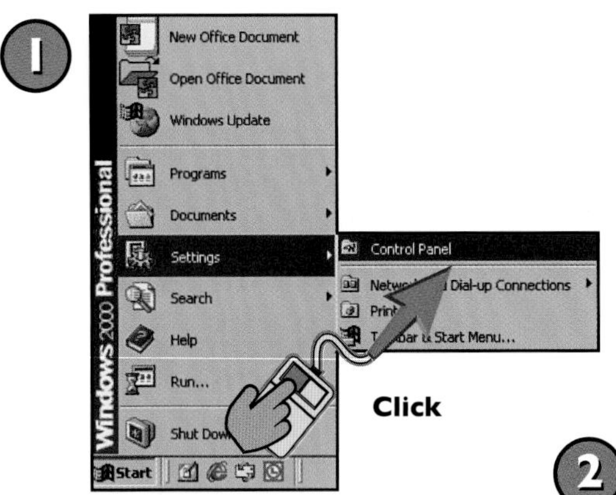

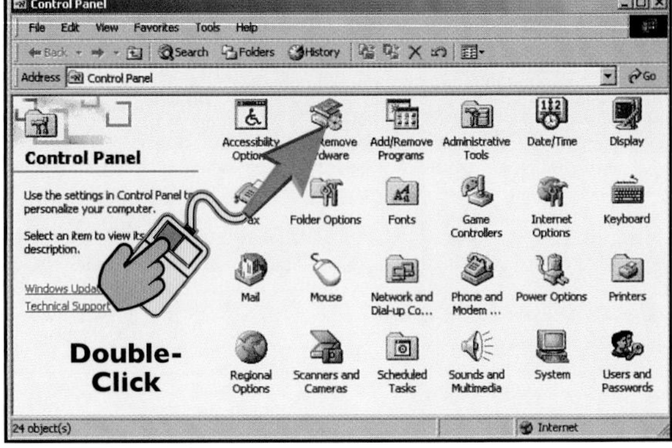

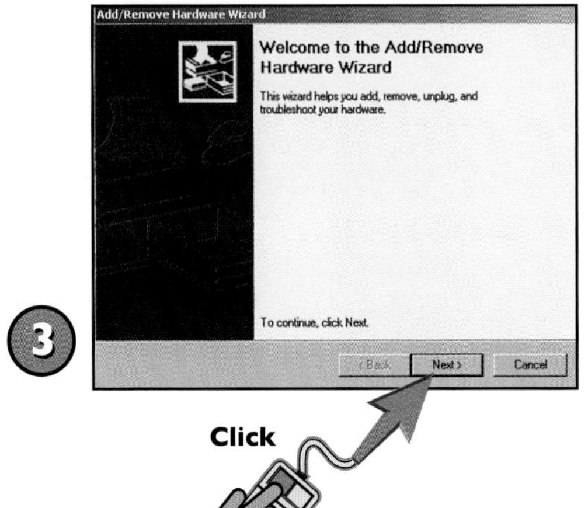

1 After you've connected the device to your computer, click **Start**, choose **Settings**, and select **Control Panel**.

2 Double-click the **Add/Remove Hardware** icon.

3 Click the **Next** button.

Connecting the New Hardware

Connect the new hardware device to your computer by following the instructions that came with the hardware device.

Canceling the Install

You can choose **Cancel** at any time to stop the process. Click **Back** to go back and change a selection you made.

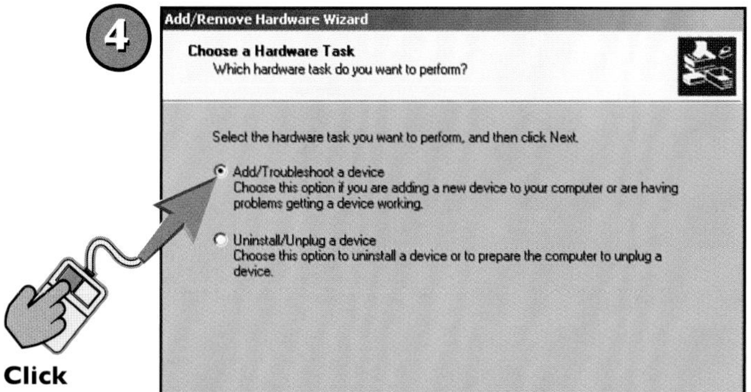

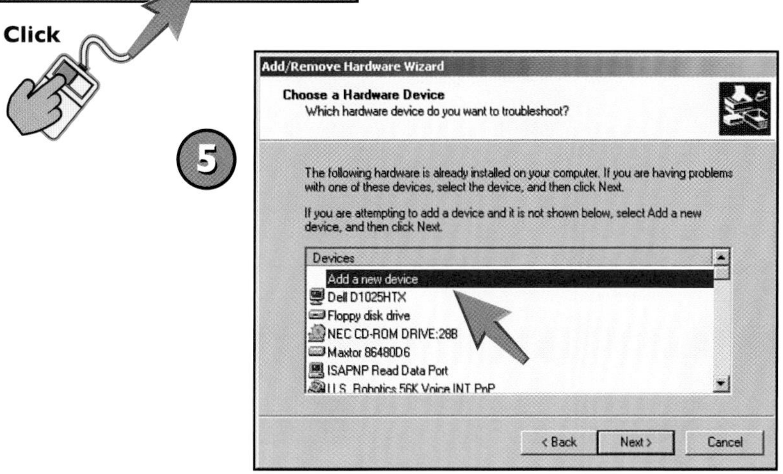

Click

Click

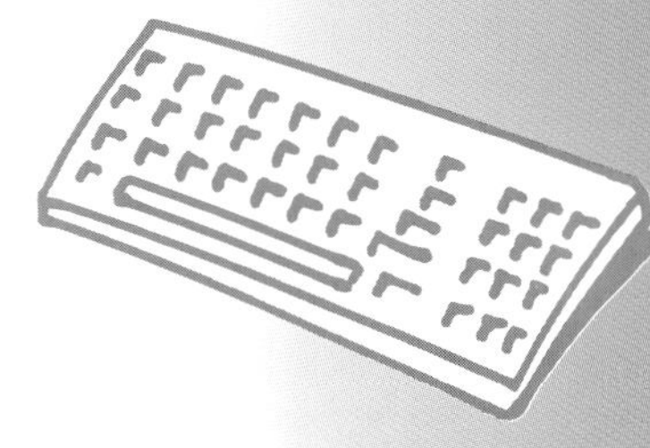

4 Select the **Add/Troubleshoot a Device** radio button. Click the **Next** button.

5 If Windows detected your hardware, it is set up automatically (you might be prompted with onscreen instructions). You'll see a list of all installed hardware.

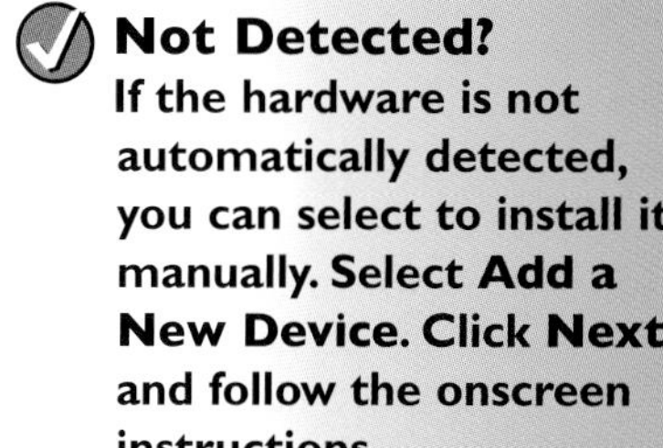

Not Detected?

If the hardware is not automatically detected, you can select to install it manually. Select Add a New Device. Click Next and follow the onscreen instructions.

Task 12: Troubleshooting Hardware

When you make changes to your system or add new hardware, you might have problems. New with Windows 2000 are troubleshooting features to help you pinpoint the problem. Windows 2000 will then suggest possible remedies.

Start Here

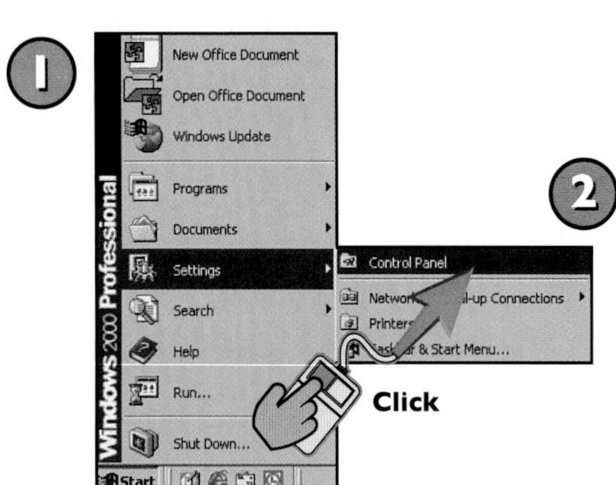

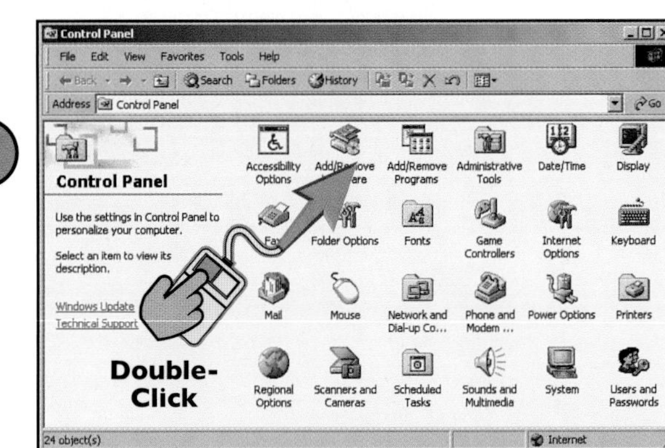

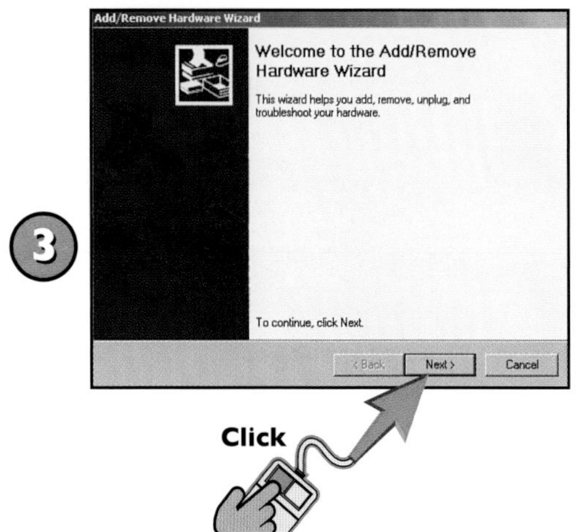

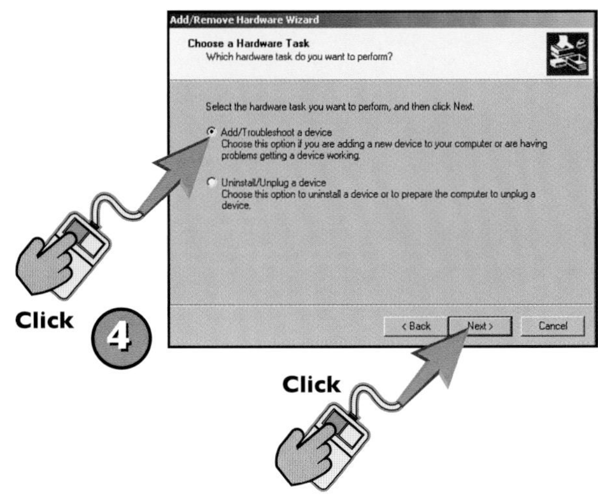

Properties Tabs
In addition to the Add/Remove Wizard, you can also find **Troubleshoot** buttons in many of the hardware properties dialog boxes. Click this button for another method of troubleshooting.

1. Click **Start**, choose **Settings**, and select **Control Panel**.
2. Double-click the **Add/Remove Hardware** icon.
3. Click the **Next** button.
4. Select the **Add/Troubleshoot a Device** radio button. Click the **Next** button.

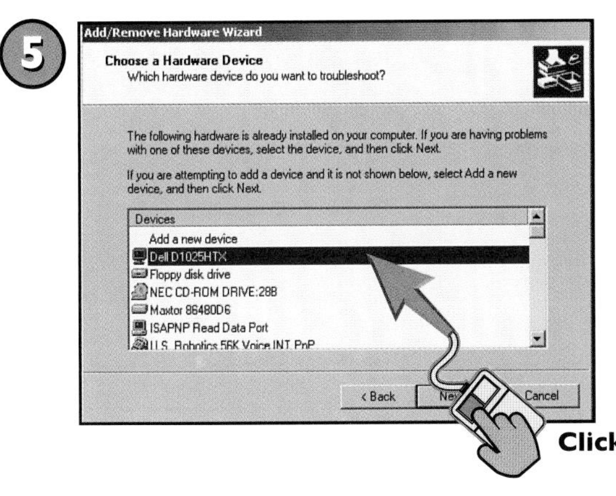

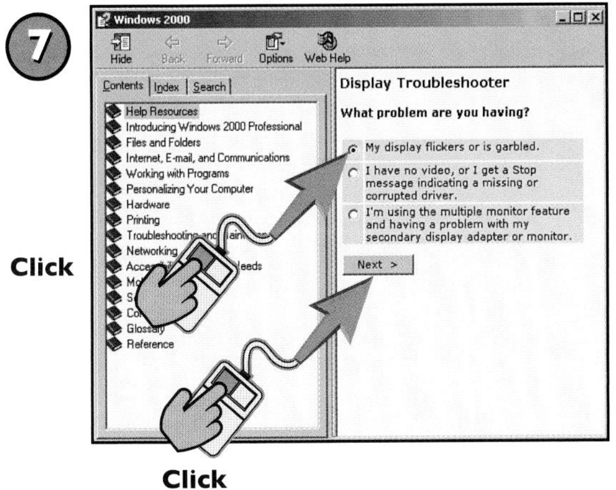

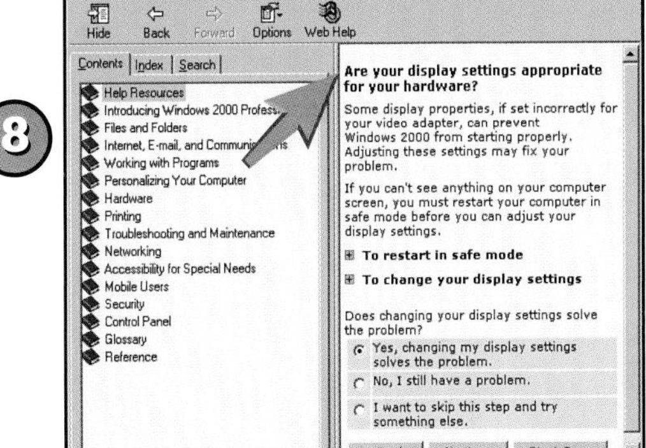

5 Windows displays a list of hardware installed on your system. Select the device to troubleshoot and click **Next**.

6 Click **Finish** to start the troubleshooter.

7 Select the problem and then click **Next**.

8 Follow the instructions in the help troubleshooter.

Task 13: Displaying System Properties

When you are troubleshooting, you sometimes need to display information about your system. You can find this information in the Properties dialog box for My Computer.

Start Here

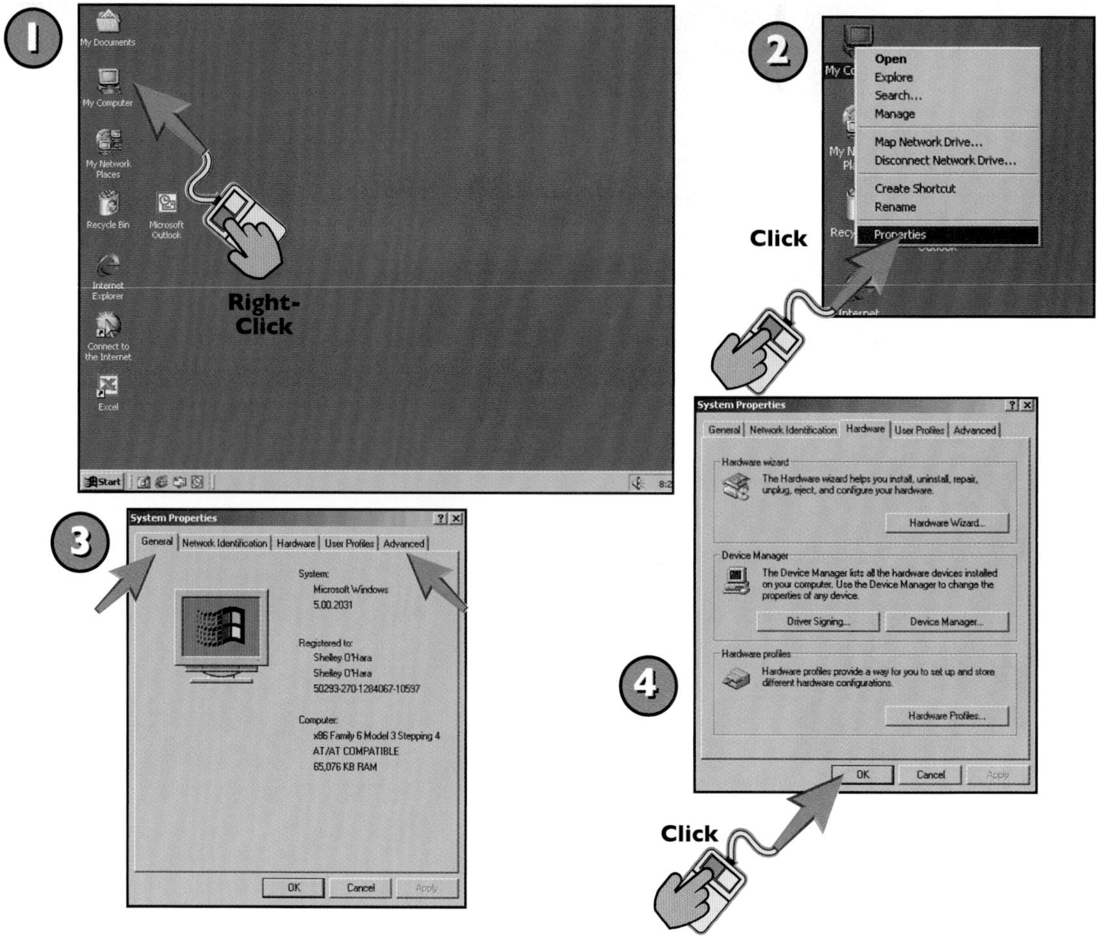

Right-Click

Click

Click

1. Right-click the **My Computer** icon.
2. Choose **Properties** from the pop-up menu that opens.
3. You see the General tab. Click any of the other tabs to display specific system information.
4. When you are finished, click the **OK** button.

Task 14: Displaying the Task Manager

Start Here

1

2

3

4

Click

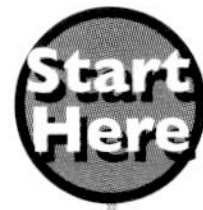

You can use the Task Manager to view a list of running programs, shut down stuck programs, and also view system performance.

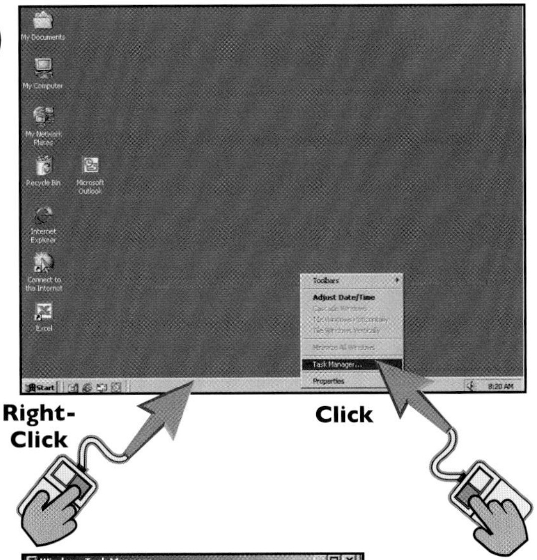

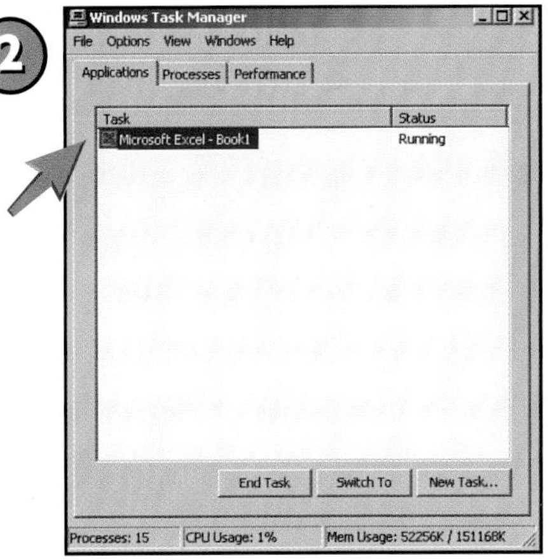

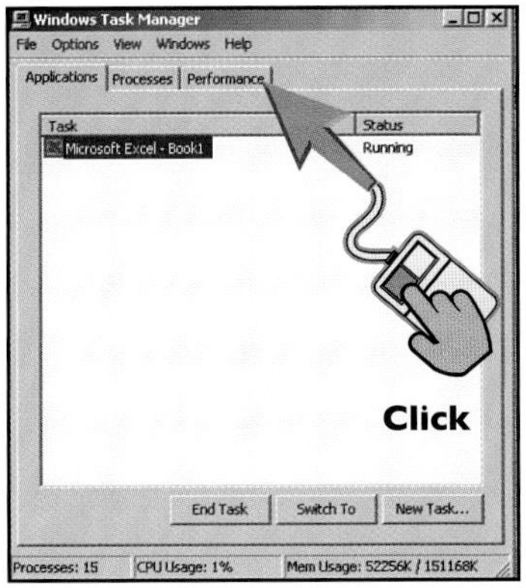

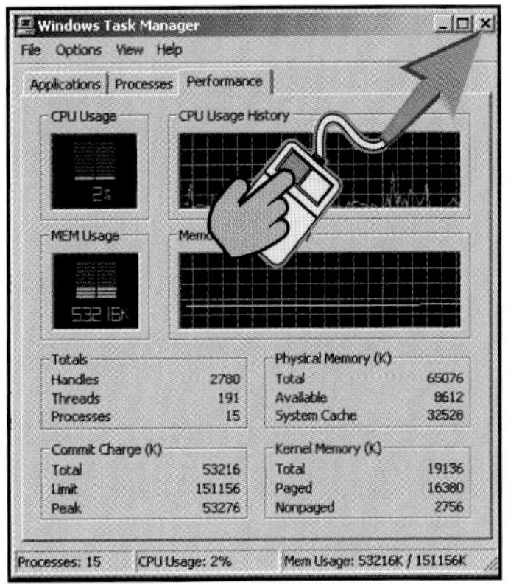

1. Right-click a blank part of the taskbar and select **Task Manager**.
2. You see the Task Manager. The Applications tab lists all running programs.
3. To view performance statistics, click the **Performance** tab.
4. The Performance tab displays data about CPU and memory usage. When you are finished reviewing this information, click the **Close** (×) button.

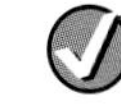

Shutting Down a Program
To shut down a program, select it in the task list (on the **Applications** tab) and then click **End Task.**

End Task

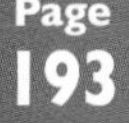

PART 9

Connecting to Online Services and the Internet

If you have a modem and an Internet connection, you can venture beyond your PC to resources available from online services, such as America Online and MSN, or from the Internet. Windows 2000 includes Internet Explorer 5, a Web browser that offers you complete and convenient browsing of the Internet. As with any browser software, you can use Internet Explorer to view World Wide Web pages, to search for specific topics, and to download and upload files. In addition to browsing the Web, you can use the Internet Explorer 5 mail program, Microsoft Outlook Express, to exchange email messages with others who are connected to the Internet. You can also use Outlook Express to participate in newsgroups.

Tasks

Task 1: Setting Up for the Internet

To explore the Internet, you must have a modem and an Internet connection. You can get this connection through online providers such as America Online or MSN, or you can get an account from an independent Internet service provider (ISP). Before you can take advantage of all the benefits of the Internet, you have to get your Internet connection set up. Windows makes it easy to set up by providing a wizard that guides you through the steps.

No Account?

If you do not have an ISP and you want Windows to find one for you, choose **I Want to Sign Up for a New Internet Account** and then follow the wizard's directions.

Getting Connected via a LAN

These steps show getting connected via a phone line. If you are connecting through a LAN, the steps will vary.

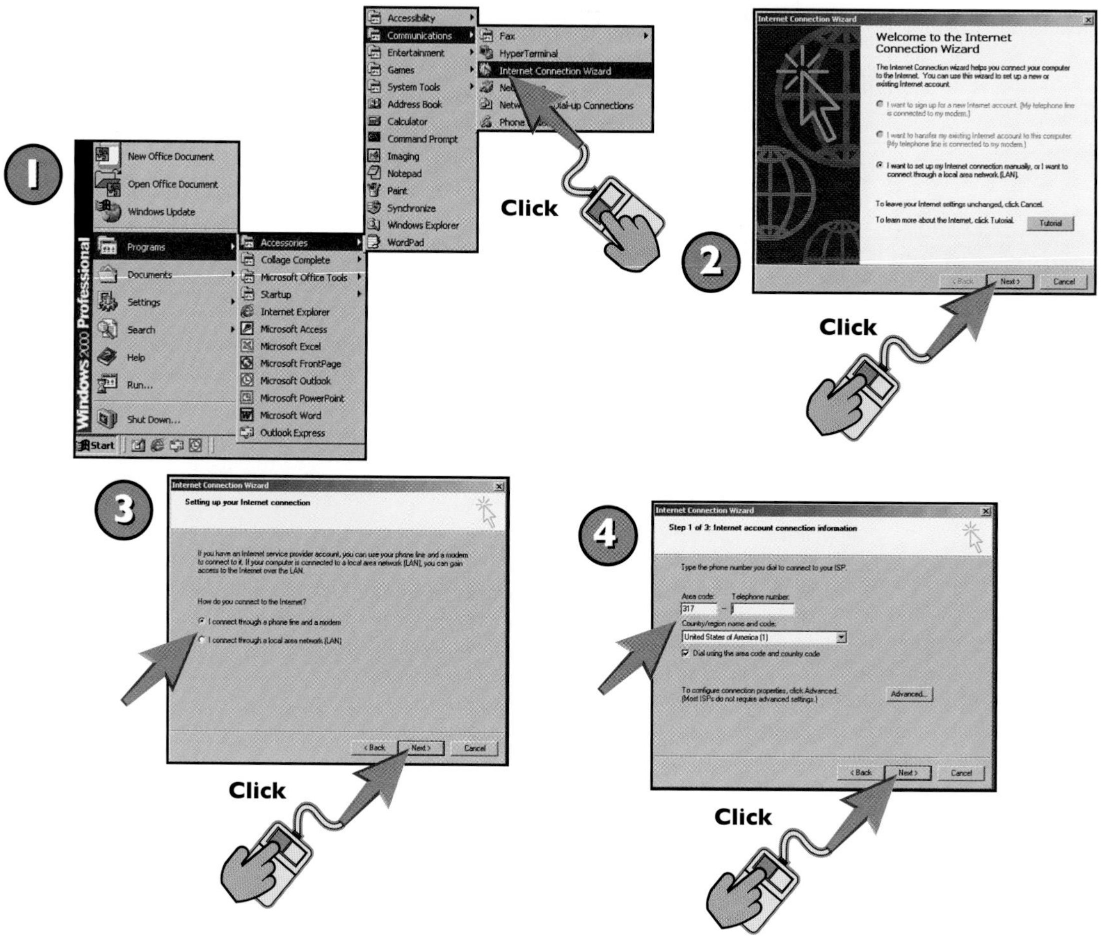

1. Click **Start**, choose **Programs**, select **Accessories**, choose **Communications**, and then click **Internet Connection Wizard**.
2. Select how you want to set up your account (new or existing) and then click **Next**.
3. Specify how you want to get connected—through your phone line or through your LAN—and then click **Next**.
4. Complete the remaining steps, providing information for your setup and ISP.

Next Step

5 Type your username and the password assigned to you by your ISP and then click **Next**.

6 Type a name for your dial-up connection (you can use any name you want) and then click **Next**.

7 Select **Yes** if you want to set up your Internet mail account and follow the steps for setting up this account. (Click **Next** to move from step to step.)

8 Select **Yes** to set up a news account. Complete the onscreen instructions, clicking **Next** to move from one dialog box to the next. Click **Finish** to complete the setup.

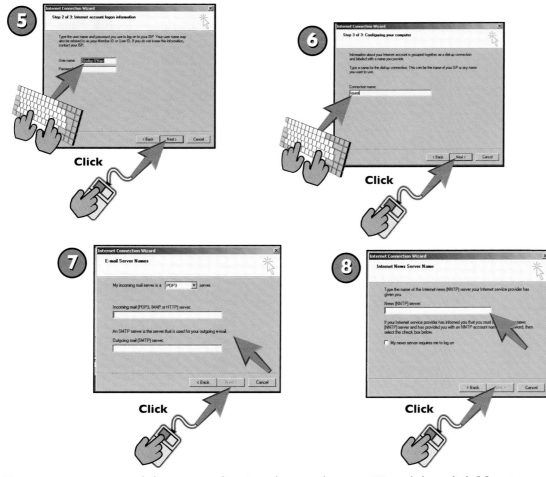

Finding an Internet Service Provider

You can find local ISPs in the Yellow Pages. There are also nationwide providers, such as AT&T WorldNet, MindSpring, and EarthLink. Be sure to compare pricing and services when selecting an ISP.

Going Back a Step

If you need to change one of your selections, click the Back button to go back through your choices.

Setting Up an Internet Mail Account

If you click Yes in step 7, you will be prompted to type your name, email address, and mail server information (you can get this information from your Internet service provider).

Setting Up an Internet News Account

If you click Yes in step 8, you will be prompted to type your name, email address, and news server information (you can get this information from your Internet service provider).

Task 2: Starting Internet Explorer

After you've gotten your Internet connection set up, you can start Internet Explorer and browse the Internet. To start, take a look at the different tools for browsing the Web.

1

Double-Click

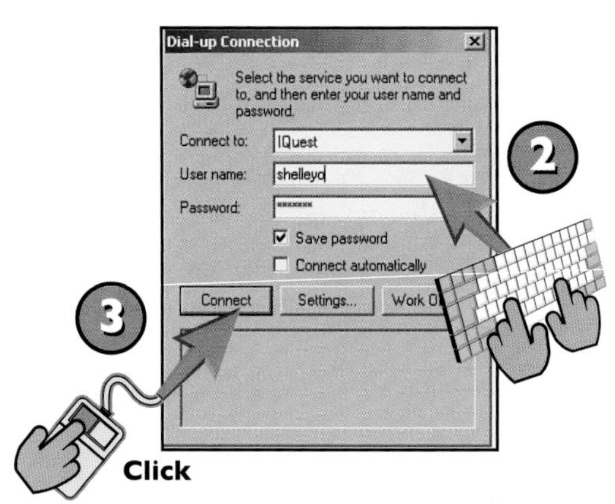

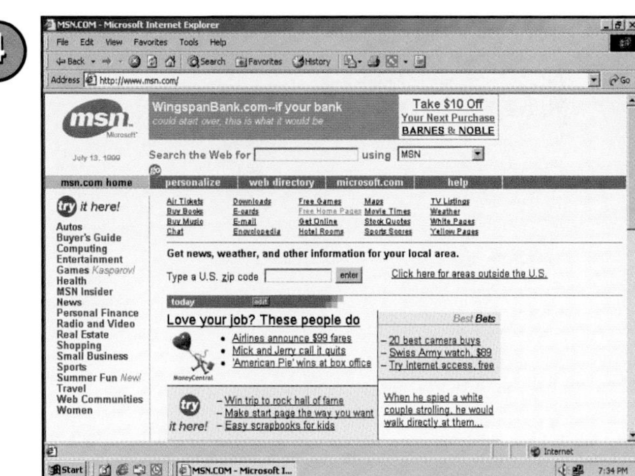

Going Home

You can go to the start page (called your home page) at any time by clicking the **Home** button.

Problems?

If you have problems connecting—the line is busy, for instance—try again. If you continue to have problems, check with your ISP.

1. Double-click the **Internet Explorer** icon.
2. Enter your username and password (some information might have been completed for you).
3. Click the **Connect** button.
4. Windows connects to your ISP. The Internet Explorer window appears, and you see your start page (in my case, the Microsoft or MSN home page).

Task 3: Typing an Address

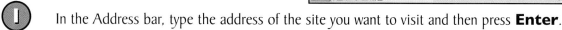

1 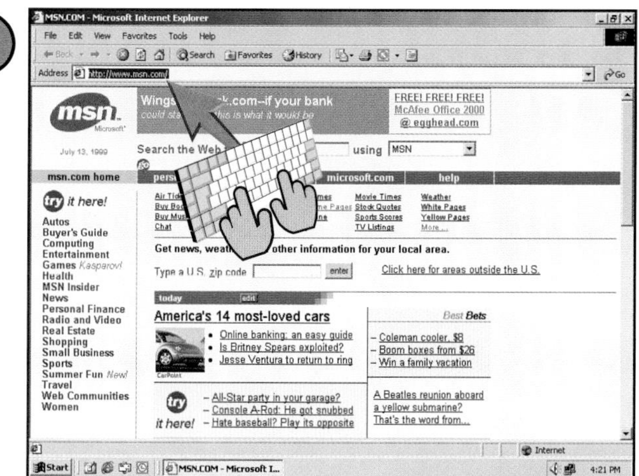

2 

Typing a site's address is the fastest way to get to that site. An address, sometimes called a *URL* (uniform resource locator), consists of the protocol (usually **http://** for Web pages) and the domain name (something like **www.cbssportsline**). The domain name might also include a path (a list of folders) to the document. The extension (usually **.com**, **.net**, **.gov**, **.edu**, or **.mil**) indicates the type of site (commercial, network resources, government, educational, or military, respectively). You can find addresses in advertisements, articles, books, and so on.

1. In the Address bar, type the address of the site you want to visit and then press **Enter**.
2. Internet Explorer displays the page associated with the URL you typed.

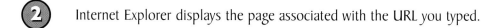

Error Message?
If you get an error message, make sure you typed the address correctly. You must type the periods, colons, slashes, and other characters in the exact order.

Task 4: Browsing with Links and Toolbar Buttons

Information on the Internet is easy to browse because documents contain *links* to other pages, documents, and sites. Simply click a link to view the associated page. You can jump from link to link, exploring all types of topics and levels of information. Links are also called *hyperlinks* and usually appear underlined and sometimes in a different color. In addition to using links, you can also use the buttons in the toolbar to navigate from page to page.

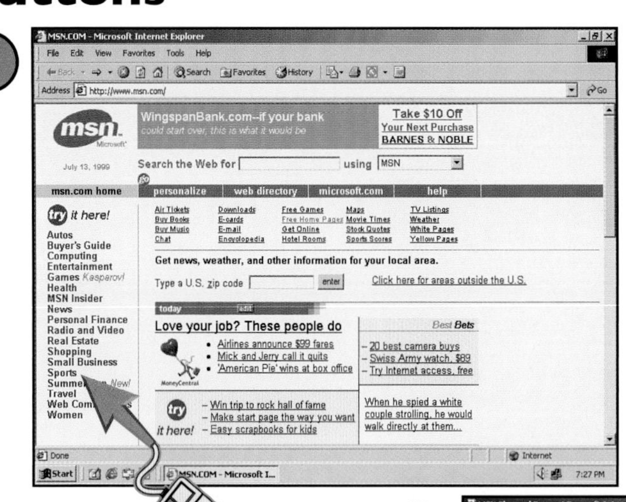

1. Click a link. For instance, on this page, click **Sports**.

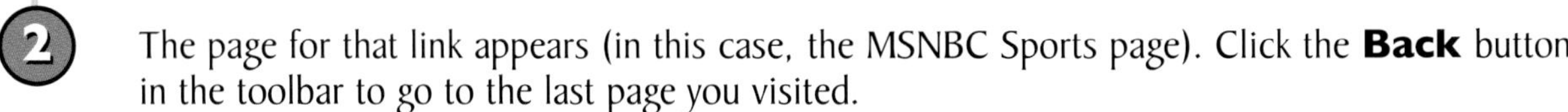

2. The page for that link appears (in this case, the MSNBC Sports page). Click the **Back** button in the toolbar to go to the last page you visited.

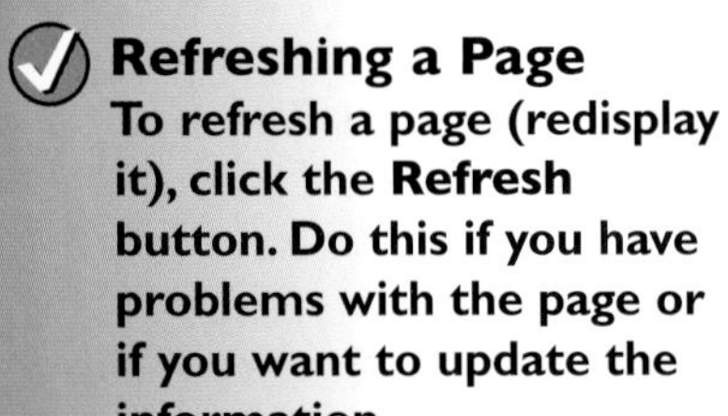

Refreshing a Page

To refresh a page (redisplay it), click the Refresh button. Do this if you have problems with the page or if you want to update the information.

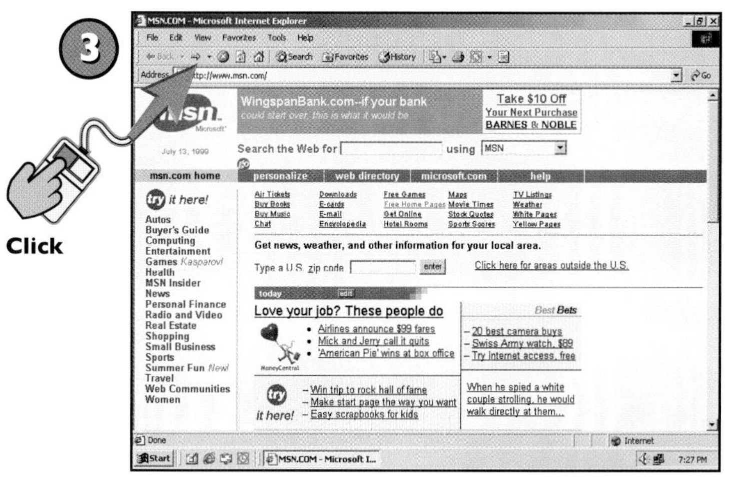

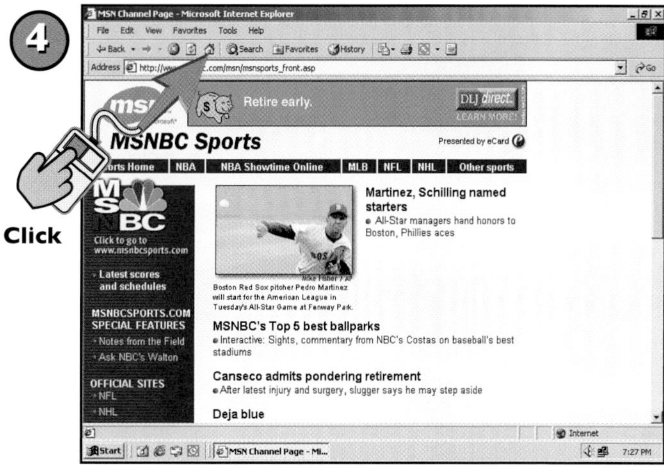

3 Click the **Forward** button to move forward through the pages you've already visited.

4 To return to the Microsoft start page, click the **Home** button in the toolbar.

Images Can Be Links
Images can serve as links. You can tell whether an image (or text) is a link by placing your mouse pointer on it; if the pointer changes into a pointing hand, the image (or text) is a link.

Stop!
To stop the display of a page, click the **Stop** button.

Forward Button Not Available?
You must have clicked the **Back** button before you can use the **Forward** button.

Task 5: Adding a Site to Your Favorites List

When you find a site that you especially like, you might want a quick way to return to it without having to browse from link to link or having to remember the address. Fortunately, Internet Explorer enables you to build a list of favorite sites and to access those sites by clicking them in the list.

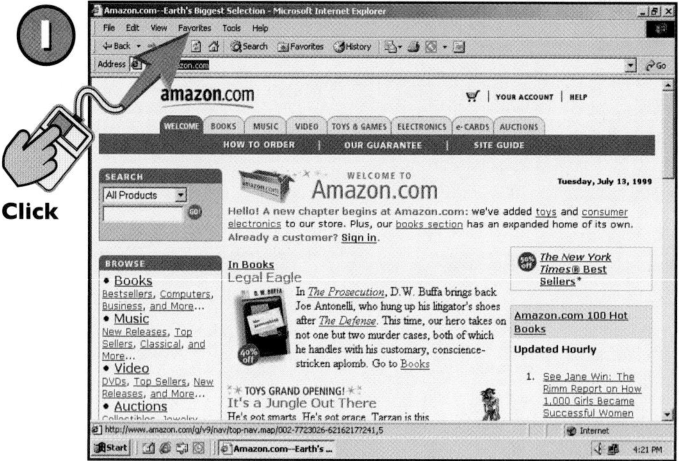

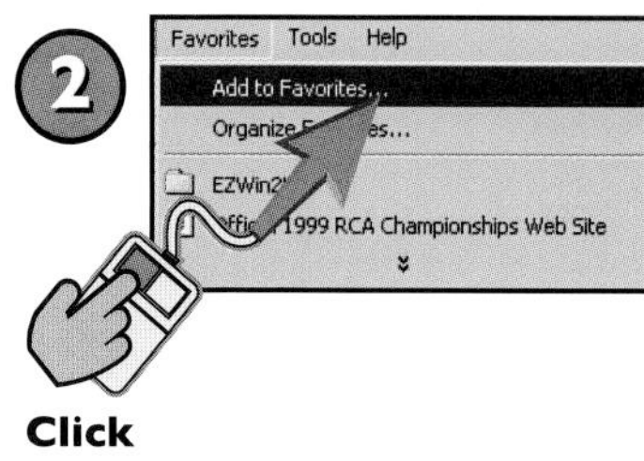

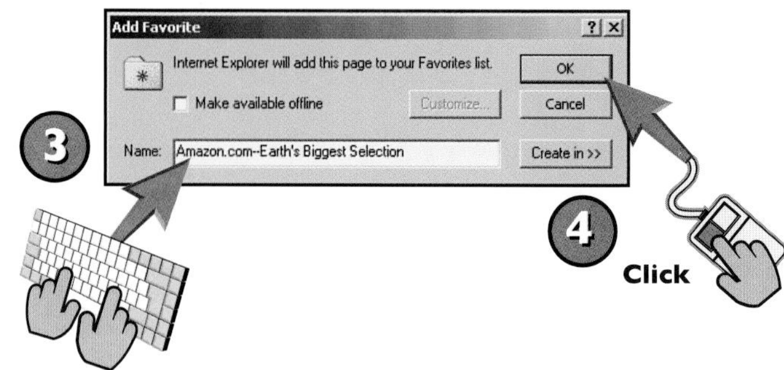

Reviewing Offline

You can review site content offline. To do so, check the **Make Available Offline** button. To customize how the content is downloaded, click the **Customize** button and follow the steps in the Offline Favorite Wizard.

Removing a Site from the List

To remove a site from your favorite list, choose **Favorites** and then click **Organize Favorites.** Select the site you want to delete and then click the **Delete** button. Confirm the deletion by clicking the **Yes** button.

1. After you've opened the Web site that you want to add to your favorites list, click the **Favorites** option in the menu bar (do not click the Favorites button in the toolbar).
2. Click the **Add to Favorites** command.
3. Type a name for the page or edit the default name.
4. Click **OK**.

Task 6: Going to a Site in Your Favorites List

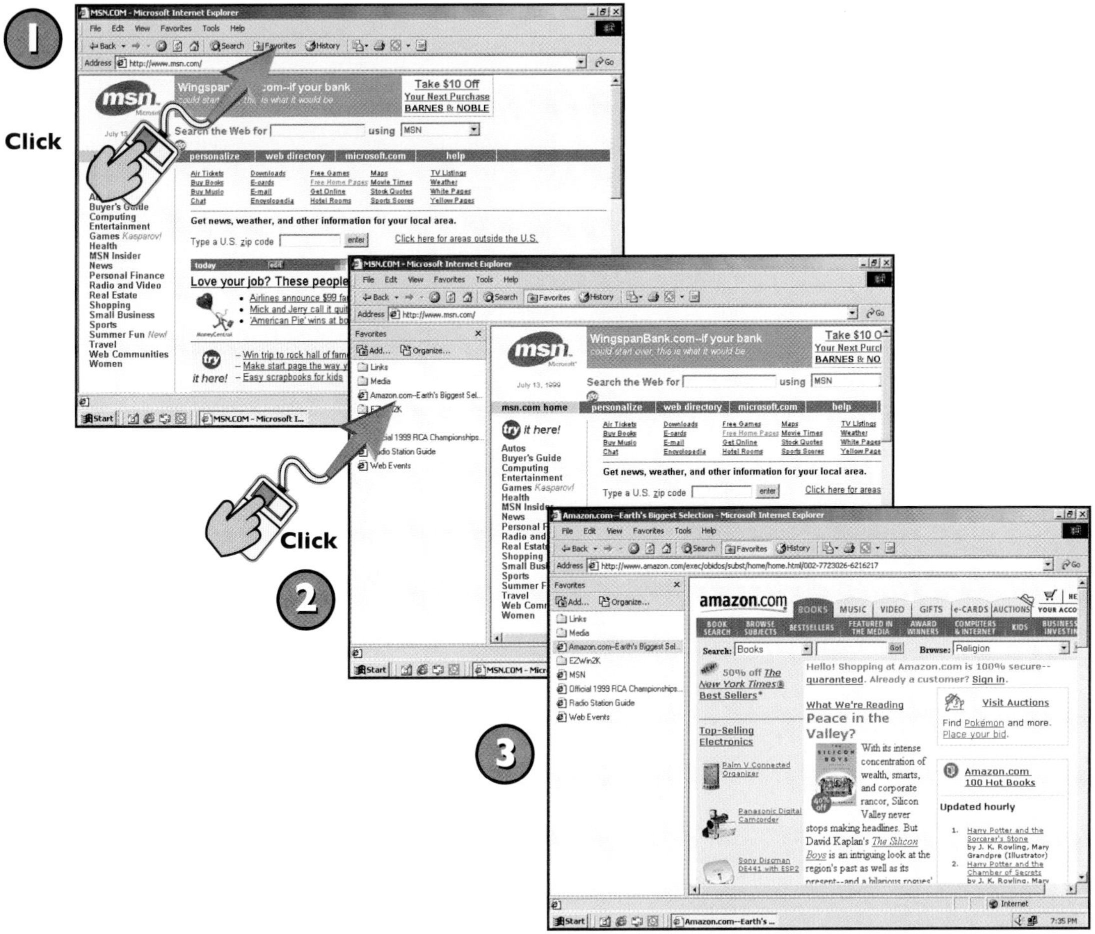

After you have added a site to your favorites list, you can easily reach that site by displaying the list and selecting the site.

Click

Click

1 Click the **Favorites** button on the toolbar.

2 The pane on the left side of the screen contains your favorites list, whereas the right pane contains the current page. Click the site in the left side that you want to visit.

3 Internet Explorer displays the site you selected from the favorites list.

Closing the List

To close the Favorites pane, click its **Close** (×) button.

Using the Menu

You can also reach a site by opening the **Favorites** menu, and you can set up folders to group sites together. All of the sites and folders are listed. Simply select the folder you want (if necessary) and then select the site you want. For more information on adding folders, see Task 7, "Rearranging Your Favorites List."

Task 7: Rearranging Your Favorites List

If you add several sites to your favorites list, it might become difficult to use. You can organize the list by grouping similar sites together in a folder. You can add new folders and move sites from one folder to another.

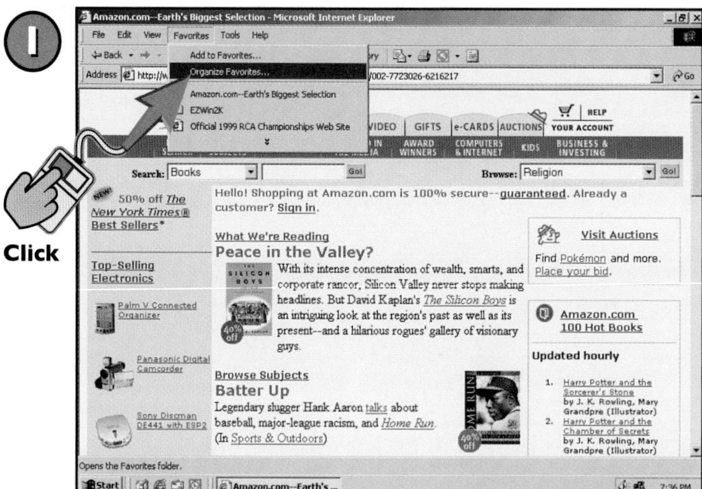

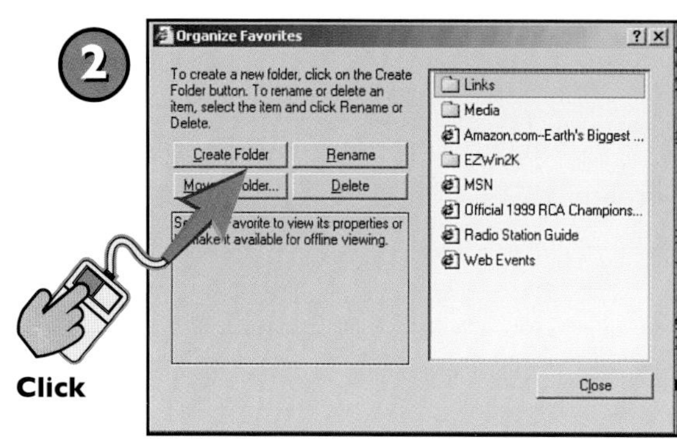

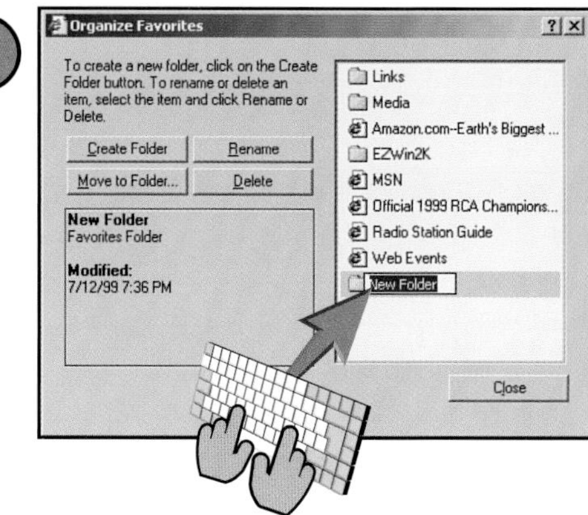

1. Click the **Favorites** option in the menu bar and then choose **Organize Favorites**.

2. To create a new folder, click the **Create Folder** button.

3. Type a name for the folder and press **Enter**.

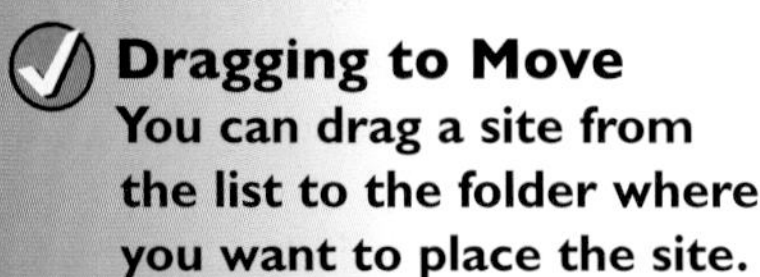

Dragging to Move
You can drag a site from the list to the folder where you want to place the site.

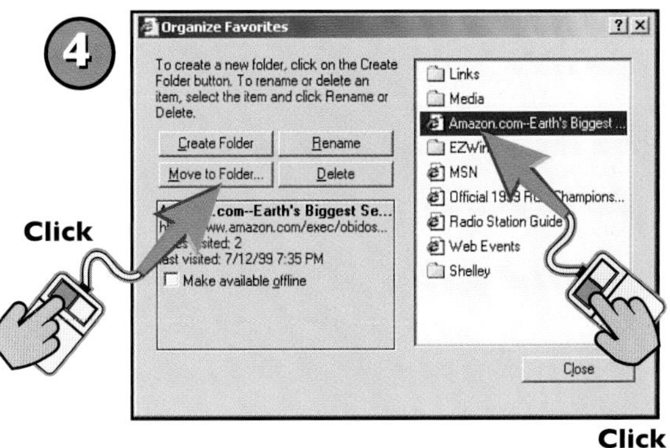

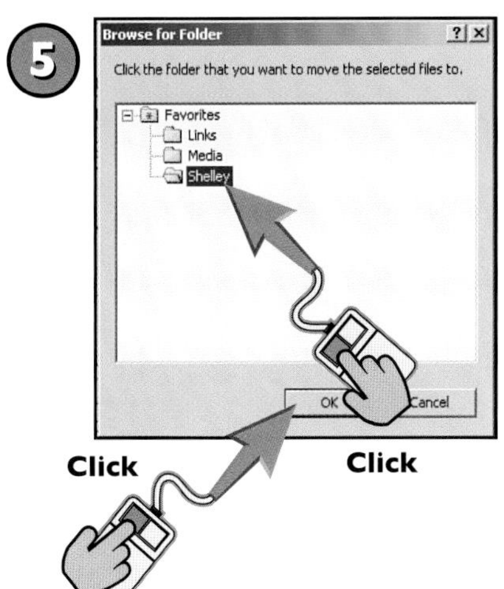

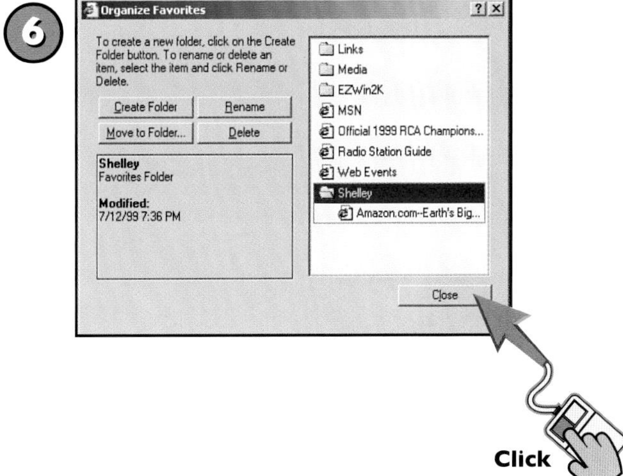

4 To move a site from one folder to another, select the site and then click the **Move to Folder** button.

5 Select the folder to which you want to move the site and then click **OK**.

6 The site is moved. When you are finished moving all the sites you want to rearrange, click the **Close** button.

Deleting a Site
To delete a site, select it and click the Delete button. Click the Yes button to confirm the deletion.

Renaming a Site
To rename a site, select the site and click the Rename button. Type a new name and press Enter.

Task 8: Searching the Internet

The Internet includes many, many, *many* different sites. Looking for the site you want by browsing can be like looking for a needle in a haystack. Instead, you can search for a topic and find all sites related to that topic. To search, you select to use either a search engine or a search index. The basic procedure is the same, but the results and special options for each search engine/index will vary.

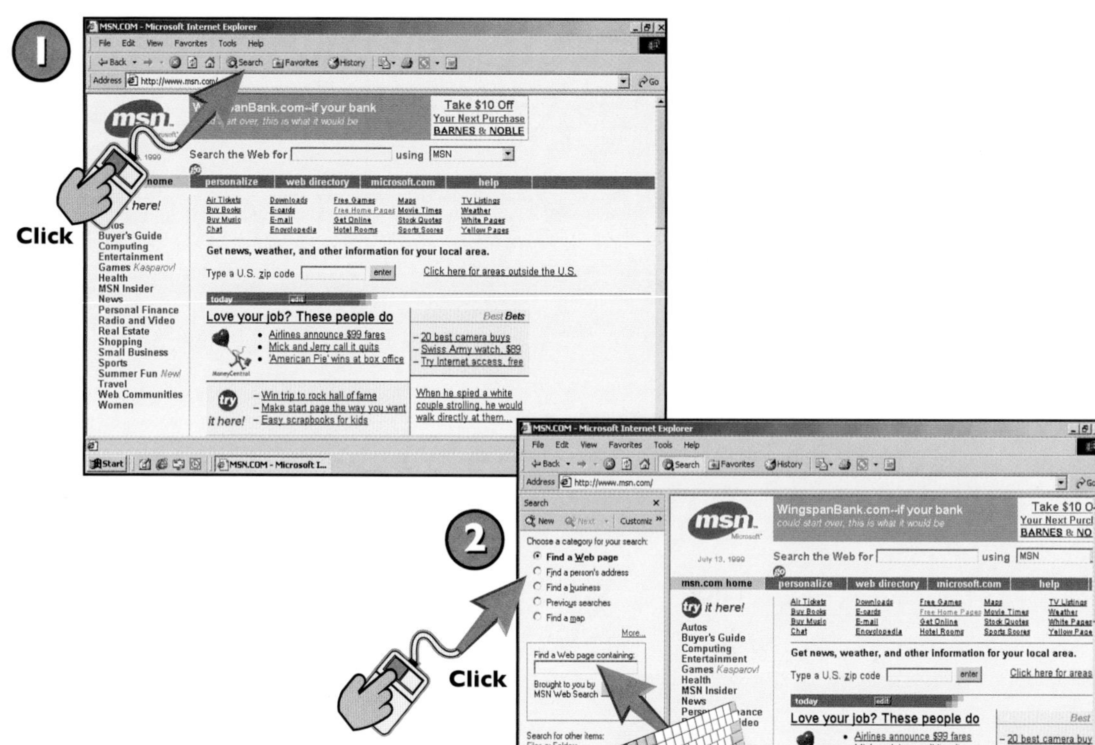

1. Click the **Search** button in the toolbar.
2. Select a category for your search.
3. Type the entry you want to find.

Customizing the Search

To customize the search, click the **Customize** button and then make any changes to how each of the categories are searched.

New Search

To start a new search, click the **New** button.

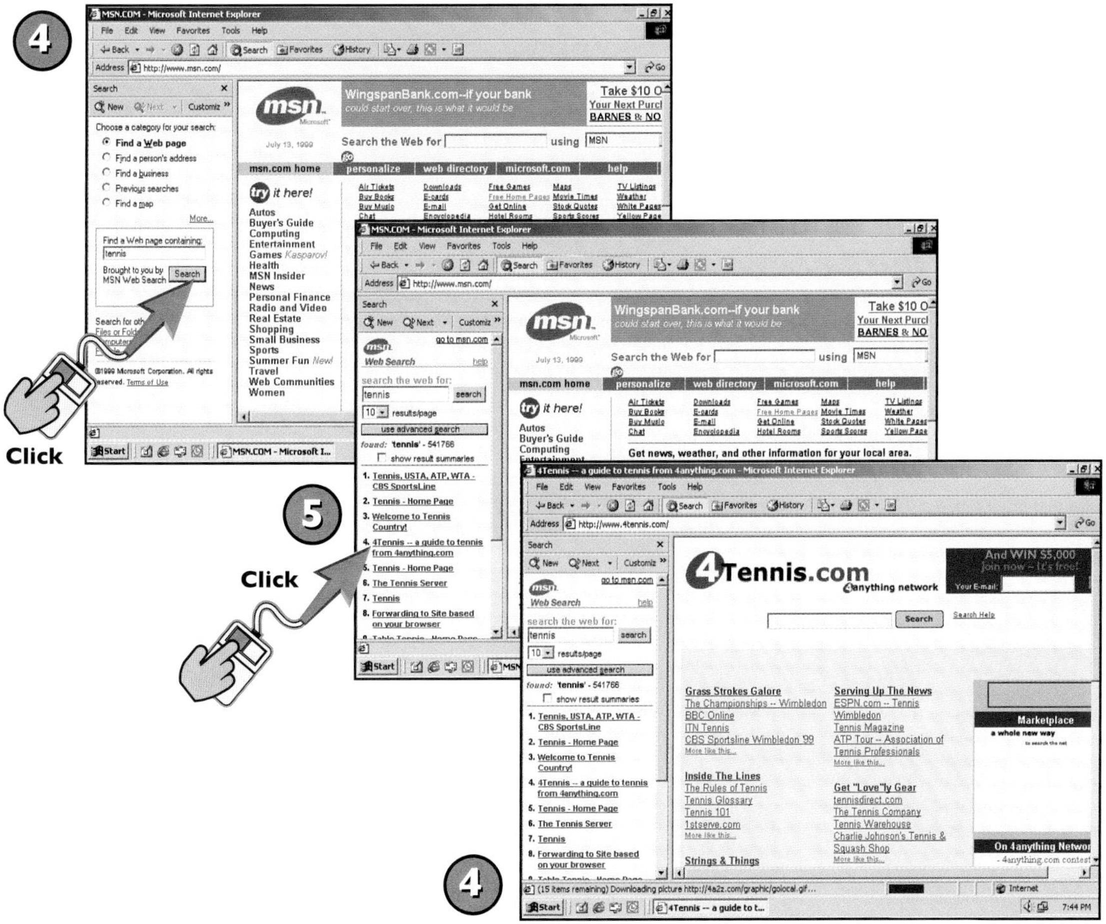

4 Click the **Search** button.

5 The left pane displays the results of the search in link format. Scroll down until you find the link you want and then click it.

6 The page you selected appears in the right pane.

Trying Another Search Provider
To select a different provider (search tool), display the **Choose Provider** drop-down list and select the provider you want to use.

More Searching
You can also visit some of the popular search engines' home pages, such as Excite (**www.excite.com**), Yahoo! (**www.yahoo.com**), Infoseek (**www.infoseek.com**), and Snap.com (**snap.com**). You can then use the search tools from those pages.

Task 9: Setting Internet Options

With Internet Explorer, you can set options about how the browser works. One common preference is to select your home page—the page that is displayed when you log on and when you click the **Home** button. You can also select how many days to keep pages in the History folder.

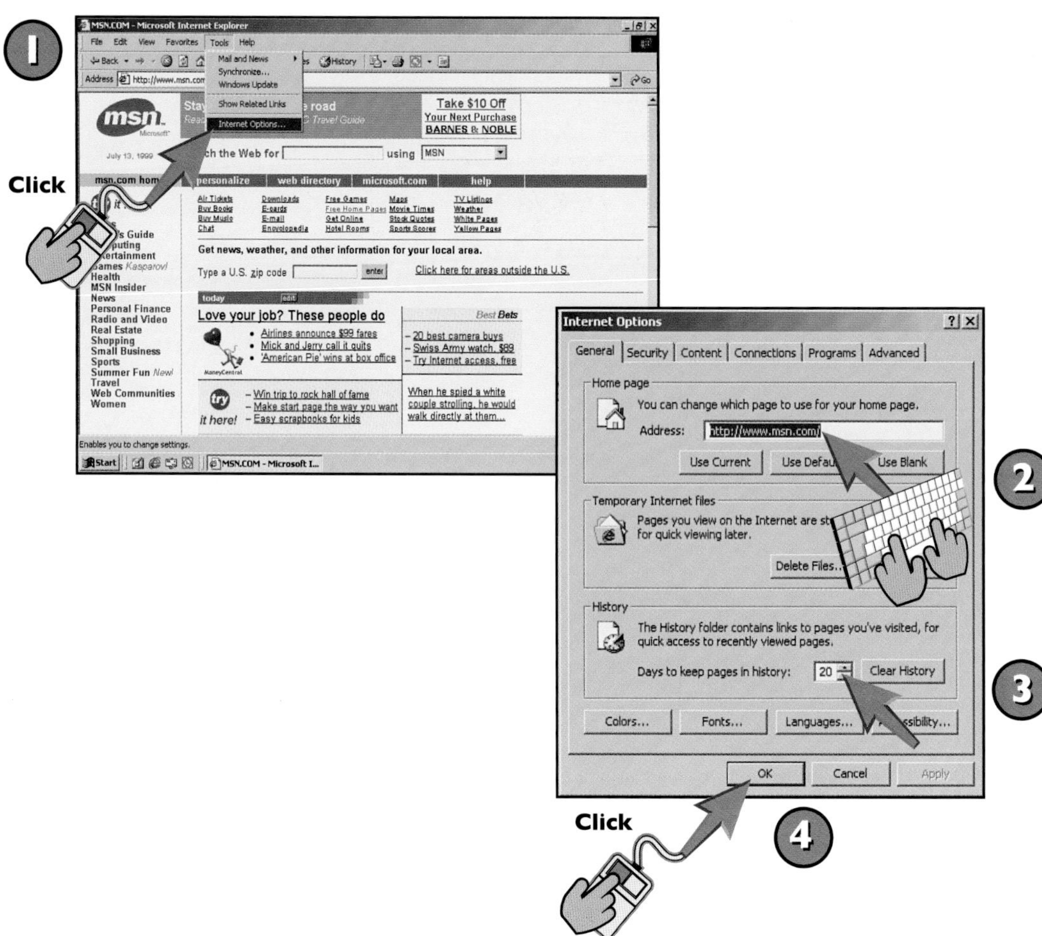

Setting Security
To set security zones, click the **Security** tab. For more information on security, review the online help. Internet Explorer devotes an entire section of its help system to security issues.

Connections
To review or make changes to your Internet connection, click the **Connections** tab. Here you can set up new connections and set options for the current connection.

1. Click **Tools** and then choose **Internet Options**.
2. Type the address to use as the home page.
3. Set the number of days to keep pages in the History folder.
4. Click **OK**.

Task 10: Using the History List

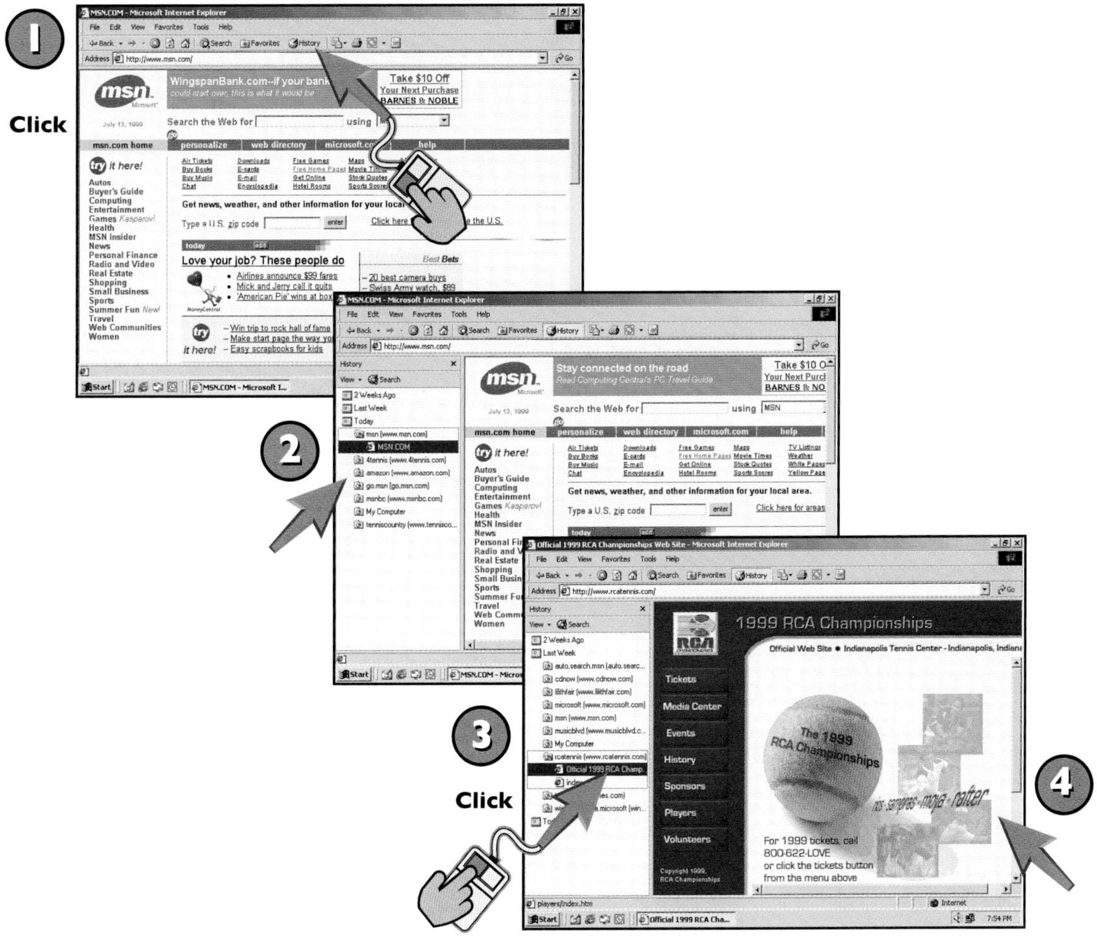

As you browse from link to link, you might remember a site that you liked, but not remember that site's name or address. You can easily return to sites you have visited by displaying the history list. From this list, you can select the week you want to review and then the site you want to visit.

1 Click the **History** button.

2 Internet Explorer displays the history list in a pane on the left side of the window. If necessary, select the week whose list you want to review.

3 Click the site you want.

4 Internet Explorer displays that site.

Closing the History List

To close the history list, click the **Close** (×) button in the top-right corner of the History pane.

Clearing the History

You can select how many days the history is kept, and you can clear the history list. Choose **Tools**, click **Internet Options**, and then select the number of days the history should be kept. To clear the history, click the **Clear History** button.

Task 11: Printing a Web Page

In some cases, you might want to print a hard copy version of a page. You can do so using the Print command.

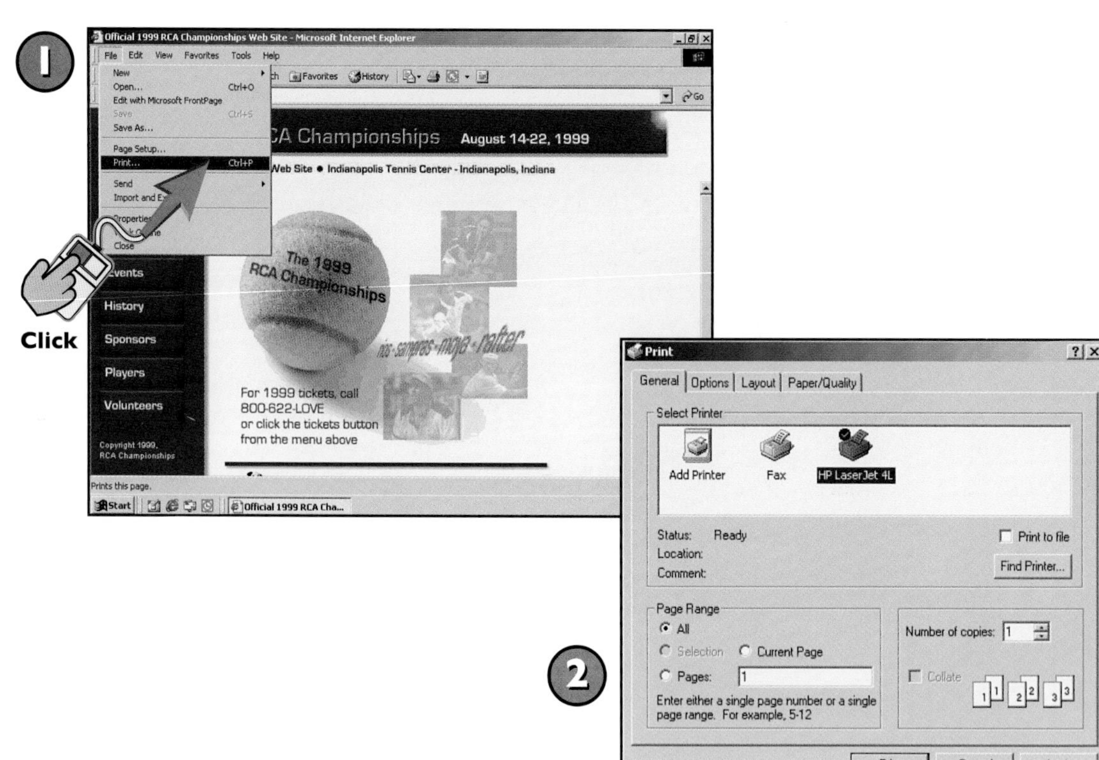

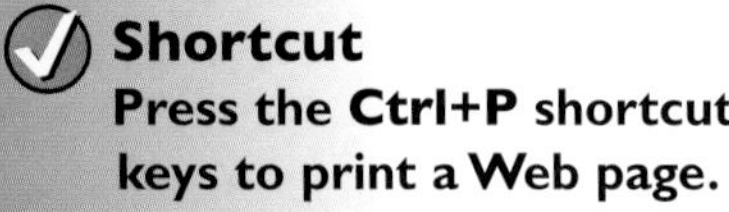

Shortcut
Press the Ctrl+P shortcut keys to print a Web page.

1. Display the page you want to print, open the **File** menu, and choose **Print**.
2. Click the **Print** button. The page is printed.

End Task

Task 12: Exiting Internet Explorer

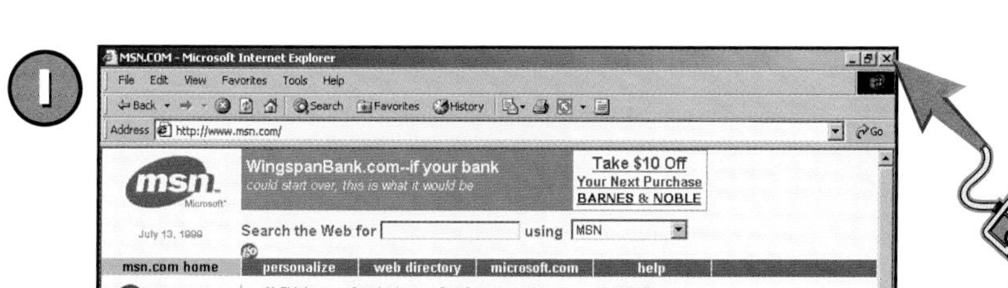

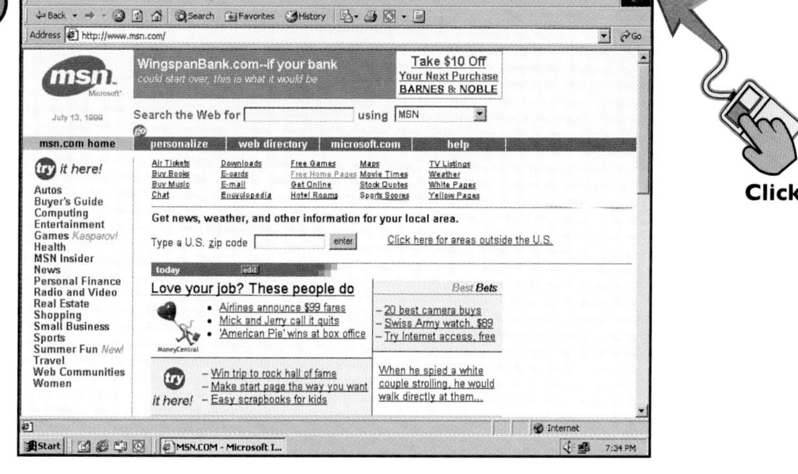

When you are finished browsing the Internet, you need to exit Internet Explorer and also end your connection to your Internet provider.

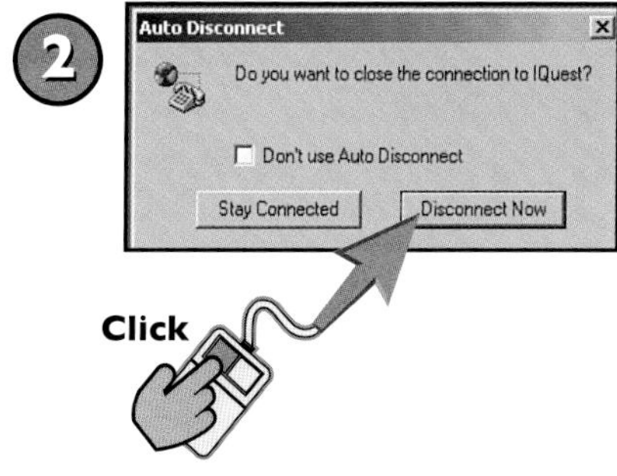

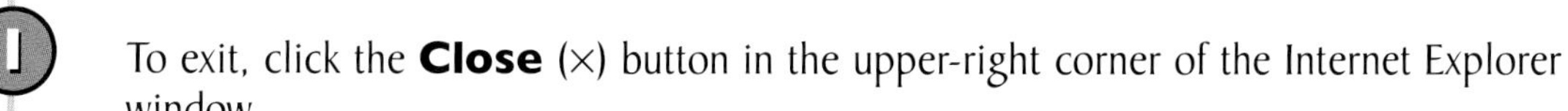

1. To exit, click the **Close** (×) button in the upper-right corner of the Internet Explorer window.

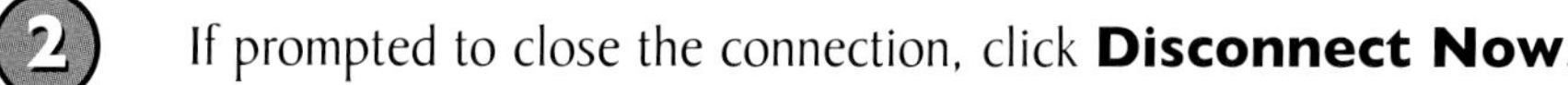

2. If prompted to close the connection, click **Disconnect Now**.

Task 13: Starting Outlook Express

You can use Outlook Express to create, send, and receive email over the Internet. You can send messages to colleagues, clients, friends, and family, and you can read and reply to messages others send you. You can also send files—such as reports, spreadsheets, pictures, and so on—by attaching them to your messages.

Setting Up an Account
To use Outlook, you must set up your mail account. Run the Internet Connection Wizard and follow the steps for setting up a mail account.

More Startup Methods
You can also start Outlook Express from Internet Explorer. To do so, click the **Mail** button and choose **Read Mail**. To start Outlook Express from the Quick Launch toolbar, click the **Launch Outlook Express** button. Finally, you can add a shortcut icon to your desktop for Outlook Express.

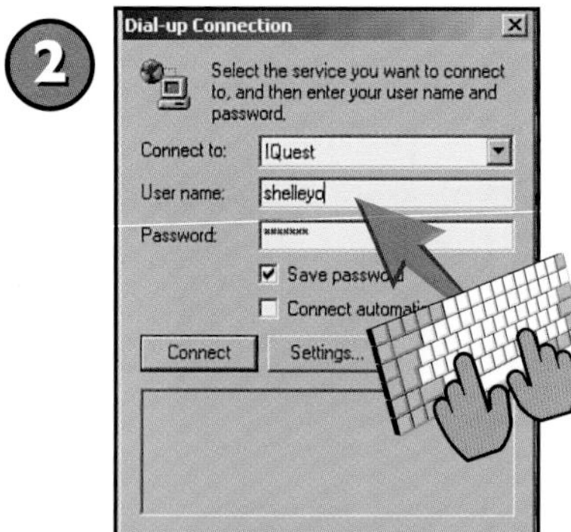

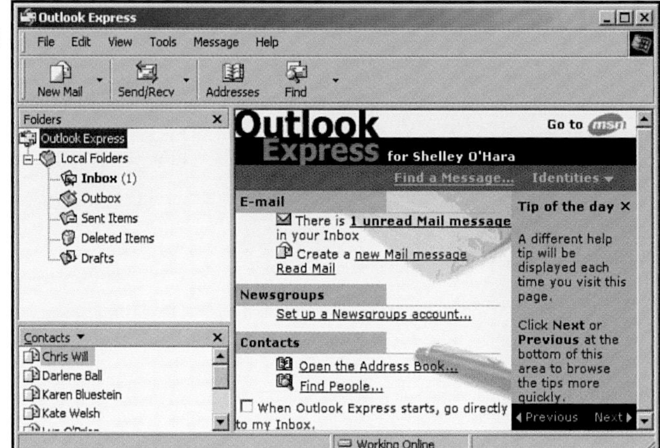

1. Click **Start**, choose the **Programs** command, and select **Outlook Express**.

2. Depending on how the program is set up, you might be prompted to connect to your ISP. Enter the appropriate logon information and click the **Connect** button.

3. Outlook Express is started. If you did connect to your provider, Outlook checks for new messages.

End Task

Task 14: Reading Mail

Click

Double-Click

When you start Outlook Express and get connected to your Internet provider, all the messages are downloaded from your Internet mail server to your computer. The number of messages in your inbox appears in parentheses next to the inbox link in the folder list (the pane on the left side of the screen). The message list (the upper-right pane) lists all messages. Messages appearing in bold have not yet been read, but you can open and read any message in the message list (whether it is bold or not).

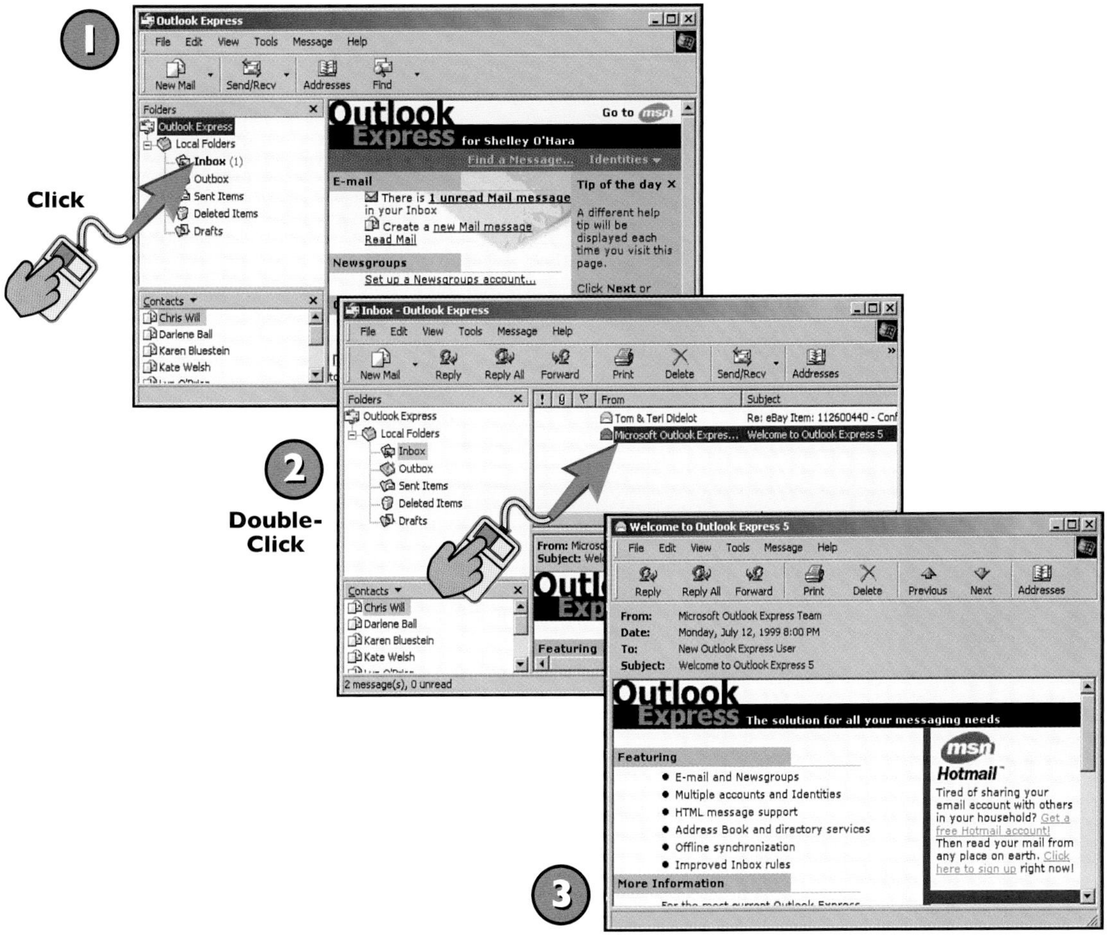

1. In the Folders list, click the **Inbox**.
2. In the message list of the Outlook Express window, double-click the message you want to read.
3. The message you selected is displayed in its own window. You can scroll through the contents to read the message.

Changing the Outlook Window

You can customize the Outlook window, selecting which bars and lists are displayed. Click **View** and then select **Layout**. Check or uncheck any of the options and then click **OK**.

Task 15: Handling Messages

When you read a message, you may want to print it, delete it, or simply read the next message. To do so, you can use the buttons in the message window.

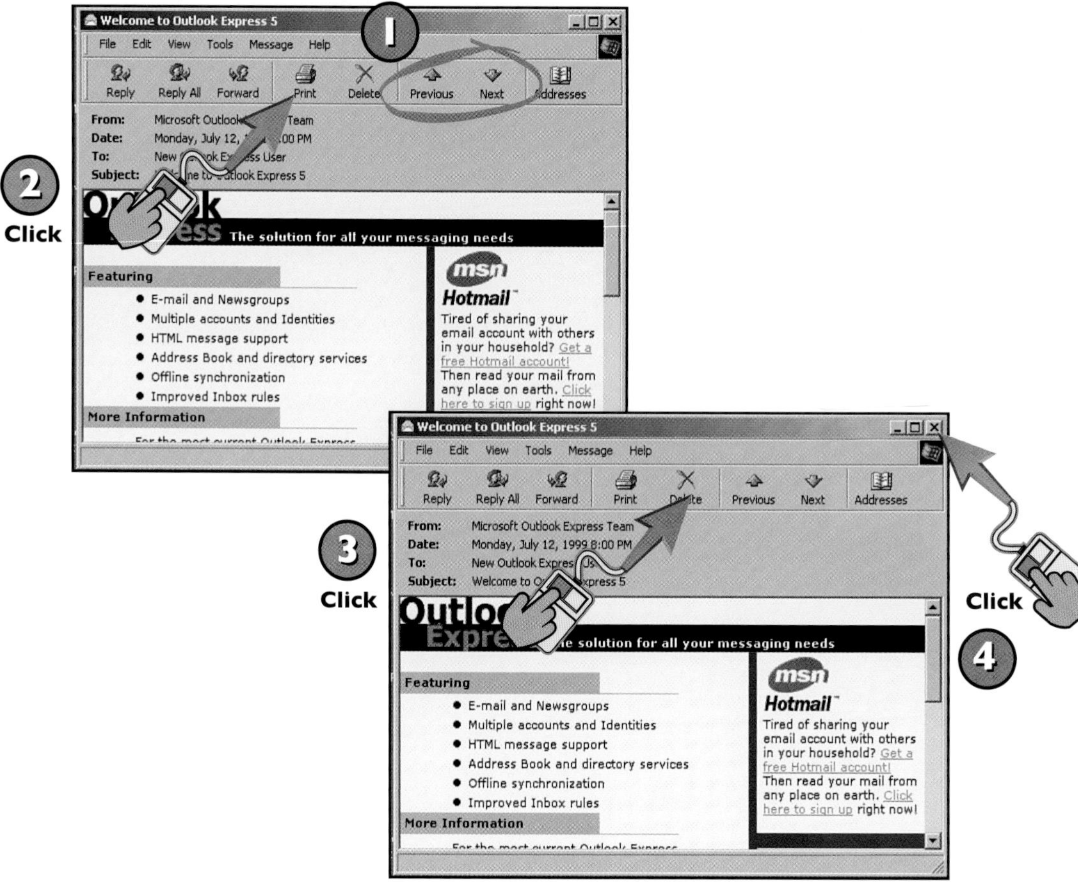

Replying to a Message
See the next task for information on replying to a message.

Checking Mail
Depending on how Outlook Express is set up on your computer, you might be prompted to connect to your Internet provider, and your mail might be automatically checked. If not, or if you choose to work offline, click the **Send/Recv** button to check for messages.

1. To display the previous message in the message list, click the **Previous** button; to display the next message in the message list, click the **Next** button.
2. To print the message, click the **Print** button and then click the **Print** button in the **Print** dialog box.
3. To delete the message, click the **Delete** button.
4. To close the message, click the **Close** (×) button.

End Task

Task 16: Responding to Mail

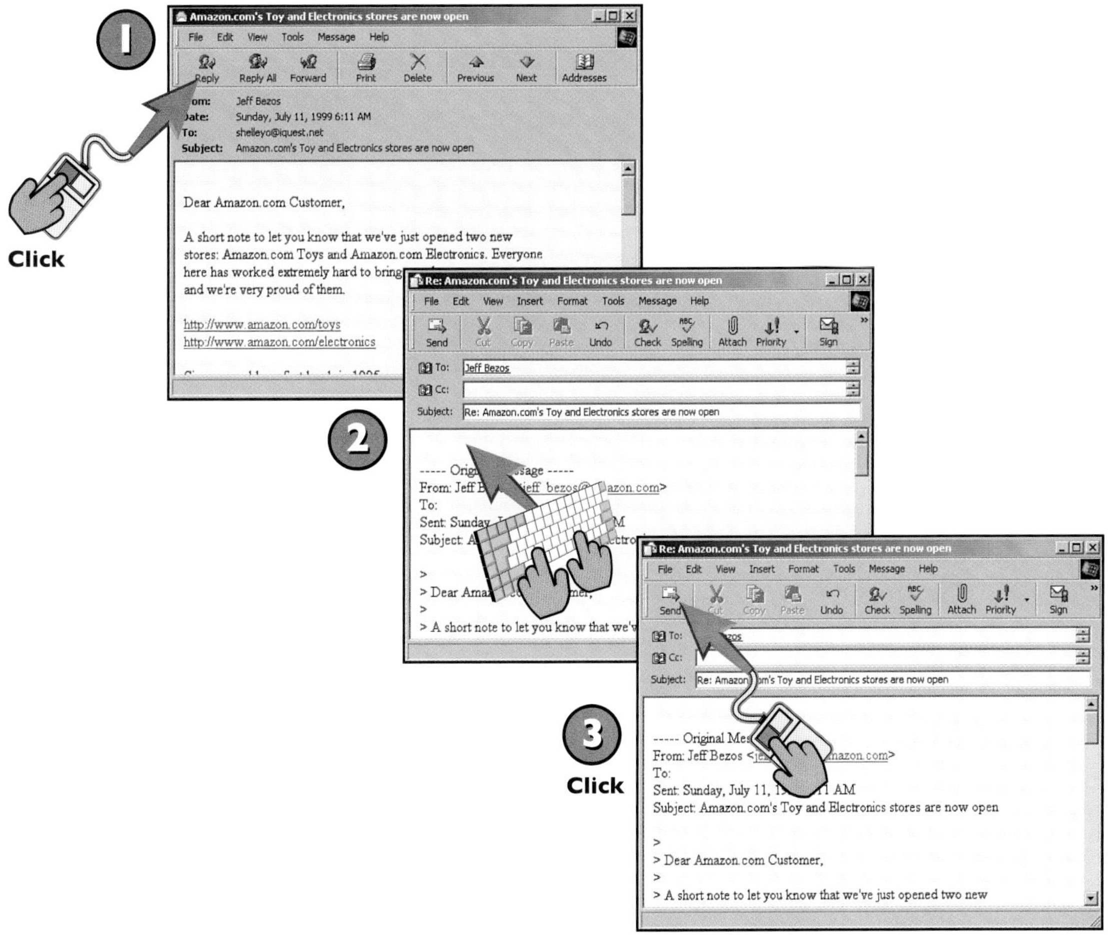

You can easily respond to a message you've received. Outlook Express completes the address and subject lines for you; you can then simply type the response.

1. Display the message to which you want to reply and click the **Reply** button.

2. The address and subject lines are completed, and the text of the original message is appended to bottom of the reply message. Type your message.

3. Click the **Send** button.

Forwarding a Message

To forward a message, open the Message menu and choose Forward, or click the Forward button. Type the address of the recipient and then click in the message area and type any message you want to include. Click the Send button.

Task 17: Creating and Sending Mail

You can send a message to anyone with an Internet email address. Simply type the recipient's email address, a subject, and the message. You can also send carbon copies (Cc) and blind carbon copies (Bcc) of messages, as well as attach files to your messages.

Toolbar Button

You can also click the **New Mail** button in the toolbar to create a new message.

Message Not Sent?

If you enter an incorrect address and the message is not sent, you most likely will receive a **Failure to Deliver** notice. Be sure to type the address in its proper format.

Attaching a File

To attach a file—such as a spreadsheet or word-processing document—to your message, click the **Attach** button. In the Insert Attachment dialog box, choose the file you want to attach and click the **Attach** button.

1. In the Outlook Express window, click **Message** and then choose **New Message**.
2. Type the recipient's address (as well any necessary Cc and Bcc addresses). Addresses are in the format ***username@domainname.ext***. Press **Tab** twice.
3. Type a subject in the **Subject** text box and then press **Tab**.

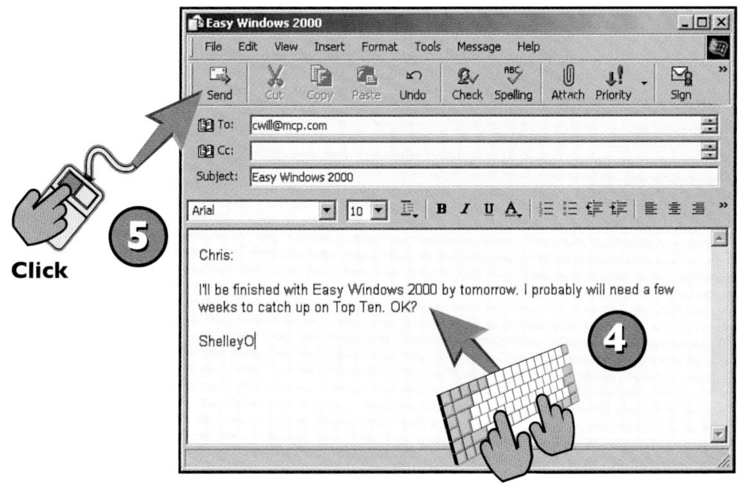

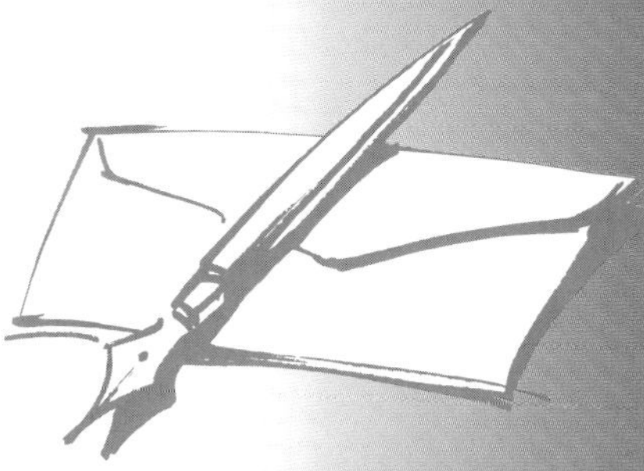

Type your message.

Click the **Send** button.

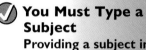

You Must Type a Subject
Providing a subject in Outlook Express is mandatory.

Send and Receive
If you are connected to the Internet, the message is sent when the Send button is clicked. If you're not connected to the Internet, Windows places the message in the outbox. You can connect and send the message by clicking the Send/Recv button from the Outlook window.

Task 18: Keeping an Address Book

If you frequently send a message to the same person, you don't need to type the address each time. Add it to your address book, and then you can select the name from a list. You can add addresses from existing messages or create new address book entries. You can also review and delete any entries, as needed.

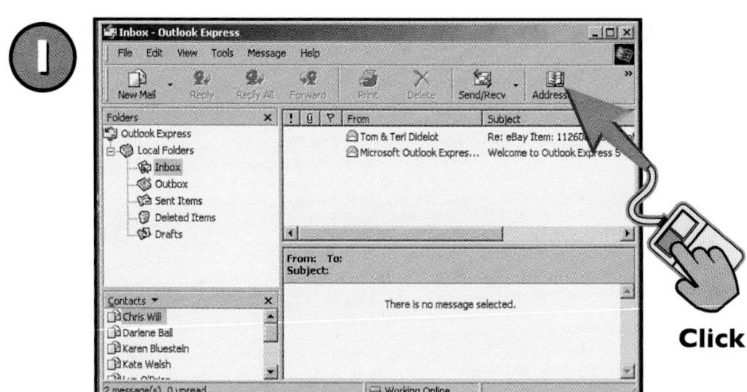

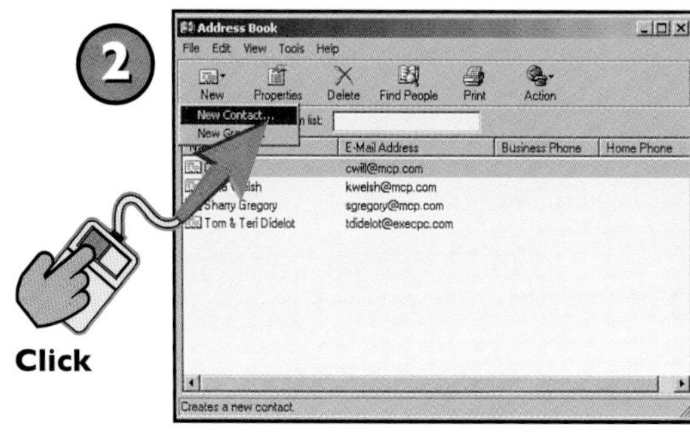

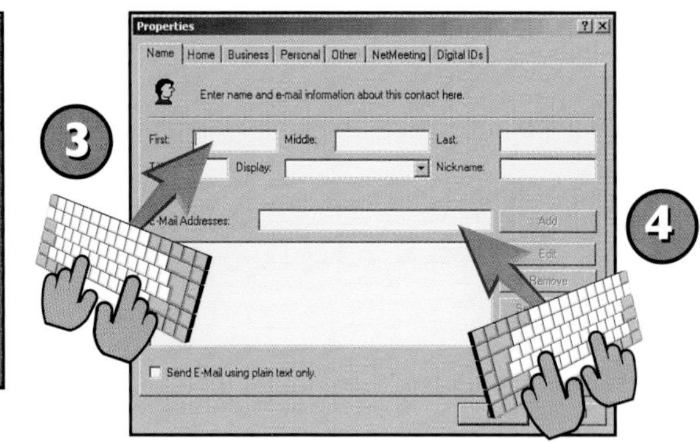

1. In the Outlook Express folder list, click the **Addresses** button.
2. You see the address book. Click the **New** button and select **New Contact**.
3. Type the person's first, middle, and last names.
4. Type the email address.

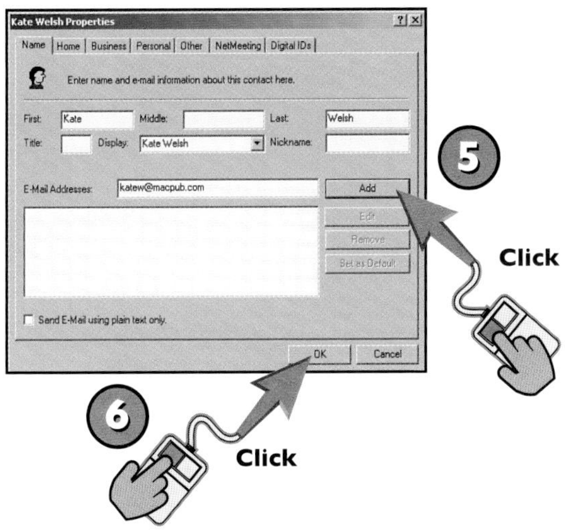

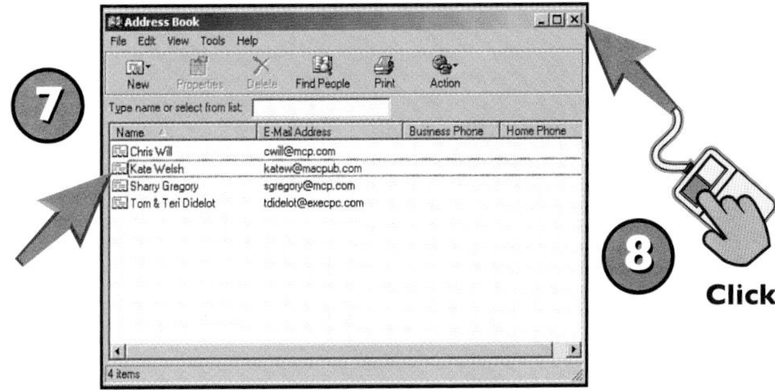

5 Click the **Add** button.

6 Click the **OK** button.

7 That person is added to your address book.

8 Click the **Close** (×) button to close the address book.

Deleting an Entry

To delete someone from your address book, select the name and then click the **Delete** button.

Reviewing Information

To review information about a person, select the name and then click the **Properties** button.

Shortcut

You can right-click the name or address from an existing message and select **Add to Address Book** from the shortcut menu.

Task 19: Looking Up an Email Address

To send a message, you must know that person's email address. If you don't know the address, you can try looking it up in one of several directories. To do so, use the address book included with Windows 2000.

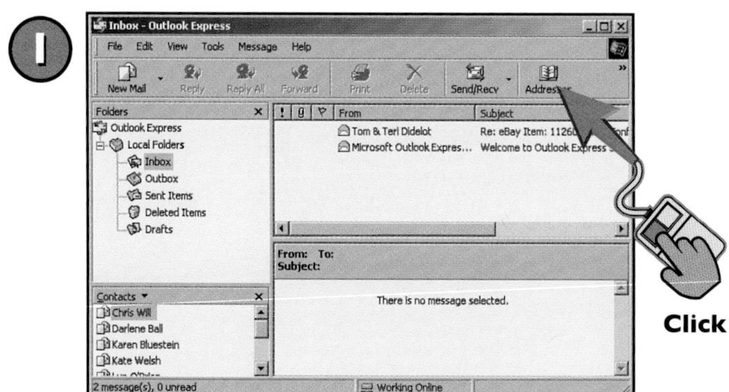

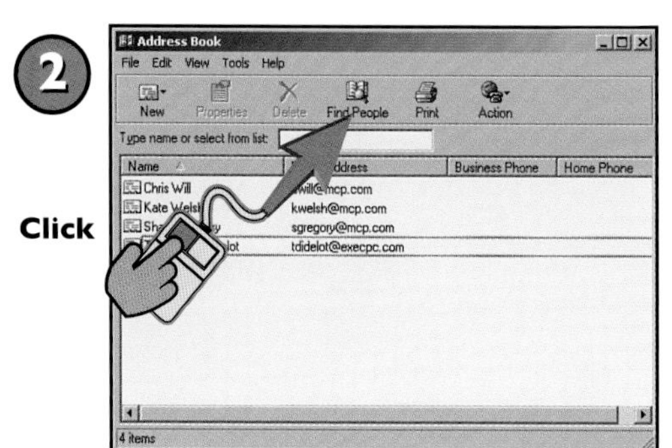

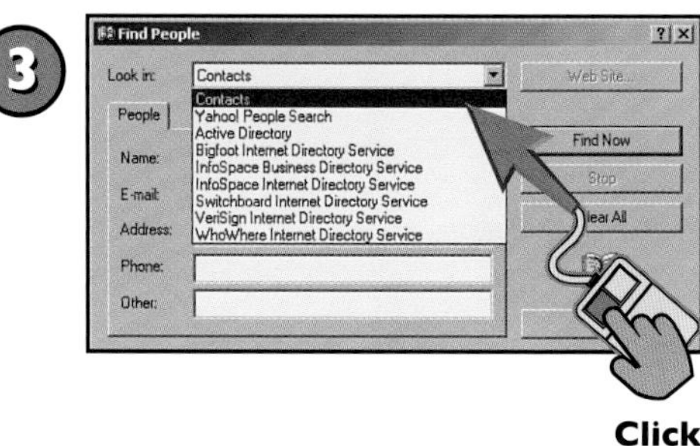

1. In the Outlook Express folder list, click the **Addresses** button.
2. You see the address book. Click the **Find People** button.
3. Display the **Look In** drop-down list and select the directory you want to search.

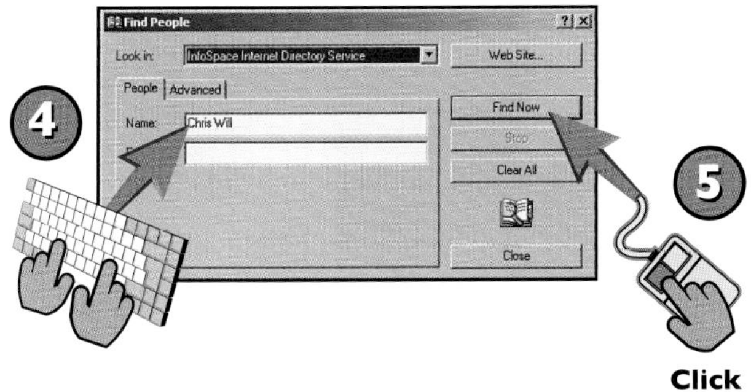

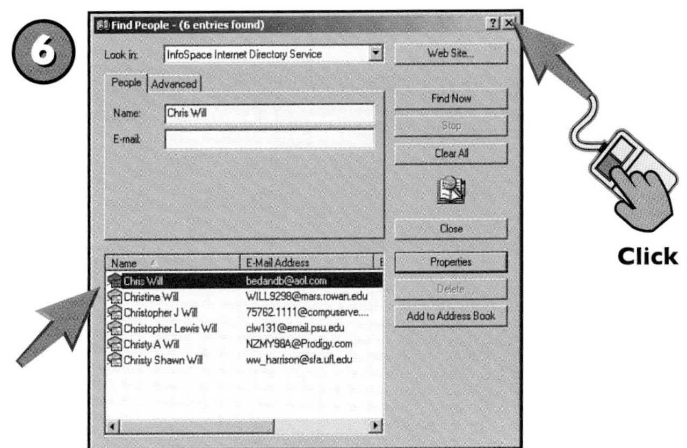

Adding the Name to Your Address Book
To add a name to your address book, select it and then click the **Add to Address Book** button.

Not Listed?
Just because you don't find an address doesn't mean the person does not have one. It means they are simply not listed in that directory. Try another one.

Do You Have the Right Person?
To be sure you have the right person (there can be several matches), click the name and click the **Properties** button. You can review other information about that person.

4. Type the name to find in the **Name** text box.

5. Click the **Find Now** button.

6. You see a list of matches. To close this dialog box, click the **Close** (×) button.

Task 20: Subscribing to Newsgroups

A *newsgroup* is a collection of messages relating to a particular topic. Anyone can post a message, and anyone who subscribes to the newsgroup can view and respond to posted messages. You can join any of hundreds of thousands of newsgroups on the Internet to exchange information and learn about hobbies, businesses, pets, computers, and more. You can use Outlook Express to send and receive newsgroup messages.

Start Here

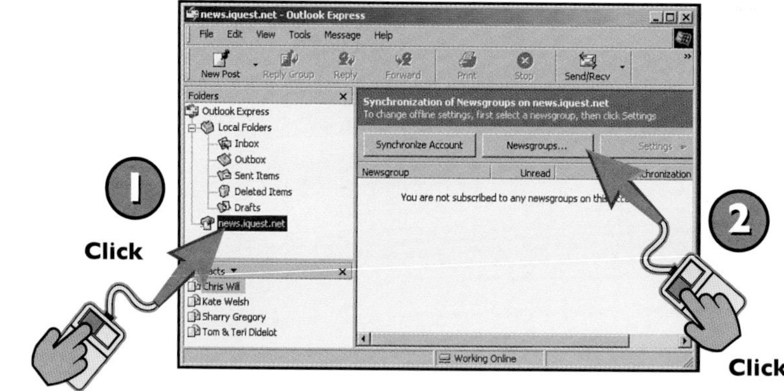

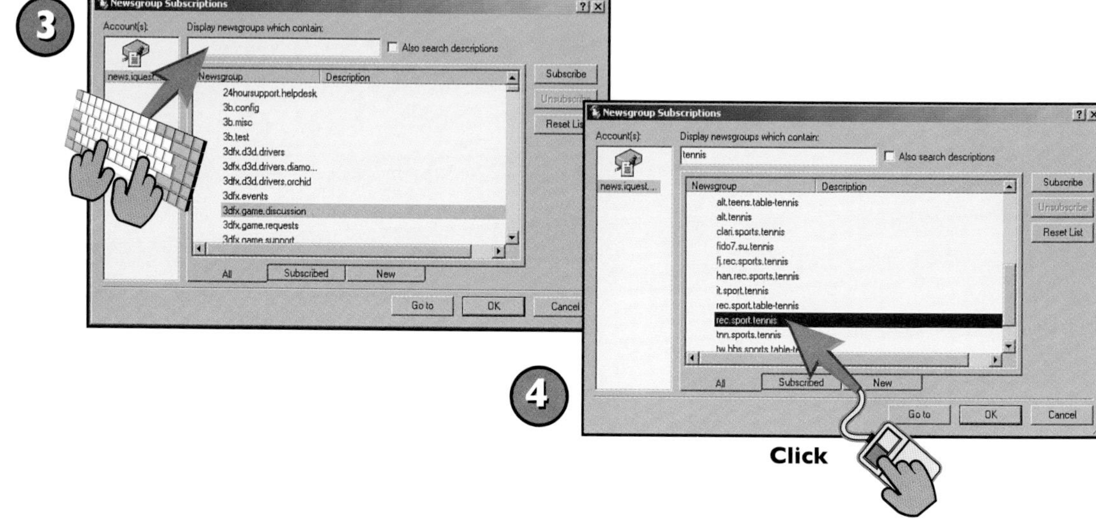

1 In the Outlook Express Folders list, click your news server.

2 Click the **Newsgroups** button.

3 Type the name of the topic area or newsgroup you want to join.

4 You see a list of matching newsgroups. Select the newsgroup you want to join.

First Time?
The first time you select your news server, you are prompted to download a list of available news-groups. Click Yes and follow the onscreen instructions.

Next Step

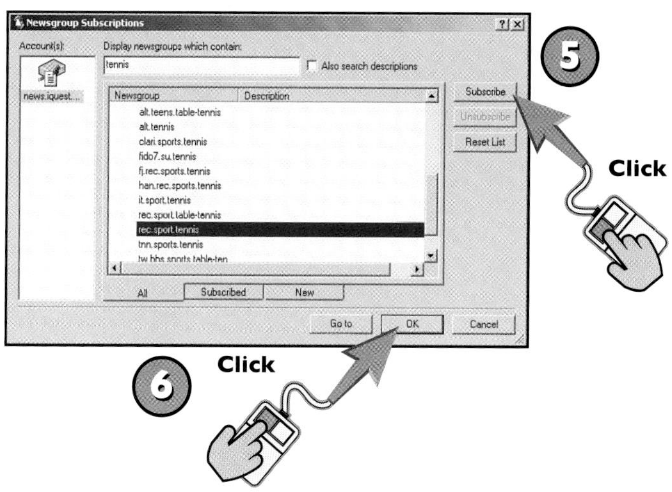

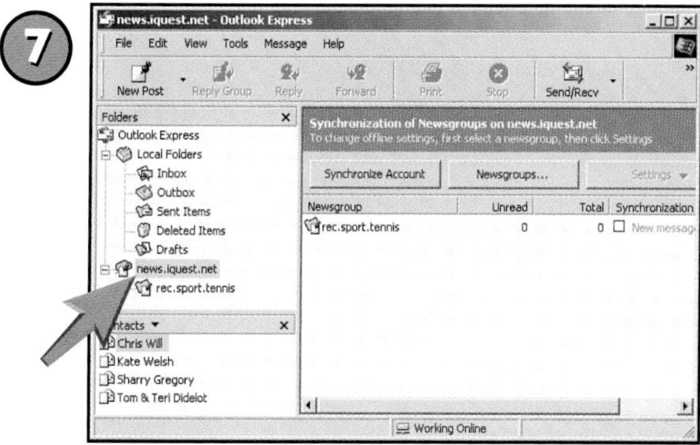

5 Click the **Subscribe** button.

6 Click **OK**.

7 You are subscribed to this newsgroup, and its name is listed under your news server in the Outlook Express Folders list.

Setting Up Newsgroups
To participate in newsgroups, you must set up your news account. You can do so when you set up your Internet connection. Alternatively, open the **Tools** menu and choose **Accounts**. Click the **News** tab and then click the **Add** button and select **News**. Follow the steps for setting up a news account.

Unsubscribing
To unsubscribe to a newsgroup, click the **Newsgroups** button. Select the newsgroup and then click the **Unsubscribe** button.

Task 21: Reading Newsgroup Messages

Start Here

After you have subscribed to a newsgroup, you can review any of the messages in that group. When a new message is posted, it starts a *thread*, and all responses are part of this thread. You can review all the current messages in the thread.

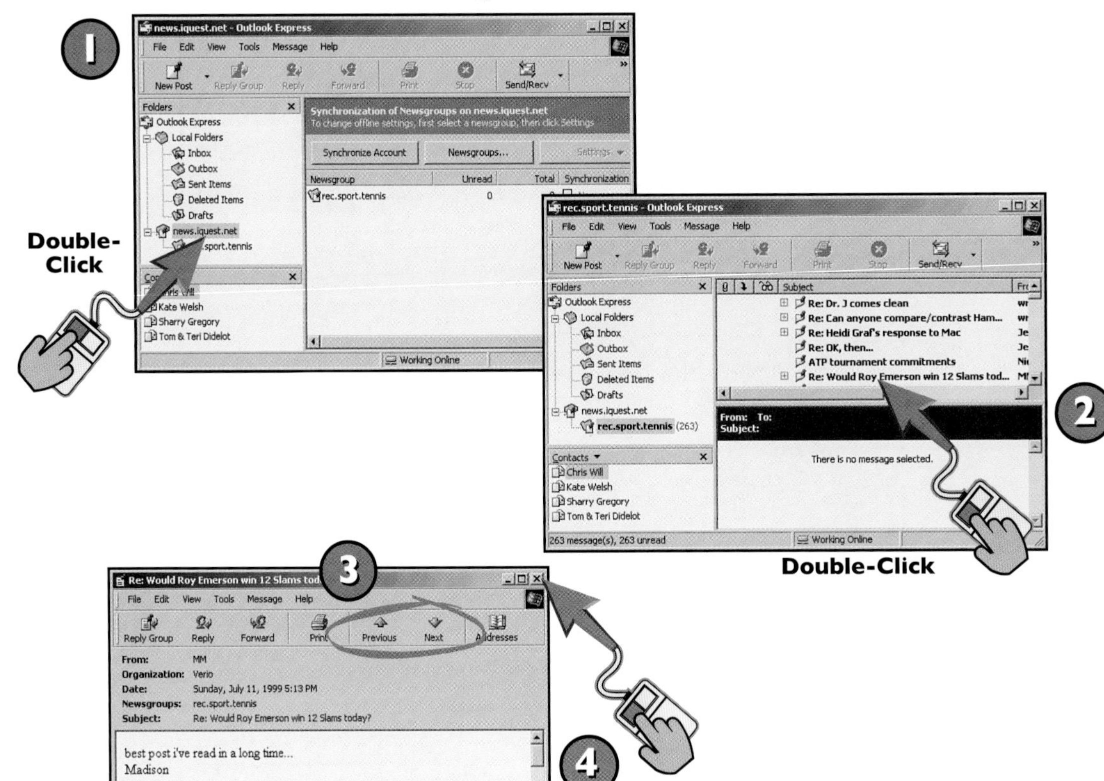

1. In the Folders list of the Outlook Express window, double-click the newsgroup you want to review.
2. A list of that newsgroup's messages appears in the message list. Messages in bold have not yet been read; messages with a plus sign have responses. Double-click the message you want to read.
3. The message appears in its own window. To display the next message, click the **Next** button; to display the previous message, click the **Previous** button.
4. To close the message, click the **Close** (×) button.

End Task

Content Not Monitored

Keep in mind that newsgroups are not usually monitored. You might come across messages that you find offensive. If so, it's best to just unsubscribe from that newsgroup.

Printing a Message

To print a message, click the **Print** button and then click **OK**.

Task 22: Replying to an Existing Newsgroup Message

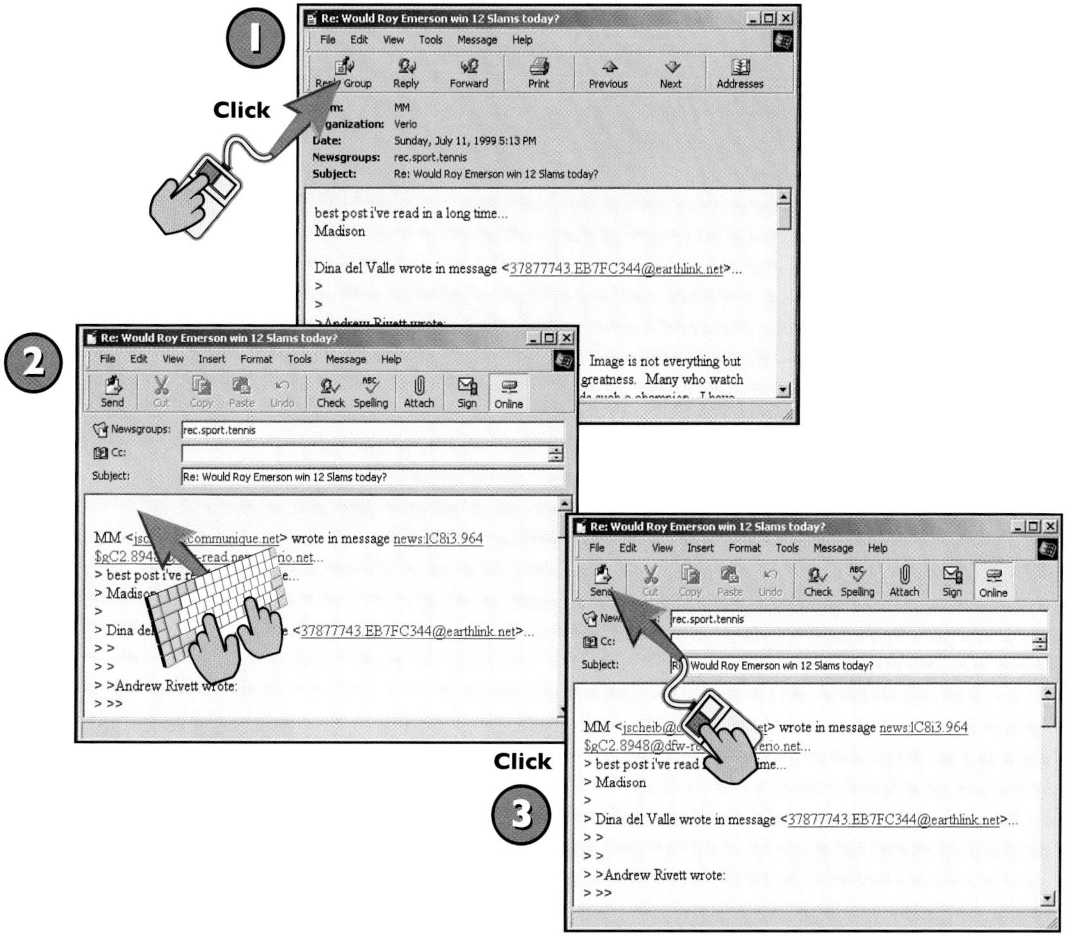

If you come across a newsgroup message to which you want to respond, you can post a reply to that message.

1 Display the message to which you want to reply and click the **Reply Group** button.

2 Type your message.

3 Click the **Send** button.

Replying via Email
You can also reply to messages privately by emailing the author. To send an email message, click the **Reply** button. Type your message and click the **Send** button.

Task 23: Posting New Messages

After you review messages, you might want to post your own opinion. One way to do this is to post a new message or start a new thread.

Start Here

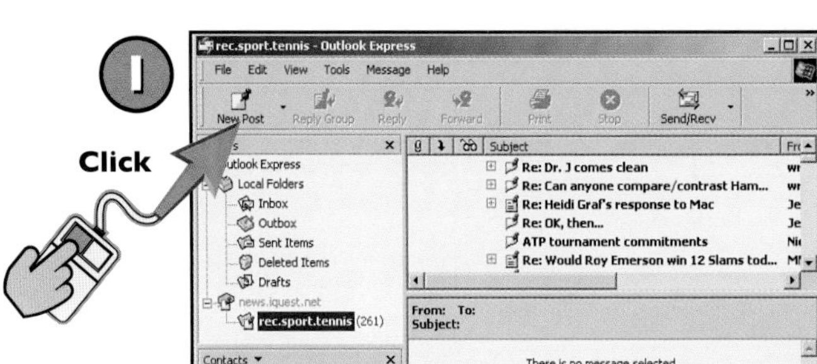

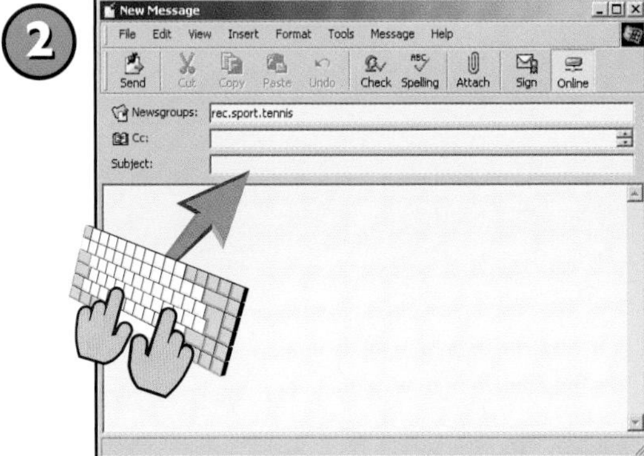

1. In the Folders list, select the newsgroup to which you want to post a new message and click the **New Post** button.
2. Type a subject.

Canceling the Message
If you change your mind about posting a message, you can cancel the message if you have not already clicked Post. Simply click the message's **Close** (×) button and, when prompted, click the **Yes** button to confirm that you don't want to save the message.

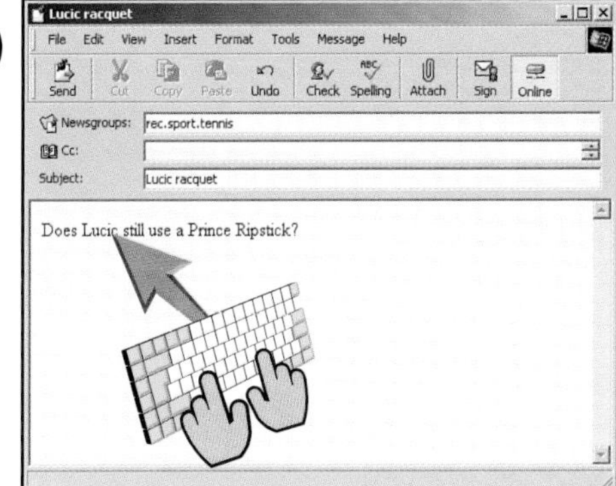

3 Type your message.

4 Click the **Send** button.

Glossary

accessory One of the mini applications that comes free with Windows 2000. Examples include WordPad, Paint, and Backup. Accessories can be found in the Accessories menu.

Active Desktop The new Windows 2000 desktop, which lets you replace a static desktop with one that can hold Web pages and mini programs (such as a clock, a stock ticker, or a weather map).

active window The window you're currently using. You can tell a window is active by looking at its title bar. If the bar shows white letters on a dark background, the window is active. Inactive windows show light gray letters on a dark gray background.

application Software that accomplishes a specific practical task. It's the same thing as a *program*.

application window A window that contains a running application, such as WordPad.

ASCII text file A file that uses only the American Standard Code for Information Interchange character set (techno-lingo for the characters you see on your keyboard).

backup job A Microsoft Backup file that includes a list of files to back up, the backup options, and the backup destination.

boot To start your computer. The term *booting* comes from the phrase "pulling oneself up by one's own bootstraps," which refers to the fact that your computer can load everything it needs to operate properly without any help from you.

bps Bits per second. The rate at which a modem or other communications device spits data through a phone line or cable.

browser A program that you use to surf sites on the World Wide Web. The browser that comes with Windows 2000 is called Internet Explorer.

byte A single character of information.

CD-ROM drive A special computer disk drive that's designed to handle CD-ROM discs, which resemble audio CDs. CD-ROMs have enormous capacity (about 500 times that of a typical floppy disk), so they're most often used to hold large applications, graphics libraries, and huge collections of shareware programs.

character formatting Changing the look of text characters by altering their font, size, style, and more.

check box A square-shaped switch that toggles a dialog box option on or off. The option is toggled on when a check mark appears in the box.

classic view The folder view used with Windows 95. That is, you click an icon to select it, and you double-click an icon to launch it. See also *Web view*.

click To quickly press and release the left mouse button.

Clipboard An area of memory that holds data temporarily during cut and paste operations.

command button A rectangular "button" (usually found in dialog boxes) that, when clicked, runs whatever command is spelled out on it.

commands The options you see in a pull-down menu. You use these commands to tell the application what you want it to do next.

data files The files used by you or your programs. See also *program files*.

delay The amount of time it takes for a second character to appear when you press and hold down a key.

desktop A metaphor for the Windows 2000 screen. Starting a Windows 2000 application is similar to putting a folder full of papers (the application window) on your desk. To do some work, you pull some papers out of the folder (the document windows) and place them on the desktop.

device driver A small program that controls the way a device (such as a mouse) works with your system.

dialog boxes Windows that pop up on the screen to ask you for information or to seek confirmation of an action you requested.

digital camera A special camera that saves pictures using digital storage (such as a memory card) instead of film.

directory See *folder*.

diskette See *floppy disk*.

document window A window opened in an application. Document windows hold whatever you're working on in the application.

double-click To quickly press and release the left mouse button twice in succession.

double-click speed The maximum amount of time Windows 2000 allows between the mouse clicks of a double-click.

drag To press and hold down the left mouse button and then move the mouse.

drag-and-drop A technique you use to run commands or move things around; you use your mouse to drag files or icons to strategic screen areas and drop them there.

drop-down list box A list box that normally shows only a single item but, when selected, displays a list of options.

DVD drive Another high-capacity storage medium, like a CD-ROM. DVD drives are relatively new and can contain more data than a CD-ROM.

Email Short for *electronic mail*. You can send messages via the Internet to anyone with an email address.

file An organized unit of information inside your computer.

floppy disk A portable storage medium that consists of a flexible disk protected by a plastic case. Floppy disks are available in a variety of sizes and capacities.

folder A storage location on your hard disk in which you keep related files together.

font A character set of a specific typeface, type style, and type size.

formatting The process of setting up a disk so that a drive can read its information and write information to it. Not to be confused with character formatting.

fragmented When a single file is chopped up and stored in separate chunks scattered around a hard disk. You can fix this by running Windows 2000's Disk Defragmenter program.

gigabyte 1,024 megabytes. Those in-the-know usually abbreviate this as G or GB when writing, and as gig when speaking. See also *byte*, *kilobyte*, and *megabyte*.

hard disk The main storage area inside your computer.

hover To place the mouse pointer over an object for a few seconds. In most Windows applications, for example, if you hover the mouse over a toolbar button, a ToolTip is displayed, showing the name of the button.

hyperlink See *link*.

icons The little pictures that Windows 2000 uses to represent programs and files.

infrared port A communications port, usually found on notebook computers and some printers. Infrared ports enable two devices to communicate by using infrared light waves instead of cables.

insertion point The blinking vertical bar you see inside a text box or in a word-processing application, such as WordPad. It indicates where the next character you type will appear.

Internet A network of networks that extends around the world. By setting up an account with an Internet service provider, you can access this network.

intranet The implementation of Internet technologies for use within a corporate organization rather than for connection to the Internet as a whole.

Jaz drive A special disk drive that uses portable disks (about the size of floppy disks) that hold 1 gigabyte of data.

Kbps One thousand bits per second (bps). Today's modern modems transmit data at either 28.8Kbps or 56Kbps.

kilobyte 1,024 bytes. This is often abbreviated to K or KB. See also *megabyte* and *gigabyte*.

LAN See *local area network*.

link A text or graphic element on a Web page that, when you click it, takes you to another page. That page might be within the same Web document, to another document at that site, or to another site entirely. Also called *hyperlink*.

list box A small window that displays a list of items such as filenames or folders.

local area network A network in which all the computers occupy a relatively small geographical area, such as a department, office, home, or building. All the connections between computers are made via network cables.

maximize To increase the size of a window to its largest extent. A maximized application window fills the entire screen (except for the taskbar). A maximized document window fills the entire application window.

Mbps One million bits per second (bps).

megabyte 1,024 kilobytes or 1,048,576 bytes. This is often abbreviated in writing to M or MB and pronounced meg. See also *gigabyte*.

menu bar The horizontal bar on the second line of an application window. The menu bar contains the application's pull-down menus.

minimize To remove a program from the desktop without closing it. A button for the program remains on the taskbar.

modem An electronic device that enables two computers to exchange data over phone lines.

multitasking The capability to run several programs at the same time.

network A collection of computers connected via special cables or other network media to share files, folders, disks, peripherals, and applications. See also *local area network*.

newsgroup An Internet discussion group devoted to a single topic. These discussions progress by "posting" messages to the group.

option buttons See *radio buttons*.

point To place the mouse pointer so that it rests on a specific screen location.

port The connection into which you plug the cable from a device such as a mouse or printer.

program files The files that run your programs. See also *data files*.

pull-down menus Hidden menus that you open from an application's menu bar to access the commands and features of the application.

radio buttons Dialog box options that appear as small circles in groups of two or more. Only one option from a group can be chosen. These are also called *option buttons*.

RAM Stands for *random access memory*. The memory in your computer that Windows 2000 uses to run your programs.

repeat rate After the initial delay, the rate at which characters appear when you press and hold down a key.

right-click To click the right mouse button instead of the usual left button. In Windows 2000, right-clicking something usually pops up a shortcut menu.

scalable font A font in which each character exists as an outline that can be scaled to different sizes. Windows 2000 includes such scalable fonts as Arial, Courier New, and Times New Roman. To use scalable fonts, you must have a software program called a *type manager* to do the scaling. Windows 2000 comes with its own type manager: TrueType.

scrollbar A bar that appears on the right side and/or bottom of a window when the window is too small to display all its contents.

shortcut A special file that points to a program or a document. Double-clicking the shortcut starts the program or opens the document.

shortcut menu A menu that contains a few commands related to an item (such as the desktop or the taskbar). You display the shortcut menu by right-clicking the object.

surf To travel from site to site on the World Wide Web.

system menu A menu, common to every Windows 2000 window, that you use to manipulate various features of the window. You activate the Control menu by clicking the Control Menu box in the upper-left corner of the window or by pressing Alt+spacebar (for an application window).

system resources Two memory areas that Windows 2000 uses to keep track of things like the position and size of open windows, dialog boxes, and your desktop configuration (wallpaper and so on).

taskbar The horizontal strip across the bottom of the Windows 2000 screen. Each running application is given its own taskbar button, and you switch to an application by clicking on its button.

text box A screen area in which you type text information, such as a description or a filename.

text editor A program that lets you edit files that contain only text. The Windows 2000 text editor is called Notepad.

title bar The area on the top line of a window that displays the window's title.

toolbar A series of application-specific buttons that typically appears beneath the menu bar.

TrueType A font management program that comes with Windows 2000.

type size A measure of the height of a font. Type size is measured in points; there are 72 points in an inch.

type style Character attributes, such as regular, bold, and italic. Other type styles (often called type *effects*) are underline and strikethrough.

typeface A distinctive graphic design of letters, numbers, and other symbols.

URL Stands for *uniform resource locator*. The address of a particular Web page.

Web integration The integration of World Wide Web techniques into the Windows 2000 interface. See also *Web view*.

Web view The folder view used when Web integration is activated. With this view, you hover the mouse over an icon to select it, and you click an icon to launch it. See also *classic view*.

window A rectangular screen area in which Windows 2000 displays applications and documents.

word wrap A word processor feature that automatically starts a new line when your typing reaches the end of the current line.

write-protection Floppy disk safeguard that prevents you from changing any information on the disk. The 5 1/4-inch disks normally have a small notch on the side of the disk. If the notch is covered with tape, the disk is write-protected. Simply remove the tape to disable the write-protection. On a 3 1/2-inch disk, write-protection is controlled by a small movable tab on the back of the disk. If the tab is toward the edge of the disk, the disk is write-protected. To disable the write-protection, slide the tab away from the edge of the disk.

Zip drive A special disk drive that uses portable disks (a little smaller than a Jaz drive disk) that hold 100 megabytes of data.

D

E

F

G-H

I-J

K-L

M

N

O

P

Q

R

S

T

U

V

W-Z

Web pages